ATLAS FOUR

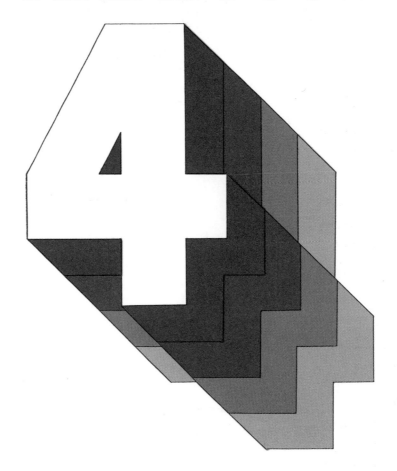

Collins◇Longman

Copyright © Collins◇Longman Atlases 1969,1970,1973, 1975,
1977, 1980

First published 1969, revised 1970, reprinted 1972
Second edition 1973, revised 1975, 1977 reprinted 1978, 1979
Third edition 1980, reprinted 1981

Wm Collins Sons & Co Ltd
PO Box
Glasgow G4 0NB

Longman Group Ltd
Longman House
Burnt Mill
Harlow
Essex

Collins ISBN 0 00 360034 3
Longman ISBN 0 582 00170 6

Printed in Hong Kong by
Sheck Wah Tong Printing Press Ltd

Preface
to the third edition

Since it first appeared in 1969 Atlas Four has received enthusiastic acclaim both for its content and presentation, and is now widely used by Secondary School Certificate Grades. During the past decade several regularly revised reprints have kept Atlas Four up-to-date and since 1973, when the metric system was adopted for teaching and examination requirements, a fully metricated edition has been available. Now, in the 1980's, with the development of new emphases in school geography and changes in 'Certificate' examination syllabii, a new, enlarged and greatly improved edition of Atlas Four is introduced to meet these current needs.

Sixteen additional pages of maps have been included in this new edition extending the coverage of South America, China and Japan, introducing a complete new series of continental human activity maps, and enlarging the world thematic section to include such topics as Climatic Regions, Tectonics and Economic Geology, Time Zones, International Organisations, Fuels, Ores, Food Crops, Beverages, Livestock and Fishing, as well as new maps and diagrams on Population and Communications. The maps of the British Isles have also been fully revised and many completely redrawn to include latest developments such as North Sea oil and gas. The statistical section preceding the maps and the geographical index of place names have likewise been up-dated from the latest available source data.

Atlas Four is a 'Certificate-level Atlas' in the sense that the needs of Secondary School pupils preparing for their final examination have been particularly borne in mind during our long and thorough researches into the educational requirements. At the same time, our chief aim has been to provide teacher and student with the best possible educational tool for the study of geography at this general level of attainment. To do this properly, and to make adequate use both of the latest developments in cartographic techniques and of the results of our researches in schools, we decided from the outset to start from first principles on a whole range of new material.

Atlas Four thus introduces original features both in content and in cartographic design, and these are discussed in the Map Notes following. Innovations, however, have been made only where there was solid evidence to show that they would be welcomed in the schools, and we have carefully avoided mere change for change's sake. In every respect—educationally, geographically and cartographically—we believe that Atlas Four represents a major step forward.

Finally, in the preparation of Atlas Four we have used only the most accurate and up-to-date sources available. Very many individuals and organisations have been generous with contributions and advice, and to all we would like to express our profound thanks. In particular, we are grateful for the professional advice of Professor J. Wreford Watson of the Department of Geography, Edinburgh University.

J. David Thompson, B.Sc.
Cartographic Editor

CONTENTS

MAP NOTES

Measurements

Metric measurements are used exclusively throughout the atlas on all general maps and thematic maps.

Symbols

For easy reference the symbols used in the general maps are explained on the inside covers. Each of the thematic maps has a key of its own. Colour schemes and symbols have been standardized wherever possible to avoid confusion and keep the range of symbols within bounds.

Projections

The projections on which the maps have been drawn have been selected to retain, as far as possible, true shape and equal area. The world maps are constructed on Winkel's Tripel Projection which, although not strictly providing equal areas, overcomes the extreme distortion of shape that afflicts all truly equal area projections.

Although it is beyond the scope of this note to explain the properties of map projections, it should be stressed that the scales indicated on the maps as representative fractions and bars are exact only along the standard parallels. The discrepencies are very slight on the larger scale maps, but can be misleading if, for instance, the world maps are used to measure distance in any direction, as the scale is correct only along the equator.

Statistics

A four page statistical section arranged by continent is included at the beginning of the atlas. Details of total population, population density, area and capital city are given for each country.

Regional Maps

In the design of the regional maps of the British Isles and the continents care has been taken to achieve a balanced presentation of the physical and human elements. Relief is represented by layer-colours, contours and hill shading.

Settlements have been selected strictly according to size and importance. It is always difficult to anticipate every individual requirement in selecting the names to be included on the reference map. While as many names as seem consistent with legibility and the general needs of this level are shown, the inclusion of too many minor settlements has been avoided. In crowded urban areas space frequently precludes the cartographer from naming quite important places, and this problem sometimes arises even at the scale of the regional maps of the British Isles.

On the maps of China the Pinyin system has been used to transliterate names. This system has now been adopted within China, by the United States Board of Geographical names and by the media.

The scales used for the regional maps vary according to the size and importance of the region or country. Thus densely settled and highly developed areas such as the Low Countries or Northeastern U.S.A. are singled out for treatment at the largest possible scale.

Thematic Maps

Apart from the detailed treatment of special topics for the British Isles the thematic maps of the rest of the world have been arranged on a continental basis. This means that the information is presented at a better scale than would have been possible if all these maps were of the world as a whole.

Maps of Physiography and Geology, Climate, Land Cover, Human Activity, Mineral Resourses and Population are included for each continent.

Where it is vital to see a subject in its global setting it has been treated as a world map and in some cases material already mapped continentally is presented again in summary form for the world as a whole. A wide range of physical, economic and demographic topics are mapped.

Index

The comprehensive index contains all names except for some of those on the thematic maps, and totals over 16,000 entries. Without discarding the use of full latitude and longitude the index has been designed so that references can be made as quickly and conveniently as possible. Further details will be found at the beginning of the index.

AFRICA

COUNTRY	Population	AREA IN SQ. KM	DENSITY	MEAN ANNUAL % INCREASE	CAPITAL	Population
ALGERIA	17 304 000	2 382 000	7.3	3.2	Algiers	1 503 000
ANGOLA	6 761 000	1 247 000	5.4	na	Luanda	480 000
BENIN	3 197 000	113 000	28	2.7	Porto Novo	104 000
BOTSWANA	693 000	600 000	1.2	3.6	Gaborone	18 000
BURUNDI	3 864 000	28 000	138	na	Bujumbura	79 000
CAMEROON	6 531 000	475 000	14	1.9	Yaoundé	274 000
CENTRAL AFRICAN EMPIRE	2 370 000	623 000	3.8	na	Bangui	187 000
CHAD	4 116 000	1 284 000	3.2	2.1	N'Djamena	179 000
COMORO ISLANDS	291 000	2 000	146	2.5	Moroni	12 000
CONGO	1 390 000	342 000	4.1	2.5	Brazzaville	290 000
DJIBOUTI	108 000	22 000	4.9		Djibouti	62 000
EGYPT	38 067 000	1 001 000	38	2.2	Cairo	5 715 000
EQUATORIAL GUINEA	316 000	28 000	11	1.7	Malabo	37 000
ETHIOPIA	28 668 000	1 222 000	23	2.6	Addis Ababa	1 161 000
GABON	530 000	268 000	2.0	1.0	Libreville	251 000
GAMBIA	538 000	11 000	49	2.5	Banjul	48 000
GHANA	10 309 000	239 000	43	2.7	Accra	738 000
GUINEA	4 529 000	246 000	18	2.4	Conakry	526 000
GUINEA BISSAU	534 000	36 000	15	0.2	Bissau	65 000
IVORY COAST	5 017 000	322 000	16	2.5	Abidjan	850 000
KENYA	13 847 000	583 000	24	3.6	Nairobi	630 000
LESOTHO	1 214 000	30 000	40	2.2	Maseru	29 000
LIBERIA	1 751 000	111 000	16	2.3	Monrovia	172 000
LIBYA	2 444 000	1 760 000	1.4	4.2	Tripoli	551 000
					Benghazi	282 000
MADAGASCAR	8 266 000	587 000	14	1.5	Tananarive	378 000
MALAWI	5 175 000	118 000	44	2.6	Lilongwe	20 000
MALI	5 844 000	1 240 000	4.7	2.5	Bamako	197 000
MAURITANIA	1 481 000	1 031 000	1.4	2.6	Nouakchott	135 000
MAURITIUS	851 000	2 000	426	1.6	Port Louis	138 000
MOCAMBIQUE	9 444 000	783 000	12	2.3	Maputo	384 000
MOROCCO	17 828 000	446 000	40	na	Rabat	597 000
NAMIBIA	852 000	824 000	1.0	2.9	Windhoek	61 000
NIGER	4 727 000	1 267 000	3.7	2.7	Niamey	130 000
NIGERIA	64 750 000	924 000	70	2.7	Lagos	1 477 000
REPUBLIC OF SOUTH AFRICA	26 129 000	1 221 000	21	2.5	Cape Town	1 097 000
					Pretoria	562 000
REUNION	474 000	2 510	189	2.4	St. Denis	85 000
RWANDA	4 289 000	26 000	165	2.7	Kigali	54 000
SENEGAL	5 115 000	196 000	26	2.4	Dakar	726 000
SEYCHELLES	59 000	280	211	2.2	Victoria	15 000
SIERRA LEONE	3 111 000	72 000	43	1.5	Freetown	214 000
SOMALI REPUBLIC	3 261 000	638 000	5.1	2.6	Mogadishu	230 000
SUDAN	16 126 000	2 506 000	6.4	2.5	Khartoum	334 000
SWAZILAND	497 000	17 000	29	3.2	Mbabane	21 000
TANZANIA	15 607 000	945 000	17	2.9	Dar es Salaam	517 000
TOGO	2 283 000	56 000	41	2.5	Lome	135 000
TUNISIA	5 737 000	164 000	35	2.4	Tunis	648 000
UGANDA	11 943 000	236 000	51	3.3	Kampala	331 000
UPPER VOLTA	6 174 000	274 000	23	2.3	Ouagadougou	125 000
WESTERN SAHARA	128 000	266 000	0.5	8.9	El Aaiun	24 000
ZAIRE	25 629 000	2 345 000	11	2.8	Kinshasa	2 008 000
ZAMBIA	5 138 000	753 000	6.8	3.2	Lusaka	448 000
ZIMBABWE	6 530 000	391 000	17	3.5	Salisbury	502 000

THE AMERICAS

COUNTRY	Population	AREA IN SQ. KM	DENSITY	MEAN ANNUAL % INCREASE	CAPITAL	Population
ANTIGUA & BARBUDA	74000	442	167.4	0.4	St. John's	25000
ARGENTINA	25719000	2 767 000	9.3	1.3	Buenos Aires	8353000
BAHAMAS	211000	14 000	15	3.6	Nassau	102 000
BARBADOS	256000	431	540	0.6	Bridgetown	12000
BELIZE	144000	23 000	6.3	3.1	Belmopan	5000
BERMUDA	57000	53	1 075	1.6	Hamilton	3000
BOLÍVIA	5789000	1 099 000	5.3	2.7	La Paz	661000
					Sucre	107000
BRAZIL	109181000	8 512 000	13	3.0	Brasilia	272000
CANADA	23143000	9 976 000	2.3	1.4	Ottowa	693000
CAYMAN ISLANDS	12000	259	46.3	1.9	Georgetown	4000
CHILE	10454000	757000	14	1.8	Santiago	3186000
COLOMBIA	24373000	1 139 000	21	2.8	Bogota	2855000
COSTA RICA	2012000	51 000	39	2.6	San Jose	395000
CUBA	9405000	115000	82	na	Havana	1009000
DOMINICA	74000	751	99	1.1	Roseau	12000
DOMINICAN REPUBLIC	4835000	49 000	99	3.0	Santo Domingo	818000
ECUADOR	7305000	284 000	26	3.4	Quito	557000
EL SALVADOR	4123000	21 000	196	3.0	San Salvador	380000
FALKLAND ISLANDS	2000	12 000	0.2	0.0	Stanley	1090
GREENLAND	50000	2 176 000	0.02	1.5	Godthaab	9032
GRENADA	105000	344	305	0.4	St. George's	9000
GUADELOUPE	342000	1 779	192	1.6	Pointe a Pitre	39000
GUATEMALA	6256000	109 000	57	2.5	Guatemala City	707000
GUIANA (FR.)	62000	91 000	0.7	3.5	Cayenne	25000
GUYANA	783000	215 000	3.6	2.2	Georgetown	164000
HAITI	4668000	28 000	168	1.6	Port-au-Prince	494000
HONDURAS	2831000	112 000	25	3.9	Tegucigalpa	302000
JAMAICA	2057000	11 000	187	1.7	Kingston	573000
MARTINIQUE	343000	1 102	311	1.6	Fort-de-France	100000
MEXICO	62329000	1 973 000	32	3.5	Mexico City	11340000
MONTSERRAT	11698	98	120	1.6	Plymouth	1267
NICARAGUA	2233000	130 000	17	3.3	Managua	500000
PANAMA	1719000	76 000	23	3.1	Panama City	404000
PARAGUAY	2724000	407 000	6.7	2.8	Asuncion	473000
PERU	16090000	1 285 000	13	3.0	Lima	3303000
PUERTO RICO	3213000	9 000	357	2.6	San Juan	695000
ST. KITTS-NEVIS	65000	357	182	0.6	Basseterre	15726
ST. LUCIA	115000	616	187	1.3	Castries	45000
ST. VINCENT	96000	388	247	2.0	Kingstown	23000
SURINAM	435000	163 000	2.7	2.6	Paramaribo	151000
TRINIDAD & TOBAGO	1067000	5 000	213	1.2	Port of Spain	68000
UNITED STATES OF AMERICA	215118000	9 363 000	23	0.8	Washington	2861000
URUGUAY	3101000	178 000	17	1.2	Montevideo	1230000
VENEZUELA	12361000	912 000	14	2.9	Caracas	2175000
VIRGIN ISLANDS (U.S.A.)	62 468	344	182	7.0	Charlotte Amalie	12220

ASIA & OCEANIA

COUNTRY	Population	AREA IN SQ. KM	DENSITY	MEAN ANNUAL % INCREASE	CAPITAL	Population
ASIA						
AFGHANISTAN	19803000	647000	31	2.4	Kabul	588000
BAHRAIN	259000	622	416	3.5	Manama	89000
BANGLADESH	76815000	144000	533	n.a.	Dacca	1730000
BHUTAN	1202000	47000	26	2.1	Thimbu	11000
BRUNEI	177000	6000	30	2.4	Bandar Seri Begawan	37000
BURMA	30834000	677000	46	2.5	Rangoon	3187000
CAMBODIA	8354000	181000	46	2.8	Phnom Penh	394000
CHINA	852133000	9561000	89	1.7	Peking	7570000
CYPRUS	639000	9000	71	0.8	Nicosia	116000
HONG KONG	4383000	1045	4194	2.0	Victoria	849000
INDIA	610077000	3287000	186	2.1	New Delhi	301000
INDONESIA	139616000	1907000	73	2.6	Jakarta	4576000
IRAN	33400000	1648000	20	2.9	Tehran	4002000
IRAQ	11505000	435000	26	3.3	Baghdad	2969000
ISRAEL	3465000	21000	165	3.1	Jerusalem	344000
JAPAN	112768000	372000	303	1.2	Tokyo	11623000
JORDAN	2779000	98000	28	3.3	Amman	598000
KOREA (NORTH)	16246000	121000	134	2.7	Pyongyang	1500000
KOREA (SOUTH)	35860000	98000	366	2.1	Seoul	6889000
KUWAIT	1031000	18000	57	6.0	Kuwait	80000
LAOS	3383000	237000	14	2.2	Vientiane	177000
LEBANON	2961000	10000	296	3.0	Beirut	702000
MACAO	249000	16	15562	1.8	Macao City	241000
MALAYSIA	12300000	330000	37	2.8	Kuala Lumpur	452000
MONGOLIA	1488000	1565000	0.9	3.0	Ulan Bator	282000
NEPAL	12904000	141000	92	2.3	Katmandu	210000
OMAN	791000	212000	3.7	n.a.	Muscat	25000
PAKISTAN	72368000	804000	90	3.0	Islamabad	77000
PHILIPPINES	43751000	300000	146	2.9	Manila	1438000
QATAR	180000	11000	16	3.1	Doha	130000
SAUDI ARABIA	9240000	2150000	4.3	3.0	Riyadh	667000
SINGAPORE	2278000	602	3784	1.6	Singapore	2250000
SOUTHERN YEMEN	1749000	333000	5.3	2.4	Aden	285000
SRI LANKA	14270000	66000	216	2.2	Colombo	618000
SYRIA	7596000	185000	41	3.3	Damascus	837000
TAIWAN	15500000	36000	431	na	Taipei	1922000
THAILAND	42960000	514000	84	2.9	Bangkok	3967000
TURKEY	40163000	781000	51	2.4	Ankara	1554000
UNITED ARAB EMIRATES	655000	84000	7.8	3.2		
VIETNAM	46523000	333000	139	2.9	Hanoi	1444000
YEMEN	6870000	195000	35	2.9	Sana	150000
OCEANIA						
AUSTRALIA	13643000	7687000	1.8	1.5	Canberra	185000
FIJI	580000	18000	32	2.0	Suva	80000
KIRIBATI	55000				Tarawa	17188
NAURU	8000	21	381			
NEW CALEDONIA	135000	19000	7.1	2.6	Noumea	74000
NEW HEBRIDES	97000	15000	6.5	2.9	Vila	16604
NEW ZEALAND	3140000	269000	12	1.9	Wellington	327000
PAPUA NEW GUINEA	2829000	462000	6.1	2.0	Port Moresby	77000
SOLOMON ISLANDS	200000	28000	7.1	3.1	Honiara	15000
TONGA	90000	699	129	3.0	Nuku'alofa	16000
TUVALU	6200	24	258	na	Funafuti	1000
WESTERN SAMOA	151000	2842	53	1.3	Apia	33000

EUROPE

COUNTRY	Population	AREA IN SQ. KM	DENSITY	MEAN ANNUAL % INCREASE	CAPITAL	Population
ALBANIA	2 548 000	29 000	88	3.0	Tirane	192 000
ANDORRA	29 000	453	64	4.9	Andorra	2 500
AUSTRIA	7 514 000	84 000	89	0.3	Vienna	1 859 000
BELGIUM	9 889 000	31 000	319	0.2	Brussels	1 075 000
BULGARIA	8 761 000	111 000	79	0.5	Sofia	963 000
CZECHOSLOVAKIA	14 918 000	128 000	117	0.6	Prague	1 096 000
DENMARK	5 073 000	43 000	118	0.5	Copenhagen	1 328 000
EAST GERMANY	16 786 000	108 000	155	-0.2	East Berlin	1 098 000
FAROE ISLANDS	37 122	1 399	27	1.1	Thorshavn	10 726
FINLAND	4 727 000	337 000	14	0.4	Helsinki	869 000
FRANCE	52 915 000	547 000	97	0.8	Paris	8 424 000
GIBRALTAR	26 833	6	4 472			
GREECE	9 165 000	132 000	69	0.6	Athens	2 101 000
HUNGARY	10 596 000	93 000	114	0.4	Budapest	2 051 000
ICELAND	220 000	103 000	2.1	1.1	Reykjavik	84 772
ITALY	56 189 000	301 000	187	0.8	Rome	2 868 000
LIECHTENSTEIN	23 700	157	151	2.4	Vaduz	4 000
LUXEMBOURG	358 000	2 586	138	1.0	Luxembourg	78 000
MALTA	304 000	316	962	-1.6	Valletta	14 049
MONACO	25 000	1.5	16 667	1.2	Monaco	24 000
NETHERLANDS	13 710 000	41 000	334	0.8	Amsterdam	996 000
NORWAY	4 027 000	324 000	12	0.7	Oslo	465 000
POLAND	34 362 000	313 000	110	0.9	Warsaw	1 400 000
PORTUGAL	9 449 000	92 000	103	0.2	Lisbon	1 012 000
REPUBLIC OF IRELAND	3 162 000	70 000	45	1.2	Dublin	815 000
ROMANIA	21 446 000	238 000	90	1.0	Bucharest	1 707 000
SAN MARINO	20 000	61	328	0.6	San Marino	5 000
SPAIN	35 971 000	505 000	71	1.0	Madrid	3 520 000
SWEDEN	8 222 000	450 000	18	0.4	Stockholm	1 354 000
SWITZERLAND	6 346 000	41 000	155	0.7	Berne	285 000
U.S.S.R.	256 670 000	22 402 000	11	0.9	Moscow	7 632 000
UNITED KINGDOM	55 928 000	244 000	229	0.2	London	7 168 000
WEST GERMANY	61 498 000	248 000	248	0.4	Bonn	283 000
YUGOSLAVIA	21 500 000	256 000	84	0.9	Belgrade	1 204 000

Urals

Caucasus

Black Sea

Baltic Shield

Baltic Sea

North European Plain

Carpathians

Alps

Pyrenees

MEDITERRANEAN SEA

North Sea

ATLANTIC OCEAN

Arctic Circle

Bonne Projection

Scale 1:20 000 000

800 km
600
400
200
0

Main trend lines
Rift valleys
Main centres of volcanic activity

Quaternary
Tertiary
Mesozoic
Palaeozoic
Precambrian

Lowland Plains & Basins
High Plains & Plateaus
Scarps & Upland Edges
Fold & Volcanic Mountains

© Collins ◇ Longman Atlas

Legend:
- Permanent ice and snow
- Tundra and alpine
- Desert
- Semi-desert
- Grassland, heath, marsh and steppe
- Forest and woodland
- Cultivated land

Scale 1:16 000 000

0 200 400 600 800 km

Conic Projection

ICELAND
Hekla 1491

North Cape

ARCTIC

NORWEGIAN SEA

Lofoten Is.

SCANDINAVIA

Tornio

2470

Gulf of Bothnia

Faroe Is.

Shetland Is.

Mälaren Åland Is. Gulf of Finland

Vänern L. Peipus

Skagerrak Vättern

Hebrides Orkney Is.

Ben Nevis 1343

NORTH SEA

Gotland

Jutland Baltic Sea

Bornholm

ATLANTIC

OCEAN

Ireland Great Britain

Thames

Land's End

English Channel

North European

Weser Elbe

Rhine Oder Vistula Bug

Dnieper

Meuse

Ardennes

Ore Mts. Sudeten Mts.

Bohemian Forest Moravian Heights Carpathians

Seine

Loire Vosges Black Forest Danube

Bay of Biscay

Jura Mts. Inn

Massif Central

Mt. Blanc 4807 The Alps Hungarian Plain

C. Finisterre

Garonne Rhône Po Drava Mures

Cevennes Transylvanian Alps

Cantabrian Mts. Pyrenees Sava

Douro Pico de Aneto 4404

Meseta Gulf of Lions Dinaric Alps Balkan

Ebro

Tagus Ligurian Sea Apennines Adriatic Sea

Guadiana Gulf of Biscay Corsica Tiber Pindus Mts.

C. St. Vincent Sierra Morena Balearic Is. Sardinia Olympus 2911

Guadalquivir

Str. of Gibraltar Sierra Nevada Tyrrhenian Sea

Ionian Sea

MEDITERRANEAN

Sicily Mt Etna 3340

Aegean Sea

High Atlas Tell Atlas Malta

Saharan Atlas

Crete

OCEAN

Kola
Peninsula

White Sea

N. Dvina

L. Onega

L. Ladoga

Plain

Central

Russian

Uplands

Dnieper

Dniester

Bug

Dnieper

Sea of Azov

Crimea

Black   Sea

Bosporus

Pontine   Range

Kizil Irmak

Anatolia

Taurus Mts.

Rhodes

Cyprus

SEA

Levant

Mesopotamia

Tigris

Euphrates

Van Gölu

Mt Ararat
5165

Urmia

Araxes

Kura

Caucasus Mts.

Elbrus
5633

Tsimlyansk Res.

Don

Donets

Don

Volga

Volga Uplands

Oka

Volga

Rybinsk Res.

Volga

Kama

URAL MOUNTAINS

Narodynaya
1894

Pechora

Ural

1639

West
Siberian
Plain

Ob

Ob

Irtysh

Tobol

Ob

Kirghiz   Steppe

L. Balkhash

Syr Darya

Aral Sea

Turanian Plain

Kyzyl Kum

Ust Urt
Plateau

Amu Darya

Caspian   Sea

Kara
Bogaz
Gol

Kara Kum

Elburz Mts.

Dasht-e-Kavir

Iranian

Zagros   Mts.   Plateau

© Collins ◊ Longman Atlases

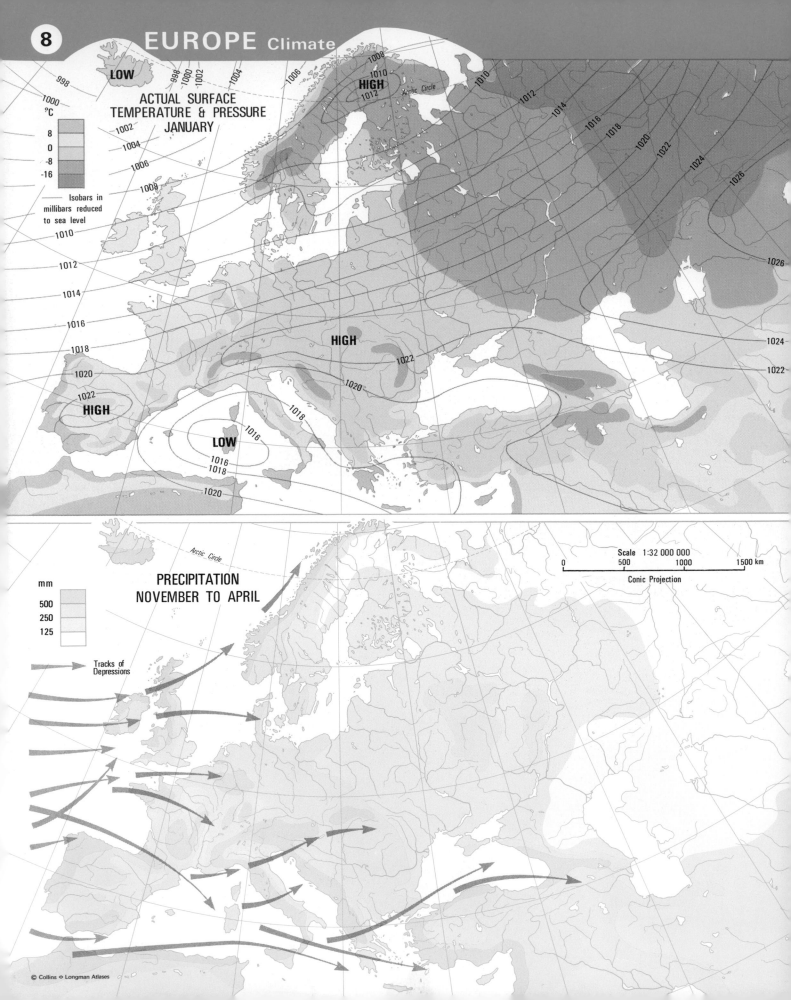

ACTUAL SURFACE TEMPERATURE & PRESSURE JANUARY

°C

8
0
-8
-16

Isobars in millibars reduced to sea level

LOW
998
1000
1002
1004
1006
1008
1010
1012
1014
1016
1018
1020
1022
1024
1026

HIGH
1012

HIGH

Arctic Circle

HIGH
1022

LOW

HIGH

1016
1018
1020

PRECIPITATION NOVEMBER TO APRIL

mm

500
250
125

Tracks of Depressions

Arctic Circle

Scale 1:32 000 000

0   500   1000   1500 km

Conic Projection

© Collins ◇ Longman Atlases

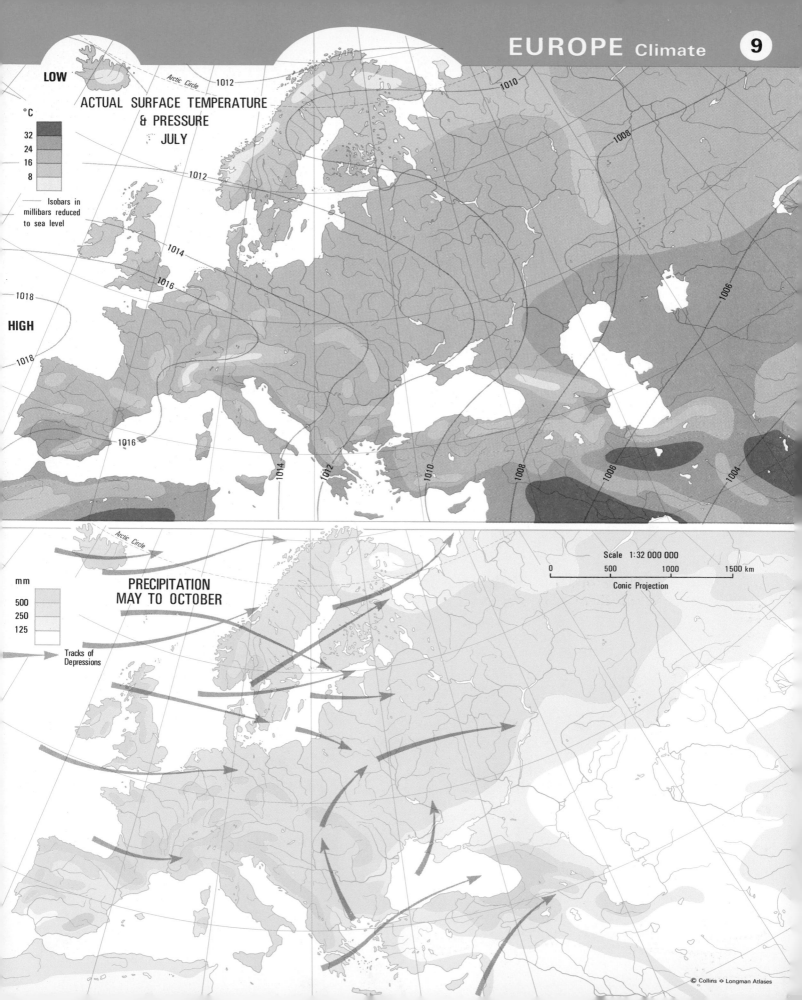

LOW

ACTUAL SURFACE TEMPERATURE & PRESSURE JULY

°C

32	
24	
16	
8	

Isobars in millibars reduced to sea level

HIGH

1012
1012
1014
1016
1018
1018
1016
1016
1014
1012
1010
1008
1006
1010
1008
1006
1004

Arctic Circle

PRECIPITATION MAY TO OCTOBER

mm

500	
250	
125	

Tracks of Depressions

Arctic Circle

Scale 1:32 000 000

0   500   1000   1500 km

Conic Projection

© Collins ◇ Longman Atlases

Little or no activity

PREDOMINANT SUBSISTENCE ECONOMY

Hunting and fishing

Traditional cultivation

Semi-intensive sedentary

Traditional pastoralism

Nomadic herding (reindeer)

Nomadic herding (sheep & goats)

Non-nomadic (sheep & goats)

PREDOMINANT COMMERCIAL ECONOMY

Intensive cultivation

Grain

Large-scale specialised (plantation)

Specialised (market gardening)

Livestock rearing

Extensive (cattle)

Extensive (sheep)

Intensive (cattle)

Intensive dairying

Lumbering

Fishing

Manufacturing/service industry

Extractive industry

Areas of mixed economies shown by banding

Scale 1:16 000 000

0   200   400   600   800 km

Conic Projection

ARCTIC

Lapland

Arctic Circle

NORTH SEA

Oslo

Stockholm

Göteborg

BALTIC SEA

Copenhagen-Malmö

Hamburg

Berlin

Warsaw

North European

Europoort

Nord

Ruhr

Liège

Frankfurt

Prague

Katowice

Paris Basin

Paris

Mannheim-Karlsruhe

Stuttgart

Clydeside

Tyneside

Merseyside

West Yorkshire

West Midlands

London

Zürich

Carpathian

Lyon

The Alps

Milan

Turin

Plain of Lombardy

Genoa

Marseille

Apennines

Meseta

Pyrénées

Madrid

Barcelona

Balkan

MEDITERRANEAN

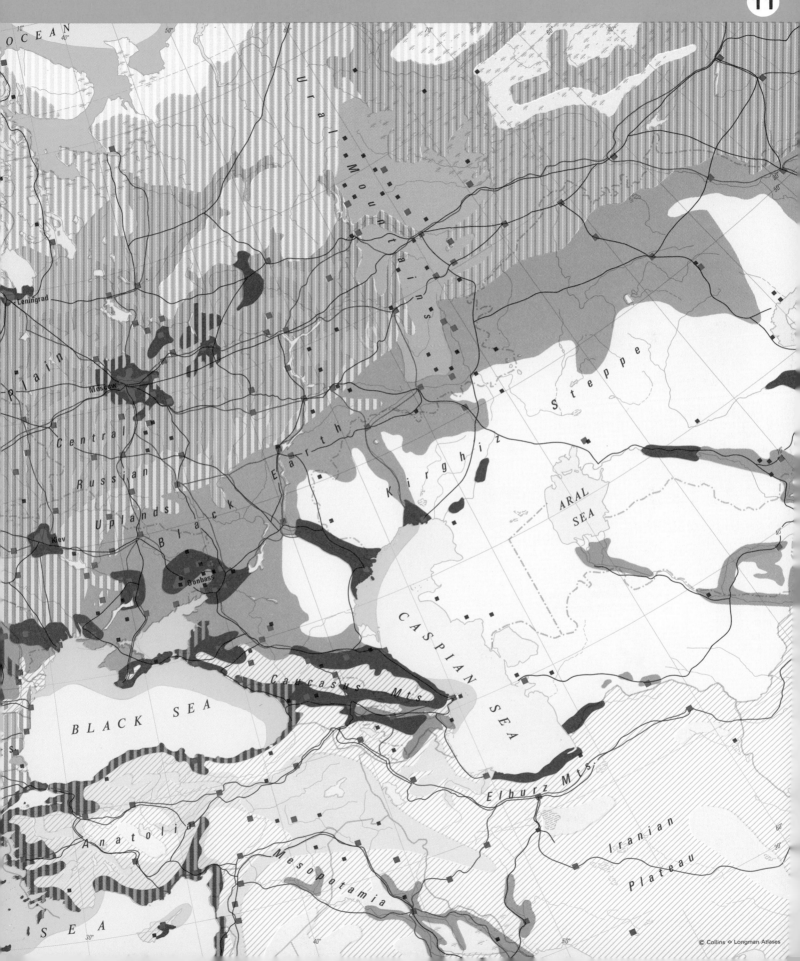

OCEAN

Ural Mountains

Steppe

Leningrad

K i r g h i z

ARAL SEA

Moscow

Central

Russian

Black Earth

Uplands

Kiev

Black

Donbass

CASPIAN SEA

Caucasus Mts.

BLACK SEA

Elburz Mts.

Anatolia

Iranian

Mesopotamia

Plateau

SEA

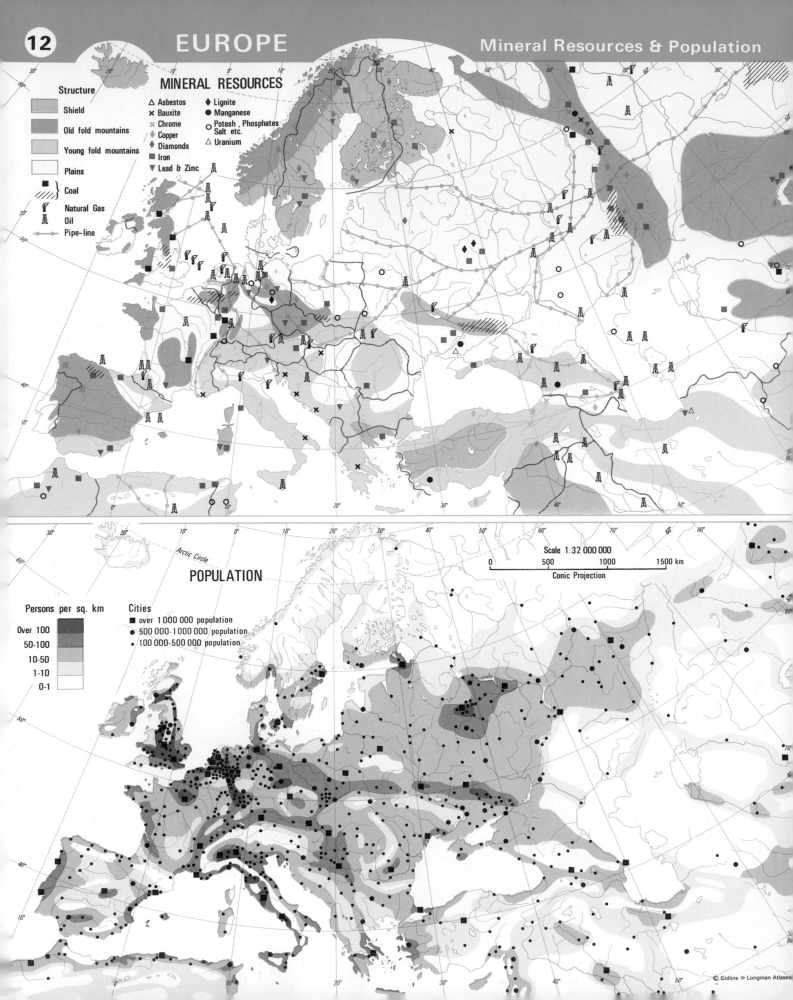

MINERAL RESOURCES

Structure
- Shield
- Old fold mountains
- Young fold mountains
- Plains

- Coal
- Natural Gas
- Oil
- Pipe-line

- △ Asbestos
- ✕ Bauxite
- ✕ Chrome
- ◆ Copper
- ◆ Diamonds
- ■ Iron
- ▼ Lead & Zinc
- ◆ Lignite
- ● Manganese
- ○ Potash , Phosphates Salt etc.
- △ Uranium

POPULATION

Persons per sq. km
- Over 100
- 50-100
- 10-50
- 1-10
- 0-1

Cities
- ■ over 1 000 000 population
- ● 500 000-1 000 000 population
- • 100 000-500 000 population

Scale 1:32 000 000

0   500   1000   1500 km

Conic Projection

Arctic Circle

© Collins ◇ Longman Atlases

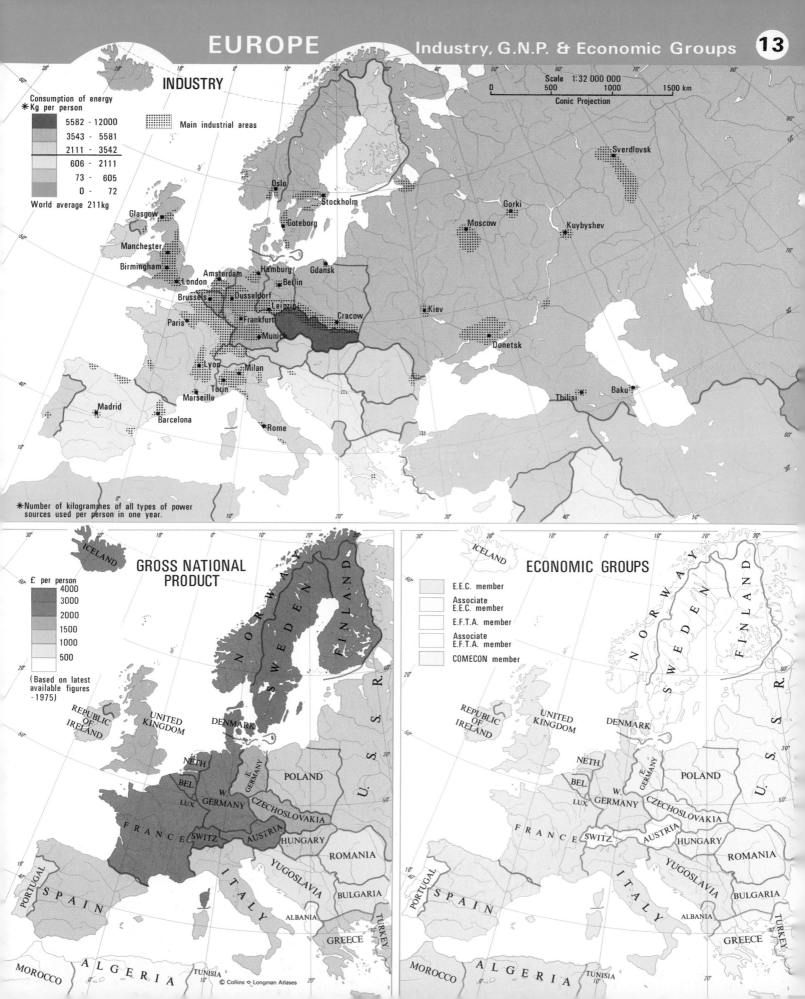

INDUSTRY

Consumption of energy
✻ Kg per person

	5582 - 12000
	3543 - 5581
	2111 - 3542
	606 - 2111
	73 - 605
	0 - 72

World average 211kg

▦ Main industrial areas

Scale 1:32 000 000
0   500   1000   1500 km
Conic Projection

Sverdlovsk

Oslo
Stockholm
Goteborg
Glasgow
Gorki
Moscow
Kuybyshev
Manchester
Birmingham
Hamburg   Gdansk
London   Amsterdam   Berlin
Brussels   Dusseldorf
Paris   Leipzig   Cracow   Kiev
Frankfurt
Munich
Donetsk
Lyon   Milan
Torin
Marseille
Baku
Madrid   Thilisi
Barcelona   Rome

✻Number of kilogrammes of all types of power
sources used per person in one year.

GROSS NATIONAL PRODUCT

£ per person

	4000
	3000
	2000
	1500
	1000
	500

(Based on latest
available figures
-1975)

ICELAND
NORWAY   SWEDEN   FINLAND
REPUBLIC OF IRELAND
UNITED KINGDOM
DENMARK
U.S.S.R.
NETH.
BEL.
E. GERMANY
POLAND
LUX.
W. GERMANY
CZECHOSLOVAKIA
U.
FRANCE   SWITZ.   AUSTRIA   HUNGARY
ROMANIA
PORTUGAL   SPAIN   ITALY   YUGOSLAVIA
BULGARIA
ALBANIA
GREECE   TURKEY
MOROCCO   ALGERIA   TUNISIA

ECONOMIC GROUPS

	E.E.C. member
	Associate E.E.C. member
	E.F.T.A. member
	Associate E.F.T.A. member
	COMECON member

ICELAND
NORWAY   SWEDEN   FINLAND
REPUBLIC OF IRELAND
UNITED KINGDOM
DENMARK
U.S.S.R.
NETH.
BEL.
E. GERMANY
POLAND
W. GERMANY
CZECHOSLOVAKIA
U.
FRANCE   SWITZ.   AUSTRIA   HUNGARY
ROMANIA
PORTUGAL   SPAIN   ITALY   YUGOSLAVIA
BULGARIA
ALBANIA
GREECE   TURKEY
MOROCCO   ALGERIA   TUNISIA

© Collins • Longman Atlases

© Collins ○ Longman Atlases

BEL : BELGIUM
L : LIECHTENSTEIN
LUX : LUXEMBOURG
NETH : NETHERLANDS
S.M : SAN MARINO
SWITZ : SWITZERLAND

Scale 1:20 000 000

Bonne Projection

800 km
600
400
200
0

ARCTIC OCEAN

ATLANTIC OCEAN

NORTH SEA

MEDITERRANEAN SEA

BLACK SEA

Caspian Sea

White Sea

Baltic Sea

Aegean Sea

Adriatic Sea

Ionian Sea

Tyrrhenian Sea

North Cape
Arctic Circle

ICELAND
Reykjavík

UNION OF SOVIET SOCIALIST REPUBLICS

NORWAY
SWEDEN
FINLAND
DENMARK

UNITED KINGDOM
REPUBLIC OF IRELAND

WEST GERMANY
EAST GERMANY
POLAND
CZECHOSLOVAKIA
AUSTRIA
HUNGARY
ROMANIA
BULGARIA
YUGOSLAVIA
ALBANIA
GREECE

FRANCE
SPAIN
PORTUGAL
ANDORRA

ITALY
MONACO
S.M.

SWITZ
NETH
BEL
LUX

TURKEY
IRAN
IRAQ
SYRIA
LEBANON
CYPRUS

ALGERIA
TUNISIA
MOROCCO

Cities and places:
Sverdlovsk, Ufa, Kuybyshev, Kazan, Saratov, Penza, Kirov, Kotlas, Syktyvkar, N.Dvina, Vologda, Gorki, Yaroslavl, Kalinin, Moscow, Tula, Orel, Voronezh, Volgograd, Rostov, Astrakhan, Grozny, Ordzhonikidze, Tbilisi, Yerevan, Tabriz, Mosul, Aleppo, Homs, Adana, Konya, Antalya, Izmir, Bursa, Istanbul, Ankara, Nicosia, Rhodes, Crete, Athens, Pátras, Thessaloníki, Sofia, Bucharest, Constanţa, Varna, Burgas, Edirne, Cluj, Ploeşti, Belgrade, Szeged, Miskolc, Košice, Cracow, Lvov, Kishinev, Odessa, Kerch, Sevastopol', Sinop, Trabzon, Batumi, Krasnodar, Donetsk, Dnepropetrovsk, Zaporozhye, Kharkov, Kiev, Minsk, Smolensk, Vilnius, Kaunas, Riga, Tallinn, Leningrad, Vyborg, Helsinki, Turku, Tampere, Vaasa, Luleå, Oulu, Murmansk, Narvik, Tromsø, Trondheim, Bergen, Stavanger, Oslo, Gothenburg, Stockholm, Sundsvall, Malmö, Copenhagen, Esbjerg, Kiel, Hamburg, Bremen, Hannover, Berlin, Dresden, Wrocław, Poznań, Gdańsk, Warsaw, Białystok, Łódź, Prague, Plzeň, Bratislava, Vienna, Budapest, Zagreb, Graz, Split, Sarajevo, Tirane, Brindisi, Taranto, Bari, Reggio, Palermo, Cagliari, Naples, Rome, Ancona, Bologna, Florence, Venice, Trieste, Milan, Genoa, Turin, Monaco, Nice, Marseille, Lyon, Geneva, Berne, Zürich, Innsbruck, Munich, Stuttgart, Frankfurt, Essen, Bonn, Luxembourg, Brussels, Lille, Strasbourg, Amsterdam, The Hague, Rotterdam, London, Birmingham, Leeds, Manchester, Liverpool, Bristol, Edinburgh, Glasgow, Belfast, Dublin, Brest, Nantes, Bordeaux, Toulouse, Paris, Barcelona, Valencia, Zaragoza, Madrid, Murcia, Granada, Seville, Bilbao, Oviedo, La Coruña, Oporto, Lisbon, Palma, Algiers, Oran, Annaba, Bizerta, Tunis, Rabat, Casablanca, Fez, Tangier, Gibraltar (Br.)

Seas and waters: Gulf of Bothnia, Skagerrak, English Channel, Bay of Biscay, Sea of Azov

Islands: Faroe Is., Shetland Is., Orkney Is., Hebrides, Gotland, Bornholm, Corsica (Fr.), Sardinia (It.), Sicily, Balearic Is. (Sp.), Lofoten, Malta, Sir. (J.)

Rivers: Ob, Pečora, Kama, Volga, Don, Donets, Dnieper, Dnestr, Prut, Danube, Vistula, Oder, Elbe, Rhine, Rhône, Loire, Seine, Garonne, Ebro, Douro, Tagus, Sava, Bug, Dvina, N.Dvina, L.Onega, L.Ladoga, Rybinsk Resr., Vättern, Vänern, Tigris, Euphrates

Tertiary
Mesozoic
Palaeozoic
Precambrian

Igneous rocks of various ages

Lowland Plains & Basins
High Plains & Plateaus
Scarps & Upland Edges
Fold & Volcanic Mountains

Main fault line

MOINE THRUST

Northwest Highlands

GREAT GLEN FAULT

Grampian Mountains

HIGHLAND BOUNDARY FAULT

Ochil Hills

SOUTHERN UPLANDS FAULT

Southern Uplands

Cheviot Hills

CRAVEN FAULT

Lake District

Pennines

Antrim Mts.

Wicklow Mts.

Macgillycuddy's Reeks

Cambrian Mountains

Cotswolds

Chiltern Hills

North Downs

South Downs

Exmoor

Dartmoor

Scale 1:5 000 000

0   50   100   150   200   250km

Conic Projection

Sub-alpine

Heath and peat

Grass moorland

Forest and woodland

Agricultural land

Urban areas

Orkney Islands

Unst
Yell
Shetland Islands
Foula Mainland
Fair Isle

Butt of Lewis
C. Wrath
Dunnet Hd.
Duncansby Hd.
Lewis
St. Kilda
Outer Hebrides
North Uist
Skye
South Uist
Barra
Inner Hebrides
Coll
Tiree
Mull ▲966
Rhum
The Minch
Ben More Assynt ▲998
Northwest Highlands
Dornoch Firth
Moray Firth
Spey
Cairngorms
Ben Macdhui ▲1311
The Great Glen
Grampians
Ben Nevis ▲1343
Tay
Strathmore
Firth of Tay
Firth of Lorn
Forth
Ochil Hills
L. Lomond

NORTH SEA

Firth of Forth
Clyde
Pentland Hills
Islay
Jura
Kintyre
Arran
Firth of Clyde
Southern Uplands
▲830
Tweed
Cheviot Hills
Malin Hd.
L. Foyle
North Channel
Antrim Plateau
Galloway
Tyne
Sperrin Mts.
Belfast L.
Lagan
Lough Neagh
Donegal Bay
L. Erne
Mull of Galloway
St. Bee's Hd.
Solway Firth
Lake District
Scafell Pike ▲978
Pennines
Mourne Mts. ▲852
Isle of Man
Morecambe Bay
Yorkshire Moors
Vale of York
York Wolds
Flamborough Hd.
Achill I.
Ribble
Spurn Hd.
IRISH SEA
Mersey
Humber
Connemara
L. Corrib
Boyne
Lincoln Wolds
Liffey
Anglesey
Snowdon ▲1085
The Peak
Vale of Trent
The Wash
Shannon
Wicklow Mts. ▲926
Cambrian Mts.
Dee
The Fens
East Anglia
L. Derg
Sl. Bloom
Cardigan Bay
Severn
Gt. Ouse
Golden Vale
Barrow
Galty Mts.
Blackwater
Carnsore Pt.
Wye
Vale of Evesham
Cotswold Hills
Chilterns
Carrauntoohill ▲1041
St. George's Channel
St. David's Hd.
Bristol Channel
Mendip Hills
Salisbury Plain
Thames
Sheppey
North Downs
The Weald
South Downs
Dungeness
Cape Clear
Lundy
Exmoor
Isle of Wight
Beachy Head
High Willhays ▲621
Dartmoor
Portland Bill
Start Point
Land's End
Isles of Scilly
Lizard Point
ENGLISH CHANNEL

Scale 1 : 4 000 000
0   50   100   150 km
Conic Projection

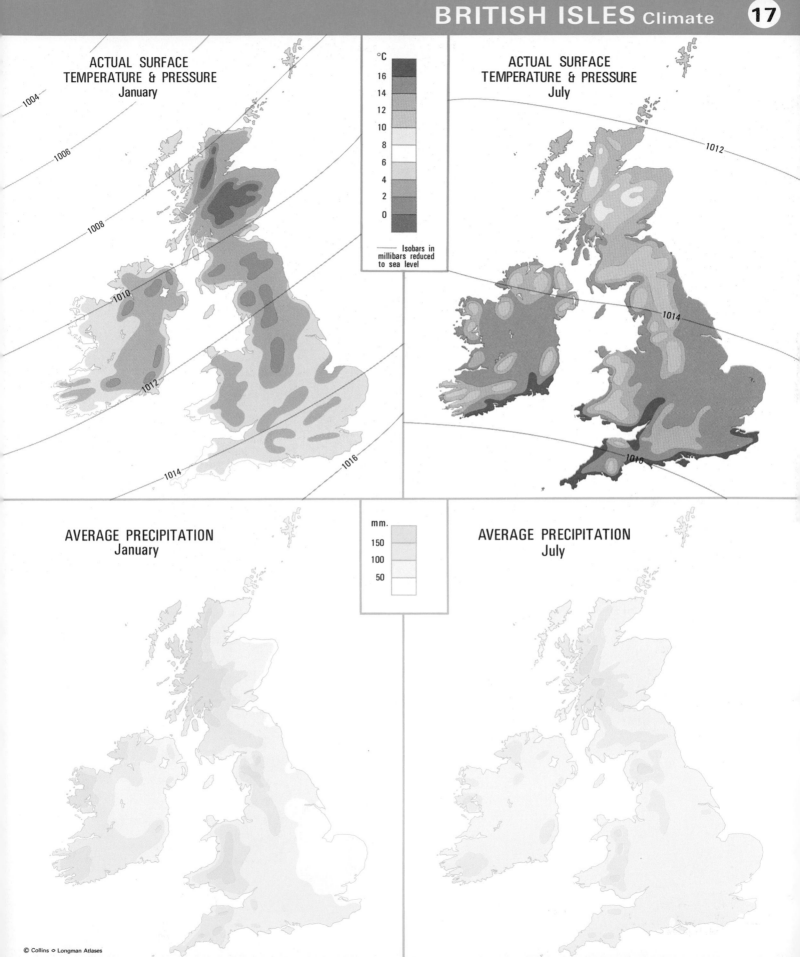

ACTUAL SURFACE
TEMPERATURE & PRESSURE
January

ACTUAL SURFACE
TEMPERATURE & PRESSURE
July

°C
16
14
12
10
8
6
4
2
0

—— Isobars in
millibars reduced
to sea level

1004
1006
1008
1010
1012
1014
1016

1012
1014
1016

AVERAGE PRECIPITATION
January

AVERAGE PRECIPITATION
July

mm.
150
100
50

PREDOMINANT COMMERCIAL ECONOMY

Intensive cultivation

Grain

Specialised (market gardening)

Livestock rearing

Extensive (sheep)

Intensive (cattle)

Intensive dairying

Manufacturing/service industry

Extractive industry

Areas of mixed economies shown by banding

ATLANTIC OCEAN

NORTH SEA

IRISH SEA

North West Highlands

Grampian Highlands

Dundee

Glasgow

Edinburgh

Southern Uplands

The Pennines

Newcastle upon Tyne

Middlesbrough

Belfast

Dublin

Bradford

Leeds

Kingston upon Hull

Liverpool

Manchester

Sheffield

Stoke-on-Trent

Derby

Nottingham

The Fens

Cambrian Mountains

Birmingham

Swansea

Cardiff

Bristol

London

Southampton

Scale 1 : 4 000 000

0   50   100   150 km

Conic Projection

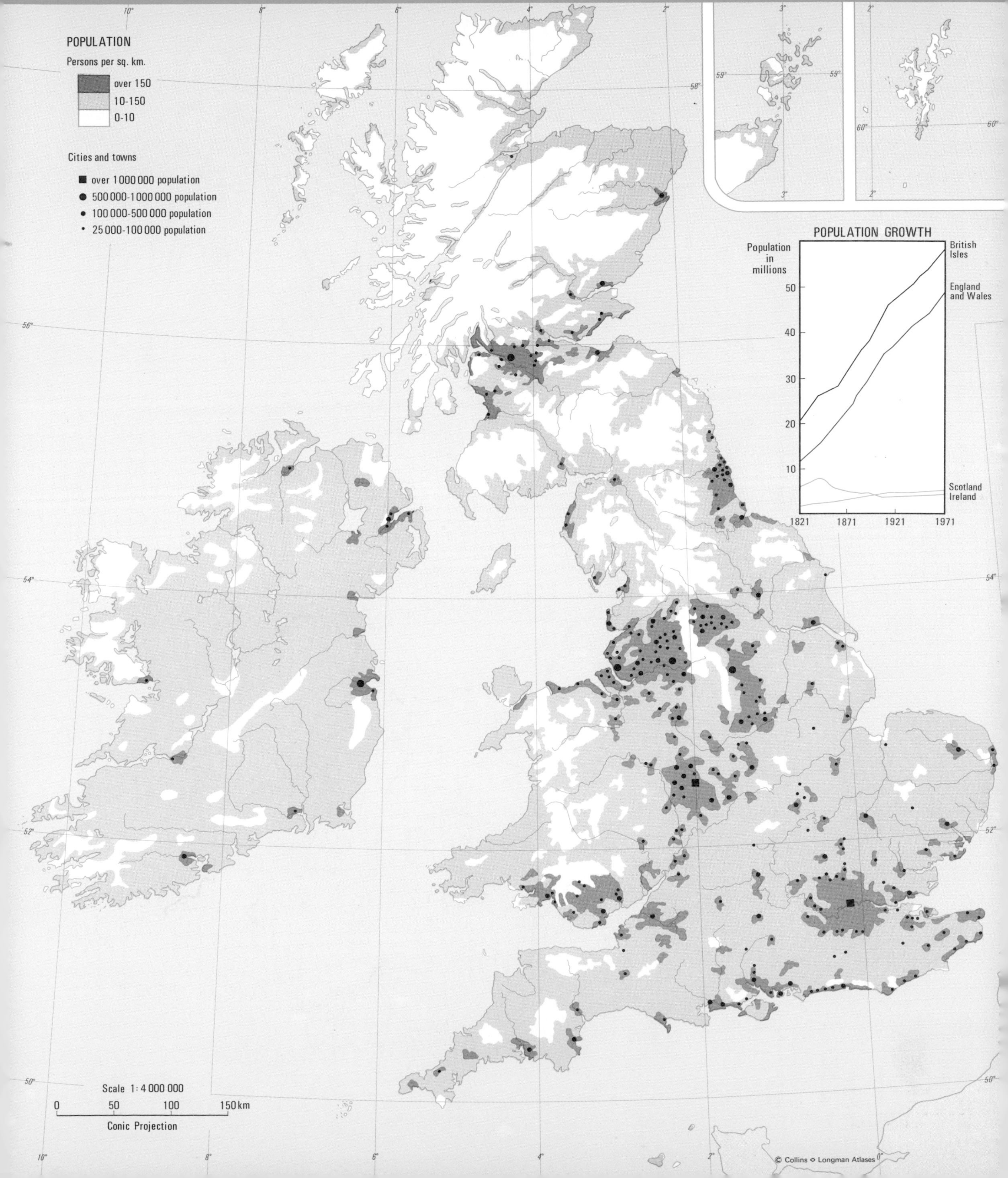

POPULATION

Persons per sq. km.

- over 150
- 10-150
- 0-10

Cities and towns

- ■ over 1 000 000 population
- ● 500 000-1 000 000 population
- ● 100 000-500 000 population
- • 25 000-100 000 population

POPULATION GROWTH

Population in millions

British Isles

England and Wales

Scotland
Ireland

50

40

30

20

10

1821   1871   1921   1971

Scale 1: 4 000 000

0   50   100   150 km

Conic Projection

© Collins ◇ Longman Atlases

Collins ○ Longman Atlases

AIR ROUTES

Internal Air Routes

> 10 return flights/day
6-10 return flights/day
3-5 return flights/day
2 return flights/day
1 return flight/day
○ Airport/Airstrip

Scale 1:7 000 000
Conic projection
0 50 100 150 200km

Lerwick
Lerwick
Sumburgh
Sanday
Stronsay
Kirkwall
Westray
Wick
Aberdeen
Inverness
Dundee
Edinburgh
Newcastle
Teesside
Humberside
Leeds/Bradford
East Midlands
Norwich
London
Heathrow
Gatwick
Southampton
Bournemouth
Manchester
Blackpool
Liverpool
Chester
Birmingham
Bristol
Cardiff
Swansea
Exeter
Plymouth
Newquay
Guernsey
Jersey
Stornoway
Skye
Benbecula
Barra
Tiree
Islay
Campbeltown
Glasgow
Isle of Man
Belfast
Dublin
Galway
Aran Is.
Shannon
Cork

ROAD, RAIL & SEA ROUTES

Motorways
Main roads
Railways
Main car ferry routes
● Car ferry terminal (only major terminals named)
Dover

Lerwick
Kirkwall
Stromness
Scrabster
Faroe Islands
Aberdeen
Ullapool
Stornoway
Uig
Tarbert
Lochmaddy
Lochboisdale
Castlebay
Armadale
Mallaig
Coll
Tiree
Craignure
Colonsay
Tobermory
Lochaline
Oban
Port Askaig
Port Ellen
Ardrossan
Brodick
Cairnryan
Stranraer
Larne
Belfast
Douglas
Fleetwood
Liverpool
Holyhead
Dun Laoghaire
Dublin
Fishguard
Pembroke
Rosslare
Cork
Newcastle
Hull
Plymouth
Weymouth
Portsmouth
Southampton
Newhaven
Folkestone
Dover
Ramsgate
Sheerness
Harwich
Felixstowe
Great Yarmouth
Boulogne
Cherbourg
St. Malo
Roscoff
Santander
Guernsey
Jersey
Dieppe
Le Havre
Rotterdam
Zeebrugge
Bergen & Stavanger
Oslo
Gothenberg
Esbjerg

C. Calais
D. Dunkirk
E. Esbjerg
F. Flushing
G. Gothenberg
H. Hamburg
Hk. Hook of Holland
K. Kristiansand
O. Ostend
Os. Oslo
S. Swinoujscie
Sc. Scheveningen
Z. Zeebrugge

EMPLOYMENT

Type of Employment
Great Britain

Agriculture, forestry & fishing
Engineering & allied industries
Other manufacturing
Construction
Mining, quarrying, gas, electricity & water
Service industries

Northern Ireland
Agriculture
Production industries
Service industries

Figures give percentage of total employed population in each category

Area of each circle is proportional to total employed population in each region

Total No. Employed by Region

8 million
5m
1m
0.5m

Standard region boundary

Regional pie charts (% employed):

SCOTLAND — 57, 15, 15, 8, 3, 2
NORTHERN — 50, 16, 19, 8, 6, 2, 1
NORTH WESTERN — 54, 16, 22, 5, 2, 1
YORKSHIRE & HUMBERSIDE — 50, 17, 19, 6, 2
EAST MIDLANDS — 47, 17, 23, 6, 5, 2
WEST MIDLANDS — 46, 32, 13, 5, 3, 1
EAST ANGLIA — 56, 13, 17, 6, 2
SOUTH EAST — 67, 13, 12, 5, 2
WALES — 54, 18, 12, 7, 6, 3
SOUTH WEST — 60, 15, 13, 6, 3
NORTHERN IRELAND — 59, 39, 2

NORTH SEA

Scale 1:7 000 000
Conic projection

0　50　100　150　200　250 km

Figures not available

POWER STATIONS

Hydro-electric (Capacity > 50MW)
Coal fired (Capacity > 500MW)
Oil fired (Capacity > 500MW)
Gas fired (Capacity > 500MW)
Nuclear (Capacity > 500MW)

FUEL

Oil pipeline
Gas pipeline
Pipeline terminal
International Boundary

Coalfield
Oilfield
Gasfield

Oil/gas fields and locations (North Sea and surrounding):
Thistle, Stratford, Dunlin, Brent, Cormorant, Hutton, Heather, Lyell, Ninian, Alwyn, Bruce, Beryl W., Beryl, Crawford, Brae, Odin, Frigg N.E., Frigg E., Frigg, Heimdal, Balder, Gudrun, Sleipner, Maureen, Thelma, Renee, Andrew, Piper, Claymore, Tartan, Buchan, Glenn, Forties, Montrose, Beatrice, Mabel, Lomond, Cod, N.W.Tor, S.E.Tor, Ekofisk, Eldfisk, Argyll, Albuskjell, Edda, Josephine, Fulmar, Auk

Sullom Voe, Flotta, Fasnakyle, Foyers, Tummel, Erochy, Cruachan, Sloy, Kincardine, Longannet, Cockenzie, Inverkip, Hunterston, St. Fergus, Peterhead, Cruden Bay, Stella, Blyth, Hartlepool, Teesside

Heysham, Morecambe, Fiddler's Ferry, Ince, Wyfa, Dinorwic, Ffestiniog, Rheidol, Skelton Grange, Eggborough, Thorpe Marsh, Ferrybridge, Drax, W. Burton, Cottam, High Marnam, Staythorpe, Willington, Rugeley, Castle Donington, Drakelow, Ironbridge, Uskmouth, Aberthaw, Pembroke

Rough, W. Sole, Indefatigable, Viking, Leman Bank, Scram, Audrey, Sean, Ann, Dotty, Hewett, Theddlethorpe, Easington, Bacton, Sizewell, W. Thurrock, Littlebrook, Northfleet, Kingsnorth, Grain, Dungeness, Didcot, Fawley, Hindey Point

Ballylumford, Coolkeeragh, Turlough Hill, Cathleen's Fall/Cliff, Ardnacrusha, Carrigadrohid/Inniscarra, Powerhead, Tarbert, Kinsale Head

IRISH SEA

English Channel

U.K.
France

© Collins © Longman Atlases

ORKNEY

SHETLAND

Kirkwall

Lerwick

Stornoway

WESTERN ISLES

HIGHLAND

STRATHCLYDE

Inverness

GRAMPIAN

Aberdeen

TAYSIDE

Dundee

CENTRAL

Cupar

FIFE

Stirling

Glasgow

Edinburgh

LOTHIAN

SCOTLAND
9 Regions
3 Island Authorities
53 Districts

Newtown
St Boswells

BORDERS

DUMFRIES &
GALLOWAY

Dumfries

NORTHUMBER-
LAND

Newcastle upon Tyne

TYNE &
WEAR

ENGLAND
39 Counties
6 Metropolitan Counties
Greater London
36 Metropolitan Districts
296 Non-Metropolitan Districts

Carlisle

Durham

DURHAM

CLEVELAND

Middlesbrough

CUMBRIA

Northallerton

NORTH
YORKSHIRE

**NORTHERN
IRELAND**
1 Region
26 Districts

DONEGAL

Lifford

Londonderry

Antrim

Tyrone

Belfast

Sligo

Fermanagh

Monaghan

Armagh

Down

ISLE OF
MAN

Douglas

Kingston upon Hull

SLIGO

LEITRIM

CAVAN

MONAGHAN

LOUTH

Dundalk

LANCASHIRE

Preston

WEST
YORKSHIRE

Wakefield

HUMBERSIDE

MAYO

Castlebar

Carrick-on-
Shannon

ROSCOMMON

Longford

Cavan

Navan

Manchester

Barnsley

SOUTH
YORKSHIRE

Lincoln

LONGFORD

MEATH

G.M.

MERSEYSIDE

Liverpool

DERBYSHIRE

Matlock

NOTTINGHAMSHIRE

LINCOLN-
SHIRE

Roscommon

WEST MEATH

Mullingar

DUBLIN

Nottingham

GALWAY

Galway

OFFALY

Tullamore

KILDARE

Dublin

Mold

CLWYD

Chester

CHESHIRE

Caernarfon

GWYNEDD

Port Laoise

Naas

WICKLOW

Stafford

STAFFORD-
SHIRE

LEICESTER-
SHIRE

Leicester

NORFOLK

Norwich

CLARE

Ennis

LAOIS

Carlow

Wicklow

Shrewsbury

SALOP

Birmingham

W.M.

Warwick

WARWICK
SHIRE

NORTHAMPTONSHIRE

Northampton

CAMBRIDGE
SHIRE

SUFFOLK

Ipswich

Limerick

TIPPERARY

KILKENNY

CARLOW

Kilkenny

WEXFORD

Bedford

BEDFORD
SHIRE

Cambridge

LIMERICK

Clonmel

POWYS

Llandrindod
Wells

HEREFORD &
WORCESTER

Worcester

Gloucester

Oxford

Aylesbury

BUCKINGHAMSHIRE

HERTFORDSHIRE

Hertford

Chelmsford

ESSEX

Tralee

KERRY

WATERFORD

Waterford

Wexford

WALES
8 Counties
37 Districts

DYFED

Carmarthen

GLOUCESTER-
SHIRE

OXFORD-
SHIRE

Reading

BERKSHIRE

Kingston
upon Thames

GREATER
LONDON

CORK

Cork

**REPUBLIC
OF IRELAND**
26 Counties

W. GLAMORGAN

Swansea

M.D.
GLAMORGAN

S.G.

GWENT

Cwmbran

Cardiff

Bristol

AVON

Trowbridge

WILTSHIRE

Maidstone

SURREY

KENT

SOMERSET

Taunton

HAMPSHIRE

Winchester

WEST
SUSSEX

Chichester

EAST
SUSSEX

Lewes

DEVON

Exeter

DORSET

Dorchester

Newport

ISLE OF
WIGHT

CORNWALL

Truro

Scale 1:4 000 000
0   50   100   150km

Conic Projection

	International boundary
	National boundary
	County or region boundary
	Historic counties in Northern Ireland
	Metropolitan county
	Greater London
•	Administrative headquarters (those underlined contain the offices of more than one county)

The local government boundaries for England & Wales shown on this map were officially approved by an Act of Parliament in October 1972, and those for Scotland and Northern Ireland in October 1973. The sub-division of Counties and Regions is not shown.

G.M. GREATER MANCHESTER
S.G. SOUTH GLAMORGAN
W.M. WEST MIDLANDS

Relief

Metres		
200	100	0

Sea Level

Scale 1:400 000

Lambert Conformal Conic Projection

Motorway
'A' Road
'B' Road
Woodland

0   5   10   15   20km

Relief

Metres	
1000	
500	
200	
100	
0	Sea Level
Land Dep.	20
	50
Metres	

Scale 1 : 1 000 000

0 10 20 30 40 50 60 km

Lambert Conformal Conic Projection

West from Greenwich 0° East from Greenwich

LINCOLNSHIRE · NORFOLK · Norfolk Broads · CAMBRIDGESHIRE · SUFFOLK · BEDFORDSHIRE · HERTFORDSHIRE · ESSEX · GREATER LONDON · London · SURREY · KENT · EAST SUSSEX · The Weald · Romney Marsh · STRAIT OF DOVER · FRANCE · PAS DE CALAIS · NORD

King's Lynn · Wisbech · Peterborough · March · Ely · Cambridge · Newmarket · Bury St. Edmunds · Thetford · Norwich · Great Yarmouth · Lowestoft · Southwold · Ipswich · Felixstowe · Harwich · Colchester · Clacton on Sea · Walton on the Naze · Chelmsford · Maldon · Southend-on-Sea · Brentwood · Romford · London · Enfield · Barnet · Harrow · Hounslow · Richmond-upon-Thames · Kingston upon Thames · Croydon · Bromley · Bexley · Dartford · Gravesend · Rochester · Chatham · Gillingham · Sittingbourne · Faversham · Whitstable · Herne Bay · Margate · Broadstairs · Ramsgate · Sandwich · Deal · Dover · Folkestone · Hythe · New Romney · Canterbury · Ashford · Maidstone · Tonbridge · Royal Tunbridge Wells · Sevenoaks · Reigate · Crawley · East Grinstead · Hastings · Bexhill · Eastbourne · Brighton · Hove · Worthing · Lewes · Newhaven · Seaford · Beachy Head · Dungeness · Rye · Lydd · Calais · Gravelines · Dunkirk · Boulogne · St Omer · Guines · Ardres · Marquise

IRISH SEA

ST GEORGE'S CHANNEL

CARDIGAN BAY

LANCASHIRE
CHESHIRE
STAFFORDSHIRE
SHROPSHIRE
HEREFORD
WORCESTER
MERSEYSIDE

Manchester
Salford
Eccles
Wilmslow
Crewe
Nantwich
Sandbach
Northwich
Winsford
Chester
Wrexham
Shrewsbury
Wellington
The Wrekin
Severn
Ludlow
Clee Hills
Wyre Forest
Kidderminster
Great Malvern
Hereford
Leominster
Bromyard

Southport
Formby
Crosby
Bootle
Liverpool
Wallasey
Birkenhead
Bebington
Ellesmere Port
Hoylake
Heswall
West Kirby

Prestatyn
Rhyl
Colwyn Bay
Llandudno
Gt Ormes Hd
Conwy
Bangor
Menai Bridge
Beaumaris
Benllech
Red Wharf Bay
Amlwch
Cemaes Bay
The Skerries
Carmel Hd
Holyhead
Holy I.
Rhosneigr
Aberffraw
Anglesey
Llangefni
Llanerchymedd

Snowdon 1085
GWYNEDD
Caernarfon
Porthmadog
Pwllheli
Abersoch
Aberdaron
Bardsey I.
Bardsey
Lleyn Peninsula
Nefyn
Tudweiliog
Criccieth
Harlech
Tremadog Bay
Barmouth
Fairbourne
Towyn
Aberdovey
Borth
Aberystwyth

Bala
Dolgellau
Machynlleth
Newtown
Llanidloes
Rhayader
Llandrindod Wells
Builth Wells
Brecon
Llandovery

CAMBRIAN MOUNTAINS
BERWYN
CLWYDIAN Range

New Quay
Aberaeron
Aberporth
Cardigan
Newport
Fishguard
Strumble Hd
St David's Hd
Ramsey
Prescelly 536
DYFED
PRESCELLY MTS

Scale 1 : 1 000 000

0 10 20 30 40 50 60km

Lambert Conformal Conic Projection

5° 4° 52° 53°

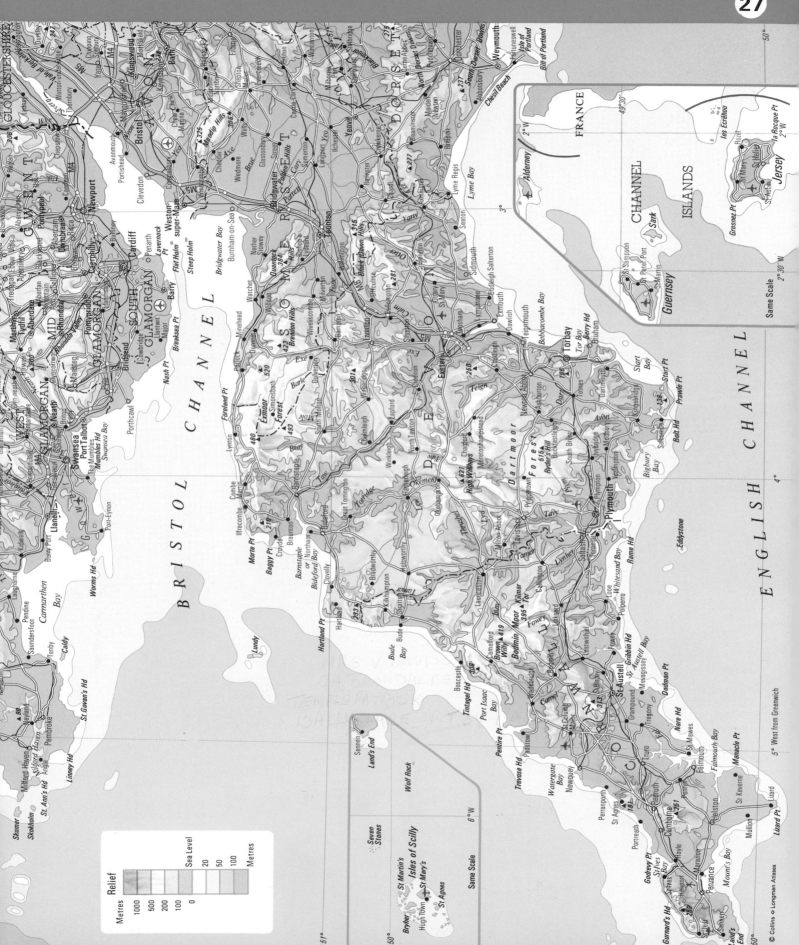

FRANCE

CHANNEL ISLANDS

Alderney
Guernsey
St Peter Port
Jersey
St Helier
Sark

Same Scale

BRISTOL CHANNEL

ENGLISH CHANNEL

GLOUCESTERSHIRE

Bristol
Bath
Weston-super-Mare
Cardiff
Newport
Swansea
Port Talbot

GWENT

SOUTH GLAMORGAN
MID GLAMORGAN
WEST GLAMORGAN

SOMERSET

DORSET

DEVON

Exmoor Forest

Dartmoor Forest

Torbay
Plymouth
Exeter
Taunton
Weymouth
Isle of Portland
Lyme Bay

CORNWALL

Land's End
Isles of Scilly
St Mary's

Seven Stones
Wolf Rock

Lizard Pt

Relief

Metres
1000
500
200
100
0

Sea Level
20
50
100
Metres

Same Scale

© Collins · Longman Atlases

The Machars
DUMFRIES AND GALLOWAY
Wigtown Bay
Port William Whithorn Garlieston
Isle of Whithorn
Burrow Hd

SOLWAY FIRTH
Silloth
Abbey Town Thursby
Wigton Wetheral
Aspatria Caldbeck
Maryport Flimby
Workington Seaton Cockermouth Keswick Skiddaw 931
Whitehaven Cleator Moor Crummock Wtr Derwent Wtr
St Bees Hd Ennerdale Wtr Scafell Pike 978
St Bees Egremont
Seascale Wast Water Coniston
Bootle Black Combe 600
Millom Ulverston Grange-over-Sands
Barrow-in-Furness Dalton-in-Furness Carnforth
Isle of Walney Morecambe Bay High Bentham
Hilpsford Pt Morecambe Heysham Lancaster Ward's Stone 560
Glasson

IRISH

SEA

Fleetwood Rossall Pt Preesall
Cleveleys Thornton Wyre Garstang
Blackpool Great Eccleston
Kirkham Ribble M55
Lytham St Anne's Preston
Southport Tarleton Leyland
Burscough Rufford
Formby Ormskirk Skelmersdale
Formby Pt
Liverpool Bay Crosby Maghull
MERSEYSIDE Bootle Kirkby
Wallasey St Helens
Birkenhead Liverpool
Hoylake West Kirby
Heswall Bebington Widnes
Neston Runcorn M56

Pt of Ayre
Andreas Bride
Jurby Hd Ramsey Bay
Ramsey
Kirk Michael Snaefell 620 Maughold Hd
Peel Laxey Clay Hd
Crosby ISLE OF MAN
South Barrule 483 Douglas
Port Erin Castletown Langness

The Skerries Cemaes Bay
Carmel Hd Amlwch
Holyhead Bay Llanerchymedd Red Wharf Bay Benllech Puffin I.
Holyhead Anglesey Gt Ormes Hd
Holy I. Llangefni Conwy Bay Llandudno
Rhosneigr Beaumaris Conwy Colwyn Bay
Aberffraw Menai Bridge Penmaenmawr Abergele
Caernarfon Bangor Llanfairfechan
Menai Str Bethesda 1062
Caernarfon Bay Llanberis Llanrwst Denbigh
Nefyn 564 1085 Betws y Coed Ruthin
Tudweiliog Snowdon 519
Pwllheli GWYNEDD CLWYD
Criccieth Blaenau Ffestiniog
Tremadog Bay Porthmadog Bala
Harlech Y Llethr 754 Llanuwchllyn
Abersoch 669 Carnedd y Filiast
Barmouth Cader Idris
Fairbourne

CUMBRIA
Lake District
Penrith
Pooley Bridge
Ullswater Appleby
Helvellyn 950 Shap
Ambleside Kirkby Stephen
Windermere Sedbergh
Kendal
Kirkby Lonsdale Ingleton
Carlisle M6 Eden Wetheral 622
NORTHUMBERLAND
Alston 561
Cross Fell 893 DURHAM
Weardale Stanhope Tow Law
Wolsingham Bishop Auckland
Middleton in Teesdale 790
Barnard Castle Gainford
Bowes Richmond Catterick
Rogan's Seat 672 Swale Leyburn
Gt Shunner Fell 713 Aysgarth
Hawes Wensleydale Cover Masham
Whernside 737 NORTH YORKSHIRE
Ingleborough 723 Pen-y-ghent 693 Gt Whernside 704 Pateley Br
Settle Wharfe 409
Hellifield Skipton Ilkley
Gargrave Barnoldswick Earby Silsden
LANCASHIRE Pendle Hill 558 Colne Nelson Keighley Guiseley
Clitheroe Whalley Brierfield Bingley Shipley WEST YORKSHIRE
Longridge Gt Harwood Burnley Hebden Bridge Bradford
Accrington Forest of Rossendale Todmorden Halifax Batley
Blackburn Bacup Brighouse Dewsbury
Darwen Haslingden Rawtenstall 468 Elland
Chorley Ramsbottom Rochdale Huddersfield Kirkbu
Adlington Horwich Bury Heywood Marsden Meltham Denby Penistone
GREATER Bolton Radcliffe Oldham Saddleworth Moor
Wigan Farnworth Middleton Ashton-under-Lyne 678
Ashton-in-Makerfield Atherton Eccles Salford Hyde Stalybridge Stocksbri
Leigh MANCHESTER Bleaklow Hill
Newton-le-Willows Urmston Sale Stockport Kinder Scout 636 High Peak
Warrington Altrincham Cheadle Marple New Mills
Widnes Wilmslow Whaley Bridge Hathersag
Runcorn M56 Knutsford Macclesfield Chapel en le Frith
Ellesmere Port Frodsham Northwich Buxton
CHESHIRE Holmes Chapel Bakewell DE
Flint Chester Kelsall Winsford Middlewich 336 Harrington
Holywell Broughton Tarporley Sandbach Biddulph Leek 489
Connah's Quay Mold 555 Farndon Nantwich Alsager Kidsgrove Dove
Buckley Crewe Newcastle-under-Lyme Stoke-on-Trent
Denbigh Ruthin Rhosllanerchrugog Audlem Trentham 254
Wrexham Whitchurch Market Drayton Stafford
POWYS Corwen Llangollen Ruabon Overton Ellesmere Wem Upper Tean Brailsfo
Llandrillo 827 Whittington West Felton Hodnet Eccleshall 139 Hatt
Llangynog Ceiriog Oswestry Harmerhill Stone
Aran Fawddwy 905 Lake Vyrnwy Llanfyllin Newport Rugeley
SALOP Wellington Telford Burton upon Tren
Llanegryn Shrewsbury STAFFORDSHIRE Cannock

Newcastle upon Tyne
Ryton Blaydon Whickham
Consett Anfield Tyne
NORTHUMBERLAND Derwent
Collier Law 516
A1(M) Willing
Crook Shildon

54°

53°

© Collins ◇ Longman Atlases

West from Greenwich   0°   East from Greenwich

Scale 1 : 1 000 000

0   10   20   30   40   50   60 km

Lambert Conformal Conic Projection

Relief

Metres	
1000	
500	
200	
100	
0	Sea Level
	20
	50
	100
	Metres

NORTH SEA

Vallsend, South Shields, Jarrow, TYNE AND WEAR, A194(M), Sunderland, Washington, Houghton-le-Spring, Seaham, Hetton-le-Hole, Easington, Peterlee, Wingate, Sedgefield, Hartlepool, Tees Bay, Newton Aycliffe, Billingham, Redcar, Marske-by-the-Sea, Saltburn-by-the-Sea, CLEVELAND, Stockton-on-Tees, Thornaby-on-Tees, Eston, Brotton, Loftus, Middlesbrough, Guisborough, Darlington, Stokesley, Whitby, Cleveland Hills, Broughton, Sleights, Robin Hood's Bay, ▲454, North York Moors, ▲292, Cloughton, Scalby, Scarborough, Northallerton, Hambleton Hills, Helmsley, Kirkbymoorside, Thirsk, Pickering, Vale of Pickering, Filey, VALE OF YORK, Hovingham, Staxton, Flamborough, Flamborough Head, NORTH YORKSHIRE, Easingwold, Malton, Norton, Burton Agnes, Bridlington, Boroughbridge, Swale, Shipton, ▲246, Sledmere, Great Driffield, Bridlington Bay, Knaresborough, Harrogate, Nidd, York, Stamford Bridge, Pocklington, Hutton Cranswick, Wetherby, Wilberfoss, Hornsea, Tadcaster, Middleton on the Wolds, Ouse, Wharfe, Market Weighton, Leven, Leeds, Cawood, Selby, Holme upon Spalding Moor, Beverley, Aldbrough, Garforth, Hambleton, South Cave, Cottingham, HUMBERSIDE, Kingston upon Hull, Morley, Rothwell, M62, Hessle, Holderness, Castleford, Howden, Hedon, Knottingley, Goole, New Holland, Keyingham, Withernsea, Wakefield, Aire, Ouse, Barton-upon-Humber, Patrington, Pontefract, Garthorpe, Whitton, Humber, Easington, Hemsworth, Royston, Askern, Winterton, Immingham, Spurn Hd, Don, Thorne, Crowle, Adwick le Street, Scunthorpe, Grimsby, Cleethorpes, Barnsley, Thurnscoe, Isle of Axholme, M180, Great Coates, Doncaster, Epworth, Brigg, Mexborough, Rossington, Trent, Caistor, Tetney, Rawmarsh, Rotherham, Conisbrough, Tickhill, Bawtry, ▲168, North Somercotes, Saltfleet, Maltby, Gainsborough, Market Rasen, Louth, Sheffield, Anston, Mablethorpe, Killamarsh, Worksop, East Retford, Dunholme, Wragby, 151▲, Burwell, Sutton on Sea, Staveley, East Markham, Torksey, Lincoln Wolds, Chesterfield, Cresswell, Bardney, Horncastle, Chapel St Leonards, Bolsover, Warsop, Boughton, Lincoln, LINCOLNSHIRE, Bain, Spilsby, Burgh le Marsh, Shirebrook, Witham, Woodhall Spa, Steeping, Skegness, Clay Cross, Sutton in Ashfield, Mansfield, Metheringham, Navenby, Coningsby, Wainfleet All Saints, Gibraltar Pt, Matlock, Kirkby in Ashfield, Southwell, Newark-on-Trent, North Kyme, Wrangle, Alfreton, Holkham Bay, Blakeney Pt, Sheringham, Belper, Heanor, Eastwood, Arnold, Carlton, Long Bennington, Sleaford, Heckington, Holland Fen, Boston, Cromer, Hunstanton, Burnham Market, Wells-next-the-Sea, Holt, Ilkeston, Stapleford, Nottingham, Bingham, Grantham, Bottesford, Donington, Kirton, THE WASH, Heacham, Docking, Dersingham, Sandringham, Saxthorpe, North Walsham, Derby, West Bridgford, Beeston, Keyworth, ▲89, Aylsham, Long Eaton, Bourne, Folkingham, The Marsh, King's Lynn, NORFOLK, Melbourne, Swadlincote, Waltham on the Wolds, ▲173, Melton Mowbray, Colsterworth, Spalding, Holbeach, Sutton Bridge, East Dereham, Hoveton, Ashby-de-la-Zouch, Shepshed, Loughborough, Coalville, LEICESTERSHIRE, Deeping Fen, Long Sutton, Glen, Mundesley, ▲4, ▲83, Colishall

NOTTINGHAMSHIRE, Sherwood Forest, Lincoln Edge, River Derwent, Yorkshire Wolds

Scale 1 : 1 000 000

0   10   20   30   40   50   60 km

Lambert Conformal Conic Projection

Relief

Metres
1000
500
200
100
0 Sea Level
20
50
100
200
Metres

N O R T H

S E A

NORTHEAST ENGLAND

SHETLAND ISLANDS
Same Scale

Scale 1 : 1 000 000

Lambert Conformal Conic Projection

Relief

Metres
- 1000
- 500
- 200
- 100
- 0

Sea Level

- 20
- 50
- 100
- 200

Metres

Foula — Ham

Same Scale

PENTLAND FIRTH

ORKNEY ISLANDS Same Scale

Mull Hd · Noup Hd · Papa Westray · North Ronaldsay · N. Ronaldsay Firth
Pierowall · The North Sound · Start Point
Westray · Sanday · Sanday Sound
Sacquoy Hd · Eday · Stronsay
Rousay · Exhallow Sd · Egilsay · Wyre · Gairsay · Stronsay Firth · Auskerry
Brough Hd · Shapinsay · Shapinsay Sd
ORKNEY · Copinsay
Stromness · Ward Hill 269 · Kirkwall · Mull Hd
Ward Hill 477 · Quoyness · St Mary's · Skaill
Hoy Sd · Scapa Flow
Rora Hd · Burray
Hoy · Flotta · St Margaret's Hope
Huchness · S. Walls · South Ronaldsay
PENTLAND FIRTH
Dunnet Hd · Stroma · John O' Groats · Muckle Skerry · Duncansby Hd · Dunnet

Brough Ness · Muckle Skerry · Stroma · John O' Groats · Duncansby Hd
Dunnet Hd · Dunnet Bay · Thurso · Dunnet
Strathy Pt · Portskerra · Dounreay · Halkirk · L. Watten · Reiss · Sinclair's Bay · Noss Hd
Whiten Hd · Durness · Eriboll · Kyle of Tongue · Strathy · Bettyhill · Reay · Strath Halladale · Wick
Ben Hutig 408 · Tongue · Beinn nam Bad Mor 390 · Kinbrace
Loch Eriboll · Ben Hope 927 · Ben Loyal 763 · Ben Loyal · L. Loyal · Kildonan 628
Ben Hee 873 · L. Naver · Ben Klibreck 961 · Ben Griam Mor 590 · 287 · Lybster
Altnaharra · Morven 706 · Dunbeath
Ben More Assynt · L. Shin · Strath · Berriedale
Oykel Bridge · Lairg · Ben Horn 520 · Brora · Helmsdale
L. More · Bonar Bridge · Golspie
Beinn Tharsuinn 692 · Dornoch · Dornoch Firth · Tarbat Ness
Portmahomack · Hill of Fearn
MORAY FIRTH · Burghead · Lossiemouth · Spey Bay · Portknockie · Cullen · Portsoy · Troup Hd · Rosehearty · Kinnairds Hd · Fraserburgh
Findhorn · Garmouth · Buckie · Banff · Macduff
Nairn · Forres · Elgin · Fochabers · Knock Hill 430 · Strichen · Rattray Hd
Cromarty Firth · Cromarty · Lossie · Keith · New Pitsligo · Buchan · Peterhead
Ben Wyvis 1045 · Dingwall · Black Isle · Beauly Firth · Rothes · Strathbogie · Deveron · Turriff · Cuminestown · Ugie
Conon · Muir of Ord · Beauly F. · Charlestown of Aberlour 840 · Huntly · New Deer · Boddam · Buchan Ness
Glen Orrin · Beauly · Inverness · Ben Rinnes 781 · Fyvie · 174 · Cruden Bay
The Aird · Cârn na Loine 548 · Strath Avon · GRAMPIAN · Insch · Oldmeldrum · Newburgh
Dores · Tomatin 659 · Grantown-on-Spey · Corryhabbie Hill · The Buck 722 · Inverurie · Ellon
Strathnairn · Findhorn · Carrbridge · Tomintoul · Cârn Mòr 803 · Lumsden · Garioch · Dyce · Don
Drumnadrochit · Strathdearn · Spey · Geal Chârn 821 · Alford · Aberdeen
Invermoriston · 810 · Aviemore · Cairn Gorm 1245 · Ben Avon 1171 · Don · Tarland · Hill of Fare 471 · Don · Dee
Fort Augustus · Monadhliath Mountains · 941 · Kingussie · 1311 Ben Macdhui · Cairngorms · Braemar · Aboyne · Banchory
L. Oich · Newtonmore · HIGHLANDS · Ballater · Dee
Creag Meagaidh 1128 · Dalwhinnie · Mt Keen 936 · 879 Mt Battock · Kerloch 592 · Stonehaven
Glen Roy · Laggan · Glen Spean · 1154 · Lochnagar · Glen Esk · Fettercairn · Inverbervie
L. Treig · Ben Alder 1148 · Loch Ericht · 1067 · Glas Maol · West Water · Edzell · Laurencekirk
Forest of Atholl · Glen Tilt · Beinn a'Ghlo 1121 · Glen Clova · Brechin
Blackwater Rest · Kinloch Rannoch · Blair Atholl · Glen Garry · Glen Prosen · S. Esk · Montrose
L. Laidon · L. Rannoch · Schiehallion 1081 · Pitlochry · Kirkmichael · Strathardle · Kirriemuir · Forfar
Rannoch Moor · Ben Lawers 1214 · Kenmore · Aberfeldy · Bridge of Cally · Blairgowrie · Alyth · Glamis · Lunan Bay
Killin · Loch Tay · Dunkeld · Coupar Angus · Sidlaw Hills 455 · Carmyllie · Arbroath
Breadalbane · Glen Lyon · Banktoot · Dundee · Monifieth · Buddon Ness

NORTH SEA

West from Greenwich · © Collins · Longman Atlases

ST. GEORGE'S CHANNEL

Scale 1:1 400 000

Lambert Conformal Conic Projection

0 10 20 30 40 50 60 70 80km

© Collins ○ Longman Atlases

FRANCE

Scale 1:5 000 000

Conic Projection

© Collins © Longman Atlases

0 50 100 150 200 km

Mediterranean Sea

Ligurian Sea

English Channel

Bay of Biscay

Gulf of Gascony

Gulf of Lions

WEST GERMANY

BELGIUM

LUXEMBOURG

SWITZERLAND

ITALY

SPAIN

ANDORRA

Massif Central

Paris
Lyon
Marseille
Bordeaux
Nantes
Rennes
Brest
Strasbourg
Nancy
Metz
Reims
Orléans
Tours
Limoges
Toulouse
Montpellier
Nîmes
Avignon
Grenoble
Nice
Cannes
Monaco
Dijon
Besançon
Clermont-Ferrand

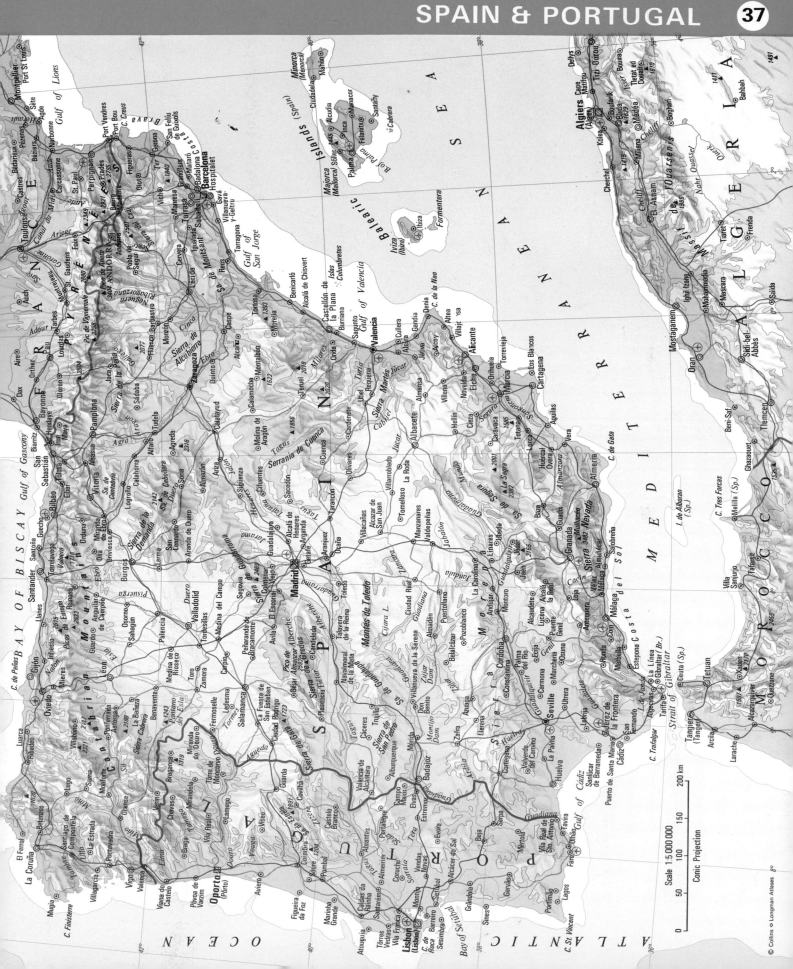

AUSTRIA

SWITZ
FRANCE
ALPS
ITALY
ALGERIA
TUNISIA

LIGURIAN SEA
ADRIATIC
TYRRHENIAN SEA
MEDITERRANEAN
Gulf of Lions
Gulf of Venice
Gulf of Genoa
Gulf of La Spezia
Gulf of Gaeta
Gulf of Naples
Gulf of Salerno
Gulf of Orosei
G. of Oristano
G. of Palmas
G. of Cagliari
G. of Valinco
G. of Asinara
Str. of Bonifacio
Str. of Messina
Gulf of Tunis
Malta Channel

Corsica (Fr.)
Sardinia (Italy)
Sicily
Minorca
Elba
Montecristo
Pianosa
Giglio
Capraia
Caprera
Asinara
San Pietro
Lipari Is.
Stromboli 926
Ustica (Italy)
Pantelleria (Italy)
Lampedusa (Italy)
Linosa
Malta
Gozo
MALTA
Valletta

Relief
Metres
5000
3000
2000
1000
500
200
0 Sea Level
Land Dep.
200
4000
7000
Metres

Lyon
St. Etienne
Roanne
Thiers
Clermont Ferrand
Montbrison
Mt-Dore 1886
St. Flour
Plomb du Cantal 1858
Le Puy
Mende
Marvejols
Sérévac
Millau
Alès
Nîmes
Béziers
Pézenas
Sète
Montpellier
Marseille
Aix-en-Provence
Salon
Arles
Avignon
Orange
Montélimar
Valence
Romans
Vienne
Villeurbanne
Grenoble
Gap
Briançon
Digne
Draguignan
Grasse
Toulon
Hyères
Îles d'Hyères
St. Tropez
Fréjus
Cannes
Antibes
Nice
Menton
Monte Carlo
MONACO
Imperia
San Remo
Ventimiglia
Var
Durance
Rhône
Loire
Allier
Cévennes
Alpes Maritimes
Mt. Pelat 3053
Les Écrins 4102
Geneva
Annecy
Mont Blanc 4807
Chamonix
Mont Cenis 4901
Simplon Tunnel
Matterhorn 4477
Mt. Rosa 4632
Gt. St. Bernard Pass 2472
Lt. St. Bernard Pass 2188
Aosta
Gran Paradiso 4061
Turin
Cuneo
Mondovì
Acqui
Asti
Alessandria
Mt. Viso 3847
Tanaro
Po
Mt. Cinto 2710
Calvi
Bastia
Corte
Ajaccio
Aleria
Sartène
Pto. Vecchio
Bonifacio
C. Corse

Locarno
Lugano
Como
L. Como
L. Maggiore
Bolzano
Merano
Wildspitze 3774
Brenner Pass 1372
Gr. Glockner 3798
Bormina 4026
Tirano
Trento
L. Garda
Bergamo
Brescia
Milan
Monza
Novara
Vercelli
Pavia
Voghera
Piacenza
Cremona
Mantua
Parma
Reggio
Modena
Ferrara
Bologna
Ravenna
Faenza
Forlì
Verona
Vicenza
Padua
Venice
Treviso
Udine
Gorizia
Trieste
Ljubljana
Rijeka
Karlovac
Sava
Drau
Villach
Klagenfurt
Celje
Maribor
Varaž
Zagreb
Triglav 2863
Gospić
Pag
Krk
Cres
Lošinj
Pula
Rovinj
Istra
Dugi Otok
Zadar
Biha
Kupa
Dinaric Alps
Dolomites
Carnic Alps
Adige
Brenta

Genoa
Savona
Chiavari
Rapallo
La Spezia
Massa
Carrara
Pisa
Leghorn
Prato
Florence
Arno
Volterra
Cecina
Piombino
Grosseto
Siena
Arezzo
SAN MARINO
San Marino
Urbino
Rimini
Pésaro
Senigallia
Ancona
Iesi
Macerata
Foligno
Perugia
L. Trasimeno
L. Bolsena
Terni
Viterbo
Civitavecchia
Rome
Velletri
Frosinone
Rieti
L'Aquila
Mt. Corno 2914
Téramo
Ascoli Piceno
Monte Vettore 2478
Pescara
Chieti
Sulmona
Avezzano
Mt. Amaro 2794
Termoli
Campobasso
San Severo
Foggia
Benevento
Ariano
Melfi
Caserta
Naples
Avellino
Vesuvius
Ischia
Capri
G. of Naples
Salerno
Potenza
Pisciotta
Sapri
G. of Policastro
Cosenza
Páola
Nicas
Palmi
Reggio
Messina
Barcellona
Cefalù
Palermo
Trápani
Marsala
Favignana
Marettimo
Alcamo
Termini
Enna
Nebrodi Mts.
Mt. Etna 3340
Adrano
Catania
Siracusa
Ragusa
Módica
Vittória
C. Passero
Caltagirone
Caltanissetta
Agrigento
Licata
Sciacca
Platani
Salso
L. Bolsena
Pontine Is.
Gaeta
Capri
Arbatax
Villaputzu
C. Carbonara
Cagliari
Iglésias
Sássari
Alghero
Bosa
Macomer
Orosei
Oristano
Tempio
Olbia
Porto Torres
C. Falcone
G. of Asinara
Coghinas
Tirso
C. Mte. Santu
C. Spartivento
Gulf of Orosei
Mannu
1834

Bejaia
Akbou
Sétif
Batna
Biskra
Barika
Constantine
Constantine Mts.
Souk Ahras
Ain Beida
Tébessa
Kasserine
Sbeitla
Thala
Le Kef
Medjerda Mts.
Medjerda
Béja
Mateur
Bizerta
Tabarka
La Calle
Skikda
Annaba
C. de Fer
C. Serrat
Galita
Tunis
Nabeul
C. Bon
Enfida
Sousse
Monastir
Msaken
Mahdia
Kairouan
W. el Hatob
W. el Fekka
el Abiod
el Arab
W. Mellègue

10° 12° 14° 16°
42° 40° 38° 36°

Scale 1:5 250 000

0   50   100   150   200 km

Conic Projection

© Collins ○ Longman Atlases

Scale 1:4 000 000

0   50   100   150 km

Conic Projection

Relief
Metres
5000
3000
2000
1000
500
200
0   Sea Level
Land Dep.
200
4000
7000

Bering Str.

I C   N
Komsomolets
October Revolution
Severnaya   Bolshevik
Zemlya
C. Chelyuskin

N

Taymyr Peninsula
Byrranga Mts.
Pyasina   Upper Taymyr   Khatangskiy G. L A P T E V
L. Taymyr   Olenekskiy Gulf   S E A
Nordvik
Khatanga
Anabar
Ust Olenek

New Siberian Is
Novaya Siberia
Kotelnyy
Bolshoi Lyakhovskiy E A S T S I B E R I A N S E A

Wrangel I.   De Long Str.
Arctic Circle   Gulf of Anadyr
Ambarchik
Anadyr
Chukchee Pen.
Gulf of Anadyr

Dudinka
Noril'sk   Kamen
2037
Putoran Mts
Kamen

Central

Siberian

S O C I A L I S T R E P U B L I C S

Bulun
Tiksi
Kazachye
G. of Tana

Verkhoyansk
Srednekolymskaya
Kolyma
Omolon

Mt Pabeda
3147
Cherskogo
Mt Chen
2682
Oymyakon
Magadan
Okhotsk

Kolyma Range
Gizhiga
Gizhiga Gulf
G. of Penzh
Pajana

Kamchatka
Ust-Kamchatsk
Klyuchevskaya

Peninsula
Petropavlovsk-Kamchatskiy

Olenek
Olenek
Tura
Markha
Vilyuy   Vilyuysk
Vilyuy   Yakutsk   Amga   Ust Maya
Aldan
Aldan

S O C I A L I S T R E P U B L I C

Lower Tunguska
R A L S O C I A L I S T R E P U B L I C S
Yeniseysk
Stony Tunguska
Angara
Chuna
Olekminsk
Lena
Aldan
Aldan
Olekma
Mt Topko
1906

Dzhugdzhur Range
Ayan
Shantar Is
Okha

S E A O F
O K H O T S K

Kirensk
Ust Kut
Lena
Stanovoy Range
Skalistyy
2482

Aleksandrovsk-Sakhalinskiy
Poronaysk
Sakhalin

Kansk
Tayshet
Bratsk
Bratsk Rezr.
Nizhneudinsk
Eastern
Sayan
Cheremkhovo
Angarsk
Irkutsk
Ulan-Ude
L. Baikal
Vitim
Vitim
Shilka
Chita
Skovorodino
Zeya
Svobodnyy
Blagoveshchensk
Amur
Amur
Komsomolsk-na-Amur
Nikolayevsk-na-Amur
Amgun
Sovetskaya Gavan
Uglegorsk
Gulf of Tartary

Kuril Islands

Yuzhno-Sakhalinsk
La Perouse Str.
Wakkanai

snoyarsk
kan
Tulun
Munku
Sardyk   3492
Kyzyl
nu Ola Re
Ubsa Nur
Petrovsk-Zabaykal'skiy
Khōtōgōl
Dalat
Nauforovo Range

Da Hinggan Ling

Khabarovsk

Birobidzhan

Sikhote Alin Range

L. Khanka
Ussuriysk
Olga

Hokkaido
Asahi-daki
2290
Sapporo
Hakodate

M O N G O L I A
Ubsa
Nur

Ulan Bator
Undur Khan

C H I N A
Harbin
Mudanjiang
Jilin

Vladivostok
Nakhodka

S E A O F
J A P A N

Honshu

J A P A N
Niigata
Tokyo
Yokohama
Fuji-san
3776
Nagoya
Kyoto
Kobe   Osaka

Gobi
i
Nen Jiang

INNER MONGOLIA
(NEI MONGGOL)
Hohhot
Zhangjiakou
Baotou
Peking
(Beijing)

Changchun
Shenyang Fushun
Anshan

NORTH
KOREA
Pyongyang

Luda
Korea Bay
Liaodong Bay

SOUTH
KOREA
Seoul

72° 84° 96° 108° 120° 132° 144° 156° 168° 180°
108° 120° 132°

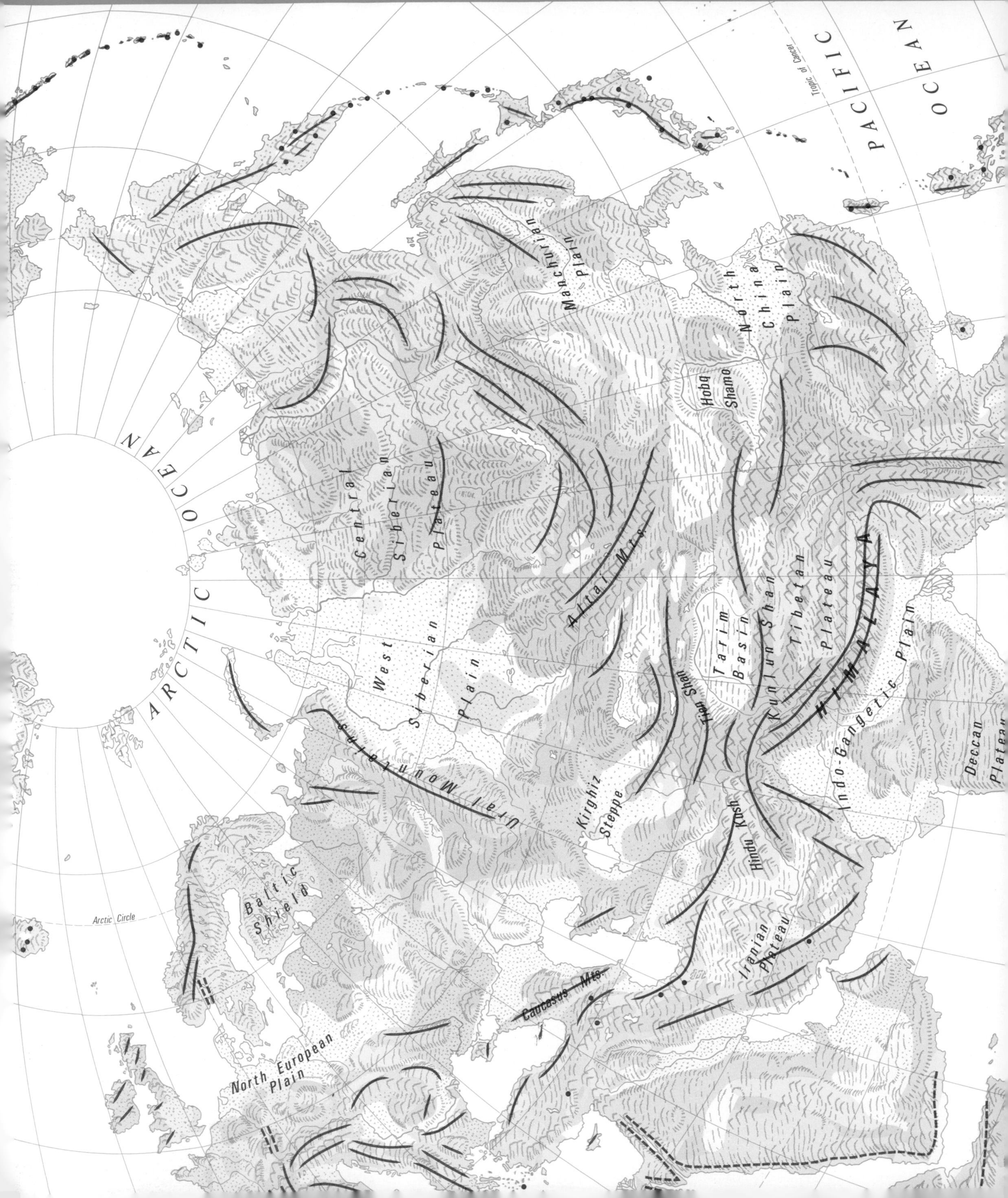

PACIFIC OCEAN

Tropic of Cancer

Manchurian Plain

North China Plain

Hobq Shamo

ARCTIC OCEAN

Central Siberian Plateau

West Siberian Plain

Altai Mts.

Tarim Basin

Tien Shan

Kunlun Shan

Tibetan Plateau

HIMALAYA

Indo-Gangetic Plain

Deccan Plateau

Ural Mountains

Kirghiz Steppe

Hindu Kush

Iranian Plateau

Caucasus Mts.

Baltic Shield

Arctic Circle

North European Plain

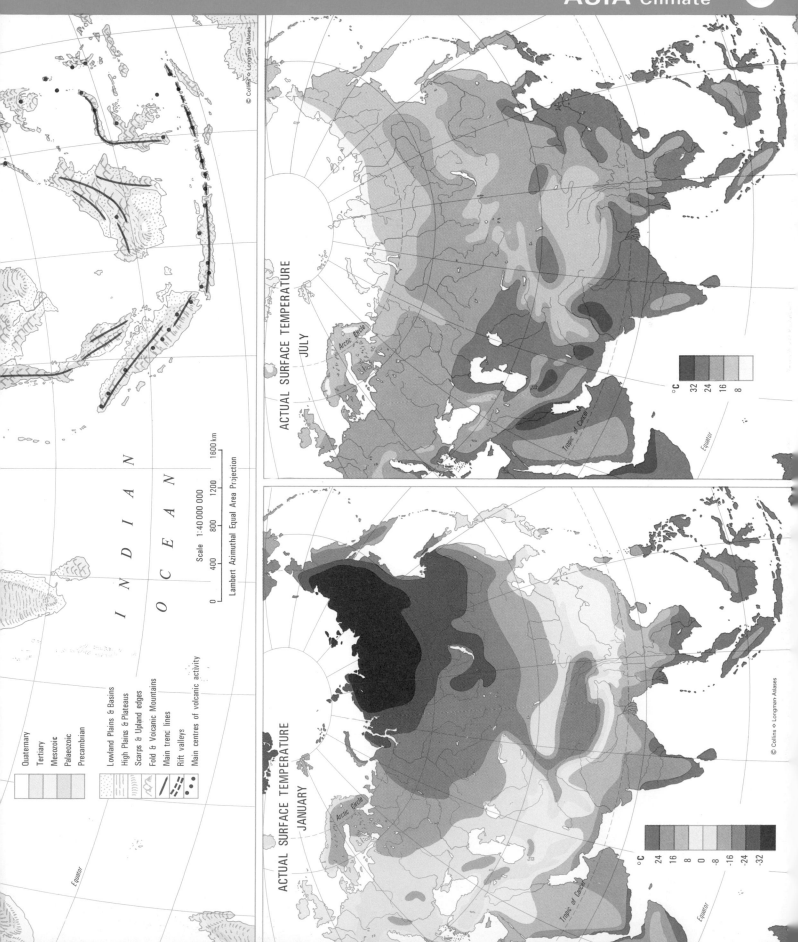

© Collins o Longman Atlases

ASIA Climate

ACTUAL SURFACE TEMPERATURE
JULY

°C 32 24 16 8

ACTUAL SURFACE TEMPERATURE
JANUARY

°C 24 16 8 0 -8 -16 -24 -32

Scale 1:40 000 000

0   400   800   1200   1600 km

Lambert Azimuthal Equal Area Projection

I N D I A N   O C E A N

Quaternary
Tertiary
Mesozoic
Palaeozoic
Precambrian

Lowland Plains & Basins
High Plains & Plateaus
Scarps & Upland edges
Fold & Volcanic Mountains
Main trenc lines
Rift valleys
Main centres of volcanic activity

Arctic Circle

Tropic of Cancer

Equator

PACIFIC OCEAN

ARCTIC OCEAN

ATLANTIC OCEAN

NORWEGIAN SEA

BARENTS SEA

BERING SEA

Bering Str.
East Cape

St. Lawrence I.

Aleutian Is.

Wrangel I.

New Siberian Is.

Severnaya Zemlya

C. Chelyuskin

Taymyr Peninsula

Franz Josef Land

Spitsbergen

Novaya Zemlya

North Cape

Kola Pen.

White Sea

N. Dvina

Pechora

NORTH SEA

British Isles

BALTIC SEA

G. of Bothnia

Scandinavia

L. Ladoga

Vistula

Dnieper

Danube

Carpathians

EUROPE

North European Plain

Central Russian Uplands

Volga

Don

Kama

Ural

Dniester

BLACK SEA

Caucasus
Elbrus 5642

Ararat 5165

Pontine Mts

Taurus Mts.

Anatolia

Cyprus

Tropic of Cancer

Jordan

Gulf of Aden

ARABIA

Syrian Desert

Euphrates

Tigris

Persian Gulf

G. of Oman

ARABIAN SEA

Rub al Khali

Socotra

C. Guardafui

Elburz Mts.

Zagros Mts.

Kuh-i-Haar

Makran

CASPIAN SEA

ARAL SEA

Amu Darya

Syr Darya

Turanian Plain

Kirghiz Steppe

Ural Mountains

West Siberian Plain

S I B E R I A

Ob

Irtysh

Yenisei

Lena

Verkhoyansk Range

Kolyma Range

Koryak Ra.

Kamchatka Peninsula

SEA OF OKHOTSK

Sakhalin

Gulf of Tartary

Kuril Islands

Hokkaido

SEA OF JAPAN

Honshu
Fuji 3776

Shikoku

Kyushu

Korean Str.

Formosa Str.

YELLOW SEA

EAST CHINA SEA

PHILIPPINE IS.

Luzon

Hainan

Formosa

RyuKyu Is.

G. of Tongking

SOUTH

Sikhote Alin Range

Amur

Argun

Da Hinggan Ling

Ussuri

Sungari

Yablonovyy Range

Stanovoy Ra.

L. Baikal

Altai Mts.

L. Balkhash

Gobi

Tarim Basin

Lop Nur

Altun Shan

Qilian Shan

Qinghai Hu

Huang He

Pei Shan

North China Plain

Qin Ling

Nan Ling

Ar Jiang

Mekong

Salween

Irrawaddy

Arakan Yoma

Khasi Hills

Brahmaputra

HIMALAYA
Everest 8848

Ganges

Jumna

Tibetan Plateau

Kunlun Shan

Tien Shan

Pamirs

Karakoram Ra.
K2 8611

Hindu Kush

Helmand

Sulaiman Ra.

Indus

Sutlej

Thar Desert

Narmada

Godavari

Western

Deccan

Bay of Bengal

Chang Jiang (Yangtze)

Red Basin

Gongga Shan 7590

Arctic Circle

PRECIPITATION MAY TO OCTOBER

mm
1000 500 250 125

Arctic Circle

Tropic of Cancer

Equator

PRECIPITATION NOVEMBER TO APRIL

mm
1000 500 250 125

Arctic Circle

Tropic of Cancer

Equator

CHINA

SEA

BORNEO

Kinabalu

Palawan

Mindanao

Moluccas

Celebes

Timor

TIMOR SEA

AUSTRALIA

Flores

JAVA

SUMATRA

Straits of Malacca

Mentawai Is.

Gulf of Siam

Andaman Is.

Nicobar Is.

INDIAN OCEAN

Ceylon

C. Comorin

Maldive Is.

Lakshadweep Is.

Chagos Archipelago

Seychelles

MADAGASCAR

Equator

Ghats

Eastern

Scale 1:40 000 000

1600 km
1200
800
400
0

Lambert Azimuthal Equal Area Projection

Permanent Ice and Snow

Tundra and Alpine

Desert

Semi-desert

Grassland including grass Steppe

Forest and Woodland

Cultivated land

© Collins ◇ Longman Atlases

ARCTIC OCEAN

Arctic Circle

West Siberian Plain

Ural Mts.

Moscow

Warsaw

Ruhr

Donbass

BLACK SEA

Anatolia

Mesopotamia

CASPIAN SEA

ARAL SEA

Kirghiz Steppe

Irtysh

Kuzbass

Aldan

Yakutsk

SEA OF JAPAN

Manchurian Plain

Changchun

Shenyang

Anshan

Peking

North China Plain

Tientsin

Hobq Shamo

Huang Ho (Yellow)

Hwang Ho

Shanghai-Wuhu

Nanking

Taipei

Canton

Hong Kong

Tokyo

Yokohama

Osaka

Nagoya

Nagasaki

Hamamatsu

Gobi

Tarim Basin

Tibetan Plateau

HIMALAYA

Red Basin

Szechwan Basin

Mekong

Irrawaddy

SOUTH

Punjab

Delhi

Indus

Baluchistan

Ganges

Asansol

Calcutta-Howrah

Bay of Bengal

Bombay

ARABIAN SEA

Rub al Khali

Persian Gulf

Tropic of Cancer

PREDOMINANT SUBSISTENCE ECONOMY

Gathering hunting and fishing

Traditional cultivation

Shifting

Semi-intensive sedentary

Intensive cropping (rice dominant)

Intensive cropping (other crop dominant)

Traditional pastoralism

Nomadic herding (reindeer)

Nomadic herding (sheep & goats)

Non-nomadic (cattle)

Non-nomadic (sheep & goats)

PREDOMINANT COMMERCIAL ECONOMY

Intensive cultivation

Grain

Large scale specialised (plantation)

Specialised (market gardening)

Livestock rearing

Extensive (cattle)

Extensive (sheep)

Intensive (cattle)

Intensive dairying

Lumbering

Fishing

Manufacturing / service industry

Extractive industry

Areas of mixed economies shown by banding

Scale 1:40 000 000

0   400   800   1200   1600 km

Lambert Azimuthal Equal Area Projection

© Collins · Longman Atlases

CHINA SEA

Hong Kong

Singapore

Jakarta

Equator

PRESSURE & WINDS MAY TO OCTOBER

Arctic Circle

Tropic of Cancer

HIGH

LOW

1000
1002
1004
1006
1008
1010
1012
1014
1016

Wind direction

Pressure

mb
1020
1016
1012
1008
1004
1000

HIGH

LOW

Isobars in millibars reduced to sea level

PRESSURE & WINDS NOVEMBER TO APRIL

Arctic Circle

Tropic of Cancer

LOW

HIGH

1008
1010
1012
1014
1016
1018
1020
1022
1024
1026
1028
1030

1010
1012
1014
1016
1018
1020

Wind direction

Pressure

mb
1032
1028
1024
1020
1016
1012
1008
1004

HIGH

LOW

Isobars in millibars reduced to sea level

ARCTIC OCEAN

PACIFIC OCEAN

PACIFIC

BERING SEA

SEA OF OKHOTSK

SEA OF JAPAN

YELLOW SEA

EAST CHINA SEA

SOUTH CHINA SEA

Bay of Bengal

ARABIAN SEA

CASPIAN SEA

BLACK SEA

BARENTS SEA

NORWEGIAN SEA

ATLANTIC OCEAN

NORTH SEA

BALTIC SEA

White Sea

Aleutian Is.
St. Lawrence I.
Bering Str.

Kuril Islands
Petropavlovsk-Kamchatskiy
Kamchatskiy
Anadyr
Magadan
Okhotsk
Ayan
Verkhoyansk
Yakutsk
Sakhalin
Hokkaido
Hakodate
Vladivostok
Komsomol'sk-na-Amure
Khabarovsk
Amur
Argun
Songhua Jiang
Shenyang
Harbin

Honshu
Nagoya Tokyo
Kyoto Osaka Yokohama
JAPAN
Str. Shikoku
Nagasaki Kyushu
Nagasaki
Hyūgū Is.

Kuril Islands

Wrangel I.
New Siberian Is.
Novosibirskiye
Lena
Nordvik
Norilsk
Dudinka
Yenisey
Tomsk
Irtysh
Yeniseysk
Krasnoyarsk
Chita
Amur
Ulan-Ude
Irkutsk
L. Baikal
Ulan Bator

MONGOLIA

SOUTH KOREA
NORTH KOREA
Seoul
Pyongyang
Pusan
KOREA
Korea Str.

Qingdao
Lüda
Tianjin
Jinan
Peking
Nanjing
Shanghai

TAIWAN
(FORMOSA)
Taipei

PHILIPPINES
Luzon
Quezon City
Manila
Samar

Franz Josef Land
Spitsbergen
Severnaya Zemlya
Novaya Zemlya
ARCTIC OCEAN

Salekhard
Ob
Pechora
Ob
Irtysh
Omsk
Novosibirsk
Semipalatinsk
Avaguz
Karaganda
Balkhash
L. Balkhash
Ürümqi

Lop Nur
Qinghai Hu

CHINA

Huang He
Xi'an
Lanzhou
Wuhan
Changsha
Chang Jiang (Yangtze)
Chong Jiang (Yangtze)
Chongqing
Kunming
Canton
Victoria
HONG KONG (U.K.)
Macao (Port.)
Hainan
Liuzhou
Xi Kiang
Guiyang

BURMA
Mandalay
Irrawaddy
Sadiya
Lhasa
TIBET
Brahmaputra
BHUTAN
NEPAL
Katmandu
Dacca
BANGLADESH
Calcutta
Ganges
Varanasi
Kanpur
New Delhi
Delhi
Agra
Yamuna (Jumna)
INDIA
Nagpur
Hyderabad
Godavari
Bombay
Ahmadabad
Narmada

ICELAND
REP. OF IRELAND
Dublin
UNITED KINGDOM
Glasgow
London
NORWAY
Oslo
SWEDEN
Stockholm
FINLAND
Helsinki
Murmansk
Arkhangel'sk
Petrozavodsk
Leningrad
Riga
Minsk
Moscow
Tula
Gorki
Rybinsk
Volga
Perm
Sverdlovsk
Kama
UNION OF SOVIET SOCIALIST REPUBLICS
Kuybyshev
Saratov
Ural
Orsk
Aralsk
ARAL SEA
Syr Darya
Amu Darya
Tashkent
Alma-Ata
Samarkand
Frunze
Guryev
Krasnovodsk
Astrakhan
Volgograd
Don
Kharkov
Donetsk
Dnieper
Kiev
Odessa
Sevastopol
Tbilisi
Baku
Tabriz
Tehran
Mashhad

AFGHANISTAN
Kabul
Islamabad
Srinagar
KASHMIR
Lahore
PAKISTAN
Indus
Karachi
Helmand
IRAN
Isfahan
Abadan
Baghdad
IRAQ
Basra
Tigris
Euphrates
Kuwait
KUWAIT
BAHRAIN
QATAR
Doha
Dubai
UNITED ARAB EMIRATES
Muscat
OMAN
The Gulf
Riyadh
SAUDI ARABIA
Mecca
Tropic of Cancer
YEMEN
Sana
SOUTHERN YEMEN
Aden
Gulf of Aden
Al Shabi
Socotra

NORTH SEA
DENMARK
Copenhagen
Amsterdam
Brussels
Paris
FRANCE
Berne
SW.
Rhine
Bonn
N.W. GER.
GER.
Berlin
Prague
CZECHOSLOVAKIA
POLAND
Warsaw
Vistula
Danube
Vienna
AUSTRIA
Budapest
HUNGARY
Bucharest
ROMANIA
Belgrade
YUGOSLAVIA
Sofia
BULGARIA
Istanbul
Ankara
TURKEY
Izmir
GREECE
CYPRUS
LEBANON
Beirut
Damascus
SYRIA
Amman
JORDAN
Jerusalem
ISRAEL
Tropic of Cancer

Arctic Circle

VIETNAM
LAOS
Hanoi
Vientiane

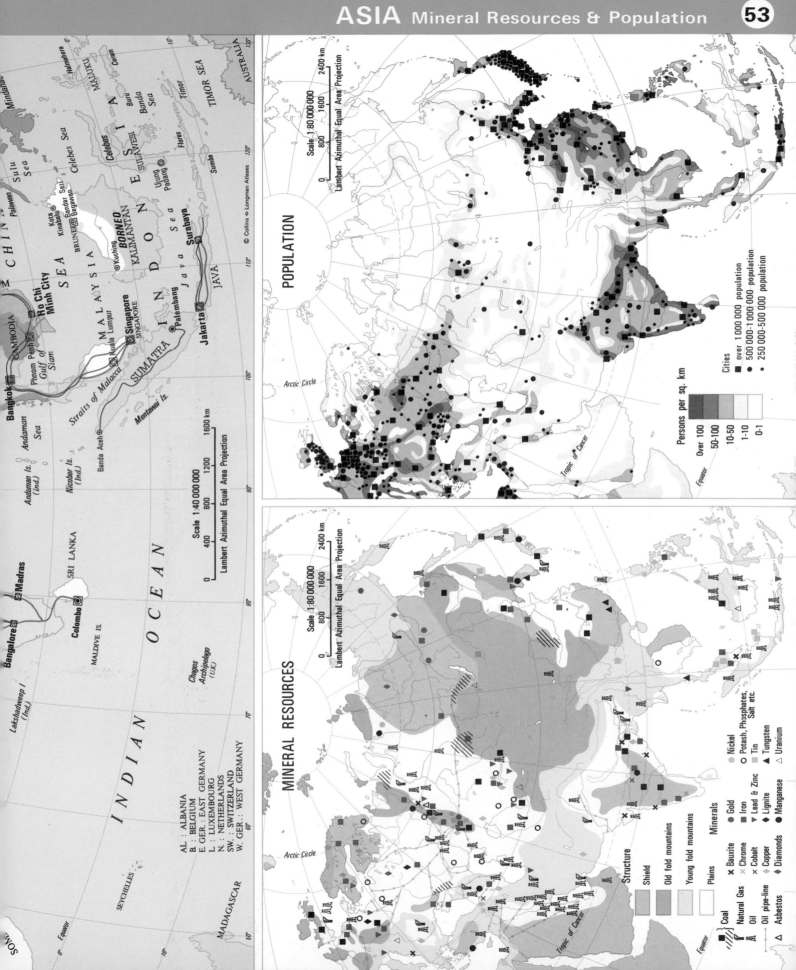

POPULATION

Scale 1:80 000 000
Lambert Azimuthal Equal Area Projection

0   800   1600   2400 km

Arctic Circle

Tropic of Cancer

Equator

Persons per sq. km
Over 100
50-100
10-50
1-10
0-1

Cities
■ over 1 000 000 population
● 500 000-1 000 000 population
· 250 000-500 000 population

MINERAL RESOURCES

Scale 1:80 000 000
Lambert Azimuthal Equal Area Projection

0   800   1600   2400 km

Arctic Circle

Tropic of Cancer

Equator

Structure
Shield
Old fold mountains
Young fold mountains
Plains

Minerals
✗ Bauxite   ● Gold   ● Nickel
✗ Chrome   ■ Iron   ○ Potash, Phosphates, Salt etc.
✗ Cobalt   ▼ Lead & Zinc   ■ Tin
◆ Copper   ◆ Lignite   ▲ Tungsten
■ Coal   ◆ Diamonds   △ Uranium
                   ● Manganese

▦ Natural Gas
⚒ Oil
→ Oil pipe-line
△ Asbestos

Mindanao
Halmahera
Ceram
MALUKU
Buru
Banda Sea
Ceram
Timor
TIMOR SEA
AUSTRALIA
130°
Flores Sea
Celebes
SULAWESI
Banda Sea
Sumba
120°
Sulu Sea
Palawan
Celebes Sea
Kota Kinabalu
Sabah
Bandar Seri Begawan
BRUNEI
BORNEO
KALIMANTAN
Ujung Padang
Kuching
I   N   D   O   N   E   S   I   A
Java Sea
Surabaya
110°
C H I N A
S E A
Ho Chi Minh City
CAMBODIA
Phnom Penh
Gulf of Siam
M A L A Y S I A
Kuala Lumpur
Singapore
SINGAPORE
SUMATRA
Palembang
Jakarta
JAVA
100°
Bangkok
Straits of Malacca
Mentawai Is.
Banda Aceh
Andaman Is. (Ind.)
Andaman Sea
Nicobar Is. (Ind.)
1600 km
Scale 1:40 000 000
0   400   800   1200
Lambert Azimuthal Equal Area Projection

SRI LANKA
Madras
Bangalore
Colombo
MALDIVE IS
Lakshadweep I (Ind.)
90°
I N D I A N   O C E A N
Chagos Archipelago (U.K.)
80°
70°
SEYCHELLES
60°
MADAGASCAR
50°
Equator

© Collins ◇ Longman Atlases

AL : ALBANIA
B : BELGIUM
E. GER. : EAST GERMANY
L : LUXEMBOURG
N. : NETHERLANDS
SW. : SWITZERLAND
W. GER. : WEST GERMANY

GREECE

Thessaloniki
Khalkidhiki
Mt Athos 2033

AEGEAN

SEA

Euboea

Athens
Piraeus
Corinth

Cyclades
Páros
Náxos
Milos
Thíra

CRETE
Réthimnon
Iráklion

GEOR

Istanbul
Üsküdar Izmit
Gebze
Bursa

ANATOLIA

T U R K E Y

Ankara

Sivas

Erzurum

Konya

TAURUS MOUNTAINS

Adana

Mersin

G. of Iskenderun

Iskenderun
Antakya

Aleppo

S Y R I A

Latakia

CYPRUS
Nicosia
Mt Olympus 1952

Hama

Homs

Palmyra

Tripoli

LEBANON
Beirut

Damascus

MEDITERRANEAN SEA

Mt Hermon 2814

Haifa

ISRAEL
Ramat Gan
Tel-Aviv-Yafo
Jerusalem
Gaza

Amman

JORDAN

Dead Sea

Alexandria

Port Said

El Arish

Nile Delta

Cairo

Suez Canal

Sinai

PETRA

Ma'an

Negev

Gulf of Aqaba

E G Y P T

Libyan

Desert

Arabian

Eastern

Desert

Gulf of Suez

R E D

S E A

Aswan
Aswan High Dam

Scale 1:9 000 000
0   100   200   300   400 km
Conic Projection

Lake Nasser

SUDAN

Nubian Desert

Wadi Halfa

60 © Collins ◇ Longman Atlases

Scale 1:10 000 000

0   100   200   300 km

Conic Projection

© Collins ⬦ Longman Atlases

JIANG UYGUR
Kunlun Shan
Karakoram Pass
6919
Tibetan Plateau
7315
(Qing Zang Gaoyuan)
Dogai Coring
(X I Z A N G)
C H I N A
QINGHAI
6800
Yushu
Huang He
NINGXIA HUIZA
4001
Taibai Shan
QIN Ling
SHAANXI
Hanzhong
Chengdu
Hechuan
Chongqing
SICHUAN
Gar
Garyarsa
7216
Tangra Yumco
Siling Co
Nam Co
Ban
7000
Lhasa
Zetang
Yarlung Zangbo Jiang
Xigaze
Gyangze
Qamdo
Batang
Lancang Jiang
Hengduan Shan
Nu Jiang
Yalong
Kangding
Gongga Shan
7590
Ya'an
Leshan
Yibin
Luzhou
Kamet
7756
Nanda Devi
7817
7728
132
NEPAL
Jumla
Dhaulagiri
8172
Mustang
Annapurna
8078
Pokhara
Kanchenjunga
8848
8586
Mt Everest
Katmandu
Thimbu
BHUTAN
Kula Kangri
7554
SIKKIM
ARUNACHAL PRADESH
Sadiya
Kedusam
5108
Namuchabawashan
7756
Putao
Dibrugarh
Degen
Zhongdian
Lijiang
Xichang
Zhaotong
Dongchuan
GUIZHOU
Guiyang
Duyun
Anshun
Darjeeling
Siliguri
Bengal
Jalpaiguri
Gauhati
MEGHALAYA
Shillong
Sylhet
Tezpur
Nowgong
A S S A M
NAGALAND
Kohima
KACHIN STATE
Myitkyina
Mogoung
Tengchong
Baoshan
Kunming
YUNNAN
Chuxiong
Xiaguan
Dali
Beijing
Hongshui He
Bareilly
Shahjahanpur
UTTAR PRADESH
Lucknow
Kanpur
Faizabad
Gorakhpur
Ghaghra
Gogra
Muzaffarpur
Darbhanga
Jaunpur
Monghyr
Saidpur
Jamalpur
Mymensingh
Silchar
MANIPUR
Imphal
Thaungdut
Mawlaik
Mogoung
Katha
Bhamo
Lashio
Longling
Lincang
Mengzi
Wenshan
Jianshui
Gejiu
Simao
Lai Chau
Ha Giang
Yaozu
Aztuxian
Hekou
2879
Jinghong
VIETNAM
Hanoi
Haiphong
Allahabad
Jhansi
Varanasi
Mirzapur
Gaya Bihar
Patna
Bhagalpur
English Bazar
BIHAR
Daltonganj
Berhampore
Pabna
Agartala
Comilla
BANGLADESH
Dacca
Narayanganj
Jessore
Khulna
Chittagong
Yeu
Shwebo
Monywa
Sagaing
Mandalay
Maymyo
SHAN STATE
Kengtung
Maymo
Phong Saly
Sam Neua
Dhanbad
Asansol
Pirulia
Burdwan
Bengal
Howrah
Calcutta
Kharagpur
Sundarbans
Ranchi
Jamshedpur
Rourkela
Neogaon
Myingyan
Meiktila
BURMA
3053
Pegu-Yoma
Magwe
Yamethin
Pyinmana
Chiang Rai
Luang Prabang
Xieng Khouang
2817
Vinh
Jabalpur
Narsimhapur
MADHYA PRADESH
Bilaspur
Raigarh
Sarangarh
Hirakud Res.
Sambalpur
Balasore
Mouths of the Ganges
Cox's Bazar
Akyab
Irrawaddy
Thayetmyo
Prome
Myanaung
Toungoo
Sittang
KAWTHOOLEI
Pegu
Chiang Mai
M.Lampang
M.Phrae
Vientiane
Nong Khai
Udon Thani
Thakhek
Savannakhet
Raipur
Nagpur
Wardha
Chanda
Kanker
Dolungii
Mahanadi
ORISSA
Cuttack
Bhubaneswar
Puri
Berhampur
Palmyras Pt
Kyaukpyu
Ramree I.
Sandoway
Henzada
Bassein
Irrawaddy Delta
C. Negrais
Rangoon
Thaton
Martaban
Moulmein
Uttaradit
P. Mong
2316
M.Phitsanulok
M.Khon Kaen
Khemmarat
Nakhon Sawan
THAILAND
Ubon Ratchathani
Surin
Warangal
Godavari
Indravati
Jagdalpur
Jeypore
Vizianagaram
Vishakhapatnam
ANDHRA PRADESH
Hyderabad
Rajahmundry
Eluru
Kakinada
Vijayawada
Guntur
Bandar
B A Y   O F
B E N G A L
Ye
Gulf of Martaban
Tavoy
TENASSERIM
Kanchanaburi
Nakhon Pathom
Bangkok
Thonburi
Chon Buri
Phet Buri
Chanthaburi
Battambang
Sisophon
Tonle Sap
CAMBODIA
Pursat
Phnom Penh
Kompot
Krishna
Kavali
Nellore
North Andaman
Middle Andaman
ANDAMAN Islands
South Andaman
Port Blair
(India)
Little Andaman
ANDAMAN
SEA
Mergui
Mergui Archipelago
Prachuap Khiri Khan
Chumphon
Isthmus of Kra
GULF OF
SIAM
Madras
Kanchipuram
Vellore
Pondicherry
Cuddalore
Kumbakonam
Karikal
Nagappattinam
Tiruchirapalli
Madurai
Car Nicobar
Nicobar
Little Andaman
Islands
Gt Nicobar
(India)
Phangnga
Krabi
Phuket
Surat Thani
Nakhon Si Thammarat
B. Kantang
B. Hat Yai
Songkhla
Alor Setar
Kota Bharu
MALAYSIA
Kuala Trengganu
Jaffna
Vavuniya
Trincomalee
Batticaloa
Gulf of Mannar
Puttalam
Kandy
2524
Colombo
Galle
SRI LANKA
George Town
Penang I.
Taiping
Ipoh
Kuala Lumpur
INDONESIA
SUMATRA
Banda Aceh

Metres | Relief
5000
3000
2000
1000
500
200
0 | Sea Level
Land Dep. | 200
4000
7000
Metres

Scale 1:14 000 000
0   200   400   600   800 km
Conic Projection

Taichung
Shanchung
Chiai
Tainan
Pingtung

TAIWAN
(FORMOSA)

Batan Is
Luzon Strait
Babuyan Is
ojeador
C. Engaño
Laoag   Aparri
Tuguegarao
Peleo   Ollagan
San Fernando
Baguio Bayombong
Dagupan
San Carlos   Cabanatuan
Quezon City
Manila
San Pablo   Daet
City   PHILIPPINES
ngas   Naga
Mindoro   Burias   Legaspi
Sorsin
Bulan
Masbate   Catarman
Calbayog   Samar
Panay   Catbalogan
Guiuan
Iloilo   Cadiz   Tacloban
Bacolod   Cebu   Leyte
Dinagat   Cape Johnson
Negros   Siargao   Depth
Tanjay   Bohol   Tagbilaran
Dumaguete   Surigao
Dipolog   Butuan
Ozamiz   Cagayan de Oro
Pagadian   Iligan
MINDANAO
Zamboanga   Davao
Basilan   Cotabato
Basilan Gulf   Datu Piang
Jolo   General
Sulu   Santos
Arch

Philippine Trench

Davao G.

PHILIPPINES

CELEBES SEA

Karakelong   Talaud Is
Sangi
Sangihe Is
Molucca Sea
Menado
Kuandang   Tondano
Belang
Gorontalo
Djailolo   Morotai
Ternate   Tobelo
Soasiu   Halmahera
Weda
Waigeo
MOLUCCAS
Dampier Str   Kwaka
Batjan   Sorong   Klamono
Togian Is   Vogelkop
Poh   Arfak
Peleng   Taliabu   Misool   Wasian
Sula Is   Obi
CERAM SEA
Banggai Is
G. of Tolo
Binaija   Rita
Namlea
Buru   Ambon   Ceram
Muna   Butung   Banda
Tukangbesi
Baubau   Is
Kai Is   Wokam
Aru   Kobroor
Is
BANDA SEA   Trangan
Nila
Damar   Jamdena   Tanimbar
Wetar   Roma   Saumlaki   Is
Selaru
Alor   Leti Is
Dili   Sermate
Timor
Maumere
Ende
Savu Sea
Sawu   Roti   Kupang

PACIFIC OCEAN

Parece Vela

Farallon de Pajaros
Asuncion
Agrihan
Pagan
Alamagan
Mariana   Guguan
Sarigan
Anatahan   Farallon de Medinilla
Islands   Saipan
Tinian
Rota
Agana   Guam   Nero Deep

Challenger Depth

Yap
Faraulep   Gaferut
Sorol   Pigailoe
Ifalik   Lamotrek
Palau   Koror
Is   Eauripik
Caroline   Islands
(U.S. Trust Territory)
Sonsurol
Merir
Tobi   Helen Reef
Mapia Is

Equator

Schouten Is
Manokwari   Biak
Biak   Bosnik
Mokmer
Japen   Sarmi
Serui
Teluk   Jayapura
Irian   Vanimo
Aitape
Membramo
IRIAN   Mts
Maoke Range
Sudirman Mts   Djajawidjaja
Puntjak Jaya   Mts
JAYA   Mondla Pk
Kokenau
NEW GUINEA
Mappi
Digoel
Kolepom   Okaba
C. Vals   Merauke   Daru
Mulgrave Is

Manus
Lorengau
Admiralty Is

Bismarck Sea

Meprik
Wewak   Angoram
Sepik   Bogia
Madang
PAPUA NEW   Wabag   Bismarck
Laiagam   Mt
GUINEA   Mt Hagen   Goroka
Mendi   Wilhelm   Kainantu
Huon Pen
Finschhafen
Lae
Wau
Kikori   Baimuru
Kerema
Gulf of   Kila Kila
Papua   Port Moresby

Torres Str.
Thursday I
Prince of Wales I   C. York

ARAFURA SEA

Coral Sea

KAZAKHSTAN SSR
U.S.S.R.
MONGO...
UZBEKISTAN SSR
KIRGIZSTAN SSR
Turkestan
TADZHIKISTAN SSR
PAMIRS
AFGHANISTAN
HINDU KUSH
KARAKORAM RANGE
PAKISTAN
JAMMU AND KASHMIR
HIMACHAL PRADESH
PUNJAB
HARYANA
RAJASTHAN
UTTAR PRADESH
MADHYA PRADESH
MAHARASHTRA
ORISSA
ANDHRA PRADESH
NEPAL
HIMALAYA
SIKKIM
BHUTAN
BANGLADESH
BENGAL
MEGHALAYA
ARUNACHAL PRADESH
ASSAM
NAGALAND
MANIPUR
MIZORAM
BURMA
Kachin State
Shan State
Chin Hills
THAILAND
LAOS
VIETNAM

XINJIANG-UYGUR
Junggar Pendi
Tian Shan
Tarim He
Taklimakan Shamo
Kunlun Shan
Altun Shan
Tibetan Plateau (Qing Zang Gaoyuan)
TIBET (XIZANG)
Tanggula Shan
QINGHAI
GANSU
NINGXIA HUIZU
SICHUAN
Red Basin
YUNNAN
GUIZHOU
CHINA

Tashkent
Chimkent
Dzambul
Alma Ata
Frunze
Lake Balkhash
Balkhash
Ayaguz
Ayaguz
Aktogay
Zaysan
Lake Zaysan
Altay
Ulan Gom
Hirgis Nur
Ubsa Nur
Khóbsógól Dalai
Lake Baikal
Irkutsk
Slyudyanka
Yenisei
Kyzyl
Sayan Mts
Belukha Mt. 4506
Ulëgey
Kara-Usa Nur
Hovd
Uliastaj
Altaj
Móron
Bulagan
Ulan Bator
Darhan
Selenga

Dushanbe
Faizabad
Pik Kommunizma 7495
Kokand
Andizhan
Namangan
Talasskiy Ala Tau
Issyk-Kul
Przhevalsk
Gulja
Bole
Ebinur Hu
Karamay
Urumqi
Turpan Pendi -154
Turpan
Hami 4925
Anxi
Dunhuang
Yumen
Ruo Shui
Hanggin Houqi
Shizuishan
Wuwei
Yinchuan

Chitral
Gilgit
K2 8611
Karakoram Pass
Peshawar
Malakand
Islamabad
Rawalpindi
Jhelum
Srinagar
Leh
Kashi
Shache
Yarkant He
Pishan
Hotan
Qarqan He
Ruoqiang
Qiemo
Lop Nur
Bosten Hu
Kuqa
Aksu
Yangi Hizu
Korla
Mangnai
Da Qaidam
Har Hu
Qinghai Hu
Xining
Lanzhou
Linxia
Lintan
Longxi
Tianshui
Qingyang
Pingliang

Lahore
Gujranwala
Sialkot
Jammu
Amritsar
Jullundur
Ludhiana
Ambala
Simla
Dehra Dun
Saharanpur
Meerut
Delhi
New Delhi
Moradabad
Bareilly
Shahjahanpur
Lucknow
Kanpur
Jaipur
Mathura
Aligarh
Agra
Gwalior
Jhansi
Allahabad
Varanasi
Patna
Darbhanga
Monghyr
Bhagalpur
Gaya
BIHAR
Ranchi
Jamshedpur
Asansol
Dacca
Calcutta
Howrah
Kharagpur
Balasore
Cuttack
Bhubaneswar
Puri
Sambalpur
Berhampur
Vishakhapatnam
Kakinada
Vijayawada
Bandar
Guntur

Nanda Devi 7816
Mt. Everest 8878
Kangchenjunga 8598
Annapurna 8078
Dhaulagiri 8172
Katmandu
Gorakhpur
Darjeeling
Jalpaiguri
Siliguri
Thimbu
Gauhati
Shillong
Sylhet
Agartala
Silchar
Imphal
Kohima
Dibrugarh
Sadiya
Tezpur
Putao
Myitkyina
Bhamo
Lashio
Mandalay
Meiktila
Myingyan
Akyab
Chittagong
Cox's Bazar
Sundarbans

Xigaze
Gyangze
Lhasa
Batang
Dege
Qamdo
Nam Co
Siling Co
Yarlung Zangbo Jiang
Nu Jiang
Yushu
Bayan Har Shan
Gangga Shan 7590
Chengdu
Chongqing
Neijiang
Zigong
Luzhou
Yibin
Zunyi
Guiyang
Kunming
Dali
Xiaguan
Baoshan
Tengchong
Lincang
Simao
Gejiu
Mengzi
Hanoi
Haiphong

Lancang Jiang
Salween
Chindwin
Irrawaddy
Mekong
Red
Taung-gyi
Kengtung
Jinghong
Luang Prabang
Vientiane
Chiang Mai
M. Lampang
Pegu Yoma
Sittang
Prome
Pyinmana
Yamethin
Toungoo
Sandoway
Tharrawaddy
Bassein

BAY OF BENGAL

Chita · Shilka · Shitka · Svobodnyy · **U.S.S.R.** · Khabarovsk · Sakhalin · Yuzhno Sakhalinsk · Kuril Islands · Iterup

Ulan Ude · Berzya · Manzhouli · Hailar · **HEILONGJIANG** · Blagoveshchensk · Sunwu · Amur · Birobidzhan · La Perouse Strait · Wakkanai · Kunashir

Hulun Chih · Xing'an · Xiao Hinggan Ling · Hegang · Fujin · Bikin · Sikhote Alin Range · Asahikawa · Asahi dake · Kushiro · **HOKKAIDO**

Kerulen · Tamsag Bulag · Qiqihar · Anda · Harbin · Jiamusi · Yilan · Hanka L. · Kikachi · Sapporo · Otaru · Muroran · Hakodate

Saynshand · Tao'an · Fuyu · Songhua Jiang · Mudanjiang · Ussuriysk · Olga · Aomori · Hachinohe

Erenhot · **JILIN** · Changchun · Jilin · Yanji · Vladivostok · Akita · Morioka

INNER MONGOLIA (NEI MONGGOL) · Shuangliao · Siping · Liaoyuan · Tonghua · Chongjin · Nakhodka · **SEA OF JAPAN** · **HONSHU** · Yamagata · Sendai

Chifeng · Shenyang · Fushun · Pingdingshan · Hamhung · **NORTH KOREA** · Niigata · Utsonomiya · **JAPAN**

Baotou · Hohhot · Jining · Zhangjiakou · Xuanhua · **LIAONING** · Fuxin · Benxi · Dandong · Hungnam · Wonsan · Toyama · Tokyo · Chiba

Huang He · Datong · Ningwu · Chengde · Anshan · Liaoyang · Sinuiju · Kanazawa · Gifu · Kawasaki · Yokohama

Great Wall · Peking (Beijing) · Tangshan · Jinzhou · Qinhuangdao · Xinjin · Pyongyang · Nampo · Kaesong · Chunchon · Kangnung · Oki gunto · Nagoya · Shizuoka · Hamamatsu

Sanggan He · **HEBEI** · Tianjin · Gulf of Chihli · Ligdong Bay · Liaodong Peninsula · Korea Bay · Seoul · Inchon · Suwon · Changju · Kyoto · Osaka · Sakai · Wakayama

Taiyuan · Shijiazhuang · Dezhou · Yantai · Weihai · Shandong Bandao · Taejon · Taegu · Ulsan · Hiroshima · Okayama · Kobe · Amagasaki · Takamatsu

SHANXI · Yuci · Xingtai · Boshan · Weifang · **YELLOW** · Kunsan · Chonju · Masan · Pusan · Shimonoseki · Matsuyama · **SHIKOKU**

Fenyang · Yanchuan · Liaocheng · Fengcheng · Jinan · Qingdao · **SEA** · Kwangju · Yosu · Tsushima · Kitakyushu · Fukuoka

SHAANXI · Zhengzhou · Anyang · Hebi · Teng Xian · Zaozhuang · Xugou · Qingjiang · Mokpo · Cheju · Korea Strait · Saseho · Kumamoto · **KYUSHU**

Xianyang · Luoyang · Kaifeng · Xuzhou · Lianyungang · Yancheng · Quelpart · Nagasaki

Xi'an · Tongguan · **HENAN** · Xuchang · Bo Xian · **JIANGSU** · Huaiyin · Huaiyin · Rugao · Nantong · Kagoshima · Osumi Gunto

Nanyang · Shangshui · **PLAIN** · Bengbu · Taizhou

Shui · Guanghua · Huai He · Huainan · Zhenjiang · **PACIFIC**

Yichang · Xiangfan · Xiangyang · Hefei · Nanjing · Changzhou · Wuxi · Shanghai · **OCEAN**

Jiangling · Shashi · Huangshi · **ANHUI** · Wuhu · Suzhou · Shengze · Jiaxing

Changde · **HUBEI** · Wuhan · Huanggang · Tongling · Hangzhou · Ningbo · **EAST**

Dongting Hu · Anqing · Shaoxing · Amami

HUNAN · Nanchang · Jiujiang · Jingdezhen · Qu Xian · Lishui · Dajing · **CHINA** · Tokuno

Changsha · Xiangtan · Tuochuanbu · Poyang Hu · Jinhua · Wenzhou · **SEA**

Shaoyang · **JIANGXI** · Qingjiang · Zhuzhou · Yian · Shangrao · **ZHEJIANG**

Hengyang · Guilin · Zhongshan · Nanping · **FUJIAN** · Fuzhou · Matsu Is. · Ryukyu Islands · Miyako · Okinawa · Naha

GUANGXI ZHUANGZU · Yingde · Mei Xian · Chao an · Fuzhou · Formosa Strait · Chilung · Hsinchu · Miyako · Iriomote

Liuzhou · Ganzhou · Changting · Putian · Taipei · Taichung · Hualien · **TAIWAN (FORMOSA)**

Xi Jiang · Wuzhou · **GUANGDONG** · Quanzhou · Zhangzhou · Xiamen · Changhua · Chia · Taitung

Nanning · Guiping · Foshan · Canton (Guangzhou) · Shantou · Chao an · Tainan · Pingtung

Maoming · Shunde · Kowloon · Chaoyang · Kaohsiung · Bashi Channel

Macao (Port.) · Victoria · **HONG KONG (U.K.)** · Pingtung · Batan Islands

Leizhou Peninsula · Zhanjiang · Haikou · **SOUTH** · Luzon Strait · Babuyan Islands

HAINAN · Dongfang · Yacheng · Yulin · **CHINA SEA** · **PHILIPPINES** · Laoag · Tuguegarao · Aparri · **LUZON**

Relief

Metres	
5000	
3000	
2000	
1000	
500	
200	
0	Sea Level
Land Dep.	
200	
4000	
7000	
Metres	

Scale 1:16 000 000

0 · 200 · 400 · 600 · 800 km

Conic Projection

© Collins ◇ Longman Atlas

Relief

Metres		Sea Level	Metres
5000		0	200
3000			4000
2000			7000
1000			
500			
200			

Scale 1 : 7 500 000

Conic Projection

0 50 100 150 200 250 300 km

© Collins • Longman Atlases

Scale 1:7 500 000

0   100   200   300 km

Conic Projection

Relief

Metres
5000
3000
2000
1000
500
200
0 Sea Level
Land Dep.
200
4000
7000
Metres

© Collins ◇ Longman Atlases

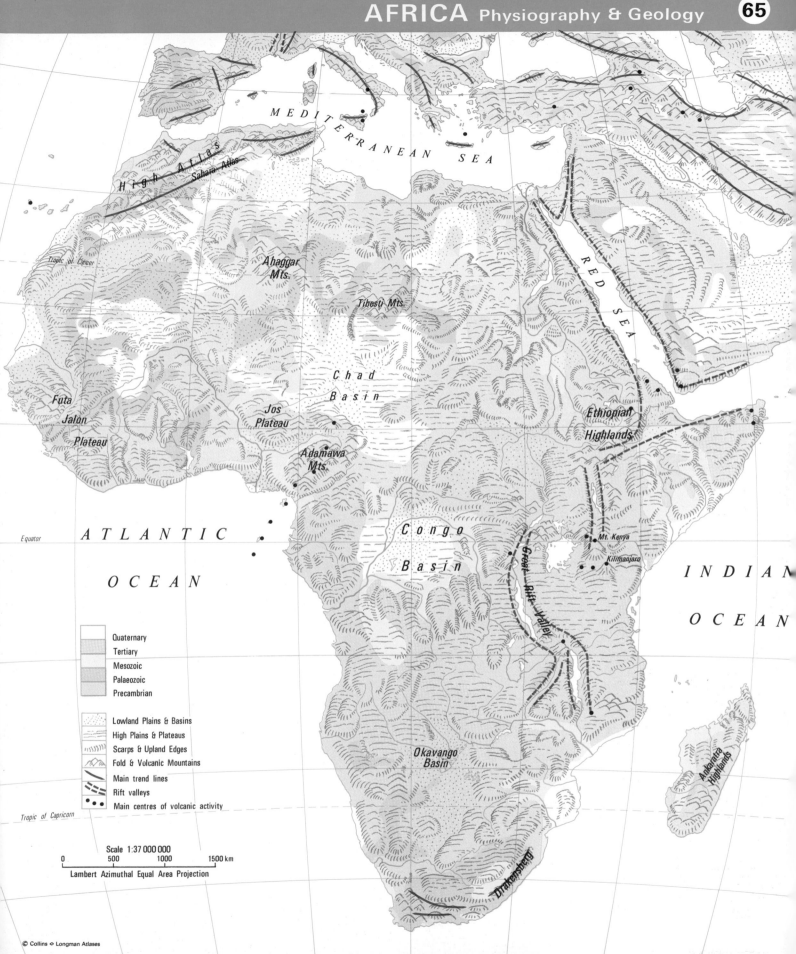

MEDITERRANEAN SEA

High Atlas

Sahara Atlas

Tropic of Cancer

Ahaggar Mts.

Tibesti Mts.

RED SEA

Chad Basin

Futa Jalon Plateau

Jos Plateau

Ethiopian Highlands

Adamawa Mts.

Equator

ATLANTIC

OCEAN

Congo Basin

Mt. Kenya

Kilimanjaro

INDIAN

OCEAN

Great Rift Valley

Okavango Basin

Ankarata Highlands

Tropic of Capricorn

Drakensberg

Quaternary
Tertiary
Mesozoic
Palaeozoic
Precambrian

Lowland Plains & Basins
High Plains & Plateaus
Scarps & Upland Edges
Fold & Volcanic Mountains
Main trend lines
Rift valleys
Main centres of volcanic activity

Scale 1:37 000 000

0   500   1000   1500 km

Lambert Azimuthal Equal Area Projection

ATLANTIC

OCEAN   Str. of Gibraltar

MEDITERRANEAN   SEA

BLACK SEA

CASPIAN SEA

Pyrenees

Danube

Madeira

High Atlas   Saharan Atlas

Sicily

Malta

Crete

Cyprus

Syrian Desert

Euphrates

Tigris

Canary Is.

S   A   H   A   R   A

Ahaggar Mts. ▲ 2918

Libyan

Desert

-133 Qattara Depression

L. Nasser

Nubian Desert

Sinai

Nile

Red Sea

Persian Gulf

Tropic of Cancer

Arabia

Tibesti Mts. ▲ 3415

Darfur ▲ 3071

Atbara

Blue Nile

Gezira

▲ 4620

L. Tana

Ethiopian

Highlands

Gulf of Aden

Niger

Senegal

Gambia

Futa

Jalon

Plateau

Volta

Niger

S   u   d   a   n

L. Chad

Benue

White Nile

Bahr el Jebel

Shebelle

G   u   i   n   e   a

Bight of Benin

Adamawa Highlands

▲ Mt. Cameroon 4070

Macias Nguema

Principe

São Tomé

Gulf of Guinea

Ubangi

Zaïre

Congo

Basin

L. Mobutu

Ruwenzori Range 5119

L. Idi Amin Dada

L. Kivu

L Turkana

L. Kyoga

▲ Mt. Elgon 4321

Owen Falls

L. Victoria

▲ Mt. Kenya 5200

Kilimanjaro ▲ 5895

INDIAN

Equator

Zaïre

Kasai

Zaïre

L. Tanganyika

Great Rift Valley

Pemba I.

Zanzibar I.

OCEAN

Aldabra Is.

Scale 1:37 000 000

0   500   1000   1500 km

Lambert Azimuthal Equal Area Projection

Bié

Plateau

Zambezi

Cuando

Cubango

Okavango Basin

L. Kariba

Victoria Falls

Zambezi

L. Malawi

Ruvuma

Comoro Is.

C. d'Ambre

M o ç a m b i q u e   C h a n n e l

M a d a g a s c a r

Namib Desert

Kalahari

Desert

Limpopo

Orange

Vaal

High Veld

Drakensberge

Tropic of Capricorn

Great Karroo

Cape of Good Hope

© Collins ◇ Longman Atlases

MINERAL RESOURCES

Structure

Shield

Old fold mountains

Young fold mountains

Plains

Minerals

■ Coal	■ Gold
⚒ Oil	■ Iron
✕ Bauxite	▼ Lead
✕ Cobalt	● Manganese
◆ Copper	○ Phosphates
◆ Diamonds	■ Tin
△ Uranium	

Desert

Semi-desert

Grassland including upland grass
and tropical grass savanna

Forest and woodland including
wood savanna

Areas where farming has substantially
altered the natural cover

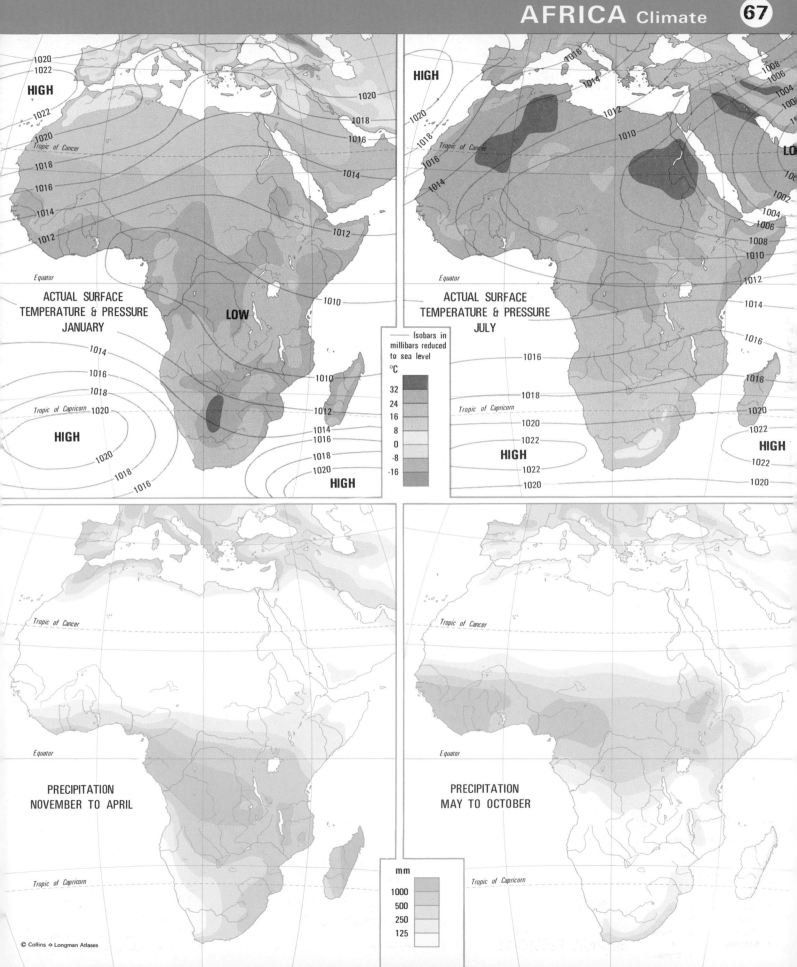

HIGH

1020
1022
1022
1020
Tropic of Cancer
1018
1016
1014
1012
1020
1018
1016
1014
1012
Equator

ACTUAL SURFACE
TEMPERATURE & PRESSURE
JANUARY

LOW

1014
1016
1018
Tropic of Capricorn 1020

HIGH

1020
1016

1010
1012
1014
1016
1018
1020

HIGH

HIGH

1016
1014
1016
1012
Tropic of Cancer
1014
1016
1012
1010
Equator

ACTUAL SURFACE
TEMPERATURE & PRESSURE
JULY

LO

1008
1006
1004
1002
1004
1006
1008
1010
1012
1014

1016
1018
1018
1020
1022
1020

1016
Tropic of Capricorn
1020
1022

HIGH

HIGH

1022
1020

Isobars in
millibars reduced
to sea level
°C
32
24
16
8
0
-8
-16

PRECIPITATION
NOVEMBER TO APRIL

PRECIPITATION
MAY TO OCTOBER

mm
1000
500
250
125

© Collins ◇ Longman Atlases

BLACK SEA

CASPIAN SEA

MEDITERRANEAN SEA

Casablanca

High Atlas

Alexandria

Cairo

Syrian Desert

Euphrates

Tigris

Persian Gulf

Tropic of Cancer

L. Nasser

SAHARA

Niger

Red Sea

Futa Jalon Plateau

Ethiopian Highlands

Addis Ababa

Benue

Ibadan

L. Volta

Lagos

Accra

Adamawa Highlands

Congo

Basin

Zaïre

Kampala

Lake Victoria

Nairobi

INDIAN

Equator

OCEAN

Lake Tanganyika

Dar es Salaam

Copper Belt

Zambezi

Salisbury

Madagascar

Tropic of Capricorn

Namib Desert

Kalahari Desert

Pretoria

Johannesburg

Orange

Drakensberg

Durban

Cape Town

Legend

Little or no activity

PREDOMINANT SUBSISTENCE ECONOMY

Gathering, hunting and fishing

Traditional cultivation

Shifting

Bush fallowing

Semi-intensive sedentary

Intensive cropping (rice dominant)

Intensive cropping (other crop dominant)

Traditional pastoralism

Nomadic herding (cattle, camels in N. Africa)

Nomadic herding (sheep and goats)

Non-nomadic (cattle)

Non-nomadic (sheep and goats)

PREDOMINANT COMMERCIAL ECONOMY

Intensive cultivation

Grain

Large-scale specialised (plantation)

Specialised (market gardening)

Livestock rearing

Extensive (cattle)

Extensive (sheep)

Intensive (cattle)

Intensive dairying

Areas of mixed economies shown by banding

Lumbering

Fishing

Manufacturing/service industry

Extractive industry

Scale 1:37 000 000

0   500   1000   1500 km

Lambert Azimuthal Equal Area Projection

© Collins ◇ Longman Atlases

FRANCE
MONACO
PORTUGAL
ANDORRA
Madrid
SPAIN
Lisbon
Corsica (Fr.)
ITALY
Rome
Sardinia (It.)
Balearic Is.
YUGOSLAVIA
Belgrade
ROMANIA
BULGARIA
Sofia
ALBANIA
Tiranë
GREECE
Athens
Black Sea
U.S.S.R.
Caspian Sea
Ankara
TURKEY
Tehran
IRAN
Tangier
Rabat
Oran
Algiers
Constantine
Annaba
Tunis
Mediterranean Sea
Sicily
MALTA
Crete
CYPRUS
SYRIA
LEBANON
Beirut
Damascus
Baghdad
IRAQ
Casablanca
Fez
TUNISIA
Tripoli
Beida
Benghazi
ISRAEL
Jerusalem
Amman
JORDAN
KUWAIT
N.T.
Marrakesh
MOROCCO
Tobruk
Alexandria
Cairo
Suez
The Gulf
Madeira (Port.)
BAHRAIN
QATAR
Canary Is. (Sp.)
Tenerife
El Aaiún
WESTERN SAHARA
ALGERIA
Reggan
Ain Salah
LIBYA
EGYPT
Nile
Aswân
Tropic of Cancer
SAUDI
RIYADH
UNITED ARAB EMIRATES
Nouadhibou
L. Nasser
Wadi Halfa
ARABIA
Nouakchott
MAURITANIA
Dongola
Port Sudan
RED SEA
MALI
Timbuktu
Niger
Gao
NIGER
Agades
CHAD
Khartoum
Atbara
Massawa
Sana
YEMEN
SOUTHERN YEMEN
St Louis
Dakar
SENEGAL
Kayes
Niamey
Sokoto
Maiduguri
N'Djamena
SUDAN
Nyala
Blue Nile
Asmara
Aden
DJIBOUTI
Djibouti
Berbera
GAMBIA
Banjul
GUINEA BISSAU
Bissau
GUINEA
Bamako
Kankan
UPPER VOLTA
Ouagadougou
Volta
Kano
Jos
Garoua
Sarh
El Muglad
White Nile
Malakal
Bahr el Jebel
Wau
Addis Ababa
Jimma
ETHIOPIA
Diredawa
Conakry
Freetown
SIERRA LEONE
IVORY
Bouaké
Tamale
GHANA
TOGO
BENIN
Savé
Ibadan
NIGERIA
Enugu
CENTRAL AFRICAN EMPIRE
Zemio
Niangara
Juba
L. Turkana
SOMALI REPUBLIC
Bardera
Monrovia
LIBERIA
COAST
Kumasi
Abidjan
Accra
Lomé
Porto-Novo
Lagos
Port Harcourt
Calabar
CAMEROON
Douala
Yaoundé
Bangui
Mobaye
Lisala
Zaïre
Mbandaka
Kisangani
UGANDA
Kampala
KENYA
Kisumu
Nairobi
Equator
Sekondi-Takoradi
Malabo
EQUATORIAL GUINEA
Bata
São Tomé
Gulf of Guinea
Libreville
Ndjolé
GABON
Franceville
CONGO
Ouesso
ZAÏRE
Kindu
RWANDA
Kigali
Lake Victoria
Mwanza
Moshi
Mombasa
Tanga
INDIAN OCEAN
ATLANTIC OCEAN
Brazzaville
Kinshasa
Ilebo
Kananga
BURUNDI
Bujumbura
Kigoma
Zanzibar
Dar es Salaam
ANGOLA
Cabinda
Kalemie
Lake Tanganyika
TANZANIA
Lindi
Aldabra Is. (U.K.)
Luanda
Malange
Mbala
Lake Tanganyika
COMORO IS.
Pemba
Lobito
Huambo
Lubumbashi
Ndola
Chipata
L. Malawi
Moçambique
Majunga
ZAMBIA
MALAWI
Lilongwe
Mongu
Menongue
Moçâmedes
Lusaka
Blantyre
Moçambique
MADAGASCAR
Tamatave
Tananarive
Salisbury
Vila de Sena
Wankie
Gwelo
Beira
ZIMBABWE
Fort Victoria
(RHODESIA)
MOÇAMBIQUE
Grootfontein
Bulawayo
Francistown
WALVIS BAY
Walvis Bay
Windhoek
BOTSWANA
Inhambane
Tuléar
Tropic of Capricorn
Fort-Dauphin
NAMIBIA
Gaborone
Pretoria
Maputo
Mbabane
SWAZILAND
Lüderitz
Johannesburg
Karasburg
Kroonstad
Maseru
LESOTHO
Ladysmith
Durban
Kimberley
Port Nolloth
REPUBLIC OF
Maseru
Calvinia
SOUTH AFRICA
East London
Cape Town
Mossel Bay
Port Elizabeth

Scale 1:37 000 000
0   500   1000   1500 km
Lambert Azimuthal Equal Area Projection

POPULATION

Persons per sq. km.
Over 100
50-100
10-50
1-10
0-1

Cities
■ Over 1 000 000 population
● 500 000-1 000 000 population
• 250 000-500 000 population

Collins ◇ Longman Atlases

FRANCE

Nice
Florence

Sarajevo

Oporto
Valladolid
ANDORRA
Marseille
Corsica (Fr.)
Rome
ITALY
Bari
Adriatic Sea
ALB

Madrid
SPAIN
Zaragoza
Barcelona
Naples
Taranto

PORTUGAL
Lisbon
Valencia
Majorca
Minorca
Sardinia (It.)
Palermo
Messina
Sicily
Catania

Seville
Cartagena
Palma
Ivira
Balearic Islands (Sp.)
MEDITERRANEAN
Cagliari
MALTA

Gibraltar (U.K.)
Tangier
Ceuta (Sp.)
Melilla (Sp.)
Algiers
Tizi Ouzou
Annaba
Bizerta
Tunis

Kenitra
Tetuan
Oran
Sidi-bel-Abbès
Bejaïa
Constantine
Kairouan
Sousse

Rabat
Fez
Oujda
Blida
Sfax

Casablanca
Meknes
Tlemcen
Biskra
G. of Gabes

Safi
Khenifra
Chott ech Chergui
Djelfa
Chott Melrhir
Gabès

MOROCCO
Tendrara
Saharan Atlas
Touggourt
Chott Djerid
Medenine

Marrakesh
Aïn Sefra
Ghardaia
Tripoli

Atlas
High
Béchar
Ouargla
Hassi Messaoud
Nalut
Misurata

Toubkal
Abadla
Ghadames
Gulf of Sirte
Sirte
Ageda

Madeira (Port.)
El Goléa
Tripolitania
Hun
El Agheila
Benghi

Wadi Draa
LIBYA
Sebha

Canary Islands (Sp.)
Lanzarote
Reggane
Aïn Salah
Fort Polignac
Murzuq

La Palma
Fuerteventura
ALGERIA
Tademaït Plateau

Tenerife
Gran Canaria
Las Palmas
Ghat

El Aaiún
Ahaggar Mts
El Qatrun

Bou Craa
Mt. Tahat 2918
Tummo

WESTERN SAHARA
Tropic of Cancer
Tamanrasset
Djado Plateau

Dakhla
Bardai
3150

Fdérik
Tibesti Mts

C. Blanc
Nouadhibou
Air or Azbine
Emi Koussi 3415

Atar
1800

MAURITANIA
Agades
Bodélé Depression

Nouakchott
Tidjikja
NIGER

St. Louis
SAHARA
Kidal
Lake Chad

C. Verde
Timbuktu
Gao
Nguigmi
CHA

Dakar
Diourbel
MALI
Niamey
Zinder
Yao

SENEGAL
Nioro
Birni N'Konni
Maradi
Nguru
N'Djamena

Banjul
Kayes
Mopti
Niger
Sokoto
Katsina
Maiduguri

GAMBIA
Tambacounda
San
Sokoto
Kaura Namoda
Kano

Bissau
Bamako
UPPER VOLTA
Ouagadougou
Kaduna
Zaria
Bauchi
Maroua

GUINEA BISSAU
Sikasso
Bobo-Dioulasso
Navrongo
Bansanné-Mango
NIGERIA
Chari

Bijagos Archipelago
Futa Jalon
Labé
Kankan
Black Volta
Tamale
Parakou
Minna
Jos
Garoua

Boké
White Volta
Ilorin
Baro
Makurdi
Adamawa Highlands

Conakry
GUINEA
Beyla
IVORY COAST
Sunyani
Lake Volta
BENIN
Ogbomosho
Benue
Ngaoundéré
Fort Crampel

SIERRA LEONE
Boo
Bouaké
GHANA
Kumasi
Savé
Ibadan
Ifesha
CENTRAL

Freetown
Daloa
Porto-Novo
Abeokuta
Onitsha
CAMEROON
EM

LIBERIA
Lomé
Cotonou
Lagos
Benin City
Enugu
Calabar
Bamenda
Ft. Sibut

Monrovia
Abidjan
Accra
Bight of Benin
Warri
Port Harcourt
Nkongsamba
Babpua

Sassandra
Sekondi-Takoradi
Niger Delta
Mt. Cameroon 4070
Bangui

C. Palmas
Douala
Mbanda

Gulf of Guinea
Malabo
Yaoundé

EQUATORIAL GUINEA
Bata

Principe
GABON
CONGO

Scale 1:20 000 000
São Tomé
Libreville

0 200 400 600 800 km
Equator
C. Lopez

Lambert Azimuthal Equal Area Projection
Lambaréné

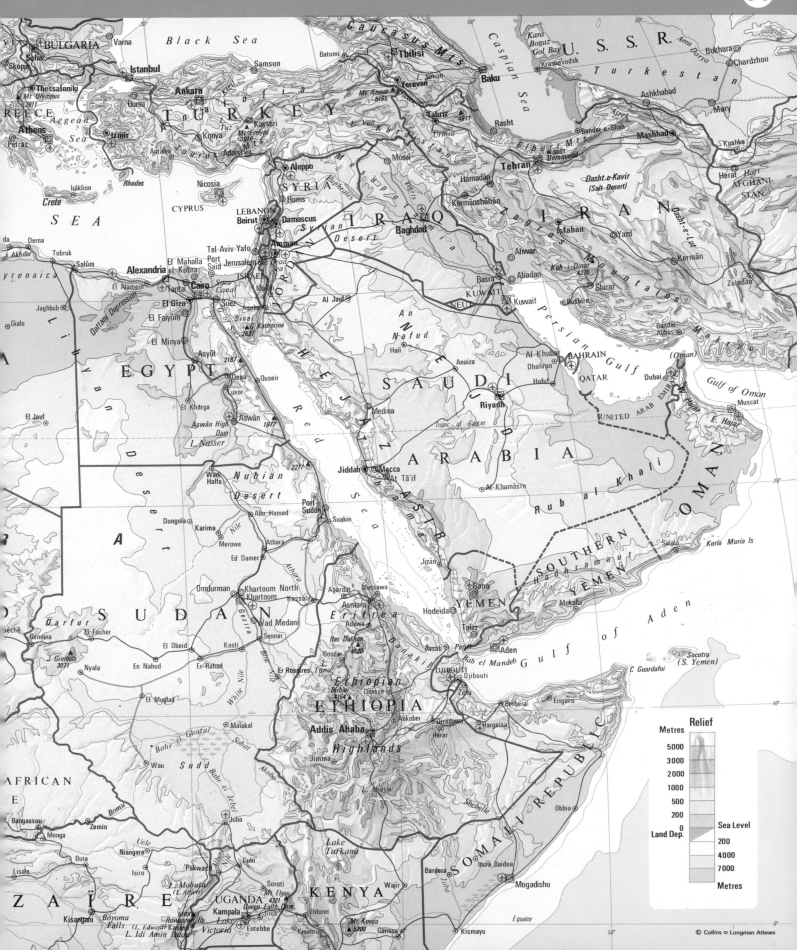

BULGARIA
Sofia
Skopje
Thessaloniki
Mt Olympus 2911
GREECE
Athens
Patras
Aegean Sea
Izmir
Iráklion
Crete
SEA
Varna
Black Sea
Istanbul
Bursa
Ankara
Konya
Antalya
Adana
Mersin
TURKEY
Taurus Mts
Kayseri
Mt Erciyas 3916
Rhodes
Nicosia
CYPRUS
LEBANON
Beirut
Aleppo
Homs
Damascus
SYRIA
Euphrates
Syrian Desert
Caucasus Mts
Batumi
Tbilisi
Yerevan
Mt Ararat 5165
Tabriz 4811
Van
Urmia
Kurdistan
Mosul
Tigris
IRAQ
Baghdad
Caspian Sea
Kara Bogaz Gol Bay
Krasnovodsk
Baku
Rasht
Elburz Mts
Demavend 5601
Tehran
Hamadan
Kermanshahan
Zagros Mountains
Isfahan
U.S.S.R.
Turkestan
Amu Darya
Bukhara
Chardzhou
Ashkhabad
Mary
Kushke
Mashhad
Herat
Hari
AFGHANI-STAN
Dasht-e-Kavir (Salt Desert)
IRAN
Yazd
Kerman
Dasht-e-Lut
Zahedan
Makran
da
Derna
El Akhdar
Tobruk
Salûm
Cyrenaica
Jaghbub
Jialo
El Jauf
Libyan Desert
EGYPT
Alexandria
El Alamein
Cairo
El Giza
Tanta
Suez Canal
Port Said
El Mahalla el Kubra
Qattara Depression
Suez
Sinai
Gulf of Suez
El Faiyûm
El Minya
Asyût 2187
Qena
Luxor
Ouseir
El Khârga
Aswân 1977
Aswân High Dam
L. Nasser
HEJAZ
Red Sea
Wadi Halfa
Nubian Desert
Abu Hamed
Dongola
Karima
Nile
Merowe
Atbara
Ed Damer
A
Desert
Tel-Aviv-Yafo
Jerusalem
ISRAEL
Port Said
JORDAN
Amman
Maan
Aqaba
G. Katherina 2637
Dead Sea
Al Jauf
An Nafud
Hail
Medina
Tropic of Cancer
HEJAZ
Jiddah
Mecca
At Tâ'if
2217
Port Sudan
Suakin
SAUDI
Anaiza
Riyadh
ARABIA
ASIR
Al Khamâsin
KUWAIT
NEUT
Basra
Abadan
Kuwait
Ahwaz
Shiraz
Bushire
Kuh-i-Dinar A4276
Persian Gulf
Hofuf
Dhahran
Al Khubar
BAHRAIN
QATAR
Bandar Abbas
Dubai
UNITED ARAB EMIRATES
(Oman)
Gulf of Oman
Muscat
W. Hajar
E. Hajar
OMAN
Rub al Khali
Salala
Kuria Muria Is
SOUTHERN
YEMEN
Hadhramaut
Mukalla
Jizân
Sana
YEMEN
Hodeida
Taizz
Assab
Perim
Bab el Mandeb
Aden
Gulf of Aden
Socotra (S. Yemen)
C. Guardafui
SUDAN
Darfur
Geneina
El Fasher
J. Gimbala 3071
Nyala
El Muglad
En Nahud
Er Rahad
El Obeid
Kosti
Sennar
Wad Medani
Khartoum North
Khartoum
Omdurman
Gezira
Atbara
Kassala
Agordat
Massawa
Asmara
Aduwa
Eritrea
Ras Dashan 4620
Gondar
L. Tana
Birhan 4154
Dessye
Ethiopian
ETHIOPIA
Highlands
Danakil
Djibouti
DJIBOUTI
Zeila
Berbera
Erigavo
AFRICAN
E
Bangassou
Monga
Lisala
ZAÏRE
Zemio
Uele
Buta
Isiro
Niangara
Kisangani
Boyoma Falls
Bahr el Ghazal
Wau
Sudd
Bahr el Jebel
Malakal
Sobat
White Nile
Blue Nile
Er Roseires
Jimma
Addis Ababa
Ankober
Dire Dawa
Harar
Hargeisa
SOMALI REPUBLIC
Obbia
Shebelle
Juba
Pakwach
Gulu
L. Mobuta (L. Albert)
Soroti
Mt Elgon 4321
Rwenzori (L. Edward) Kasese
L. Idi Amin Dada
UGANDA
Kampala
Entebbe
Jinja
Owen Falls Dam
Lake Victoria
Kisumu
Eldoret
KENYA
Mt Kenya 5200
Wajir
Garissa
Lake Turkana
L. Abaya
Bardera
Iscia Baidoa
Juba
Mogadishu
Kismayu
Equator

Relief	
Metres	
5000	
3000	
2000	
1000	
500	
200	
0	Sea Level
Land Dep.	
200	
4000	
7000	
Metres	

© Collins ◇ Longman Atlases

WESTERN
SAHARA

Fdérik Zouerate

SAOURA

Nouadhibou
C Blanc

Atar

Taoudenni

S   A   H

20°

Akjoujt

M A U R I T A N I A

Araouane

Tidjikja

Nouakchott

Méderdra

Bogué
Podor   Kaédi
Dagana
St. Louis   Matam
Louga   Senegal
Linguère

Kiffa

Néma

Timbuktu
Goundam

Bamba   Bourem
Gourma-Rarous   Niger   Gao

15°
C Verde
Dakar Rufisque
Thiès Diourbel
Kaolack

S E N E G A L

Bakel
Kayes

Nioro

Nara

Sokolo

Douentza

Mopti

Dori

Yata

Banjul
Bignona
GAMBIA
Ziguinchor Sédhiou Farim
GUINEA
Bissau BISSAU
Bolama
Bijagos
Archipelago

Tambacounda
Gambia

Kédougou Satadougou

Bafoulabé

Kita

Bani

Koulikoro
Bamako
Kati

Ségou

Bougouni

San

Djenne

Ouagadougou

Ouahigouya

U P P E R

V O L T A

Fada-
N'Gourma

Boké
Telimélé
Boffa
Kindia

Daboua
Yambering
Kabé
Pita

Fouta
Jalon

Dabola
Mamou Faranah

Kouroussa

Siguiri

Kankan

Koutiala

Sikasso

Houndé

Bobo-Dioulasso

Po

Lawra Navrongo

UPPER

Black Volta

Red Volta

Sansanné
Mango

10°

A T L A N T I C

Conakry
Forécariah

SIERRA
Makeni LEONE
Port Loko Rokel
Magburaka
Freetown Sefadu
Bo
Pujehun
Kenema
Pendembu

Kabala

Kissidougou

Macenta

N'zérékoré
Mt. Nimba

Odienné

Beyla

Touba

Man

Boundiali

Korhogo

Ferkéssédougou

Bouna

Bole

Black Volta

Wa

White Volta

NORTHERN

Tamale

Ho

Sherbro I.

L I B E R I A

Monrovia

Buchanan

Greenville

Daloa

Séguéla

Mankono

Dabakala

Bouaké

I V O R Y

C O A S T

Dimbokro

Bondoukou

Sunyani

BRONG-AHAFO

GHANA

Kétè
Krachi

Lake
Volta

ASHANTI

Kumasi

EASTERN

O C E A N

5°

Sassandra

Tabou

C Palmas

Gagnoa

Agboville

Abidjan

Bingerville

Port
Bouet

Grand
Bassam

Enchi

Awaso Obuasi
Dunkwa
Presteal Kade Oda
WESTERN
Tarkwa
Axim Cape Coast
Sekondi-Takoradi

Kade Kade
CENTRAL

Accra
Winneba Tema

Metres
5000
3000
2000
1000
500
200
0
Land Dep.
Sea Level
200
4000
7000
Metres

Relief

Scale 1:10 000 000

0   100   200   300   400   500 km

Lambert Azimuthal Equal Area Projection

© Collins ◇ Longman Atlases

ALGERIA

Ahaggar Mts

▲ *Mt Tahat*
2918
Tamanrasset

O A S I S

Adrar
des
Iforas

Sidal

Tropic of Cancer

Djado
Plateau

● Djado

Tibesti
▲ *3150*
● Bardai
▲ *3265*

LIBYA

Mountains

▲ *3325*

▲ *3415*
Emi Koussi

● Bilma

Aïr
or
Azbine

N I G E R

● Agades

Bodélé
Depression

Tillabéri

Tanout

Niamey
Dosso

Birni
N'Konn

Maradi

Tessaoua

Zinder

● Gouré

Nguigmi ●

Plain
of
Bornu

Bosso ●

Lake
Chad

C H A D

Bahr el Ghazal

● Moussoro

● Yao
L.
Fittri

Batha

Bokoro

N'Djamena

Abou Deia ●

Ba-Mbassa

● Melfi

Chari

Sokoto

Sokoto

Kaura Namoda

Katsina

Nguru

Geidam

Hadejia

Azare

BORNO

Damaturu

Dikwa

● Maiduguri

Chari

SOKOTO

Birnin
Kebbi

Gaya

Gusau

Zamfara

Gulbin-Ka

KANO

Kano

Hadejia

Komadugu Gana

Potiskum

Buni

Gongola

Biu ●

Mubi ●

Mandara
Mts

Maroua ●

Kandi

Yelwa

Zaria

KADUNA

Kaduna

BAUCHI

Bauchi

Gombe

Yola

Garoua ●

Benue

Boumo ●

Lai ●

B. Salamat

Sarh

Bahr Aouk

Mekrou

Kontagora

NIGER

Zungeru

Minna

Kafanchan

Jos
Plateau

1585

Gongola

Shebshi
Mts

Deo

Kentcha

Meissala ●

Outham

Logone

Natitingou

Kaiama

N I G E R I A

PLATEAU

Wamba
Nasarawa

Adamawa
Highlands

Ngaoundéré ●

Pende

Outham

Ft.
Crampel

Djougou

B
E
N
I
N

Parakou

Jebba

Lafiagi

Bida

FED. CAP.
TER.

Baro

Ilorin

KWARA

Lokoja

Kabba

Makurdi

BENUE

Benue

Ibi ●

Katsina Ala

Mayo Darle

Banyo

Tibati

Dyerem

C E N T R A L

Bossangoa ●

A F R I C A N

Ogbomosho

Oyo

Oshogbo

Ilesha

OYO

Iwo

Ife

Ibadan

Idah

Nsukka

Ogoja

Bamenda
Highlands

Bamenda

Foumban

Yoko ●

Bétaré Oya ●

Bouar ●

Bahoua ●

E M P I R E

Ft. Sibut

Save

Pobé

Saketé
Porto-
Novo

Abeokuta

Ijebu Ode

ONDO

Okitipupa

Benin City

Enugu

ANAMBRA

Onitsha

Afikpo

Abakaliki

Mamfe

Dschang

Carnot ●

Mambere

Berbérati ●

Bangui

Ilaro

OGUN

LAGOS

BENDEL

Warri

Ughelli

Owerri

IMO

Umuahia

Aba

Uyo

CROSS

Calabar

Mamfe

Kumba

Nkongsamba

Batra

Bertoua ●

Batouri ●

Doumé ●

M'Baiki

Nola ●

Libenge

Anécho
né

Cotonou

Bight of Benin

RIVERS

Yenagoa

Port Harcourt

Brass

Bonny

Niger
Delta

Mt Cameroon
4070

Buea

EQUATORIAL

Victoria
Malabo
3008

Douala

Sanaga

Edéa

Kumba

Yaoundé

Yokadouma ●

ZAÏRE

Gulf
of
Guinea

Bight of Bonny

Principe

GUINEA

Bata

GABON

Kribi

Nyong

Ebolowa

Lomié ●

C O N G O

Campo

Impfondo ●

Ubangi

Relief

Metres	
5000	
3000	
2000	
1000	
500	
200	
0	Sea Level
Land Dep.	
200	
4000	
7000	
Metres	

Scale 1:10 750 000

0   100   200   300   400   500 km

Lambert Azimuthal Equal Area Projection

© Collins ○ Longman Atlases

Oceans: INDIAN OCEAN, ATLANTIC OCEAN

Countries / Regions: MALAWI, MOÇAMBIQUE, ZAMBIA, ANGOLA, HUILA, CUANDO-CUBANGO, NAMIBIA, BOTSWANA, ZIMBABWE (RHODESIA), Mashonaland, Matabeleland, TRANSVAAL, ORANGE FREE STATE, REPUBLIC OF SOUTH AFRICA, CAPE PROVICE, NATAL, SWAZILAND, LESOTHO, Transkei, SOFALA, TETE, GAZA, INHAMBANE, Kwa Zulu, Ovambo

Deserts / Physical: KALAHARI DESERT, NAMIB DESERT, Great Nama Land, Bushmanland, Ngamiland, Okavango Basin, Karroo, Great Karroo, Little Karroo, Makarikari Salt Pan, Matopo Hills, Zuurberg, Caprivi Strip

Water features: Lake Kariba, Lake Xau, L. Ngami, Zambezi, Limpopo, Orange, Cubango, Okavango, Cuando, Cuito, Vaal, Great Fish, Olifants, Nossob, Molopo, Shashi, Shangani, Lundi, Sabi, Crocodile

Cities: Durban, Pretoria, Johannesburg, Soweto, Bloemfontein, Kimberley, Cape Town, Port Elizabeth, East London, Maputo, Salisbury, Bulawayo, Lusaka, Livingstone, Windhoek, Walvis Bay, Swakopmund, Lüderitz, Gaborone, Maseru, Mbabane, Beira, Pietermaritzburg, Maun, Ghanzi, Francistown, Grahamstown, Port Nolloth, Simonstown

Legend:

Scale 1:10 750 000
Lambert Azimuthal Equal Area Projection

0 100 200 300 400 km

Relief

Metres: 5000, 3000, 2000, 1000, 500, 200, 0
Land Dep.: 200
Sea Level, 200, 4000, 7000 Metres

Tropic of Capricorn
Cape of Good Hope
C. Agulhas

Equator

PACIFIC OCEAN

Tropic of Capricorn

Scale 1 : 27 000 000

Lambert Azimuthal Equal Area Projection

1500 km

1000

500

0

Southern Alps

Bismarck Ra.

Maoke Range

GREAT DIVIDING RANGE

GREAT DIVIDING RANGE

Barkly Tableland

Lake Eyre Basin

Macdonnell Ranges

Musgrave Range

Nullarbor Plain

Hamersley Ra.

INDIAN OCEAN

Quaternary
Tertiary
Mesozoic
Palaeozoic
Precambrian

Lowland Plains & Basins
High Plains & Plateaus
Scarps & Upland edges
Fold & Volcanic Mountains
Main trend lines
Main centres of volcanic activity

Celebes
3440 ▲ Rantekombola
Butung
Buru
3055 ▲ Ceram
Sula Is
Misool
Vogelkop
Japen
Admiralty Is
New Hanover
New Ireland
Bismarck Sea
New Britain

Kabia

B A N D A   S E A

Wokam   Aru Is
Trangan

Maoke
Putjak Djaja ▲ Range
5030
NEW GUINEA
Sepik
Mt. Wilhelm
4694 ▲

F L O R E S   S E A

Bali
Lombok
Sumbawa
Flores
Alor
Wetar
Jamdena
Tanimbar Is
Kolepom
C. Vals

Fly
Mt. Victoria
3987 ▲
D'Entrecasteaux Is

Sumba
Sawu
Roti
Timor

A R A F U R A   S E A

Gulf of
Papua
Torres Strait
Owen Stanley Range

T I M O R   S E A

C. Londonderry
Joseph
Bonaparte
Gulf
Melville I.
Bathurst I.
Van
Diemen
Gulf
Cobourg Pen.
C. Wessel
C. Arnhem
Arnhem Land
C. York
Cape
York
Peninsula
C. Melville

C O R A L
S E A

C. Lévêque
King Leopold
Ranges
Ord
Daly
Victoria
Roper
Groote
Eylandt
Limmen
Bight
Gulf of
Carpentaria
Sir Edward
Pellew Group
Wellesley Is.
Mitchell

Atherton
Mt Bartle Frere
1611 ▲
Plateau

Eighty Mile Beach
Barkly Tableland
Leichhardt
Flinders
Gregory Ra.

Great Barrier Reef

Monte
Bello Is.
Barrow I.
North
West C.
De Grey
Great Sandy Desert
L.Mackay

Great Dividing Range

Fortescue
Hamersley Range
Mt Bruce
1227 ▲
Ashburton
L.Disappointment
Mt Ziel
1510 ▲
Macdonnell Ranges
James Ra.
Finke
Simpson
Desert

G r e a t

Tropic of Capricorn
Gascoyne
Gibson Desert
L. Amadeus

A r t e s i a n

Dirk Hartogs I.
Murchison
L.Carnegie
Mt Woodroffe
1515 ▲
Musgrave Ranges
Everard Range

B a s i n

Warburton
Cooper Creek
L.Eyre
Grey Range
Warrego
Culgoa
Darling
Downs
1510 ▲
New
England
Range
Round Mt.
1615 ▲

L. Barlee
L.Moore
Great Victoria Desert
L.Cowan

Nullarbor plain
L. Torrens
L.Gairdner
Flinders Range
Barwon

Darling Range
Geographe Bay
Swanland
C. Leeuwin
W. Cape Howe

Great Australian Bight
Eyre
Peninsula
Spencer Gulf
Murray
Murrumbidgee
Riverina
Murray
Mt Kosciusko
2230 ▲ Snowy
Mts

Darling

Kangaroo I.
Great

Dividing Ran

I N D I A N   O C E A N

Wilson's
Promontory
King I.
Bass Strait
Hunter Is.
Flinders I.
Cape Barren I.

T A S M A N
S E A
C. Howe

South East Cape

Mt Ossa
1617 ▲

Desert
Semi-Desert
Grassland
Forest and Woodland
Cultivated land

Scale 1:20 000 000

0   200   400   600   800   1000 km

Lambert Azimuthal Equal Area Projection

© Collins ◊ Longman Atlases

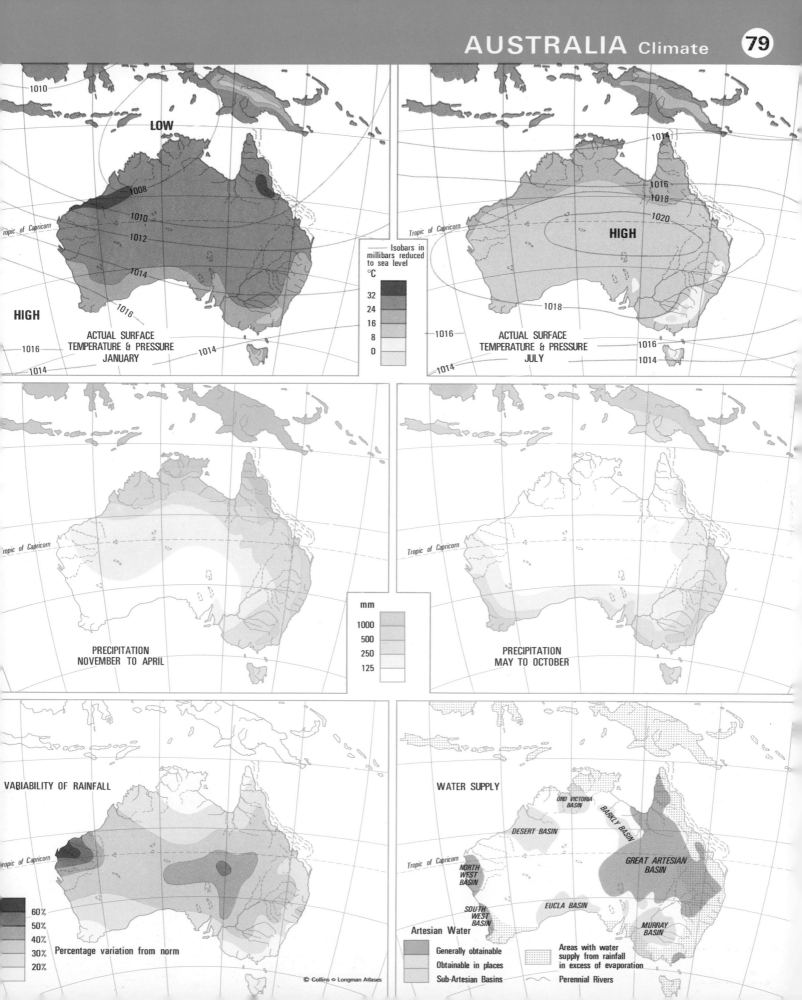

ACTUAL SURFACE TEMPERATURE & PRESSURE JANUARY

LOW

HIGH

1010
1008
1010
1012
1014
1016
1016
1014

ACTUAL SURFACE TEMPERATURE & PRESSURE JULY

HIGH

1014
1016
1018
1020
1018
1016
1014

Isobars in millibars reduced to sea level

°C
32
24
16
8
0

Tropic of Capricorn

PRECIPITATION NOVEMBER TO APRIL

PRECIPITATION MAY TO OCTOBER

mm
1000
500
250
125

VARIABILITY OF RAINFALL

60%
50%
40%
30%
20%

Percentage variation from norm

WATER SUPPLY

ORD VICTORIA BASIN
BARKLY BASIN
DESERT BASIN
NORTH WEST BASIN
GREAT ARTESIAN BASIN
SOUTH WEST BASIN
EUCLA BASIN
MURRAY BASIN

Artesian Water

Generally obtainable

Obtainable in places

Sub-Artesian Basins

Areas with water supply from rainfall in excess of evaporation

Perennial Rivers

© Collins ◇ Longman Atlases

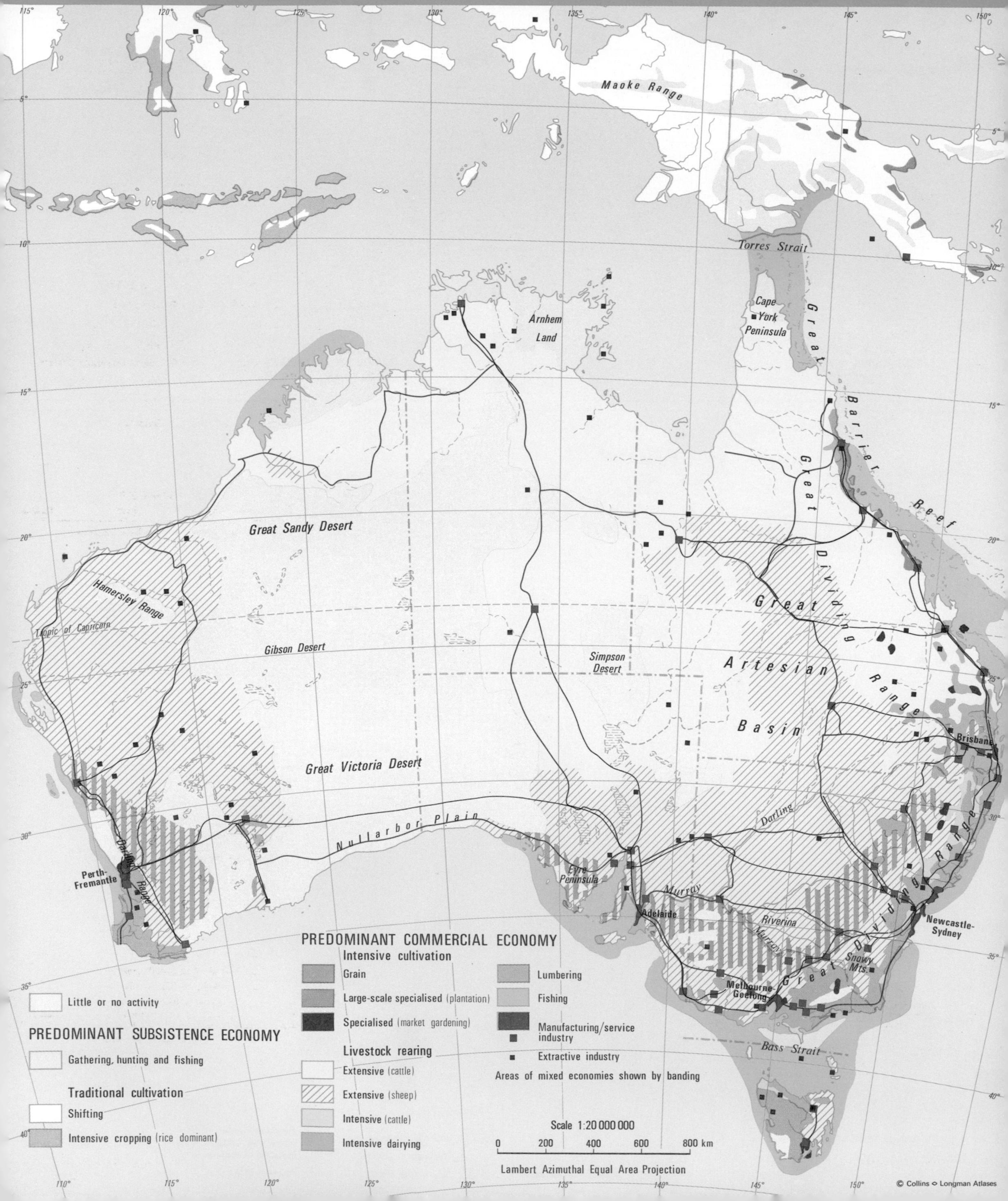

Maoke Range

Torres Strait

Arnhem Land

Cape York Peninsula

Great Barrier Reef

Great Sandy Desert

Hamersley Range

Tropic of Capricorn

Gibson Desert

Great Dividing Range

Great Artesian Basin

Simpson Desert

Great Victoria Desert

Brisbane

Darling Range

Nullarbor Plain

Eyre Peninsula

Darling

Perth-Fremantle

Adelaide

Murray

Murray

Riverina

Newcastle-Sydney

Snowy Mts

Melbourne-Geelong

Great Dividing Range

Bass Strait

PREDOMINANT COMMERCIAL ECONOMY

Intensive cultivation

Grain

Large-scale specialised (plantation)

Specialised (market gardening)

Lumbering

Fishing

Manufacturing/service industry

Extractive industry

Areas of mixed economies shown by banding

Livestock rearing

Extensive (cattle)

Extensive (sheep)

Intensive (cattle)

Intensive dairying

Little or no activity

PREDOMINANT SUBSISTENCE ECONOMY

Gathering, hunting and fishing

Traditional cultivation

Shifting

Intensive cropping (rice dominant)

Scale 1:20 000 000

0   200   400   600   800 km

Lambert Azimuthal Equal Area Projection

© Collins ◇ Longman Atlases

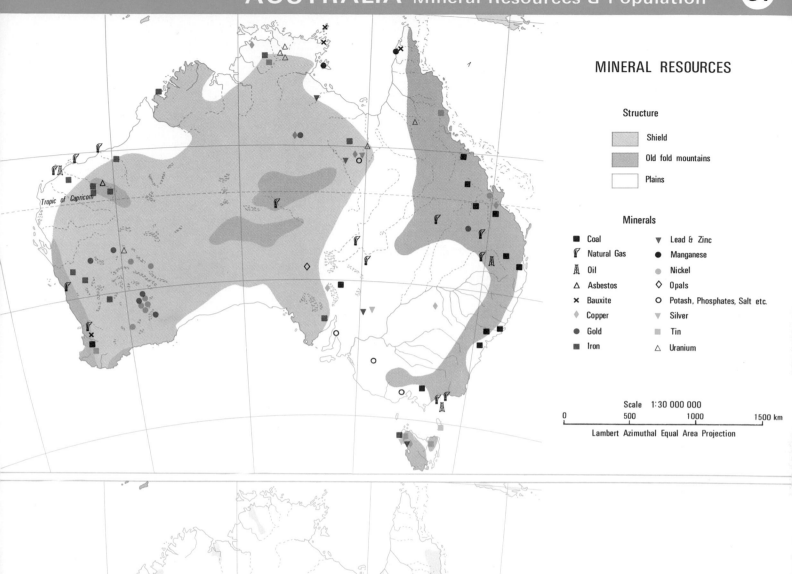

MINERAL RESOURCES

Structure

	Shield
	Old fold mountains
	Plains

Minerals

■	Coal	▼	Lead & Zinc
	Natural Gas	●	Manganese
	Oil		Nickel
△	Asbestos	◇	Opals
✕	Bauxite	○	Potash, Phosphates, Salt etc.
◆	Copper	▼	Silver
●	Gold	■	Tin
■	Iron	△	Uranium

Tropic of Capricorn

Scale   1:30 000 000

0   500   1000   1500 km

Lambert Azimuthal Equal Area Projection

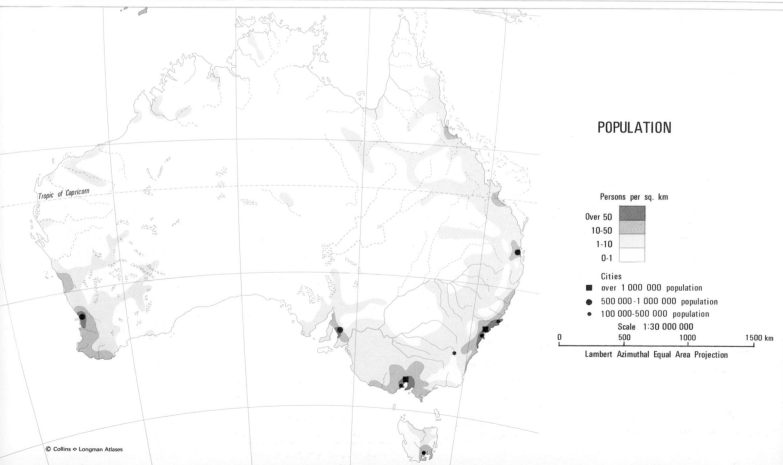

POPULATION

Tropic of Capricorn

Persons per sq. km

	Over 50
	10-50
	1-10
	0-1

Cities

■	over 1 000 000 population
●	500 000 - 1 000 000 population
●	100 000 - 500 000 population

Scale   1:30 000 000

0   500   1000   1500 km

Lambert Azimuthal Equal Area Projection

© Collins ○ Longman Atlases

Scale 1:20,000,000

| 0 | 200 | 400 | 600 | 800 km |

Lambert Azimuthal Equal Area Projection

© Collins ○ Longman Atlases

QUEENSLAND

Surat
Dalby
Toowoomba
Sandgate
Ipswich ⊕ **Brisbane**
Southport
Warwick 1328
Macpherson
Range
Murwillumbah
Kyogle
Stanthorpe
Casino
Tenterfield
Lismore
Maclean
Grafton
Coff's Harbour
Urunga

Cooper Creek
Wilson
Range
Cooper Creek
Grey Range
Bulloo
Thargomindah
Cunnamulla
St. George
Dirranbandi
Thallon
Goondiwindi
Boggabilla
Mungindi

Sturt Desert
Hungerford
Wooroorooka
Paroo
Warrego
Culgoa
Hebel
Goodooga
Lightning Ridge
Moree
Warialda
Bingara
Inverell
Glen Innes
Ben Lomond 1520
Nandewar Range
1510

L. Gregory
L. Blanche
Tibooburra
Milparinka
Wanaaring
Yantabulla
Collerina
Narran L.
Brewarrina
Walgett
Burren Junction
Wee Waa
Gwabegar
Narrabri 1495
Round Mt. 1615
Uralla
Armidale
Walcha

SOUTH

L. Callabonna
Lake Frome
Callabonna
Flinders Range
Wilcannia
Bourke
Louth
Darling
Byrock
Cobar
Hermidale
Nyngan
Coonamble
Baradine
Coonabarabran
Mullaley 1372
Gunnedah
Tamworth
Werris Creek
Quirindi
Murrurundi
Wauchope
Kendal
Port Macquarie

Leigh Creek
Lake Torrens

AUSTRALIA

Quorn
Menindee
Broken Hill
Main Barrier Range
Nymagee
Gilgunnia 573
Tullamore
Peak Hill
Wellington
Gulgong
Mudgee
Coolah
Oxley's Pk. 1372
Craboon
Scone
Liverpool Ra. 1585
Mt. Barrington
Taree
Forster
C. Hawke

Cockburn
Olary
Nevertire
Trangie
Narromine
Dubbo
Gilgandra
Merrygoen
Muswellbrook
Maitland

NEW SOUTH WALES

Peterborough
Port Pirie
Jamestown
Spalding
Burra
Clare
Morgan
Renmark
Mildura
Wentworth
Ivanhoe
Roto
Condobolin
Bogan Gate
Parkes
Forbes
Orange
Molong
Bathurst
Kandos
Cessnock
Toronto
Newcastle

Waikerie
Berri
Loxton
Mossgiel
Hillston
Ungarie
L. Cargelligo
L. Cowal
Cowra
Lithgow
Blue Mts.
Gosford

Gawler
Port Adelaide
Adelaide
Angaston
Peebinga
Hatfield
Oxley
West Wyalong
Young
Orange
Wyangala Dam
Katoomba
Penrith
Manly
Parramatta ⊕ **Sydney**
Botany Bay

Murray Bridge
Yinkanie
Morkalla
Meribah
Yungera
Piangil
Maude
Hay
Griffith
Leeton
Temora
Cootamundra
Camden
Campbelltown
Wollongong
Port Kembla
Shellharbour

Willunga
Murray
Robinvale
Balranald
Murrumbidgee
Narrandera
Junee
Wagga Wagga
Goulburn
Moss Vale

RIVERINA
Ouyen
Wanganella
Urana
Henty
Yass
Canberra
George
COMMONWEALTH TERRITORY

Lameroo
Pinnaroo
L. Tyrrell
Sea Lake
Swan Hill
Deniliquin
Jerilderie
Tocumwal
AUST. CAPITAL TERRITORY
Queanbeyan
Ulladulla

Victor Harbor
Hopetoun
Kerang
Murray
Corowa
Hume Mts.
L. Holbrook
Hume Weir
Cooma
Moruya

Kangaroo Island
The Coorong
L. Hindmarsh
Warracknabeal
Charlton
Echuca
Albury
Wodonga
Wangaratta
Mt. Townsend 2209
Mt. Kosciusko 2230
Snowy Mts.
Nimmitabel
Narooma
Bermagui
Bega

Kingston
C. Jaffa
Bordertown
Wolseley
Nhill
Donald
St. Arnaud
Bendigo
Euroa
Benalla
Bright
Mt. Bogong 1986
Bombala
Eden

Naracoorte
Horsham
Murtoa
Maryborough
Castlemaine
Mansfield
1807
Mt. Howitt
Mt. Buller 1742
Disaster Bay
C. Howe
Mallacoota

VICTORIA
Rocklands Res.
Casterton
Stawell
Ararat
Ballarat
Kilmore
Eildon Res.
Bairnsdale
Orbost
C. Everard

Beachport
Millicent
Mount Gambier
Hamilton
GREAT
Melbourne
Dandenong
Yallourn
Sale
Ninety Mile Beach

Portland
C. Nelson
Warrnambool
Camperdown
Colac
L. Corangamite
Geelong
Port Phillip Bay
Warragul
Traralgon
Morwell
Woodside

C. Otway
Waratah Bay
Wilson's Promontory
Wonthaggi

TASMAN SEA

INDIAN OCEAN

King I.
Bass Strait
Furneaux
Flinders I.
Group
Cape Barren I.

Clarke I.
Banks Strait
C. Portland
Eddystone Pt.

C. Grim
Stanley
George Town
Scottsdale
Herrick
Marrawah
Burnie
Devonport
Launceston
Corinna
Cradle Mt. 1545
Longford
Leggs Tor 1573
St. Marys
Zeehan
1617 Mt. Ossa
Great L.
Strahan
Queenstown
Freycinet Pen.

TASMANIA
Frenchman's Cap 1449
Derwent
Oyster Bay

New Norfolk
Maydena
Hobart
Bellerive
Tasman Pen.
Mt. Picton 1326
Port Arthur
Bruny I.
S. West C.
S. East C.

Relief	
Metres	
5000	
3000	
2000	
1000	
500	
200	
	Sea Level
Land Dep.	
200	
4000	
7000	
Metres	

Scale 1:7 500 000

0   100   200   300 km

Lambert Azimuthal Equal Area Projection

© Collins ◇ Longman Atlases

BROAD CLIMATIC TYPES

- Very wet and cool throughout year
- Warm, wet winters Hot, dry summers
- Mild winters, warm summers Moderate rain throughout year
- Cool, dry winters Warm, moist summers
- Very dry, cold winters Dry, warm summers
- Cold all year
- Cold winters cool summers Moderate rain throughout year

Scale 1:12 000 000

0   100   200   300 km

Conic Projection

Alpine

Forest and Woodland

Grassland

Cultivated land

NORTH ISLAND

North Cape
Ninety Mile Beach
Doubtless Bay
Kaipara Har.
Great Barrier I.
Hauraki Gulf
Manukau Har.
Coromandel Peninsula
Waikato
Bay of Plenty
L. Rotorua
Hikurangi 1753 ▲
East Cape
Waikato
Rangitaiki
Motu
Raukumara Ra.
Lake Taupo
Kaimanawa Ra.
Huiarau Ra.
Mohaka
Ngauruhoe 2291 ▲
Ngaruroro
Mt Egmont 2518
Ruapehu 2797 ▲
Mahia Peninsula
Wanganui
Hawke Bay
Ruahine Ra.
Tararua Ra.

SOUTH ISLAND

Cape Farewell
Farewell Spit
Golden Bay
D'Urville I.
Tasman Mts
Tasman Bay
Cook Strait
Wairau
Cape Foulwind
Buller
Mt Travers 2338 ▲
Spenser Mts
Awatere Ra.
Cape Campbell
Cape Palliser
Grey
Lewis Pass
Kaikoura Ra.
Clarence
Waiau
Arthur's Pass
Hurunui
SOUTHERN ALPS
Waimakariri
Pegasus Bay
Rakaia
Mt Cook 1764 ▲
L. Tekapo
Banks Peninsula
L. Pukaki
Mt Aspiring 3035 ▲
L. Ohau
Canterbury Bight
L. Wanaka
L. Hawea
Waitaki
Homer Tunnel
Clutha
L. Te Anau
L. Wakatipu
Resolution I.
L. Manapouri
Oreti
Clutha
Otago Peninsula
Mataura
Foveaux Strait
Ruapuke I.
STEWART ISLAND
Southwest Cape

Scale 1:6 000 000

0   50   100   150   200 km

Conic Projection

Scale 1:12 000 000

0   100   200   300 km

Conic Projection

MINERAL RESOURCES

Structure

- Young fold mountains
- Plains
- ■ Coal
- ⌐ Natural gas
- ● Gold
- ■ Ironsands

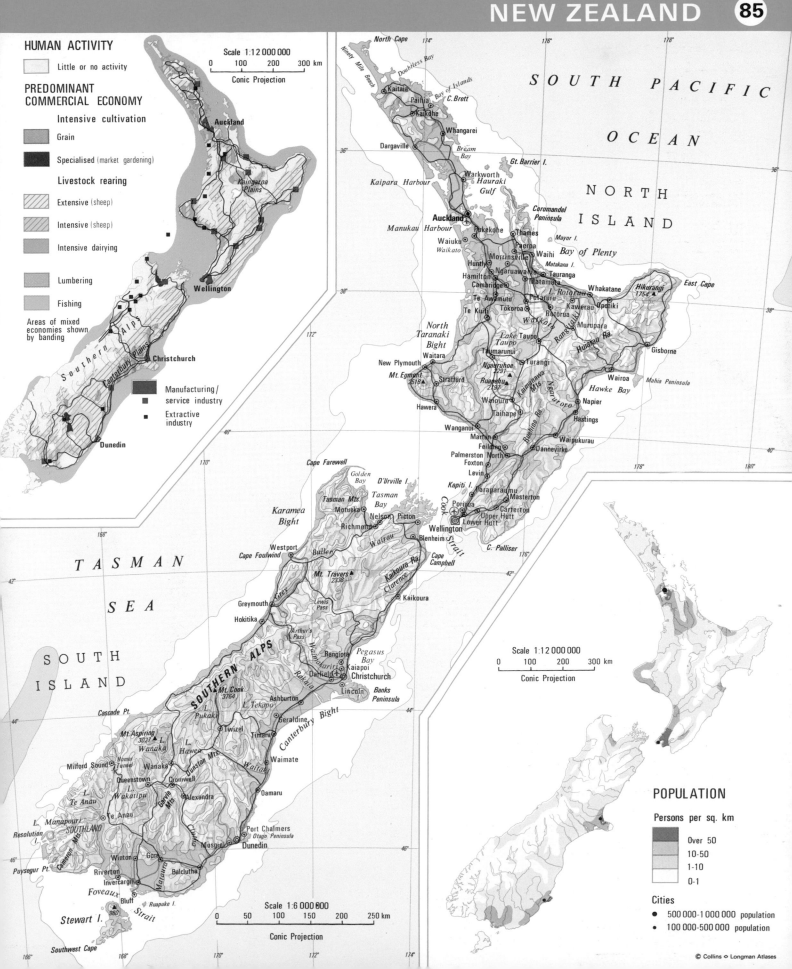

HUMAN ACTIVITY

Little or no activity

PREDOMINANT COMMERCIAL ECONOMY

Intensive cultivation

Grain

Specialised (market gardening)

Livestock rearing

Extensive (sheep)

Intensive (sheep)

Intensive dairying

Lumbering

Fishing

Areas of mixed economies shown by banding

Manufacturing / service industry

Extractive industry

Scale 1:12 000 000
0 100 200 300 km
Conic Projection

Auckland

Wellington

Christchurch

Dunedin

Southern Alps

Canterbury Plains

Kaingaroa Plains

SOUTH PACIFIC

OCEAN

NORTH ISLAND

North Cape
Ninety Mile Beach
Doubtless Bay
Kaitaia
Paihia
Bay of Islands
C. Brett
Kaikohe
Whangarei
Dargaville
Bream Bay
Gt. Barrier I.
Kaipara Harbour
Warkworth
Hauraki Gulf
Coromandel Peninsula
Auckland
Manukau Harbour
Pukekohe
Thames
Mayor I.
Waiuku
Waikato
Paeroa
Waihi
Bay of Plenty
Huntly
Morrinsville
Matakana I.
Hamilton
Ngaruawahia
Tauranga
Cambridge
Matamata
Te Awamutu
Putaruru
L. Rotorua
Whakatane
Hikurangi 1754
East Cape
Te Kuiti
Tokoroa
Rotorua
Kawerau
Opotiki
North Taranaki Bight
Waikato
Murupara
Huiakau Ra.
New Plymouth
Waitara
Lake Taupo
Taumarunui
Rangitaiki
Gisborne
Mt. Egmont 2518
Stratford
Ngauruhoe 2291
Turangi
Kaimanawa Mts
Wairoa
Hawera
Ruapehu 2797
Ngaruroro
Mahia Peninsula
Waiouru
Kaweka Ra.
Hawke Bay
Taihape
Ruahine Ra.
Napier
Wanganui
Hastings
Marton
Waipukurau
Feilding
Dannevirke
Palmerston North
Foxton
Levin
Kapiti I.
Paraparaumu
Masterton
Porirua
Carterton
Upper Hutt
Lower Hutt
Wellington
Cook Strait
C. Palliser

Cape Farewell
Golden Bay
D'Urville I.
Tasman Mts
Tasman Bay
Karamea Bight
Motueka
Nelson
Picton
Richmond
Wairau
Westport
Buller
Blenheim
Cape Foulwind
Cape Campbell
Mt. Travers 2338
Kaikoura Ra.
Clarence
Greymouth
Lewis Pass
Kaikoura
Hokitika
Arthur's Pass
Waimakariri
Rangiora
Pegasus Bay
Kaiapoi
SOUTHERN ALPS
Oxford
Christchurch
Mt. Cook 3764
Rakaia
Lincoln
Banks Peninsula
L. Pukaki
Ashburton
L. Tekapo
Geraldine
Canterbury Bight
Mt. Aspiring 3027
Twizel
Timaru
L. Wanaka
L. Hawea
Waimate
Milford Sound
Homer Tunnel
Wanaka
Dunstan Mts
Waitaki
Queenstown
Cromwell
Oamaru
L. Te Anau
L. Wakatipu
Garvie Mts
Alexandra
Port Chalmers
Te Anau
Otago Peninsula
L. Manapouri
SOUTHLAND
Mosgiel
Dunedin
Resolution I.
Cameron Mts
Clutha
Winton
Gore
Puysegur Pt.
Riverton
Balclutha
Invercargill
Mataura
Foveaux
Bluff
Ruapuke I.
Strait
Stewart I.
980
Southwest Cape

TASMAN

SEA

SOUTH ISLAND

Scale 1:6 000 000
0 50 100 150 200 250 km
Conic Projection

Scale 1:12 000 000
0 100 200 300 km
Conic Projection

POPULATION

Persons per sq. km

Over 50

10-50

1-10

0-1

Cities

500 000-1 000 000 population

100 000-500 000 population

© Collins ♦ Longman Atlases

Iceland

Denmark Str.

GREENLAND

Arctic Circle

C. Farewell

Denmark Str.

Davis Strait

Baffin Bay

Baffin Island

Foxe Basin

Hudson Strait

C. Chidley

Ungava Peninsula

Ellesmere Island

Ellesmere

Devon I.

Queen

Elizabeth

Islands

Prince of Wales I.

Melville I.

Southampton Island

Hudson Bay

James Bay

Labrador

Newfoundland

Anticosti I.

Gulf of St. Lawrence

St. Lawrence

Cape Breton I.

Nova Scotia

C. Cod

Long I.

Green Mts

St. Lawrence

Appalachian Mountains

L. Ontario

Niagara Falls

L. Erie

L. Huron

L. Superior

L. Michigan

Mississippi

ARCTIC

OCEAN

Banks I.

Victoria Island

Black

Gt. Bear Lake

Gt. Slave Lake

Mackenzie

Beaufort Sea

Peace

L. Athabasca

Saskatchewan

Nelson

Severn

Albany

Lake Winnipeg

Canadian Shield

The Great Plains

Mt. Robson 3954

Selkirk Mts

ROCKY MOUNTAINS

Peace River Res.

Fraser

Coast Mountains

Mt. Rainier 4392

Columbia

Cascade Range

Missouri

Snake

Great Salt Lake

Great Basin

Sierra

Coast Range

Brooks Range

Yukon

Alaska Range

Mt. McKinley 6194

Mt. Logan 6050

Mt. St. Elias 5489

Queen Charlotte Islands

Vancouver I.

Siberia

Bering Str.

Alaska Pen.

Kodiak I.

ATLANTIC

OCEAN

C. Hatteras

Mt. Mitchell 2037

Appalachian Mts

Tennessee

Ohio

Bahama Islands

C. Sable

Hispaniola

Cuba

Greater Antilles

Jamaica

Caribbean Sea

Yucatan Channel

Gulf of Panama

L. Nicaragua

Gulf of Mexico

Gulf of Honduras

Yucatan Peninsula

C. San Francisco

Equator

Mississippi

Missouri

Ozark Plateau

Arkansas

Red

Colorado

Campeche Bay

Sierra Madre

Citlaltepetl 5699

Rio Grande

Sierra Madre Oriental

Sierra Madre del Sur

Altiplano Mexicano

Sierra Madre Occidental

Colorado Plateau

Gila

Galapagos Is.

Clipperton I.

Gulf of California

Colorado

Lower California

C. San Lucas

Revilla Gigedo Is.

OCEAN

Nevada

Guadalupe I.

Tropic of Cancer

CIFIC

Scale 1:25 000 000

Bonne Projection

| 0 | 250 | 500 | 750 | 1000 | 1250 km |

Permanent ice and snow

Tundra and alpine

Forest and woodland

Semi-desert

Desert

Grassland including prairie and savanna

Cultivated land

ARCTIC
OCEAN

Brooks Range

Alaska Range

Coast Mountains

R O C K Y

Cascade Ra.

Coast Range

Jasper

Sierra Nevada

Great Basin

M o u n t a i n s

C a n a d i a n

The Great Plains

S h i e l d

Hudson
Bay

Arctic Circle

PACIFIC

OCEAN

Ozark Plateau

Appalachian Mts

Blue Ridge

ATLANTIC

OCEAN

Sierra Madre Occidental

Altiplano Mexicano

Sa. Madre Oriental

Sa. Madre del Sur

Tropic of Cancer

Gulf of Mexico

Sierra Madre

CARIBBEAN   SEA

	Tertiary
	Mesozoic
	Palaeozoic
	Precambrian

	Lowland Plains & Basins
	High Plains & Plateaus
	Scarps & Upland Edges
	Fold & Volcanic Mountains
	Main trend lines
	Main centres of volcanic activity

Scale 1:35 000 000

0   400   800   1200   1600 km

Bonne Projection

© Collins ◇ Longman Atlases

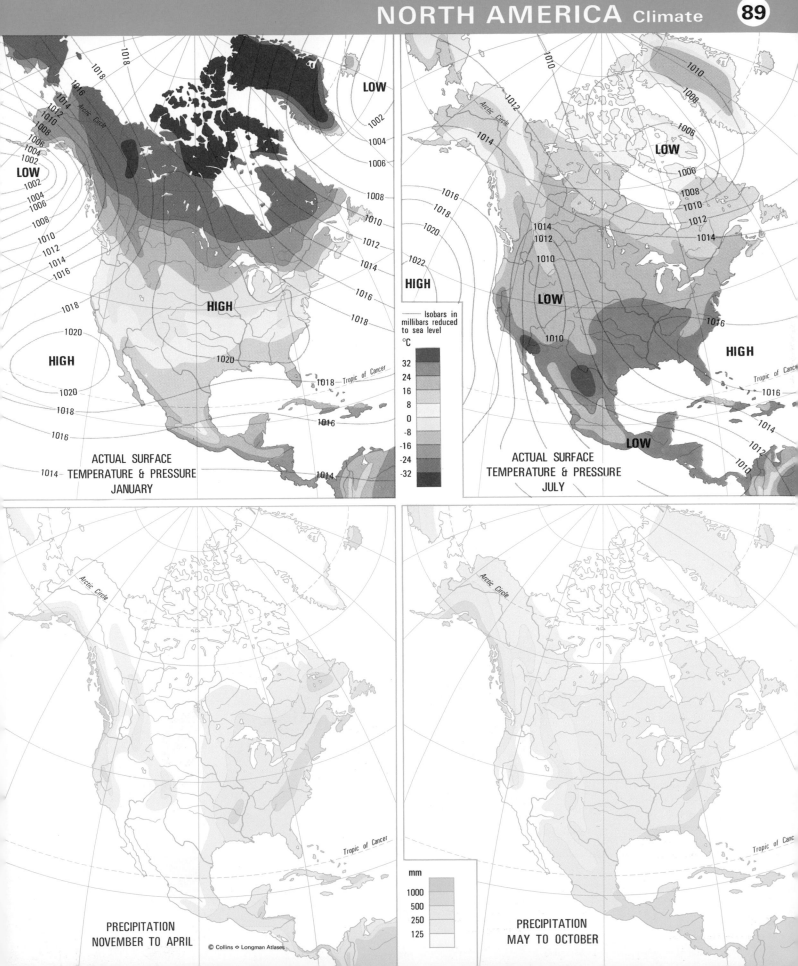

LOW

1002
1004
1006
1008
1010
1012
1014
1016
1018

HIGH

HIGH

HIGH

LOW

1002
1004
1006
1008
1010
1012
1014
1016
1018
1020

Arctic Circle

Tropic of Cancer

ACTUAL SURFACE
TEMPERATURE & PRESSURE
JANUARY

— Isobars in
millibars reduced
to sea level

°C

32
24
16
8
0
-8
-16
-24
-32

LOW

LOW

HIGH

LOW

Arctic Circle

Tropic of Cancer

ACTUAL SURFACE
TEMPERATURE & PRESSURE
JULY

Arctic Circle

Tropic of Cancer

PRECIPITATION
NOVEMBER TO APRIL

© Collins ◇ Longman Atlases

mm

1000
500
250
125

Arctic Circle

Tropic of Canc

PRECIPITATION
MAY TO OCTOBER

ARCTIC OCEAN

Greenland

Alaska Range

Rocky

Great Slave Lake

Peace

Hudson Bay

Canadian Shield

Saskatchewan

Prairies

Lake Winnipeg

Arctic Circle

PACIFIC OCEAN

Seattle

Columbia Basin

Mountains

Winnipeg

L. Superior

Montreal

Green Mts

St. Lawrence

Boston

San Francisco

Great Basin

Colorado

The Great Plains

Missouri

L. Michigan

L. Huron

Toronto-Hamilton

Ontario

L. Erie

Detroit

Cleveland

Chicago

New York

Washington-Philadelphia

Los Angeles

Sierra

Arkansas

St. Louis

Ozark Mts.

Tennessee

Appalachian Mts.

ATLANTIC OCEAN

Dallas-Fort Worth

Red

Mississippi

New Orleans

Tropic of Cancer

Sierra Madre Occidental

Gulf of Mexico

Cuba

Mexico City

Yucatan Pen.

CARIBBEAN SEA

Isthmus of Panama

Scale 1:35 000 000

0   400   800   1200   1600 km

Bonne Projection

Legend

| | Little or no activity |

PREDOMINANT SUBSISTENCE ECONOMY

| | Gathering, hunting and fishing |

Traditional cultivation

| | Shifting |
| | Semi-intensive sedentary |

Traditional pastoralism

| | Nomadic herding (cattle, reindeer in Asia) |
| | Non-nomadic (cattle) |

PREDOMINANT COMMERCIAL ECONOMY

Intensive cultivation

	Grain
	Large-scale specialised (plantation)
	Specialised (market gardening)

Livestock rearing

	Extensive (cattle)
	Extensive (sheep)
	Intensive (cattle)
	Intensive dairying

	Lumbering
	Fishing
■	Manufacturing/service industry
▪	Extractive industry

Areas of mixed economies shown by banding

© Collins ◇ Longman Atlases

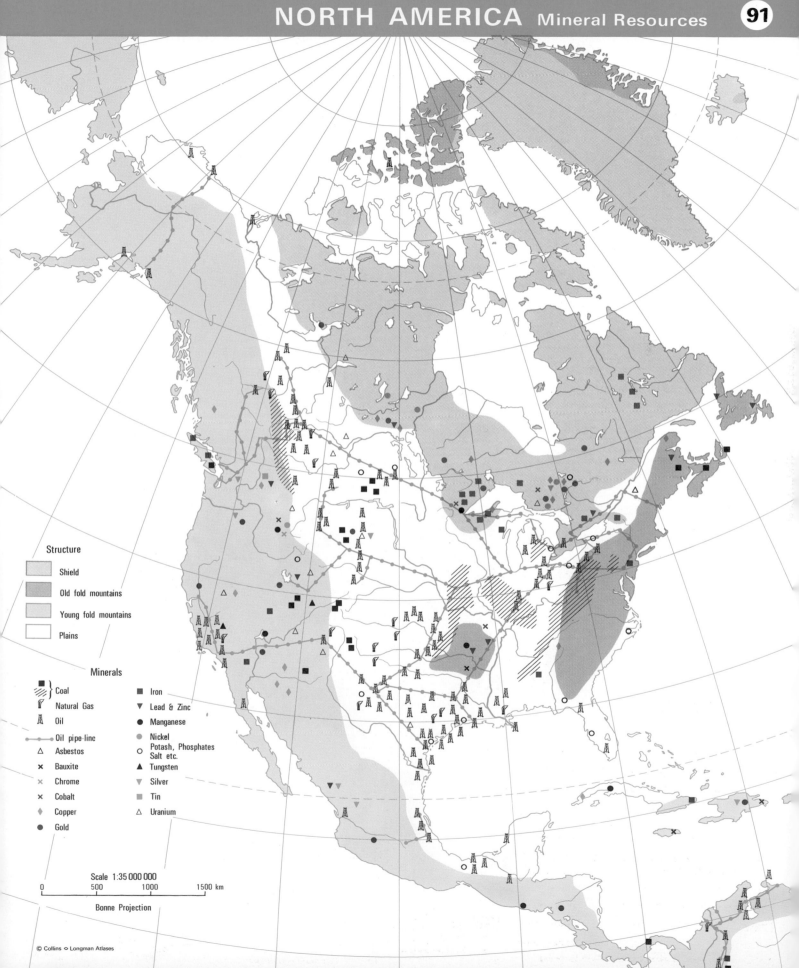

Structure

- Shield
- Old fold mountains
- Young fold mountains
- Plains

Minerals

- } Coal
- Natural Gas
- Oil
- Oil pipe-line
- △ Asbestos
- ✕ Bauxite
- ✕ Chrome
- ✕ Cobalt
- ◆ Copper
- ● Gold

- ■ Iron
- ▼ Lead & Zinc
- ● Manganese
- ● Nickel
- ○ Potash, Phosphates Salt etc.
- ▲ Tungsten
- ▼ Silver
- ■ Tin
- △ Uranium

Scale 1:35 000 000

0   500   1000   1500 km

Bonne Projection

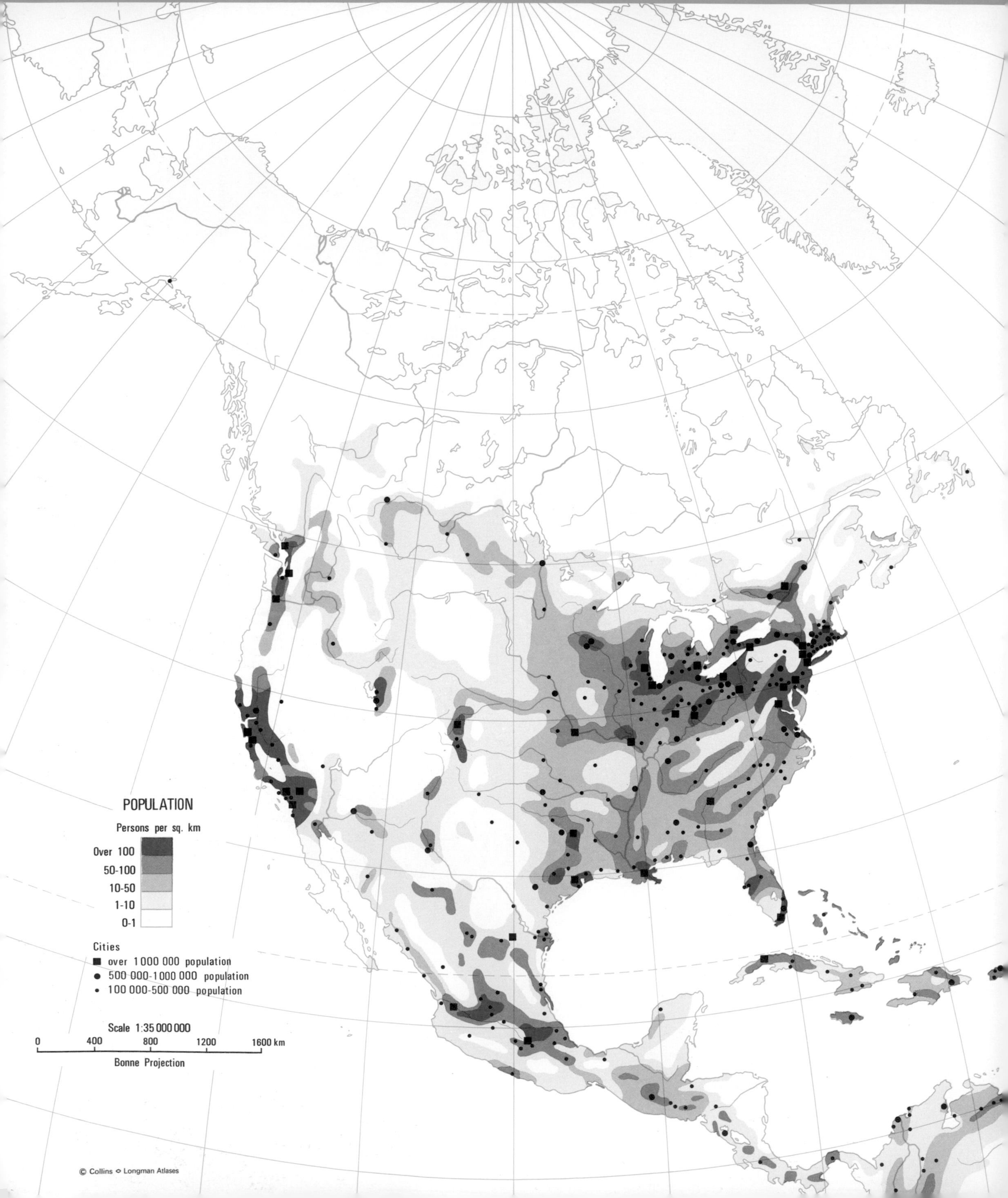

POPULATION

Persons per sq. km

Over 100

50-100

10-50

1-10

0-1

Cities

■ over 1 000 000 population

● 500 000-1 000 000 population

• 100 000-500 000 population

Scale 1:35 000 000

| 0 | 400 | 800 | 1200 | 1600 km |

Bonne Projection

© Collins ◇ Longman Atlases

U.S.S.R.

St. Lawrence I.

Bering Strait

ARCTIC OCEAN

GREENLAND (Denmark)

Ellesmere Island

Reykjavik

ICELAND

Arctic Circle

Parry Islands

Banks I.

Pr. of Wales I.

Baffin Bay

Victoria Island

Baffin Island

Davis Strait

Godthaab

U.S.A.

ALASKA

Yukon

Fairbanks

Anchorage

Kodiak I.

Mackenzie

Gt. Bear Lake

Southampton I.

Hudson Strait

Gt. Slave Lake

L. Athabasca

Peace

Churchill

Hudson Bay

James Bay

Newfoundland

PACIFIC OCEAN

Prince Rupert

Vancouver I.

Fraser

Edmonton

Calgary

Saskatchewan

Regina

C A N A D A

Churchill

Nelson

Lake Winnipeg

Albany

Ottawa

St. Lawrence

Gulf of St. Lawrence

St. John's

Cape Breton I.

Seattle

Vancouver

Spokane

Winnipeg

Missouri

Quebec

Montreal

Halifax

Portland

Columbia

Snake

Duluth

L. Superior

Minneapolis

St. Paul

Milwaukee

L. Michigan

Ottawa

Toronto

L. Ontario

L. Huron

Detroit

L. Erie

Buffalo

Cleveland

Pittsburgh

Boston

Paterson

New York

Philadelphia

Gt. Salt Lake

Salt Lake City

Platte

Omaha

Chicago

Cincinnati

Indianapolis

Ohio

Baltimore

Washington

San Francisco

Colorado

Denver

Kansas City

St. Louis

Arkansas

UNITED STATES OF AMERICA

Tennessee

ATLANTIC

Bermuda

Los Angeles

San Diego

Phoenix

Albuquerque

Oklahoma City

Red

Memphis

Birmingham

OCEAN

Tucson

El Paso

Dallas

Mississippi

Mobile

Jacksonville

Guadalupe (Mex.)

Gulf of California

San Antonio

New Orleans

Houston

Revilla Gigedo Is (Mex.)

Rio Grande

Monterrey

Gulf of Mexico

Miami

Nassau

BAHAMAS

Tropic of Cancer

La Paz

MEXICO

Havana

C U B A

DOMINICAN REP.

Guadalajara

San Luis Potosi

Tampico

Mérida

Greater Antilles

HAITI

Santo Domingo

Mexico City

Veracruz

Kingston

JAMAICA

Port-au-Prince

CARIBBEAN SEA

Belmopan

BELIZE

GUATEMALA

Guatemala City

HONDURAS

Tegucigalpa

NICARAGUA

San José

VENEZUELA

EL SALVADOR

San Salvador

Managua

San José

PANAMA CANAL ZONE (U.S.)

COLOMBIA

COSTA RICA

Panama City

Scale 1:35 000 000

0   500   1000   1500 km

Bonne Projection

© Collins ◇ Longman Atlases

B E R I N G

S E A

U.S.S.R.

St. Lawrence I.

Providenia

Bering Str.

Arctic Circle

C. Lisburne

Wainwright

Barrow

Pt. Alfred C.

B E A U F O R T

S E A

Borden I.

Prince Patrick I.

Mackenzie King I.

Parr

Melville I.

McClure Strait

Viscount Sou

Banks Island

Amundsen Gulf

Victoria Island

Cambridge Bay

Coppermine

Coronation Gulf

Bathurst Inlet

A L A S K A

Brooks Range

Endicott Mts

Yukon

Fairbanks

Anchorage

Valdez

Mt. McKinley 6194

Alaska Range

Kuskokwim Mts

Nome

Norton Sound

Seward Pen.

Kotzebue

Korabuk

Kobuk

Alatak…

Koyukuk

Galena

Tanana

McGrath

Nenana

Willow

Talkeetna

Northway

Tanacross

Whitehorse

Alaska Highway

N O R T H

T E R R.

Yellowknife

Fort Reliance

Gt. Slave Lake

Fort Resolution

Hay River

Caribou Mts

Uranium City

Fond du Lac

L. Athabasca

Wollaston L.

Reindeer Lake

Churchill Lake

M A C K E N Z I E

Mackenzie Mountains

Selwyn Mountains

Keele Pk.

Norman Wells

Fort Good Hope

Gt. Bear Lake

Fort Norman

Wrigley

Fort Simpson

Fort Liard

Fort Nelson

Liard

S. Nahanni

Watson Lake

Y U K O N

Dawson

Mayo

Keno Hill

Carmacks

Pelly

Stikine Mountains

Coast Mountains

Old Crow

Fort McPherson

Inuvik

Peel

Arctic Red

Anderson

Horton

Mackenzie

Dolphin a Union Str.

C. Bathurst

Porcupine

Fort Yukon

St. Lawrence I.

B R I T I S H

C O L U M B I A

Prince Rupert

Kitimat

Prince George

Quesnel

Kamloops

Revelstoke

Vancouver

Victoria

Nanaimo

Kelowna

Penticton

Nelson

Trail

Vancouver Island

Queen Charlotte Islands

Dixon Entrance

Hecate Str.

Qn. Charlotte Str.

Alexander Archipelago

Chichagof I.

Baranof I.

Pr. of Wales I.

Sitka

Juneau

Wrangell

Ketchikan

Stewart

Hazelton

Skagway

Haines

Mt. Fairweather 4670

Mt. St. Elias 5488

Mt. Logan 6050

Gulf of Alaska

P A C I F I C

O C E A N

Peace River Res.

Finlay

Peace River

Dawson Creek

Grande Prairie

Fort St. John

Athabasca

Lesser Slave Lake

A L B E R T A

Edmonton

Red Deer

Camrose

Jasper

Mt. Robson 3954

Athabasca

Fort Vermilion

Fort Chipewyan

McMurray

La Ronge

Peace River

S A S K A T C H E W A N

Lloydminster

North Battleford

Prince Albert

Saskatoon

Rosetown

Swift Current

Regina

Moose Jaw

Yorkt

Estevan

Medicine Hat

Calgary

Drumheller

Lethbridge

Banff

Kicking Horse Pass

Crowsnest Pass

Trans Canada Highway

Cranbrook

R O C K Y

M O U N T A I N S

S E L K I R K M T S

C O L U M B I A

Mountains

Mt. Woddington 4041

W A S H I N G T O N

Seattle

Tacoma

Spokane

Yakima

Mt. Rainier 4392

Columbia

Astoria

Portland

Eugene

O R E G O N

Snake

I D A H O

Boise

Idaho Falls

Twin Falls

Borah Pk. 3857

Great Falls

Helena

Butte

Bozeman

Yellowstone

Billings

M O N T A N A

Missoula

Missouri

Miles City

Glendive

Havre

Grand Teton 4196

Big Horn

Buffalo

Casper

W Y O M I N G

N E V A D A

C A L I F.

Klamath Falls

Mt. Shasta 4317

Eureka

C. Mendocino

U N I T E D

S T A T E S

Redeer

Bristol Bay

Alaska Pen.

Aleutian Range

Naknek

Homer

Kodiak

Kodiak I.

Shelikof Strait

Shumagin Is.

Aleutian

Vsevidof Ml.

Fort Randall

Numivak I.

Scammon Bay

Platinum

Bethel

Aniak

Anvik

Yukon

Numvak I.

Relief

Metres

5000

3000

2000

1000

500

200

0 Sea Level

Land Dep.

200

4000

7000

Metres

Scale 1:17 000 000

0   200   400   600   800 km

Bonne Projection

© Collins ◇ Longman Atlases

Hawaiian Islands (U.S.A.)

PACIFIC OCEAN

Tropic of Cancer

Kauai
Lihue
Oahu
Honolulu
Molokai
Maui
Hawaii 4206▲ Hilo
Pahala

Scale 1:20 000 000

PACIFIC OCEAN

Vancouver Island
Nanaimo
Vancouver
Victoria
C. Flattery
Port Angeles
Aberdeen
Tacoma
Seattle
Bellingham
Astoria
WASHINGTON
Mt. Baker 3285
Glacier Pk. 3211
Mt. Rainier 4392
Mt. Adams 3751
Portland
Albany
Eugene
North Bend
C. Blanco
Roseburg
OREGON
Bend
CASCADE Range
COAST Range
Crescent City
Grants Pass
Klamath Falls
Goose L.
Lakeview
Eureka
C. Mendocino
Redding
Red Bluff
Chico
Ukiah
Point Arena
SIERRA
NEVADA
Sacramento
Stockton
San Francisco
Oakland
San Jose
Monterey Bay
Monterey
CALIFORNIA
Fresno
Merced
Mt. Lyell 3997
Mt. Whitney 4418
Death Valley
Bakersfield
Delano
San Luis Obispo
Santa Maria
Point Conception
Santa Barbara
Los Angeles
Pasadena
Long Beach
Santa Ana
San Bernardino
Palm Springs
San Diego
Tijuana
Ensenada
Mexicali
Salton Sea
Brawley

BRITISH COLUMBIA
Kamloops
Revelstoke
Kelowna
Penticton
Nelson
Trail
Cranbrook
Kicking Horse
Golden
Banff
Mt. Assiniboine 4351
Calgary
Drumheller
Red Deer
ALBERTA
Medicine Hat
Lethbridge
Coleman
Crowsnest
IDAHO
ROCKY MOUNTAINS
Sandpoint
Spokane
Kalispell
Flathead L.
Shelby
Great Falls
Helena
Butte
Dillon
Bozeman
MONTANA
Missoula
Big Snowy Mt. 2661
Roundup
Billings
Boise
Salmon River Mts.
Borah Pk. 3857
Hyndman Pk. 3682
Idaho Falls
Pocatello
Twin Falls
Burley
Yellowstone
Grand Teton 4196
Gannett Pk. 4202
WYOMING
Cloud Pk. 4016
Sheridan
Worland
Buffalo
Casper
Seminoe Resr.
Pathfinder Resr.
Rawlins
Laramie
Cheyenne
Rock Springs
Flaming Gorge Resr.
Green
Uinta Mts.
Ogden
Salt Lake City
Provo
Delta
UTAH
NEVADA
Great Salt Lake
GREAT BASIN
Elko
Reno
Carson City
Hawthorne
Mt. Jefferson 3598
Boundary Pk. 4007
White Mt. Pk. 4341
Wheeler Pk. 3980
Caliente
Cedar City
Las Vegas
L. Mead
Hoover Dam
Needles
Parker Dam
COLORADO
L. Powell
Mt. Ellen 3540
Grand Canyon
Grand Canyon
Nelson
Humphreys Pk. 3862
Flagstaff
PLATEAU
Prescott
Holbrook
ARIZONA
Phoenix
Theodore Roosevelt L.
Eloy
Tucson
Silver City
Lordsburg
Nogales
Imperial Dam
Laguna Dam
Yuma
Gila
C. Colnett
San Felipe
Puerto Penasco
BAJA CALIFORNIA
Gulf of California
Lower California

CANADA
Saskatoon
Kamsack
Quill Lakes
Yorkton
Melville
Dauphin
Swan River
L. Winnipegosis
Regina
Qu'Appelle
Moose Jaw
SASKATCHEWAN
Swift Current
Weyburn
Estevan
Brandon
MANITOBA
L. Manitoba
Portage la Prairie
Rugby
Devils Lake
NORTH DAKOTA
Williston
Minot
Bismarck
Jamestown
Dickinson
Lemmon
Mobridge
Aberdeen
Huron
SOUTH DAKOTA
Oahe Resr.
Pierre
Rapid City
White
Newcastle
UNITED
Lusk
Niobrara
Alliance
Scottsbluff
NEBRASKA
North Platte
L. McConaughy
Kingsley Dam
Grand Island
Kearney
McCook
Republi
Fort Collins
Boulder
Longs Pk. 4345
Greeley
Sterling
Denver
COLORADO
Grand Junction
Mt. Elbert 4399
Pikes Pk. 4301
Colorado Springs
Pueblo
Mt. Peale 3878
Montrose
Canon City
Mt. Wilson 4343
San Juan Mts.
Uncompahgre Pk.
Alamosa
La Junta
Lamar
Great Bend
KANSAS
Dodge City
Liberal
Hutchin
Gunnison
Wheeler Pk. 4009
Raton
Clayton
N. Canadian
OKLA
Alva
Roof Butte 2989
Gallup
Belen
Albuquerque
Santa Fe
N. Truchas Pk. 3970
Mt. Taylor 3444
NEW MEXICO
Vaughn
Tucumcari
Amarillo
Borger
Pampa
Canadian
Red
AMERICA
Elephant Butte Resr.
Sierra Blanca 3659
Clovis
Lubbock
Wichita Falls
Las Cruces
El Paso
Ciudad Juárez
TEXAS
Pecos
Odessa
Big Spring
Sweetwater
Abilene
Mt. Livermore 2555
Alpine
San Antonio

Rio Grande
MEXICO
SONORA
Magdalena
Hermosillo
Sonora
CHIHUAHUA
Chmati Pk. 2356
Emory Pk. 2388
Del Rio
Eagle Pass
Piedras Negras
Ciudad Guerrero
Chihuahua
Delicias
Ciudad Camargo
COAHUILA
Sabinas
Nuevo Laredo
Laredo
Guaymas
Ciudad Obregon
Santa Rosalia
Guadalupe I. (Mex.)
PTA. San Antonio
Angel de la Guarda
Tiburon I.
Cedros I.
Sebastian Vizcaino Bay
Punta Eugenia
Ballenas Bay

PACIFIC OCEAN

© Collins · Longman Atlases

Scale 1:12 000 000

0   100   200   300   400   500   600 km

Bonne Projection

Relief

Metres	
5000	
3000	
2000	
1000	
500	
200	
0	Sea Level
200	
4000	
7000	
Metres	

Land Dep.

C A N A D A

Minnesota

Fort Frances
Rainy L.
International Falls
Atikokan
Fly
Virginia
Eveleth
Grand Rapids
Duluth
Cloquet
Two Harbors
Superior
Ashland
Spooner
Ladysmith
Chippewa Falls
Eau Claire
Marshfield

L. Nipigon
Nipigon
Thunder Bay
Dog L.
Long L.
Pic
Heron Bay
Hearst
Kapuskasing
Cochrane
Iroquois Falls
Oba
Missinaibi
Nakusimi
Groundhog
Mattagami
Franz
Timmins
Kenogamissi L.
Kirkland Lake
Tip Top Mtn. 653
▲ 390
Michipicoten Harbour
Michipicoten I.
Chapleau
Elk Lake ⊙
Eagle Mtn. ▲701
Grand Marais
Isle Royale
Lake Superior
Keweenaw Pt.
Whitefish Pt.
Montreal
Batchawana Mtn. ▲649
Biskotasi L.
Timagami L.
Apostle Is.
Hancock
Keweenaw Bay
Ontonagon
597 ▲
Ironwood
571 ▲
Mt. Curwood 604
Marquette
Negaunee
Iron River
Newberry
Munising
Sault Sainte Marie
Sault Sainte Marie
North Channel
Blind River
Little Current
Capreol
Sudbury
Sturgeon Falls
L. Nipissing
Ludgate

M I C H I G A N

Iron Mountain
Rhinelander
Manistique
Escanaba
Mackinaw City
Beaver I.
Cheboygan
Rogers City
Manitoulin I.
Georgian Bay
Parry Sound
C. Hurd
Minneapolis
St. Paul
Roseville
Richfield
Bloomington
Hastings
Chippewa
Chippewa Falls
591 ▲
Antigo
Wausau
Shawano
Marinette
Green Bay
Manitou Is.
Traverse City
Alpena
North Pt.
Owen Sound
Midland
Collingwood

W I S C O N S I N

Marshfield
Wisconsin Rapids
Appleton
Green Bay
Manistee
Au Sable
Grayling
Au Sable Pt.
Winona
Rochester
Sparta
L. Winnebago
Oshkosh
Manitowoc
Cadillac
Sterling Heights
Port Austin
Goderich
Austin
La Crosse
Fond du Lac
Sheboygan
Ludington
Clare
Saginaw Bay
Waterloo
Kitchener
Stratford
Galt
Portage
695 ▲
Watertown
Muskegon
Midland
Bay City
Saginaw
London
Brantford
Cedar Falls
Waterloo
Dubuque
Madison
Wauwatosa
Waukesha
West Allis
Milwaukee
Muskegon
Grand Rapids
Wyoming
Owosso
Flint
Port Huron
Sarnia
St. Thomas
Waterloo
Mississa

I O W A

Cedar Rapids
Janesville
Beloit
Holland
Kalamazoo
Lansing
East Lansing
Pontiac
Birmingham
L. St. Clair
Port Burwell
Long
Iowa City
Davenport
Rock Island
Moline
Clinton
Freeport
Rockford
Waukegan
North Chicago
South Haven
Battle Creek
Livonia
Warren
Windsor
Chatham
Leamington
Erie
Ottumwa
Burlington
Galesburg
Arlington Heights
Skokie
Evanston
Benton Harbor
Jackson
Ann Arbor
Dearborn
Detroit
Wyandotte
Pt. Pelee
Fort Madison
Peoria
Elgin
Oak Park
Cicero
Chicago
Gary
Michigan City
South Bend
Elkhart
Mishawaka
Adrian
Monroe
Toledo
Sandusky
Lorain
Lakewood
Euclid
Painesville
Ashtabula

U N I T E D

Aurora
Oak Lawn
Joliet
La Salle
Fox
Park Forest
Chicago Heights
Hammond
Harvey
E. Chicago
Plymouth
Fort Wayne
Defiance
Findlay
Fostoria
Elyria
Parma
Cleveland
Warren
Mentor
Cleveland Heights
Meadville
Niles
Youngstown
New Cast
Kankakee
Cuyahoga Falls
Akron
Barberton
Boardman
Canton
Alliance
Sharon
Aliquippa
Glenshaw
Pittsburgh
Pekin
Bloomington
Logansport
Peru
Decatur
Wabash
Lima
Mansfield
Marion
Wooster
Massillon
Steubenville
Weirton
Mount Lebanon
Quincy
Lafayette
Kokomo
Marion
Portland
326 ▲
Champaign
Urbana
Danville
Anderson
Muncie
Piqua
Newark
Coshocton
Cambridge
Wheeling

I L L I N O I S

Jacksonville
Decatur
Springfield
Tuscola
Indianapolis
Richmond
Springfield
Columbus
Zanesville
Mexico
Terre Haute
Franklin
Dayton
Kettering
Fairborn
Athens
Fairmont
Clarksburg
Hannibal
Effingham
Bloomington
Hamilton
Middletown
Chillicothe
Parkersburg
Florissant
Alton
Salem
Vincennes
Seymour
Bedford
Cincinnati
Newport
Covington
Portsmouth
Elkins

I N D I A N A

O H I O

St. Louis
East St. Louis
Belleville
Centralia
Princeton
Lawrenceville
Jefferson City
Mexico

M I S S O U R I

K E N T U C K Y

W E S T V I R G I N I A

O F A M E R

Mississippi
St. Croix
Mille Lacs L.
Black
Wolf
Wisconsin
Turkey
Rock
Cedar
Illinois
Wabash
White
Kaskaskia
Scioto
Muskingum
Ohio
Lake Michigan
Lake Huron
Lake Erie
Green Bay

Scale 1:5 000 000

0   50   100   150   200   250   300 km

Bonne Projection

Relief

Metres	
5000	
3000	
2000	
1000	
500	
200	
0	Sea Level

Land Dep.

200	
4000	
7000	
Metres	

© Collins · Longman Atlases

GULF OF MEXICO

PACIFIC OCEAN

Mexican States numbered on map.
1 FEDERAL DISTRICT
2 TLAXCALA
3 AGUASCALIENTES
4 MORELOS

Scale 1:12 500 000

0 100 200 300 400 500 600 700 800 km

Lambert Azimuthal Equal Area Projection

Relief

Metres	
5000	
3000	
2000	
1000	
500	
200	
0	Sea Level
Land Dep.	
200	
4000	
7000	
Metres	

© Collins · Longman Atlases

Countries and regions: TEXAS, LOUISIANA, MISSISSIPPI, ALABAMA, GEORGIA, FLORIDA, CHIHUAHUA, COAHUILA, DURANGO, NUEVO LEON, TAMAULIPAS, SAN LUIS POTOSI, NAYARIT, JALISCO, GUANAJUATO, MICHOACAN, GUERRERO, OAXACA, CHIAPAS, TABASCO, VERACRUZ, HIDALGO, PUEBLA, YUCATAN, QUINTANA ROO, CAMPECHE, GUATEMALA, BELIZE, HONDURAS, EL SALVADOR, NICARAGUA, COSTA RICA, CUBA

Cities: Houston, San Antonio, New Orleans, Monterrey, Tampico, Guadalajara, Mexico City, Puebla, Veracruz, Acapulco, Oaxaca, Mérida, Campeche, Belmopan, Belize, Guatemala City, San Salvador, Tegucigalpa, Managua, Havana

Water features: Gulf of Mexico, Campeche Bay, Pacific Ocean, Gulf of Honduras, Gulf of Fonseca, Yucatan Channel, Lake Nicaragua, Gulf of Tehuantepec

Physical features: Edwards Plateau, Sierra Madre Occidental, Sierra Madre Oriental, Sierra Madre del Sur, Isthmus of Tehuantepec, Yucatan Peninsula, Mosquito Coast, Padre Island

ATLANTIC

OCEAN

WEST

INDIES

Tropic of Cancer

CARIBBEAN SEA

Hamilton BERMUDA

BAHAMAS

West Palm Beach
Freeport
Grand Bahama I.
Great Abaco I.
Fort Lauderdale
Miami
New Providence
Eleuthera I.
Nassau
Cat I.
San Salvador
Andros I.
Exuma Is.
Rum Cay
Long I.
Samana Cay
Gt. Exuma
Crooked
French Cays
Fortune
Acklin's
Mayaguana I.
Little Inagua
Caicos Is. (U.K.)
Turks Is. (U.K.)
Great Inagua I.

Cape Kennedy
Florida

Archo. de Sabana
Archo. de Camaguey
VILLAS
Cienfuegos
Caibarién
Morón
CAMAGUEY
Nuevitas
Sancti Spíritus
Ciego de Avila
Camagüey
Holguín
Victoria de las Tunas
Banes
Jardines de la Reina
Manzanillo
Bayamo
ORIENTE
S. Luis
Turquino
Sa. Maestra
Santiago de Cuba
Guantánamo
Baracoa
1971
C. Cruz
Cayman Brac
Cayman Is. (U.K.)

B A   Greater   Antilles

Montego Bay
St. Ann's Bay
Port Antonio
Black River
JAMAICA   Kingston

Windward Passage
Tortue
Cap Haïtien
Gonaïves
G. of Gonâve
Jérémie
Gonâve I.
2414
HAITI
Les Cayes   Port-au-Prince   2680
Hispaniola

DOMINICAN
REPUBLIC
Puerto Plata
Samana
Valverde
Santiago
La Vega
8528
San Francisco de Macorís
Azua
S. Cristóbal
S. Pedro
La Romana
Santo Domingo
Barahona
Saona

Puerto Rico Trench

PUERTO RICO
(U.S.)
Arecibo   San Juan
Mayagüez   1338
Ponce   Caguas
Mona

St. Thomas
(U.S.)
Virgin Is.
Vieques Is.
St. Croix
(U.S.)

Anegada (U.K.)
Tortola (U.K.)
Virgin Gorda (U.K.)
Anguilla (U.K.)
St. Martin (Fr-Neth)
Sint Maarten (Neth)
Saba (Neth)
Sint Eustatius (Neth)
St. Kitts (U.K.)
Nevis
Montserrat (U.K.)

St. Barthélemy (Fr.)
Barbuda (U.K.)
ANTIGUA
St. John's

Leeward Islands

Guadeloupe
(Fr.)   1484
Pointe-à-Pitre
Marie Galante (Fr.)

Lesser   Antilles

Roseau   DOMINICA

Fort-de-France   Martinique (Fr.)

Castries   ST. LUCIA

St. Vincent (U.K.)   Kingstown
The Grenadines (U.K.)
Carriacou (U.K.)
St. George's   GRENADA

BARBADOS
Bridgetown

Windward Islands

Lesser   Antilles

Aruba (Netherlands)
Curaçao
Bonaire
Orchila
La Blanquilla

Guajira
Paraguaná Pen.
Willemstad
Los Roques

Riohacha
Penin.
Gulf of Venezuela
El Cardon
Coro
Margarita I.
Porlamar
Tortuga
Araya Pen.
Carúpano
Paria Pen.
Dragon's Mouth
TOBAGO
Port of Spain
TRINIDAD

Sta. Marta
Sa. Nevada
de Sta. Marta
Colón
Cienaga
Valledupar
Maracaibo
Altagracia
Cabimas
San Felipe
Tucacas
Pto. Cabello
Maracay
La Guaira
Cumaná
S. Fernando
Gulf of Paria
Serpent's Mouth

Barranquilla
Soledad
Cartagena
Calamar
Arjona
Magangué
Lake
Maracaibo
Barquisimeto
Valencia
Caracas
Valencia
San Juan de los Morros
Barcelona
Pto. La Cruz
Orinoco Delta
Maturín
Curiapo

CANAL ZONE (U.S.)
Colón
Balboa
Panama City
Penonomé
Gulf of Panamá
Archo. de las Perlas
Insula
El Real
Gulf of Darién
G. of Urabá
Monteria
Rosucio
Atrato
Magdalena
S. Jorge
El Banco
Ocaña
Sierra de Perija
Trujillo
Acarigua
Mérida
5007
Barinas
Cordillera de Mérida
Valle
El Tigre
S. Félix
Barrage
Ciudad Bolívar

Gulf of Darién
COLOMBIA
Cauca
Bello
Medellín
Itagüí
5393
Sa. Nevada de Cocuy
Bucaramanga
Barrancabermeja
Cúcuta
San Cristóbal
Pamplona
Apure
Arauca
VENEZUELA
Bolívar
Guanare
Cojedes
Coro
Guárico
Meta
S. Fernando
Orinoco
Puerto Carreño
Caroní
Caura
Angel Falls
Cuyuni
GUYANA

Tropic of Cancer

A T L A N T I C

O C E A N

Bahama Islands

C. Sable

Cuba

Yucatan Channel

Jamaica

Greater   Antilles

Yucatan
Pen.

Gulf of
Honduras

Sierra Madre L. Nicaragua

Isthmus of Panama

Gulf of
Panama

Gulf of
Darien

Hispaniola

Puerto
Rico

Lesser   Antilles

Leeward
Islands

Windward
Islands

Caribbean

Sea

Curacao

C. Gallinas

L. Maracaibo

Trinidad

Cordillera Occidental

Cordillera Central

Cordillera Oriental

Cotopaxi
5896

Mt. Chimborazo
6272

C. San Francisco

G. de Guayaquil

C. Negra

C. Orange

Guiana

Highlands

Mt. Roraima
2810

Essequibo

Orinoco

Meta

Negro

Amazon

Japura

Jurua

Amazon

Marañon

Ucayali

Purus

Madeira

Tapajos

Xingu

Tocantins

Araguaia

Guapore

Mamore

L. Titicaca

Boli
Ata

Selvas

Mato

Grosso

Highlands

São Francisco

Parnaíba

Paranaíba

C. São Roque

Equator

Manajó I.

S o u t h

A N D E S

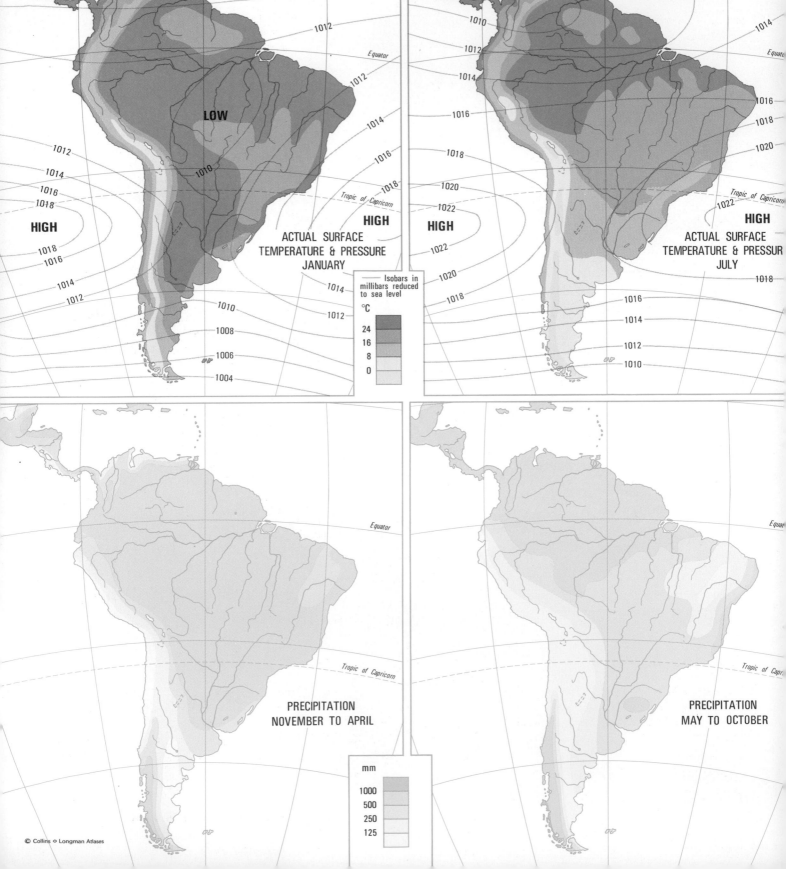

ACTUAL SURFACE
TEMPERATURE & PRESSURE
JANUARY

LOW

HIGH

HIGH

1016
1014
1012
1012
1014
1016
1018

Equator

Tropic of Capricorn

1012
1014
1016
1018
1016
1014
1012
1010
1008
1006
1004

Isobars in
millibars reduced
to sea level

°C
24
16
8
0

ACTUAL SURFACE
TEMPERATURE & PRESSURE
JULY

LOW

HIGH

HIGH

1010
1010
1012
1014
1016
1014
1016
1018
1020

Equator

Tropic of Capricorn

1018
1020
1022
1022
1020
1018
1022
1016
1014
1012
1010

PRECIPITATION
NOVEMBER TO APRIL

Equator

Tropic of Capricorn

PRECIPITATION
MAY TO OCTOBER

Equator

Tropic of Capri

mm
1000
500
250
125

© Collins ◇ Longman Atlases

ATLANTIC OCEAN

Caribbean Sea

Yucatan
Pen.

Isthmus of Panama

Caracas

Llanos

Guiana Highlands

Negro

Amazon

Amazon

Equator

S e l v a s

PACIFIC OCEAN

Lima

A N D E S

Atacama Desert

Recife

São Francisco

Brazilian

Mato

Grosso

Highlands

Upland

Gran Chaco

Paraná

São Paulo

Rio de
Janeiro

Tropic of Capricorn

SOUTH

ATLANTIC

OCEAN

Paraná

Pampas

Santiago

Buenos
Aires

Montevideo

Patagonia

Scale 1:35 000 000

0   500   1000   1500 km

Lambert Azimuthal Equal Area Projection

Falkland
Is.

	Little or no activity

PREDOMINANT SUBSISTENCE ECONOMY

Gathering hunting and fishing

Traditional cultivation

Shifting

Semi-intensive sedentary

Intensive cropping
(rice dominant)

Intensive cropping
(other crop dominant)

Traditional pastoralism

Nomadic herding (cattle)

Non-nomadic (cattle, with
llamas and alpacas on
S.Andes)

Non-nomadic (sheep)

PREDOMINANT COMMERCIAL ECONOMY

Intensive cultivation

Grain

Large-scale specialised
(plantation)

Specialised (market gardening)

Livestock rearing

Extensive (cattle)

Extensive (sheep)

Intensive (cattle)

Intensive (sheep)

Intensive dairying

Lumbering

Fishing

Manufacturing/service
industry

Extractive industry

Areas of mixed economies shown by banding

© Collins ◇ Longman Atlases

MINERAL RESOURCES

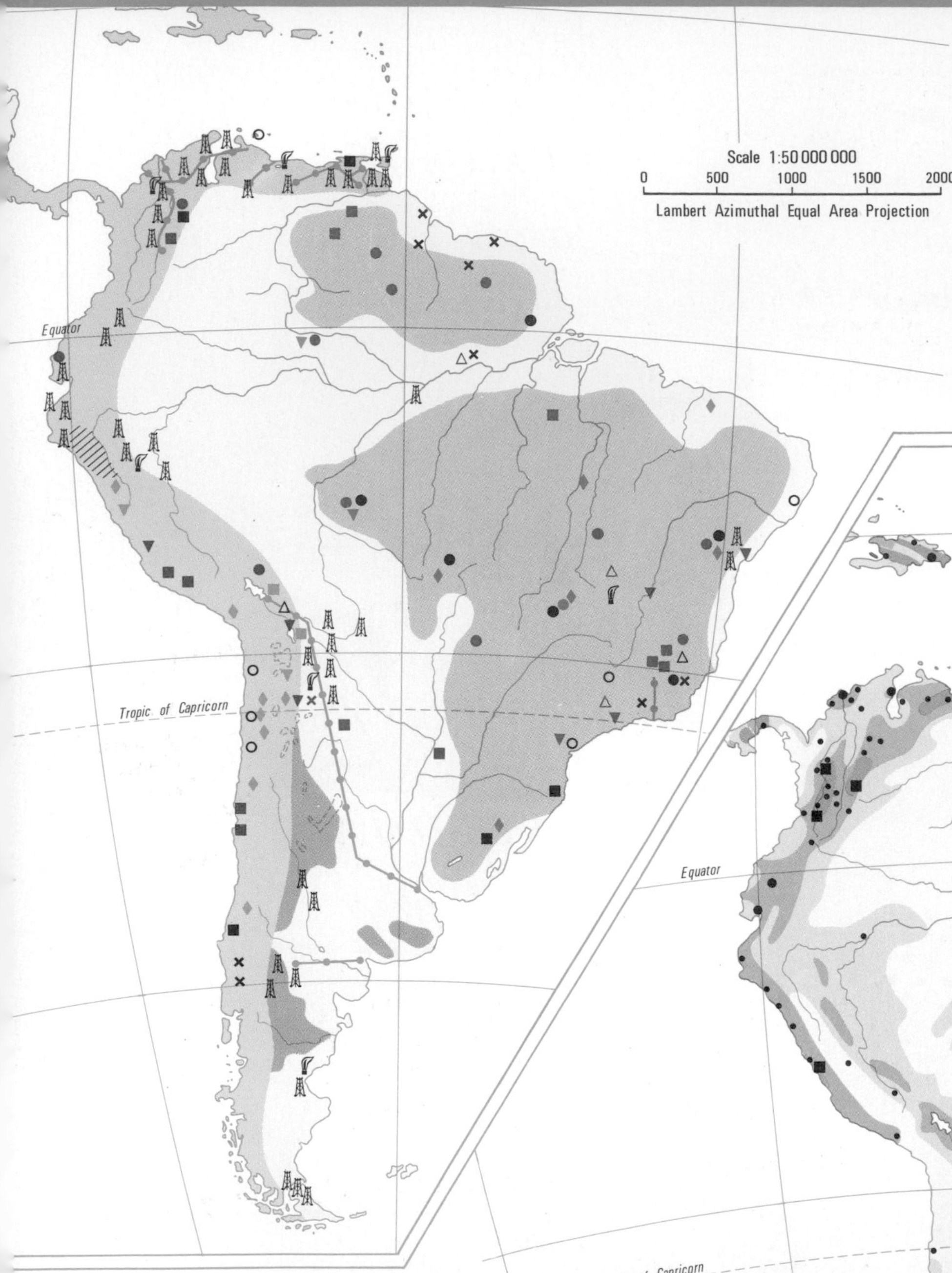

Structure

Shield

Old fold mountains

Young fold mountains

Plains

} Coal

Natural Gas

Oil

Oil pipe-line

Minerals

△ Asbestos
✕ Bauxite
✕ Cobalt
◆ Copper
■ Iron
▼ Lead & Zinc
● Manganese
● Nickel
○ Phosphates, Potash, Nitrates
▼ Silver
■ Tin
△ Uranium

Scale 1:50 000 000

0 500 1000 1500 2000 km

Lambert Azimuthal Equal Area Projection

Equator

Tropic of Capricorn

POPULATION

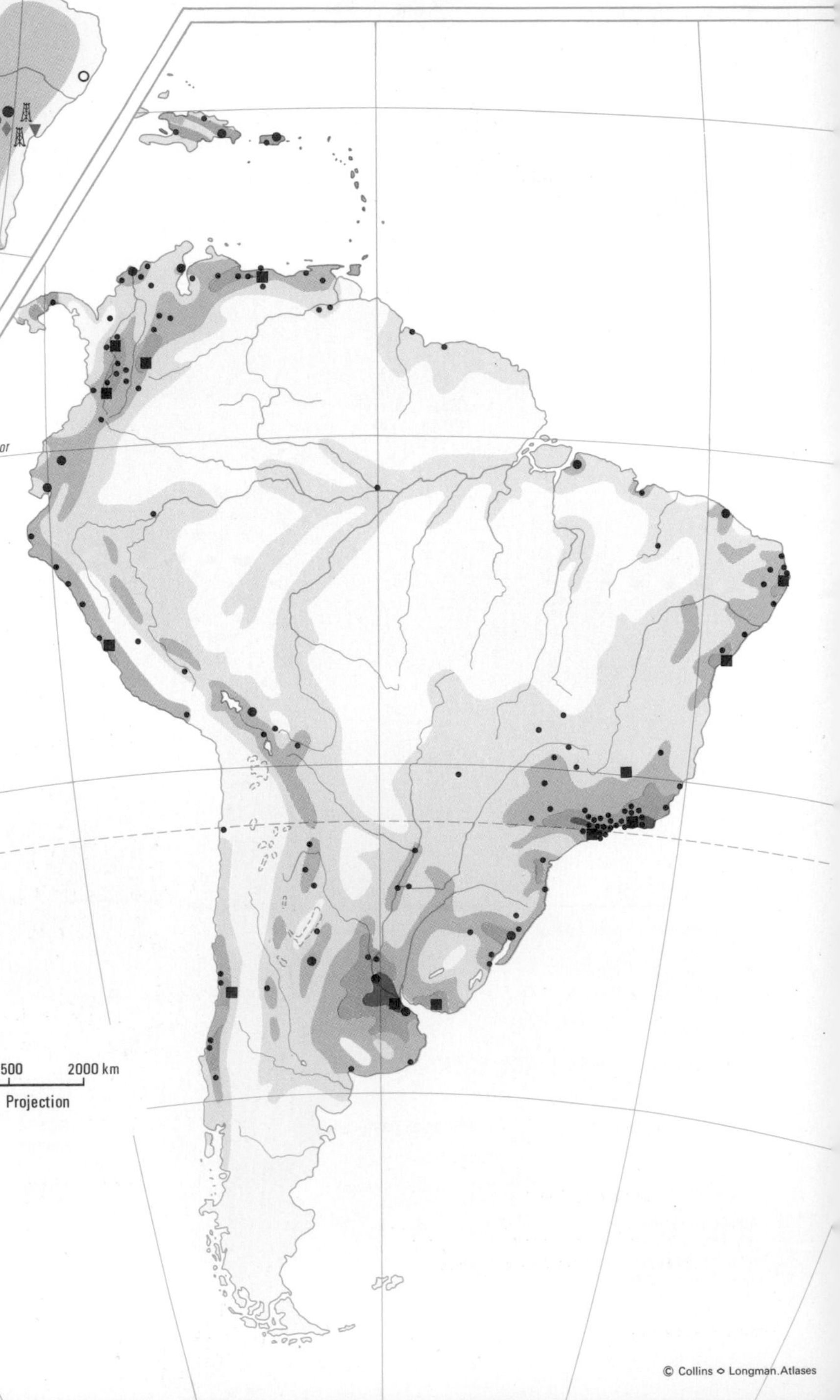

Persons per sq. km

Over 100

50-100

10-50

1-10

0-1

Cities

■ over 1 000 000 population

● 500 000 - 1 000 000 population

• 100 000 - 500 000 population

Scale 1:50 000 000

0 500 1000 1500 2000 km

Lambert Azimuthal Equal Area Projection

Equator

Tropic of Capricorn

© Collins ◇ Longman Atlases

ATLANTIC OCEAN

PACIFIC OCEAN

SOUTH ATLANTIC OCEAN

Tropic of Cancer

Tropic of Capricorn

Equator

MEXICO

Yucatan Channel

Havana
CUBA
BAHAMAS

Greater Antilles

BELIZE
Belmopan

GUATEMALA
Guatemala City
San Salvador
EL SALVADOR

HONDURAS
Tegucigalpa

NICARAGUA
Managua
L. Nicaragua

San José
COSTA RICA

PANAMA
Panamá City
CANAL ZONE (U.S.)

HAITI
Port-au-Prince
JAMAICA
Kingston

DOMINICAN REP.
Santo Domingo

PUERTO RICO
San Juan

Leeward Is.

Lesser Antilles

Windward Is.

Caribbean Sea

C. Gallinas
Curaçao

Barranquilla
Cartagena
Maracaibo
L. Maracaibo
Cúcuta

Medellín
Manizales

Bogotá

COLOMBIA

Cali

Quito
ECUADOR

Guayaquil

Galapagos Is. (Ec.)

Caracas
Ciudad Bolívar

VENEZUELA

Orinoco

TRINIDAD
Port of Spain

Georgetown
Paramaribo
Cayenne

GUYANA
Essequibo
SURINAM
GUIANA (Fr.)

Negro

Iquitos

PERU

Pucallpa

Trujillo

Callao
Lima

Cuzco

Arequipa

Arica

Iquique

Antofagasta

Manaus

Amazon

Amazon

Madeira

Trans Amazon

L. Titicaca
La Paz
Cochabamba
Santa Cruz
Sucre

BOLIVIA

PARAGUAY

Paraguay

Belém
São Luís

Tapajós

Xingu

Highway

Araguaia

Tocantins

Fortaleza
Teresina

Natal
João Pessoa
Recife
Maceió
Aracaju

Salvador

Cuiabá

Goiânia
Brasília

São Francisco

BRAZIL

Belo Horizonte
Vitória

Ribeirão Prêto
Rio de Janeiro
Niterói
São Paulo

Curitiba

Florianópolis

Pôrto Alegre
Pelotas

Salta

San Miguel de Tucumán

Salado

CHILE

ARGENTINA

Córdoba
Santa Fé

Valparaíso
Santiago

Mendoza

Rosario

Talca
Concepción

Juan Fernandez Is. (Chile)

Buenos Aires

Mar del Plata

Bahía Blanca

San Antonio Oeste

G. of San Matias

Puerto Montt

Chiloé I.

Trelew

Comodoro Rivadavia

Parará

Uruguay

URUGUAY
Montevideo

Rio de la Plata

Asunción

Paraná

Falkland Is. (Br.)

Punta Arenas
Tierra del Fuego

Scale 1:35 000 000

0   500   1000   1500 km

Lambert Azimuthal Equal Area Projection

© Collins ◇ Longman Atlases

Tropic of Cancer

A T L A N T I C   O C E A N

Equator

C. São Roque
Natal
João Pessoa
Recife
Campina Grande
Caruaru
Maceió
Aracaju
Mossoró
Fortaleza
Sobral
Teresina
São Luís
Belém
Marajó I.
Amazon Delta

B R A Z I L

Brazilian Highlands

Feira
Salvador
Itabuna
Januária
Vitória
Montes
Brasília
Goiânia
Cuiabá
Mato Grosso

Mato Grosso

Tocantins
Araguaia
Xingu
Amazon
Santarém
Amazon Highway
Trans-Amazon Highway
Tapajós
Roosevelt
Madeira
Pôrto Velho
Guajará Mirim
Trinidad
Mamoré
Guaporé

Cayenne
C. Orange
Macapá
FRENCH GUIANA (Fr.)
SURINAM
Paramaribo
Nieuw Amsterdam
New Amsterdam
Georgetown
Essequibo
GUYANA
Guiana Highlands
Boa Vista
Branco
Negro
Manaus
São Paulo de Olivença
Letícia
Japurá
Iquitos
Juruá
Putumayo
Purus
Javari
Ucayali
Marañón

B O L I V I A

La Paz
Cobija
Rio Branco
Madre de Dios
Beni
Puno
Cochabamba

P E R U

A N D E S

Cordillera
Callao
Lima
Trujillo
Chiclayo
Chimbote
Huánuco
Cerro de Pasco
La Oroya
Huancayo
Cuzco
Arequipa
Mollendo
Tacna
Arica

ECUADOR
Quito
Guayaquil
Gulf of Guayaquil
Chimborazo
Riobamba
Cuenca
Loja
Sullana
C. Negra
C. San Francisco
Tumaco
Buenaventura

C O L O M B I A
Bogotá
Medellín
Cali
Cordillera Occidental
Cordillera Central
Cordillera Oriental
Cartagena
Barranquilla
Ciénaga
Magdalena
Montería
G. of Darien
Armenia
Ibagué
Pasto
Pereira
Manizales
Cúcuta
Bucaramanga
Valledupar
San Cristóbal
Mérida

V E N E Z U E L A
Caracas
Maracaibo
Maracay
Valencia
Barquisimeto
Cabimas
Barcelona
El Tigre
Ciudad Bolívar
Ciudad Guayana
Santo Tomé
Barrancas
Cumaná
Güiria
Orinoco
Orinoco Delta
San Fernando
Apure
Meta
Arauca
Puerto Carreño
Guaviare
Vaupés
Cerro Marahuaca
Mt. Roraima

TRINIDAD
Port of Spain
BARBADOS
Windward Islands
Martinique (Fr.)
DOMINICA
Guadeloupe (Fr.)
ANTIGUA
Leeward Islands
Lesser Antilles
Curaçao (Neth.)
Willemstad
Netherlands Antilles
C. Gallinas

Caribbean Sea

Greater Antilles
PUERTO RICO
San Juan
Ponce
DOMINICAN REP.
Santo Domingo
Santiago
Puerto Plata
La Vega
HAITI
Port-au-Prince
Gonaïves
Caicos Is. (Br.)
Gt. Inagua I.
Windward Passage

JAMAICA
Kingston
Guantánamo
Santiago de Cuba
Holguín
Camagüey
C U B A
Santa Clara
Cienfuegos
Havana
Guane
BAHAMAS
Nassau
Grand Bahama I.
Gt. Abaco I.
Andros I.
Straits of Florida

U.S.A.
Miami
Fort Lauderdale
West Palm Beach
Orlando
C. Kennedy
Tampa
St. Petersburg
Key West
Florida
Puerto Juárez
Yucatan Pen.
Yucatan Channel

BELIZE
Belmopan
GUATEMALA
HONDURAS
San Pedro Sula
Tegucigalpa
Gulf of Honduras
C. Gracias á Dios
NICARAGUA
Managua
L. Nicaragua
COSTA RICA
San José
Limón
PANAMA
Panamá
Colón
CANAL ZONE
Panama Canal
Gulf of Panamá

Puerto Rico Trench

BENI

BOLIVIA

SANTA

CRUZ

CHUQUISACA

TARIJA

SALTA

TUCUMÁN

SANTIAGO
DEL ESTERO

MARCA

RIOJA

La Rioja

CÓRDOBA

LA PAMPA

MENDOZA

A R G E N T I N A

BUENOS
AIRES

Cuiabá

Cáceres

M A T O

G R O S S O

P A R A G U A Y

FORMOSA

CHACO

SANTA FÉ

ENTRE
RIOS

URUGUAY

MISIONES

CORRIENTES

B R A Z I L

GOIÁS

Brasília
Fed. Dist.

Formosa

MINAS

GERAIS

Belo
Horizonte

S Ã O
P A U L O

São Paulo

Rio de
Janeiro

P A R A N Á

Curitiba

SANTA CATARINA

Florianópolis

RIO GRANDE

DO SUL

Pôrto Alegre

S O U T H

A T L A N T I C

O C E A N

Rosario

Buenos
Aires

Montevideo

Mar del Plata

Bahía Blanca

Gulf of
San Matías

Metres	Relief
5000	
3000	
2000	
1000	
500	
200	
0	Sea Level
Land Dep.	
200	
4000	
7000	
Metres	

Scale 1:12 000 000

0   100   200   300   400   500   600 km

Lambert Azimuthal Equal Area Projection

© Collins ◇ Longman Atlases

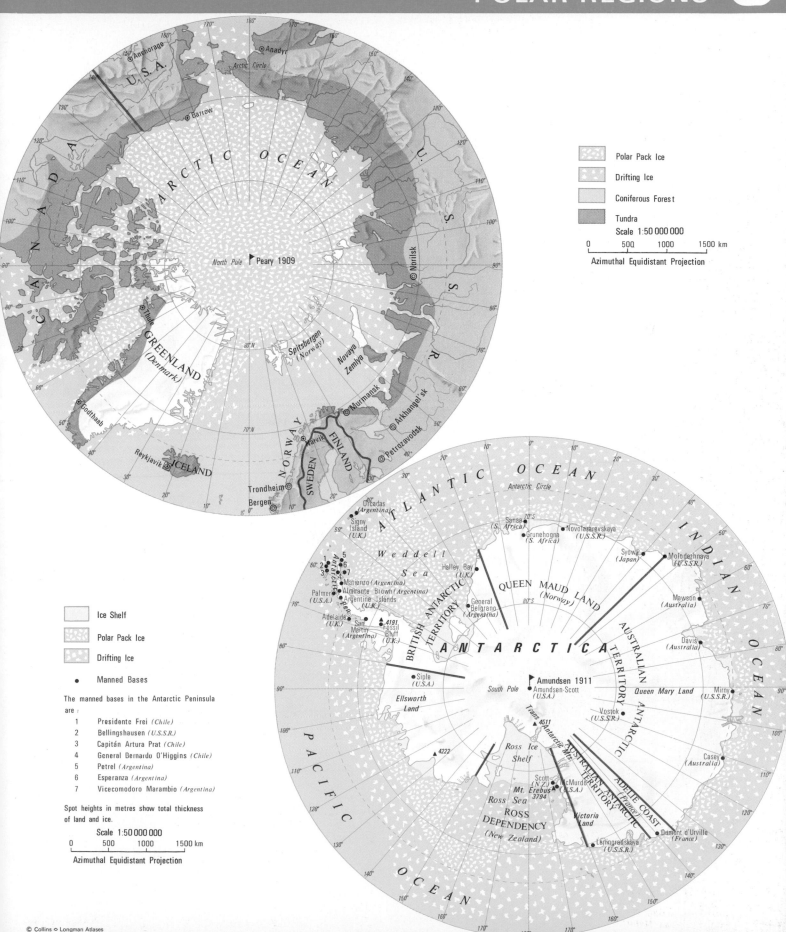

Legend (top right):
- Polar Pack Ice
- Drifting Ice
- Coniferous Forest
- Tundra

Scale 1:50 000 000

0 500 1000 1500 km

Azimuthal Equidistant Projection

Arctic map labels:

U.S.A.
Anchorage
Anadyr
Arctic Circle
Barrow
CANADA
ARCTIC OCEAN
U.S.S.R.
North Pole ▶ Peary 1909
Norilsk
Thule
GREENLAND (Denmark)
Spitsbergen (Norway)
Novaya Zemlya
80°N
70°N
Godthaab
Murmansk
Arkhangel'sk
NORWAY
Narvik
SWEDEN
FINLAND
Petrozavodsk
Reykjavik ICELAND
Trondheim
Bergen

Legend (lower left):
- Ice Shelf
- Polar Pack Ice
- Drifting Ice
- • Manned Bases

The manned bases in the Antarctic Peninsula are :

1   Presidente Frei *(Chile)*
2   Bellingshausen *(U.S.S.R.)*
3   Capitán Artura Prat *(Chile)*
4   General Bernardo O'Higgins *(Chile)*
5   Petrel *(Argentina)*
6   Esperanza *(Argentina)*
7   Vicecomodoro Marambio *(Argentina)*

Spot heights in metres show total thickness of land and ice.

Scale 1:50 000 000

0 500 1000 1500 km

Azimuthal Equidistant Projection

Antarctic map labels:

ATLANTIC OCEAN
Antarctic Circle
Orcadas (Argentina)
Signy Island (U.K.)
Sanae (S. Africa)
Grunehogna (S. Africa)
Novolazarevskaya (U.S.S.R.)
Syowa (Japan)
Molodezhnaya (U.S.S.R.)
Weddell Sea
INDIAN OCEAN
Halley Bay (U.K.)
QUEEN MAUD LAND (Norway)
Mawson (Australia)
Matienzo (Argentina)
Almirante Brown (Argentina)
Palmer (U.S.A.)
Argentine Islands (U.K.)
BRITISH ANTARCTIC TERRITORY
General Belgrano (Argentina)
AUSTRALIAN ANTARCTIC TERRITORY
Davis (Australia)
Adelaide (U.K.)
San Martin (Argentina)
4191 Fossil Bluff (U.K.)
ANTARCTICA
Siple (U.S.A.)
Amundsen 1911 ▶
South Pole
Amundsen-Scott (U.S.A.)
Queen Mary Land
Mirny (U.S.S.R.)
Ellsworth Land
Vostok (U.S.S.R.)
4511
Trans Antarctic Mts.
Casey (Australia)
4222
Ross Ice Shelf
Scott (N.Z.)
McMurdo (U.S.A.)
ADÉLIE COAST (France)
Mt. Erebus 3794
Ross Sea
Victoria Land
Dumont d'Urville (France)
ROSS DEPENDENCY (New Zealand)
Leningradskaya (U.S.S.R.)
PACIFIC OCEAN

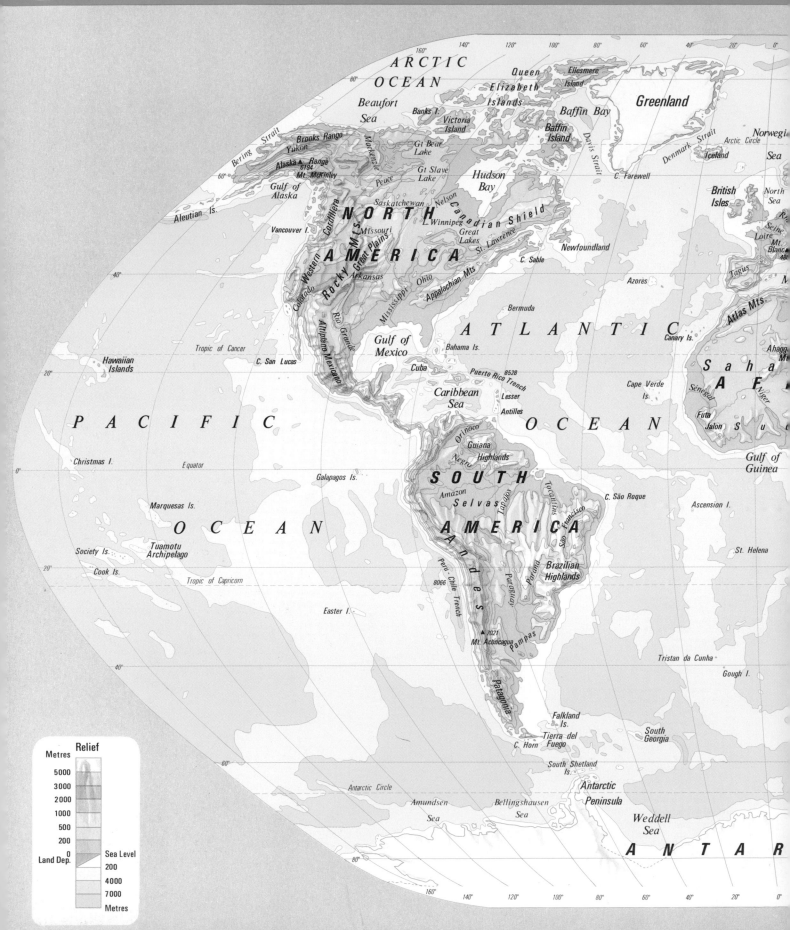

ARCTIC
OCEAN

Queen
Elizabeth
Islands
Ellesmere
Island

Greenland

Beaufort
Sea

Banks I.

Baffin Bay

Victoria
Island

Baffin
Island

Davis Strait

Denmark Strait

Arctic Circle

Norwegi
Sea

Iceland

Brooks Range

Yukon

Gt Bear
Lake

Mackenzie

C. Farewell

British
Isles

North
Sea

Alaska ▲ Range
6194
Mt. McKinley

Peace

Gt Slave
Lake

Hudson
Bay

Seine

Gulf of
Alaska

Saskatchewan

Nelson

Canadian Shield

Loire

Mt.
Blanc
481

Aleutian Is.

NORTH

L. Winnipeg

Great
Lakes

St. Lawrence

Newfoundland

Tagus

Vancouver I.

Cordillera

AMERICA

Missouri

Western

Great Plains

Rocky Mts.

Arkansas

Ohio

C. Sable

Atlas Mts.

Colorado

Mississippi

Appalachian Mts.

Azores

Rio Grande

Altiplano Mexicano

Bermuda

ATLANTIC

Canary Is.

Saha

A F

Tropic of Cancer

C. San Lucas

Gulf of
Mexico

Bahama Is.

Puerto Rico Trench
8528

Hawaiian
Islands

Cuba

Cape Verde
Is.

Sénégal

Niger

Caribbean
Sea

Lesser
Antilles

OCEAN

Futa
Jalon

Gulf of
Guinea

PACIFIC

Christmas I.

Orinoco

Negro

Guiana
Highlands

Ascension I.

Equator

Galapagos Is.

SOUTH

Amazon

Selvas

Tocantins

C. São Roque

Marquesas Is.

AMERICA

São Francisco

St. Helena

OCEAN

Andes

Tapajós

Brazilian
Highlands

Society Is.

Tuamotu
Archipelago

Madeira

Paraguay

Paraná

Tropic of Capricorn

Cook Is.

8066
Peru-Chile Trench

Easter I.

▲ 7021
Mt. Aconcagua

Pampas

Tristan da Cunha

Gough I.

Patagonia

Falkland
Is.

South
Georgia

Tierra del
Fuego
C. Horn

South Shetland
Is.

Antarctic
Peninsula

Antarctic Circle

Amundsen
Sea

Bellingshausen
Sea

Weddell
Sea

ANTAR

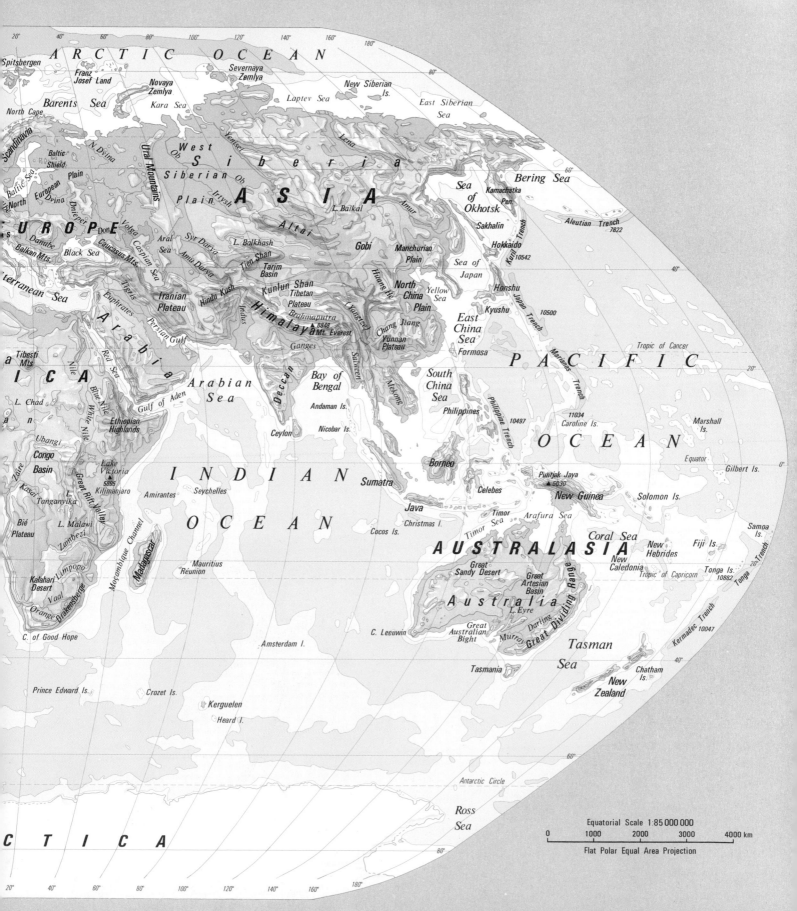

ARCTIC OCEAN

Spitsbergen
Franz
Josef Land
Novaya
Zemlya
Severnaya
Zemlya
New Siberian
Is.
North Cape
Barents Sea
Kara Sea
Laptev Sea
East Siberian
Sea
Scandinavia
N. Dvina
Ural Mountains
West
Siberian
Plain
Siberian
Plain
Yenisei
Lena
Baltic
Shield
Plain
Ob
Ob
Irtysh
S i b e r i a
Bering Sea
Baltic
Sea
European
Dvina
N Dvina
A S I A
Sea
of
Okhotsk
Kamachatka
Pen.
Sakhalin
EUROPE
Don
Volga
Caspian Sea
L. Baikal
Altai
Amur
Manchurian
Plain
Aleutian Trench
7822
Hokkaido
Kuril Trench
10542
Danube
Balkan Mts.
Black Sea
Caucasus Mts.
Aral
Sea
Syr Darya
L. Balkhash
Tien Shan
Gobi
Sea of
Japan
Honshu
Japan Trench
Amu Darya
Tarim
Basin
Huang He
North
China
Plain
Yellow
Sea
Kyushu
10500
Mediterranean Sea
Tigris
Euphrates
Iranian
Plateau
Hindu Kush
Kunlun Shan
Tibetan
Plateau
(Yangtze)
Chang Jiang
East
China
Sea
Mariana Trench
Tropic of Cancer
A R I C A
Arabia
Persian Gulf
Indus
Himalaya
8848
Mt. Everest
Brahmaputra
Yunnan
Plateau
Formosa
PACIFIC
Tibesti
Mts.
Nile
Red Sea
Ganges
Deccan
Bay of
Bengal
Salween
Mekong
South
China
Sea
Philippine Trench
10497
11034
Caroline Is.
Marshall
Is.
L. Chad
Blue Nile
White Nile
Gulf of Aden
Arabian
Sea
Andaman Is.
Philippines
OCEAN
Ubangi
Congo
Basin
Ethiopian
Highlands
Ceylon
Nicobar Is.
Borneo
Equator
Gilbert Is.
Zaire
Kasai
L.
Victoria
5895
Kilimanjaro
Amirantes
Seychelles
I N D I A N
Sumatra
Celebes
Puntjak Jaya
5030
New Guinea
Solomon Is.
L. Tanganyika
Great Rift Valley
Java
Christmas I.
Timor
Arafura Sea
Bié
Plateau
L. Malawi
Zambezi
O C E A N
Cocos Is.
Timor
Sea
AUSTRALASIA
Coral Sea
New
Hebrides
Fiji Is.
Samoa
Is.
Mozambique Channel
Madagascar
Mauritius
Réunion
Great
Sandy Desert
Great
Artesian
Basin
New
Caledonia
Tropic of Capricorn
Tonga Is.
10882
Tonga Trench
Kalahari
Desert
Vaal
Drakensberg
Australia
L. Eyre
Great Dividing Range
Orange
Limpopo
C. Leeuwin
Great
Australian
Bight
Darling
Murray
Tasman
Sea
Kermadec Trench
10047
C. of Good Hope
Amsterdam I.
Tasmania
Chatham
Is.
New
Zealand
Prince Edward Is.
Crozet Is.
Kerguelen
Heard I.
Antarctic Circle
C T I C A
Ross
Sea

Equatorial Scale 1:85 000 000
0   1000   2000   3000   4000 km
Flat Polar Equal Area Projection

© Collins ◇ Longman Atlases

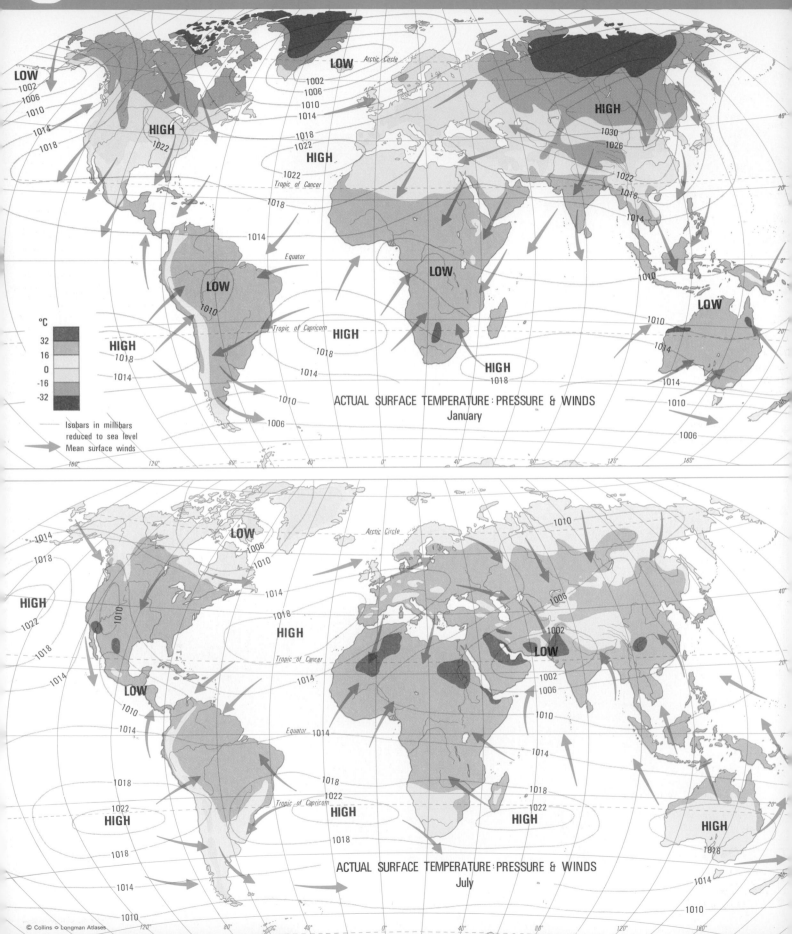

°C
32
16
0
-16
-32

Isobars in millibars
reduced to sea level
Mean surface winds

ACTUAL SURFACE TEMPERATURE: PRESSURE & WINDS
January

ACTUAL SURFACE TEMPERATURE: PRESSURE & WINDS
July

© Collins ○ Longman Atlases

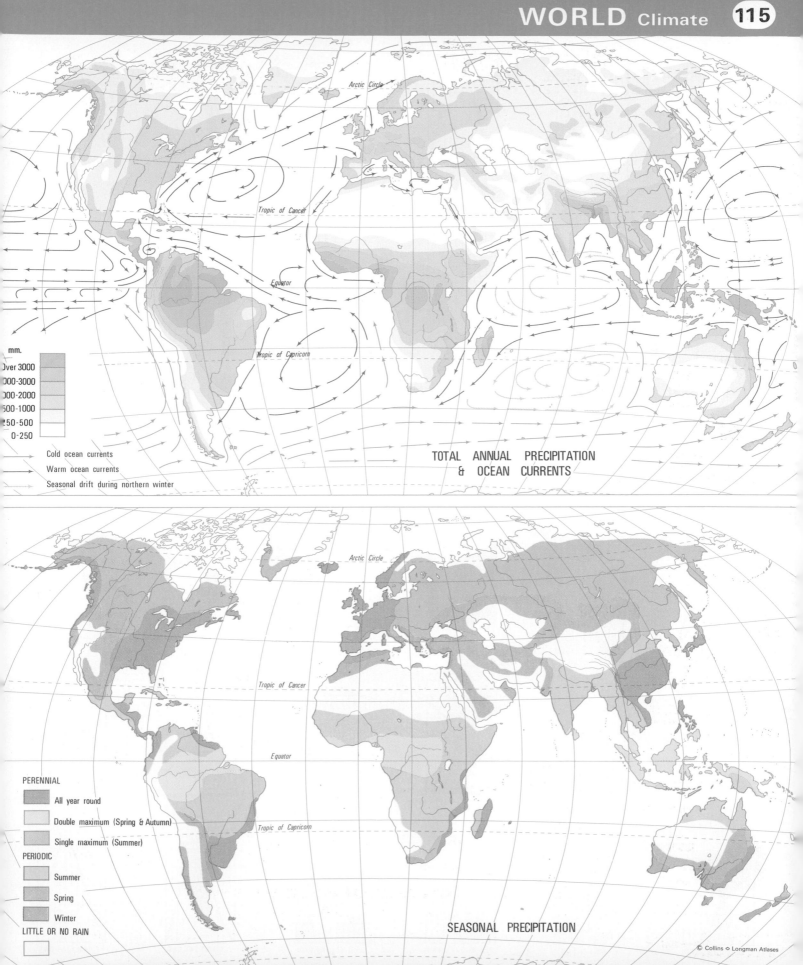

mm.
Over 3000
000-3000
000-2000
500-1000
250-500
0-250

→ Cold ocean currents
→ Warm ocean currents
→ Seasonal drift during northern winter

TOTAL ANNUAL PRECIPITATION
& OCEAN CURRENTS

PERENNIAL
All year round
Double maximum (Spring & Autumn)
Single maximum (Summer)

PERIODIC
Summer
Spring
Winter

LITTLE OR NO RAIN

SEASONAL PRECIPITATION

© Collins ◇ Longman Atlases

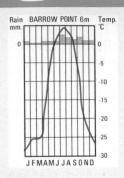

Rain mm. / BARROW POINT 6m / Temp. °C

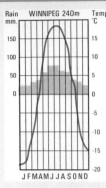

Rain mm. / WINNIPEG 240m / Temp. °C

Rain mm. / BOSTON 38m / Temp. °C

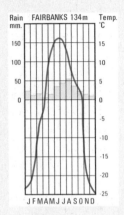

Rain mm. / FAIRBANKS 134m / Temp. °C

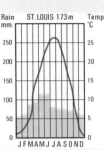

Rain mm. / ST. LOUIS 173m / Temp. °C

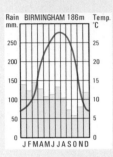

Rain mm. / BIRMINGHAM 186m / Temp. °C

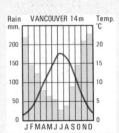

Rain mm. / VANCOUVER 14m / Temp. °C

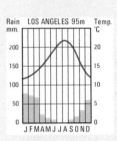

Rain mm. / LOS ANGELES 95m / Temp. °C

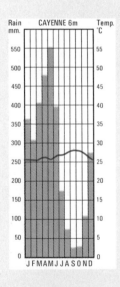

Rain / CAYENNE 6m / Temp.

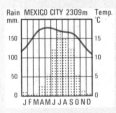

Rain mm. / MEXICO CITY 2309m / Temp. °C

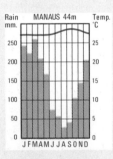

Rain mm. / MANAUS 44m / Temp. °C

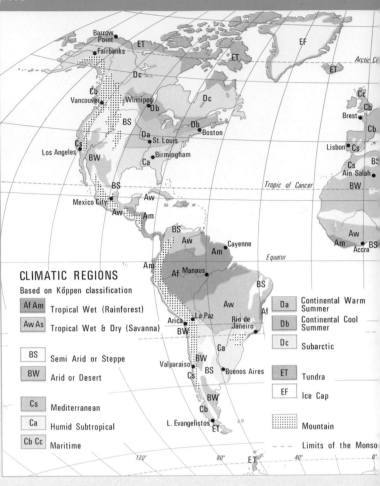

CLIMATIC REGIONS
Based on Köppen classification

Af Am	Tropical Wet (Rainforest)
Aw As	Tropical Wet & Dry (Savanna)
BS	Semi Arid or Steppe
BW	Arid or Desert
Cs	Mediterranean
Ca	Humid Subtropical
Cb Cc	Maritime

Da	Continental Warm Summer
Db	Continental Cool Summer
Dc	Subarctic
ET	Tundra
EF	Ice Cap
	Mountain
	Limits of the Monsoon

Height in metres above sea level.

Mean monthly temperature.

Average monthly rainfall.

CLIMATIC GRAPHS

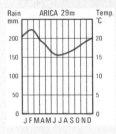

Rain mm. / ARICA 29m / Temp. °C

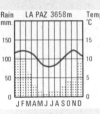

Rain mm. / LA PAZ 3658m / Temp. °C

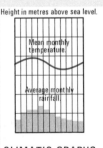

Rain mm. / RIO DE JANEIRO 61m / Temp. °C

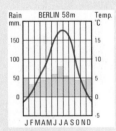

Rain mm. / BREST 17m / Temp. °C

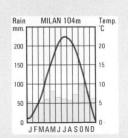

Rain mm. / BERLIN 58m / Temp. °C

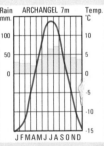

Rain mm. / ARCHANGEL 7m / Temp. °C

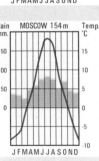

Rain mm. / MOSCOW 154m / Temp. °C

Rain mm. / VALPARAISO 41m / Temp. °C

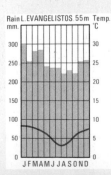

Rain mm. / L. EVANGELISTOS 55m / Temp. °C

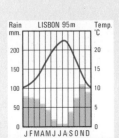

Rain mm. / BUENOS AIRES 27m / Temp. °C

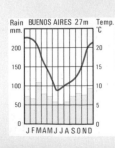

Rain mm. / LISBON 95m / Temp. °C

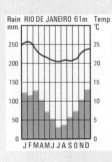

Rain mm. / MILAN 104m / Temp. °C

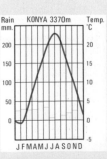

Rain mm. / KONYA 3370m / Temp. °C

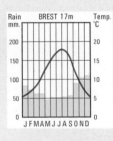

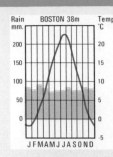

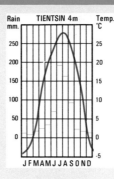 YAKUTSK 163m
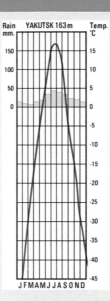 BOMBAY 11m
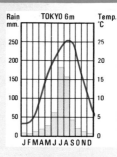 TIENTSIN 4m
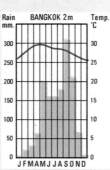 BANGKOK 2m
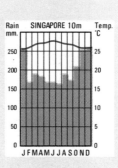 SINGAPORE 10m
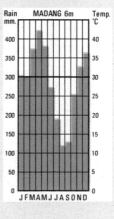 MADANG 6m
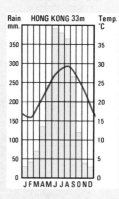 TOKYO 6m
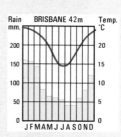 HONG KONG 33m
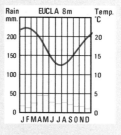 BRISBANE 42m
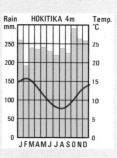 EUCLA 8m
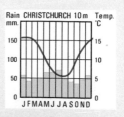 CHRISTCHURCH 10m
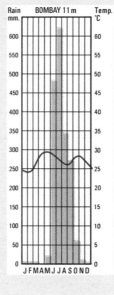 ALICE SPRINGS 579m
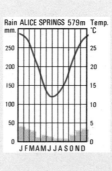 DARWIN 30m
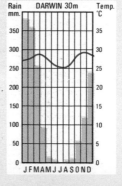 HOKITIKA 4m
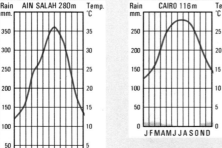 AIN SALAH, CAIRO, TASHKENT
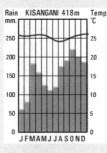 ACCRA
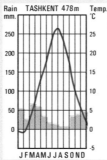 KISANGANI, ADDIS ABABA
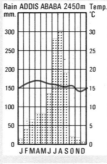 BEIRA
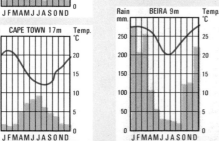 CAPE TOWN, DURBAN, ADELAIDE
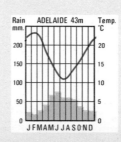 ADELAIDE
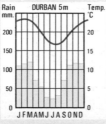

STRUCTURAL REGIONS

- Pre-Cambrian shield (exposed)
- Old fold mountains (Hercynian & Caledonian)
- Young fold mountains (Mesozoic & Alpine)
- Sedimentary basins (Tertiary & Quaternary)
- Permanent ice cap

Ocean depths
Metres
0
Continental shelf
200
4000
7000

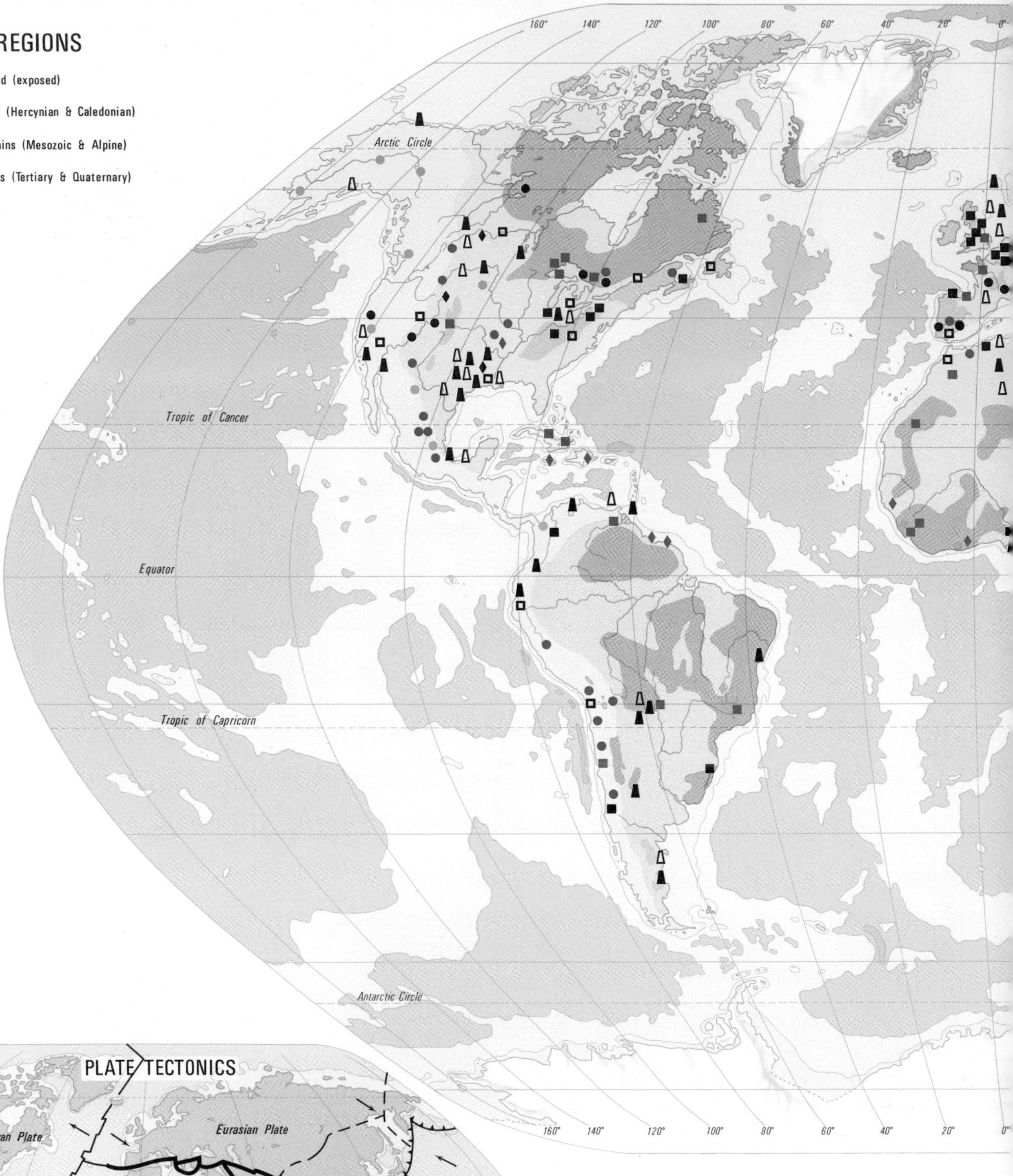

160°
140°
120°
100°
80°
60°
40°
20°
0°
Arctic Circle
Tropic of Cancer
Equator
Tropic of Capricorn
Antarctic Circle

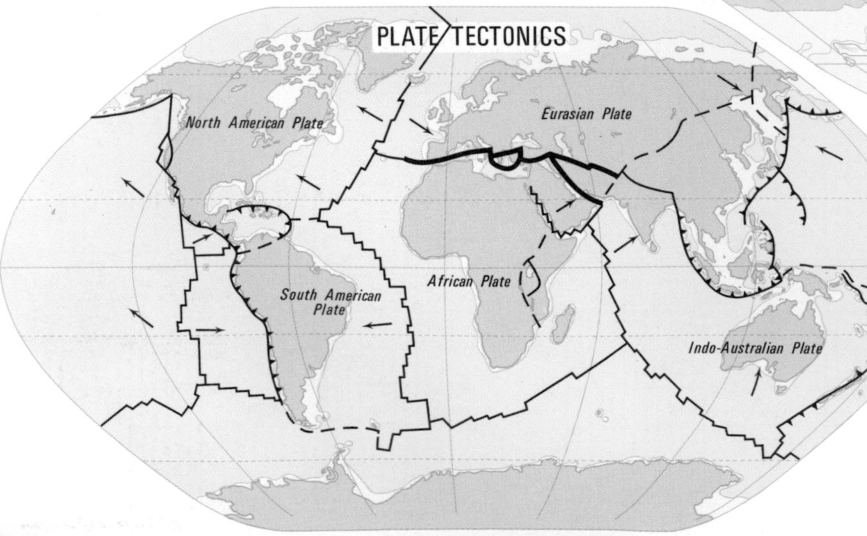

PLATE TECTONICS
North American Plate
Eurasian Plate
African Plate
South American Plate
Indo-Australian Plate

- Continental shelf
- Spreading ridge offset by faults
- Direction of plate movement
- Subduction zone
- Collision zone
- Uncertain plate boundary

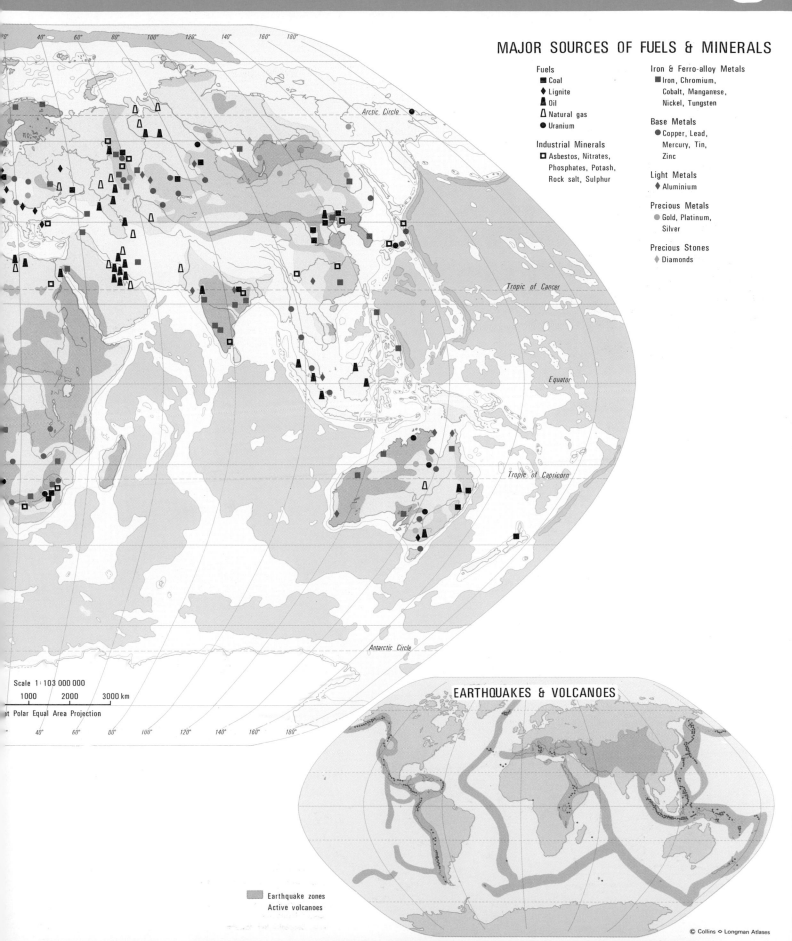

MAJOR SOURCES OF FUELS & MINERALS

Fuels
- ■ Coal
- ◆ Lignite
- ▲ Oil
- △ Natural gas
- ● Uranium

Industrial Minerals
- ☐ Asbestos, Nitrates, Phosphates, Potash, Rock salt, Sulphur

Iron & Ferro-alloy Metals
- ■ Iron, Chromium, Cobalt, Manganese, Nickel, Tungsten

Base Metals
- ● Copper, Lead, Mercury, Tin, Zinc

Light Metals
- ◆ Aluminium

Precious Metals
- ● Gold, Platinum, Silver

Precious Stones
- ◆ Diamonds

Arctic Circle

Tropic of Cancer

Equator

Tropic of Capricorn

Antarctic Circle

Scale 1:103 000 000
1000 2000 3000 km

Polar Equal Area Projection

EARTHQUAKES & VOLCANOES

Earthquake zones
Active volcanoes

© Collins ◇ Longman Atlases

ARCTIC O

Greenland

ARCTIC

Arctic Circle

Hudson
Bay

Canadian Shield

London North European P
Katowic
Ruhr

Seattle

Rocky Mountains
Great
Basin

Great Plains

Chicago Detroit

Boston
New York

St. Lawrence

San Francisco
Los Angeles

Washington-
Philadelphia

Mississippi

Mediterranean

Alps

Da

Atlas Mts

Tropic of Cancer

20°

ATLANTIC

Sahara

Niger

Caribbean Sea

OCEAN

Futa
Jalon
Plateau

Lagos
Accra
Gulf of
Guinea

Co
Ba

Equator

Llanos

Guiana
Highlands

PACIFIC

Amazon

Selvas

Kinshasa

OCEAN

Andes

Atacama Desert

Mato Grosso
Upland

Brazilian
Highlands

Rio de
Janeiro

Tropic of Capricorn

Pampas

Buenos Aires

Cape Town

Little or no activity

PREDOMINANT SUBSISTENCE ECONOMY

Gathering, hunting and fishing

Traditional cultivation

Shifting

Bush fallowing

Semi-intensive sedentary

Intensive cropping (rice dominant)

Intensive cropping (other crop dominant)

Traditional pastoralism

Nomadic herding (cattle,
reindeer in Eurasian Tundra)

Nomadic herding (sheep, goats)

Non-nomadic (cattle)

Non-nomadic (sheep, goats)

Areas of mixed econom

Patagonia

Scale 1:72 500 000

0   500   1000   1500   2000   2500   3000 km

Winkel Projection

40° · 60° · 80° · 100° · 120° · 140° · 160° · 180° · 160°

AN

West
Ob
Siberian
Plain

Ural Mts

Novosibirsk

Moscow
Central
Russian
Uplands

Black Earth
Donbass

Kirghiz Steppe

Caspian Sea

Black Sea

Tashkent

Iranian
Plateau

*Tibetan
Plateau*

Gobi

Huang He

North
China
Plain

Sea
of
Japan

Osaka

Tokyo

P A C I F I C

Cairo

Himalaya

Punjab

Indus

Delhi

Ganges

Red
Basin

Chang Jiang

Calcutta

Rub al Khali

Arabian Sea

Bay of
Bengal

South
China
Sea

O C E A N

Nile

Ethiopian
Highlands

Nairobi

Madagascar

Zambezi

I N D I A N   O C E A N

Singapore

Pretoria
Johannesburg

PREDOMINANT COMMERCIAL ECONOMY

Intensive cultivation

Grain

Large-scale specialised (plantation)

Specialised (horticulture,
market gardening)

Livestock rearing

Extensive (cattle)

Extensive (sheep)

Intensive (cattle)

Intensive (sheep)

Intensive dairying

Lumbering

Fishing

Manufacturing/service
industry

Extractive industry

Great Sandy
Desert

Great
Artesian
Basin

Great Victoria
Desert

Darling

Murray

Newcastle-
Sydney

Melbourne-
Geelong

Wellington

wn by banding

© Collins ◇ Longman Atlases

© Collins ◇ Longman Atlases

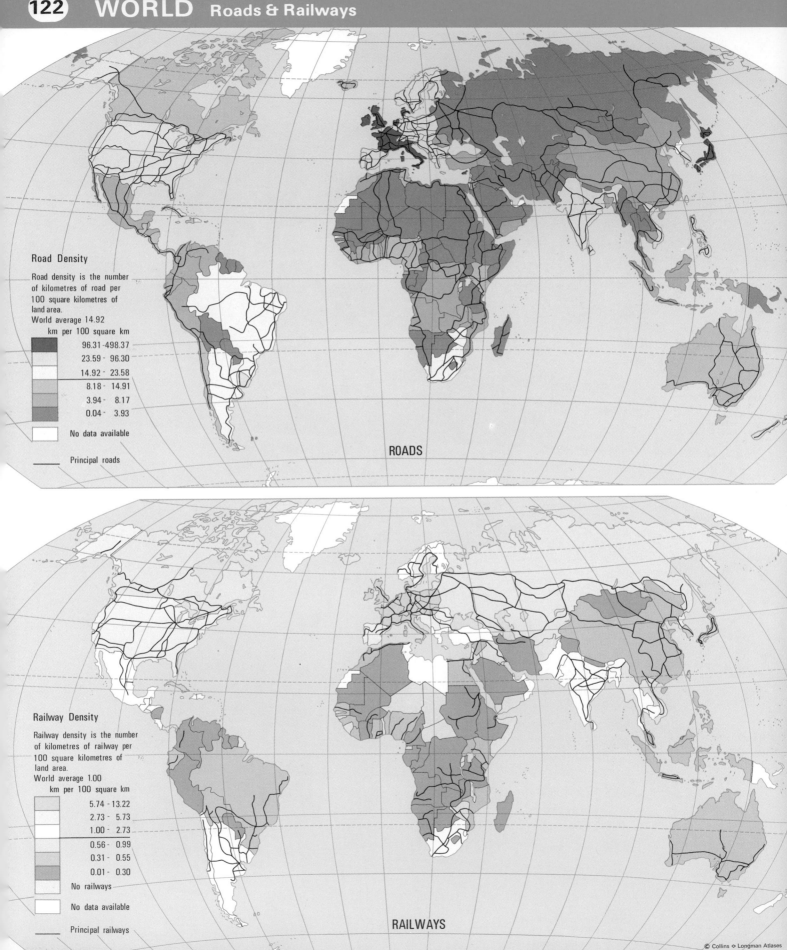

Road Density

Road density is the number
of kilometres of road per
100 square kilometres of
land area.
World average 14.92
    km per 100 square km

- 96.31 - 498.37
- 23.59 - 96.30
- 14.92 - 23.58
- 8.18 - 14.91
- 3.94 - 8.17
- 0.04 - 3.93

No data available

Principal roads

ROADS

Railway Density

Railway density is the number
of kilometres of railway per
100 square kilometres of
land area.
World average 1.00
    km per 100 square km

- 5.74 - 13.22
- 2.73 - 5.73
- 1.00 - 2.73
- 0.56 - 0.99
- 0.31 - 0.55
- 0.01 - 0.30

No railways

No data available

Principal railways

RAILWAYS

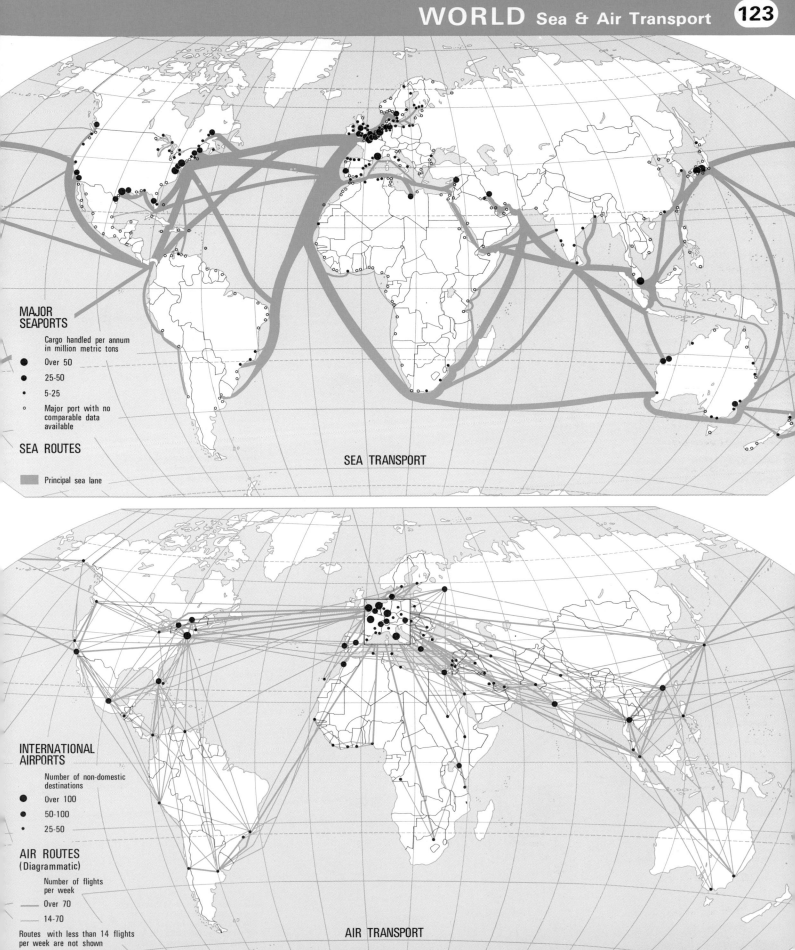

MAJOR SEAPORTS

Cargo handled per annum in million metric tons

● Over 50

● 25-50

• 5-25

○ Major port with no comparable data available

SEA ROUTES

▬ Principal sea lane

SEA TRANSPORT

INTERNATIONAL AIRPORTS

Number of non-domestic destinations

● Over 100

● 50-100

• 25-50

AIR ROUTES
(Diagrammatic)

Number of flights per week

— Over 70

— 14-70

Routes with less than 14 flights per week are not shown

AIR TRANSPORT

FOOD CROPS

Production

Percentage of total
World production

25
10
5

Wheat
Maize
Rice

Exports

Percentage of World exports by product
(Only exports >2% World total are shown)

1mm - 10%   eg:- 50%

Wheat (unmilled)
Maize (unmilled)
Rice

Canada
U.S.A.
Mexico
E.E.C.
Hungary
Romania
Spain
Yugoslavia
Turkey
Egypt
Iran
Pakistan
U.S.S.R.
China
Bangladesh
Burma
India
Thailand
Vietnam
South Korea
Japan
Philippines
Indonesia
Australia
Brazil
South Africa
Argentina

Intercontinental trade only is shown except
where international trade is significant.
Flow lines indicate direction of trade and
not necessarily trade routes. No data
on trade for USSR and China is available.

BEVERAGES

Production

Percentage of
total World production

25
10
5

Cocoa (Cocoa Beans)
Tea
Coffee

Exports

Percentage of World exports by product
(Only exports >2% World total are shown)

1mm - 10%   eg:- 50%

Cocoa
Tea & Maté
Coffee

Sweden
E.E.C.
U.S.A.
U.S.S.R.
Turkey
Egypt
Iraq
Pakistan
Japan
China
Mexico
Guatemala
El Salvador
Costa Rica
Dominican Republic
Colombia
Ivory Coast
Ghana
Nigeria
Ethiopia
Cameroon
Uganda
Kenya
India
Bangladesh
Sri Lanka
Ecuador
Angola
Madagascar
Indonesia
Papua New Guinea
Brazil
Australia

Intercontinental trade only is shown except
where international trade is significant.
Flow lines indicate direction of trade and
not necessarily trade routes. No data
on trade for USSR and China is available.

© Collins ◇ Longman Atlases

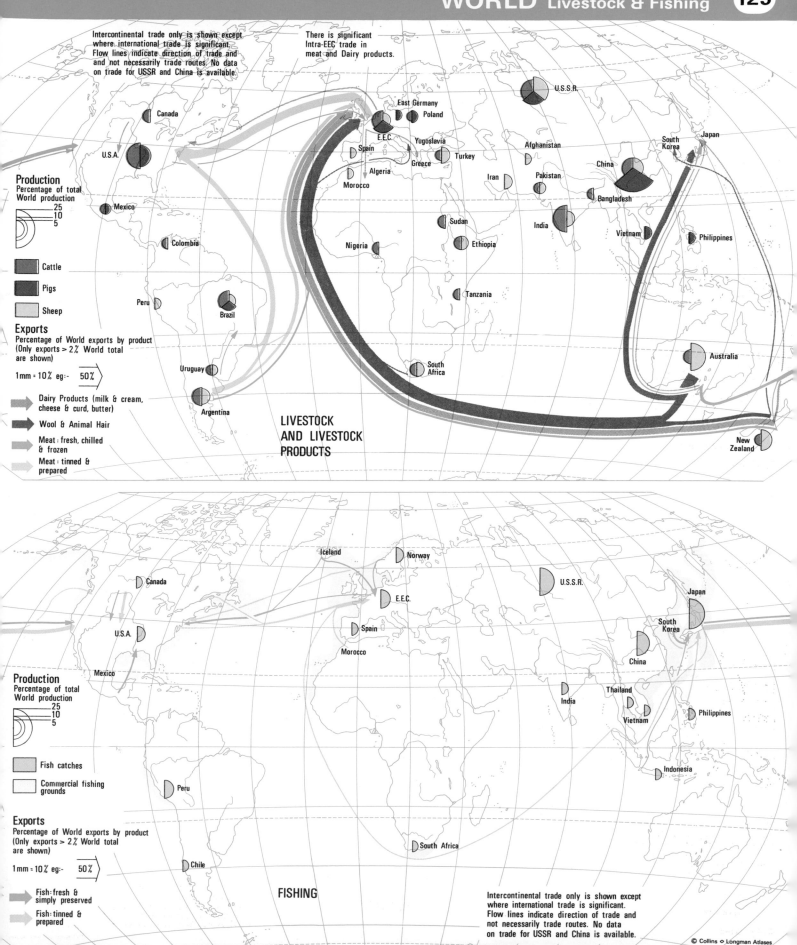

Intercontinental trade only is shown except where international trade is significant. Flow lines indicate direction of trade and and not necessarily trade routes. No data on trade for USSR and China is available.

There is significant Intra-EEC trade in meat and Dairy products.

Production
Percentage of total World production
25
10
5

■ Cattle
■ Pigs
□ Sheep

Exports
Percentage of World exports by product
(Only exports > 2% World total are shown)

1mm = 10% eg:- 50%

➤ Dairy Products (milk & cream, cheese & curd, butter)

➤ Wool & Animal Hair

➤ Meat : fresh, chilled & frozen

➤ Meat : tinned & prepared

LIVESTOCK AND LIVESTOCK PRODUCTS

Canada
U.S.A.
Mexico
Colombia
Peru
Brazil
Uruguay
Argentina

East Germany
Poland
E.E.C.
Spain
Yugoslavia
Greece
Turkey
Algeria
Morocco
Nigeria
Sudan
Ethiopia
Tanzania
South Africa
Afghanistan
Iran
Pakistan
India
Bangladesh
U.S.S.R.
China
Vietnam
South Korea
Japan
Philippines
Australia
New Zealand

Production
Percentage of total World production
25
10
5

□ Fish catches
□ Commercial fishing grounds

Exports
Percentage of World exports by product
(Only exports > 2% World total are shown)

1mm = 10% eg:- 50%

➤ Fish: fresh & simply preserved

➤ Fish: tinned & prepared

FISHING

Iceland
Norway
Canada
E.E.C.
U.S.A.
Spain
Morocco
Mexico
Peru
Chile
South Africa
U.S.S.R.
China
India
Thailand
Vietnam
Japan
South Korea
Philippines
Indonesia

Intercontinental trade only is shown except where international trade is significant. Flow lines indicate direction of trade and not necessarily trade routes. No data on trade for USSR and China is available.

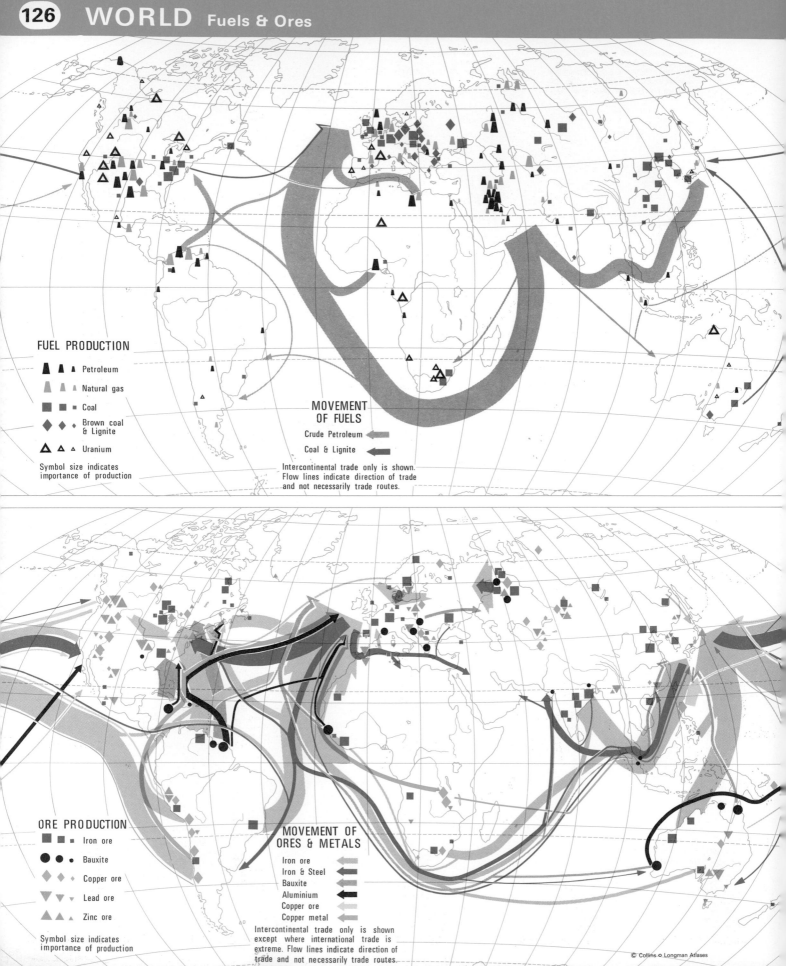

FUEL PRODUCTION

▲ ▲ ▴ Petroleum
▲ ▲ ▴ Natural gas
■ ■ ▪ Coal
◆ ◆ ◆ Brown coal & Lignite
△ △ △ Uranium

Symbol size indicates importance of production

MOVEMENT OF FUELS

Crude Petroleum ⬅
Coal & Lignite ⬅

Intercontinental trade only is shown. Flow lines indicate direction of trade and not necessarily trade routes.

ORE PRODUCTION

■ ■ ▪ Iron ore
● ● • Bauxite
◆ ◆ ◆ Copper ore
▼ ▼ ▾ Lead ore
▲ ▲ ▴ Zinc ore

Symbol size indicates importance of production

MOVEMENT OF ORES & METALS

Iron ore ⬅
Iron & Steel ⬅
Bauxite ⬅
Aluminium ⬅
Copper ore ⬅
Copper metal ⬅

Intercontinental trade only is shown except where international trade is extreme. Flow lines indicate direction of trade and not necessarily trade routes.

© Collins ○ Longman Atlases

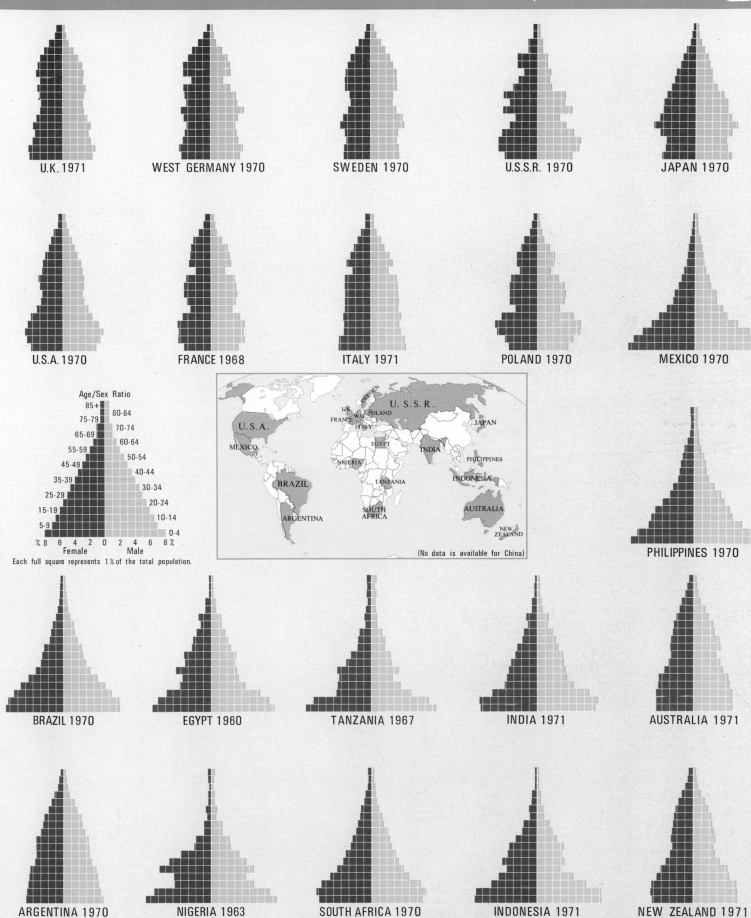

U.K. 1971

WEST GERMANY 1970

SWEDEN 1970

U.S.S.R. 1970

JAPAN 1970

U.S.A. 1970

FRANCE 1968

ITALY 1971

POLAND 1970

MEXICO 1970

Age/Sex Ratio

Female		Male
	85+	
75-79		80-84
65-69		70-74
55-59		60-64
45-49		50-54
35-39		40-44
25-29		30-34
15-19		20-24
5-9		10-14
		0-4

% 8 6 4 2 0 2 4 6 8 %
Female   Male

Each full square represents 1% of the total population.

(No data is available for China)

PHILIPPINES 1970

BRAZIL 1970

EGYPT 1960

TANZANIA 1967

INDIA 1971

AUSTRALIA 1971

ARGENTINA 1970

NIGERIA 1963

SOUTH AFRICA 1970

INDONESIA 1971

NEW ZEALAND 1971

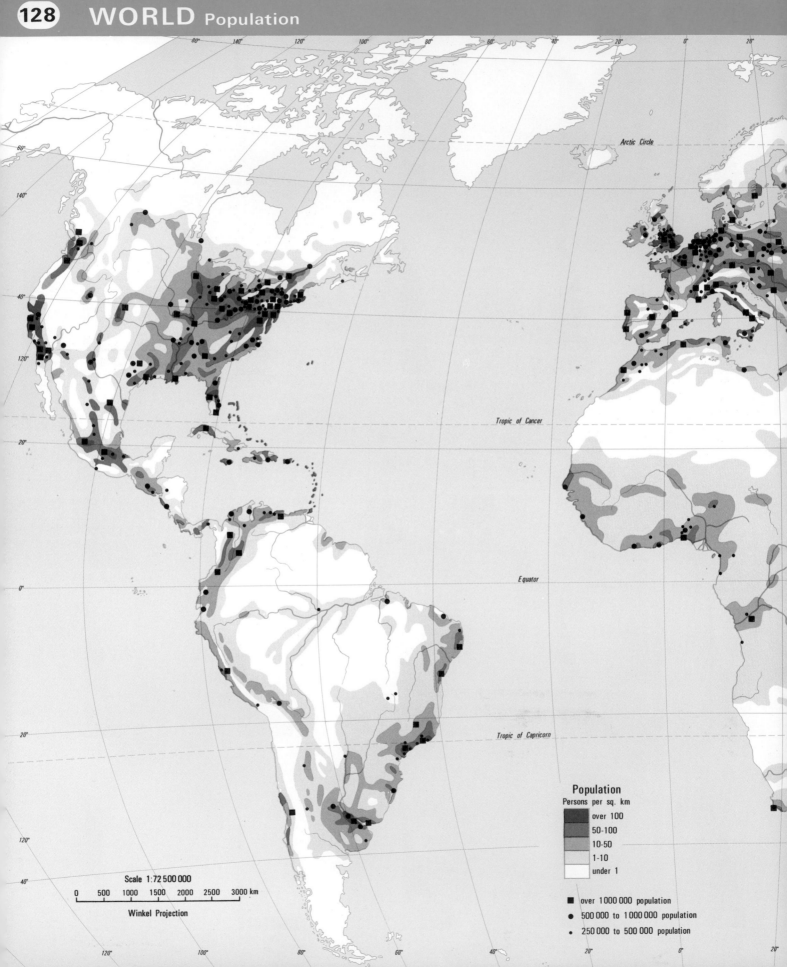

Arctic Circle

Tropic of Cancer

Equator

Tropic of Capricorn

Population
Persons per sq. km

- over 100
- 50-100
- 10-50
- 1-10
- under 1

■ over 1 000 000 population

● 500 000 to 1 000 000 population

• 250 000 to 500 000 population

Scale 1:72 500 000

0   500   1000 1500 2000 2500 3000 km

Winkel Projection

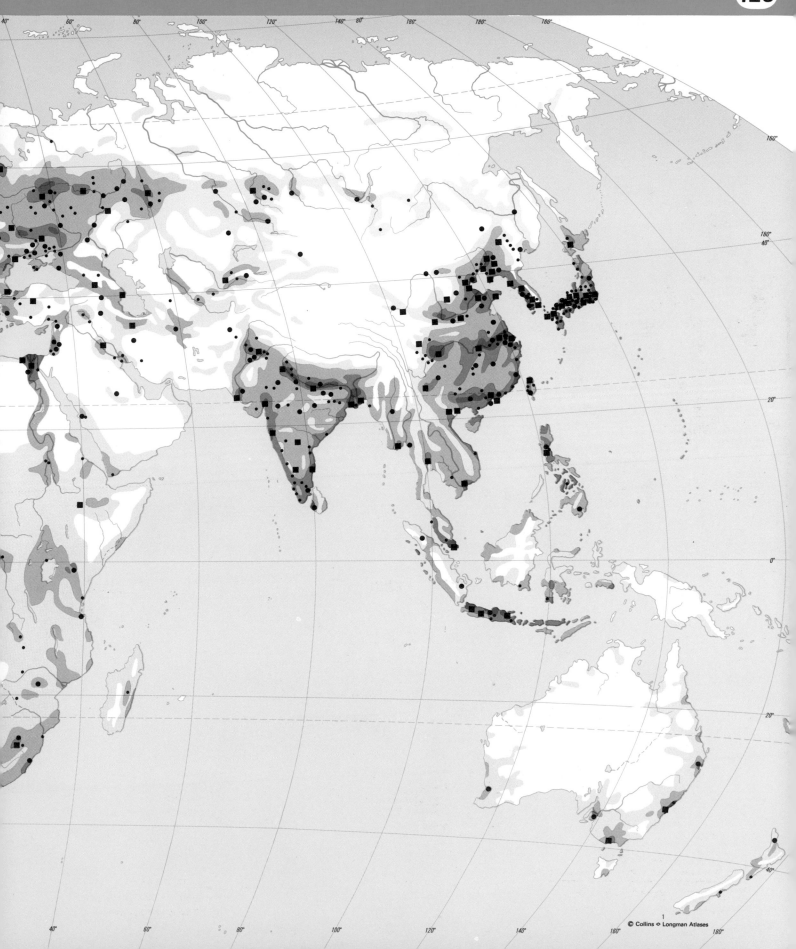

© Collins ◇ Longman Atlases

A. : AUSTRIA
BELG. : BELGIUM
CZECH. : CZECHOSLOVAKIA
D. : DJIBOUTI
E. GER. : EAST GERMANY
H. : HUNGARY
L. : LUXEMBOURG
MAL. : MALAŴI
NETH. : NETHERLANDS
ROM. : ROMANIA
SWITZ. : SWITZERLAND
YUGO. : YUGOSLAVIA

OCEAN

Arctic Circle

160°

Aleutian Is.
(U.S.A.)

○ Arkhangel'sk

UNION OF SOVIET SOCIALIST REPUBLICS

Leningrad

⊠ Gorki   ⊠ Sverdlovsk   ⊠ Novosibirsk
Minsk Moscow   Omsk
w ⊠ Kiev   Kharkov
Odessa   Aral
⊠ Bucharest   Sea
GARIA Black Sea   ⊠ Tashkent
Istanbul   ⊠ Baku   Caspian Sea
⊠ Ankara
TURKEY

40°   180°

Ulan Bator ◎
MONGOLIA

Shenyang ⊠   NORTH
KOREA
Peking ⊠   ⊠ Pyongyang
⊠ Seoul
SOUTH
KOREA

JAPAN
⊠ Tokyo
Osaka

PACIFIC

CHINA

CYPRUS
LEBANON   ⊠ Tehran   KASHMIR
A SYRIA Iraq   Kabul ◎
ISRAEL JORDAN Baghdad ⊠ IRAN AFGHANI-
Cairo ⊠   STAN   ◎ Islamabad
EGYPT   Lahore ⊠
KUWAIT   PAKISTAN   Delhi ⊠
BAHRAIN   New Delhi
SAUDI QATAR Karachi ⊠   NEPAL
Riyadh ◎ UNITED ARAB ○ Muscat   Katmandu ◎ BHUTAN
ARABIA EMIRATES   Ahmadabad ⊠ INDIA
◎ Mecca   OMAN

Chongqing   Nanjing
Wuhan ⊠ ⊠ Shanghai

⊠ Taipei
TAIWAN
(FORMOSA)
Tropic of Cancer

Canton
⊠ Victoria
HONG KONG
(U.K.)

20°

Mariana Is.
(U.S.A.)

Bombay ⊠
Khartoum ○ Sana SOUTHERN YEMEN
SUDAN YEMEN Aden
D.

Addis Ababa
ETHIOPIA

Dacca ⊠
BANGLA-
DESH BURMA Hanoi ⊠

Hyderabad ⊠
Rangoon ⊠ Vientiane ○
LAOS VIETNAM
THAI-
LAND
Bangkok ⊠
Madras ⊠ Andaman Is. CAMBODIA
(Ind.) Phnom Penh ○
Ho Chi
Minh City

OCEAN

Lakshadweep Is.
(Ind.)

SRI
LANKA
Colombo ◎

Nicobar Is.
(Ind.)

○ Quezon City
⊠ Manila
PHILIPPINES

Caroline Is.
(U.S.A.)

UGANDA
KENYA
◎ Kampala
● Nairobi
RWANDA
BURUNDI
TANZANIA

SOMALI REPUBLIC
○ Mogadishu

SEYCHELLES

MALDIVE
ISLANDS

BRUNEI
Kuala Lumpur ◎ MALAYSIA
● Singapore
SINGAPORE

Equator   0°

INDONESIA

Amirantes
(U.K.)
● Dar es Salaam

PAPUA
NEW GUINEA

SOLOMON
IS

AMBIA MAL.
aka ● Lilongwe
isbury MOÇAMBIQUE
ZIMBABWE
(RHODESIA)

MADAGASCAR
○ Tananarive

MAURITIUS

INDIAN   OCEAN

Jakarta ⊠ ⊠ Surabaya

Christmas I.
(Austl.)

Cocos Is.
(Austl.)

20°
New Caledonia
(Fr.)
Tropic of Capricorn

NA
● Gaborone
● Pretoria
● Maputo
SWAZILAND
Johannesburg
● Durban
RICA

AUSTRALIA

● Brisbane

Scale 1:72 500 000

0 500 1000 1500 2000 2500 3000 km

Winkel Projection

Prince Edward Is.
(S. Africa)

Crozet Is.
(Fr.)

Kerguelen
(Fr.)

St. Paul Amsterdam I.
(Fr.) (Fr.)

Perth ◎

● Adelaide ⊠ Sydney
◎ Canberra
⊠ Melbourne
NEW
ZEALAND

Auckland ○

Wellington ◎

40°
180°

40° 60° 80° 100° 120° 140° 160° 180°
© Collins ◇ Longman Atlases

Heard I.
(Austl.)

| A.M. | | | | | | | | | | | Noon | | P.M. | | | | | | | | | | Midnight | A. |

| 1.00 | 2.00 | 3.00 | 4.00 | 5.00 | 6.00 | 7.00 | 8.00 | 9.00 | 10.00 | 11.00 | 12.00 | 13.00 | 14.00 | 15.00 | 16.00 | 17.00 | 18.00 | 19.00 | 20.00 | 21.00 | 22.00 | 23.00 | 24.00 |

| 165° | 150° | 135° | 120° | 105° | 90° | 75° | 60° | 45° | 30° | 15° | 0° | 15° | 30° | 45° | 60° | 75° | 90° | 105° | 120° | 135° | 150° | 165° | 180° |

Greenwich Meridian

8.30

19.00

15.00 16.00 17.00 18.00 19.00 21.00 22.00 23.00 24.00

1.00 (Tuesday)

Monday Sunday

20.00

20.30

6.15

15.30 16.30

7.30 8.15 8.20

15.30 17.30

Equator 18.30

International Date Line

Equator

23.30

1.30 19.30

18.30

1.00 (Tuesday)

30° 21.30 23.30

Monday Sunday

8.30

0.15 (Tuesday)

TIME ZONES

Monday Noon

| 1.00 | 2.00 | 3.00 | 4.00 | 5.00 | 6.00 | 7.00 | 8.00 | 9.00 | 10.00 | 11.00 | 12.00 | 13.00 | 14.00 | 15.00 | 16.00 | 17.00 | 18.00 | 19.00 | 20.00 | 21.00 | 22.00 | 23.00 | 24.00 |

The Earth turns through 360°, one complete revolution, in 24 hours so each hour it turns through 15°. The surface of the Earth is divided into 24 Time Zones each of 15° longitude or 1 hour of time. The times shown for each zone are the standard times kept on land and sea when it is 12 noon on the Greenwich Meridian. Daylight saving time observed by certain countries for part of the year is not shown.

Standard Time Zones time

Less than half hour difference from Standard Time Zone time

Half hour difference from Standard Time Zone time

1 hour in advance of Standard Time Zone time

| 150° | 120° | 90° | 60° | 30° | 0° | 30° | 60° | 90° | 120° | 150° | 180° |

60°

30°

Equator Equator

30°

INTERNATIONAL ORGANIZATIONS

Independent countries not represented
in the United Nations on 1st. January 1978
N.Korea, S.Korea, Switzerland, Taiwan

Organization of American States (O.A.S.)

Organization of African Unity (O.A.U.)

The Commonwealth

Council for Mutual Economic Aid (COMECON)

Organization of Petroleum Exporting Countries (OPEC)

European Free Trade Association (E.F.T.A.)

European Economic Community (E.E.C.)

© Collins ◇ Longman Atlases

INDEX

All names in the atlas, except for some of those on the thematic maps, will be found in this index, printed in bold type. Each entry indicates the country or region of the world in which the name is located. This is followed by the number of the most appropriate page on which the name appears—generally the largest scale map. Lastly the latitude and longitude is given. Where the name applies to a very large area of the map these co-ordinates are sometimes omitted. For names that do apply to an area the reference is to the centre of the feature, which will usually also be the position of the name. In the case of rivers the mouth or confluence is always taken as the point of reference. Therefore it is necessary to follow the river upstream from this point to find its name on the map.

Towns listed in the index are not described as such unless the name could be misleading. Thus Whitley Bay is followed by 'town' in italic. Elsewhere, when the name itself does not indicate clearly what it is, a description is always added in italic immediately after. These descriptions have had to be abbreviated in many cases.

Abbreviations used in the index are explained below.

Abbreviations

Afghan.	Afghanistan	*mts.*, **Mts.**	mountains, Mountains
Bangla.	Bangladesh	Neth.	Netherlands
b., **B.**	bay, Bay	N. Ireland	Northern Ireland
Beds.	Bedfordshire	Northants.	Northamptonshire
Berks.	Berkshire	Northum.	Northumberland
Bucks.	Buckinghamshire	N. Korea	North Korea
Cambs.	Cambridgeshire	N. Yorks.	North Yorkshire
c., **C.**	cape, Cape	Notts.	Nottinghamshire
C.A.E.	Central African Empire	Oxon.	Oxfordshire
Czech.	Czechoslovakia	P.N.G.	Papua New Guinea
d.	internal division eg. county, region, state	*pen.*, **Pen.**	peninsula, Peninsula
Derbys.	Derbyshire	Phil.	Philippines
des.	desert	**Pt.**	Point
Dom. Rep.	Dominican Republic	*r.*, **R.**	river, River
D. and G.	Dumfries and Galloway	Rep. of Ire.	Republic of Ireland
E. Germany	East Germany	R.S.A.	Republic of South Africa
E. Sussex	East Sussex	**Resr.**	Reservoir
Equat. Guinea	Equatorial Guinea	Somali Rep.	Somali Republic
est.	estuary	**Sd.**	Sound
f.	physical feature eg. valley, plain, geographic district or region	S. Yemen	Southern Yemen
		S.G.	South Glamorgan
Glos.	Gloucestershire	S. Korea	South Korea
G.L.	Greater London	S. Yorks.	South Yorkshire
G.M.	Greater Manchester	Staffs.	Staffordshire
g. **G.**	Gulf	*str.*, **Str.**	strait, Strait
Hants.	Hampshire	Strath.	Strathclyde
H. and W.	Hereford and Worcester	Switz.	Switzerland
Herts.	Hertfordshire	T. and W.	Tyne and Wear
Humber.	Humberside	U.A.E.	United Arab Emirates
i., **I.**, *is.*, **Is.**	island, Island, islands, Islands	U.S.S.R.	Union of Soviet Socialist Republics
I.o.M.	Isle of Man	U.K.	United Kingdom
I.o.W.	Isle of Wight	U.S.A.	United States of America
l., **L.**	lake, Lake	U. Volta	Upper Volta
Lancs.	Lancashire	Warwicks.	Warwickshire
Leics.	Leicestershire	W. Germany	West Germany
Liech.	Liechtenstein	W.G.	West Glamorgan
Lincs.	Lincolnshire	W. Isles	Western Isles
Lux.	Luxembourg	W. Midlands	West Midlands
Mersey.	Merseyside	W. Sahara	Western Sahara
M.G.	Mid Glamorgan	W. Sussex	West Sussex
Mt.	Mount	W. Yorks.	West Yorkshire
mtn., **Mtn.**	mountain, Mountain	Wilts.	Wiltshire
		Yugo.	Yugoslavia

A

Aa *r.* France **25** 51.00N 2.06E
Aachen W. Germany **41** 50.46N 6.06E
Aalen W. Germany **40** 48.50N 10.07E
Äänekoski Finland **42** 62.36N 25.44E
Aarau Switz. **40** 47.24N 8.04E
Aardenburg Neth. **41** 51.16N 3.26E
Aare *r.* Switz. **36** 47.03N 7.18E
Aarschot Belgium **41** 50.59N 4.50E
Aba Nigeria **73** 5.06N 7.21E
Abadan Iran **55** 30.21N 48.15E
Abadan I. Iran **55** 30.10N 48.30E
Abadeh Iran **55** 31.10N 52.40E
Abadla Algeria **70** 31.01N 2.45W
Abakaliki Nigeria **73** 6.17N 8.04E
Abakan U.S.S.R. **45** 53.43N 91.25E
Abashiri wan *b.* Japan **64** 44.02N 144.17E
Abaya, L. Ethiopia **71** 6.20N 38.00E
Abbeville France **36** 50.06N 1.51E
Abbeyfeale Rep. of Ire. **35** 52.23N 9.18W
Abbeyleix Rep. of Ire. **35** 52.55N 7.22W
Abbey Town England **28** 54.50N 3.18W
Abbotsbury England **24** 50.40N 2.36W
Abbots Langley England **23** 51.43N 0.25W
Abéché Chad **71** 13.49N 20.49E
Abengourou Ivory Coast **72** 6.42N 3.27W
Åbenrå Denmark **42** 55.03N 9.26E
Abeokuta Nigeria **73** 7.10N 3.26E
Aberayron Wales **26** 52.15N 4.16W
Abercarn Wales **27** 51.39N 3.09W
Aberdare Wales **27** 51.43N 3.27W
Aberdare Range *mts.* Kenya **75** 0.20S 36.40E
Aberdaron Wales **26** 52.48N 4.41W
Aberdeen Scotland **33** 57.08N 2.07W
Aberdeen S. Dak. U.S.A. **96** 45.28N 98.30W
Aberdeen Wash. U.S.A. **96** 46.58N 123.49W
Aberdovey Wales **26** 52.33N 4.03W
Aberfan Wales **27** 51.42N 3.20W
Aberfeldy Scotland **31** 56.37N 3.54W
Aberffraw Wales **26** 53.11N 4.28W
Aberfoyle Scotland **30** 56.11N 4.23W
Abergavenny Wales **26** 51.49N 3.01W
Abergele Wales **26** 53.17N 3.34W
Abernethy Scotland **31** 56.20N 3.19W
Aberporth Wales **26** 52.08N 4.33W
Abersoch Wales **26** 52.50N 4.31W
Abersychan Wales **24** 51.44N 3.03W
Abertillery Wales **27** 51.44N 3.09W
Aberystwyth Wales **26** 52.25N 4.06W
Ab-i-Diz *r.* Iran **55** 31.38N 48.54E
Abidjan Ivory Coast **72** 5.19N 4.01W
Abilene U.S.A. **96** 32.27N 99.45W
Abingdon England **24** 51.40N 1.17W
Abington Scotland **31** 55.29N 3.42W
Abitibi *r.* Canada **97** 51.15N 81.30W
Abitibi, L. Canada **99** 48.40N 79.35W
Abomey Benin **73** 7.14N 2.00E
Abou Deia Chad **73** 11.20N 19.20E
Aboyne Scotland **33** 57.05N 2.48W
Abqaiq Saudi Arabia **55** 25.55N 49.40E
Abrantes Portugal **37** 39.28N 8.12W
Abridge England **23** 51.40N 0.08E
Abu Dhabi U.A.E. **55** 24.27N 54.23E
Abu Hamed Sudan **71** 19.32N 33.20E
Abu Simbel Egypt **54** 22.18N 31.40E
Abu Tig Egypt **54** 27.06N 31.17E
Abu Zenîma Egypt **54** 29.03N 33.06E
Acámbaro Mexico **100** 20.01N 101.42W
Acapulco Mexico **100** 16.51N 99.56W
Acarigua Venezuela **101** 9.35N 69.12W
Acatlán Mexico **100** 18.12N 98.02W
Accra Ghana **72** 5.33N 0.15W
Accrington England **28** 53.46N 2.22W
Achahoish Scotland **30** 55.57N 5.30W
à Chairn Bhain, Loch Scotland **32** 58.16N 5.05W
Achill Head Rep. of Ire. **34** 53.59N 10.15W
Achill I. Rep. of Ire. **34** 53.57N 10.00W
Achill Sound *town* Rep. of Ire. **34** 53.56N 9.56W
Achinsk U.S.S.R. **44** 56.10N 90.10E
Achnasheen Scotland **32** 57.34N 5.05W
A'Chràlaig *mtn.* Scotland **32** 57.11N 5.09W
Acklin's I. Bahamas **101** 22.30N 74.10W
Ackworth Moor Top *town* England **29** 53.39N 1.20W
Aconcagua, Mt. Argentina **109** 32.37S 70.00W
Acqui Italy **38** 44.41N 8.28E
Acton England **23** 51.31N 0.17W
Adamantina Brazil **110** 21.41S 51.04W
Adamawa Highlands Nigeria/Cameroon **73** 7.05N 12.00E
Adams, Mt. U.S.A. **96** 46.13N 121.29W
Adana Turkey **54** 37.00N 35.19E
Adapazari Turkey **54** 40.45N 30.23E
Adare Rep. of Ire. **35** 52.33N 8.48W
Adda *r.* Italy **36** 45.08N 9.55E
Ad Dahana *des.* Saudi Arabia **55** 26.00N 47.00E
Adderbury England **24** 52.01N 1.19W
Addis Ababa Ethiopia **71** 9.03N 38.42E

Ad Diwaniya Iraq **55** 31.59N 44.57E
Addlestone England **23** 51.22N 0.31W
Adelaide Australia **83** 34.56S 138.36E
Adélie Coast Antarctica **111** 80.00S 140.00E
Aden S. Yemen **71** 12.50N 45.00E
Aden, G. of Indian Oc. **71** 13.00N 50.00E
Adi *i.* Asia **59** 4.10S 133.10E
Adige *r.* Italy **38** 45.10N 12.20E
Adirondack Mts. U.S.A. **99** 44.00N 74.15W
Adiyaman Turkey **54** 37.46N 38.15E
Adlington England **28** 53.37N 2.36W
Adour *r.* France **36** 43.28N 1.35W
Adrano Italy **38** 37.39N 14.49E
Adrar des Iforas *mts.* Algeria **73** 20.00N 2.30E
Adrian U.S.A. **98** 41.55N 84.01W
Adraskand *r.* Afghan. **55** 33.17N 62.08E
Adriatic Sea Med. Sea **38** 42.30N 16.00E
Adur *r.* England **25** 50.50N 0.16W
Aduwa Ethiopia **71** 14.12N 38.56E
Adwick le Street England **29** 53.35N 1.12W
Aegean Sea Med. Sea **39** 39.00N 25.00E
Aeron *r.* Wales **26** 52.14N 4.16W
Afghanistan Asia **56** 34.00N 65.30E
Afif Saudi Arabia **54** 23.53N 42.59E
Afikpo Nigeria **73** 5.53N 7.55E
Africa **69**
Afyon Turkey **54** 38.46N 30.32E
Agadès Niger **73** 17.00N 7.56E
Agana Asia **59** 13.28N 144.45E
Agano *r.* Japan **64** 37.58N 139.02E
Agartala India **57** 23.49N 91.15E
Agboville Ivory Coast **72** 5.55N 4.15W
Agde France **37** 43.25N 3.30E
Agedabia Libya **70** 30.48N 20.15E
Agen France **36** 44.12N 0.38E
Agger *r.* W. Germany **41** 50.45N 7.06E
Aghada Rep. of Ire. **35** 51.50N 8.13W
Aghda Iran **55** 32.25N 53.38E
Aghleam Rep. of Ire. **34** 54.08N 10.06W
Agnew's Hill N. Ireland **34** 54.51N 5.59W
Agordat Ethiopia **71** 15.35N 37.55E
Agout *r.* France **37** 43.40N 1.40E
Agra India **56** 27.09N 78.00E
Agra *r.* Spain **37** 42.12N 1.43W
Agreda Spain **37** 41.51N 1.55W
Agri *r.* Italy **39** 40.13N 16.45E
Agri Turkey **54** 39.44N 43.04E
Agrigento Italy **38** 37.19N 13.36E
Agrihan *i.* Asia **59** 18.44N 145.39E
Aguascalientes Mexico **100** 21.51N 102.18W
Aguascalientes *d.* Mexico **100** 22.00N 102.00W
Agueda *r.* Spain **37** 41.00N 6.56W
Aguilar de Campóo Spain **36** 42.47N 4.15W
Aguilas Spain **37** 37.25N 1.35W
Agulhas, C. R.S.A. **76** 34.50S 20.00E
Agulhas Negras *mtn.* Brazil **109** 22.20S 44.43W
Ahaggar Mts. Algeria **73** 24.00N 5.50E
Ahar Iran **55** 38.25N 47.07E
Ahaus W. Germany **41** 52.04N 7.01E
Ahlen W. Germany **40** 51.46N 7.53E
Ahmadabad India **56** 23.03N 72.40E
Ahmadnagar India **56** 19.08N 74.48E
Ahr *r.* W. Germany **41** 50.34N 7.16E
Ahwaz Iran **55** 31.17N 48.44E
Aigun China **61** 49.40N 127.10E
Ailette *r.* France **41** 49.35N 3.09E
Ailsa Craig *i.* Scotland **30** 55.15N 5.07W
Ain *r.* France **36** 45.47N 5.12E
Aïna *r.* Gabon **74** 0.38N 12.47E
Ain Beida Algeria **38** 35.50N 7.29E
Ain Salah Algeria **70** 27.12N 2.29E
Aïn Sefra Algeria **70** 32.45N 0.35W
Aïr *mts.* Niger **73** 18.30N 8.30E
Aird Brenish *c.* Scotland **32** 58.08N 7.08W
Airdrie Scotland **31** 55.52N 3.59W
Aire *r.* England **29** 53.42N 0.54W
Aire France **36** 43.39N 0.15W
Airedale *f.* England **28** 53.56N 1.54W
Aisne *r.* France **41** 49.27N 2.51E
Aitape P.N.G. **59** 3.10S 142.17E
Aith Scotland **32** 60.17N 1.23W
Aix-en-Provence France **36** 43.31N 5.27E
Aiyina *i.* Greece **39** 37.43N 23.30E
Aizuwakamatsu Japan **64** 37.30N 139.58E
Ajaccio France **36** 41.55N 8.43E
Ajama U.A.E. **55** 25.23N 55.26E
Ajmer India **56** 26.29N 74.40E
Akaishi san *mts.* Japan **64** 35.20N 138.05E
Akashi Japan **64** 34.39N 135.00E
Akbou Algeria **38** 36.26N 4.33E
Aketi Zaire **74** 2.46N 23.51E
Akhaltsikhe U.S.S.R. **54** 41.37N 42.59E
Akhdar, Jebel *mts.* Libya **71** 32.10N 22.00E
Akhdar, Jebel *mts.* Oman **55** 23.10N 57.25E
Akhdar, Wadi *r.* Saudi Arabia **54** 28.30N 36.48E
Akheloós Greece **39** 38.20N 21.04E

Akhisar Turkey **39** 38.54N 27.49E
Akimiski I. Canada **95** 53.00N 81.20W
Akita Japan **64** 39.44N 140.05E
Akjoujt Mauritania **72** 19.44N 14.26W
Akkajaure *l.* Sweden **42** 67.40N 17.30E
Akobo *r.* Sudan/Ethiopia **71** 8.30N 33.15E
Akola India **56** 20.40N 77.02E
Akpatok I. Canada **95** 60.30N 68.30W
Akron U.S.A. **98** 41.04N 81.31W
Aksaray Turkey **54** 38.22N 34.02E
Akşehir Turkey **54** 38.22N 31.24E
Aksu China **60** 41.15N 80.15E
Aktogay U.S.S.R. **60** 46.59N 79.42E
Aktyubinsk U.S.S.R. **44** 50.16N 57.13E
Akure Nigeria **73** 7.14N 5.08E
Akureyri Iceland **42** 65.41N 18.04W
Akuse Ghana **72** 6.04N 0.12E
Akyab Burma **57** 20.09N 92.55E
Alabama *d.* U.S.A. **97** 33.00N 87.00W
Alabama *r.* U.S.A. **97** 31.05N 87.55W
Alagez U.S.S.R. **55** 40.32N 44.11E
Al Ain, Wadi *r.* Oman **55** 22.18N 55.35E
Alakol, L. U.S.S.R. **60** 46.00N 81.40E
Alakurtti U.S.S.R. **42** 67.00N 30.23E
Alamagan *i.* Asia **59** 17.35N 145.50E
Alamosa U.S.A. **96** 37.28N 105.54W
Åland Is. Finland **42** 60.20N 20.00E
Alanya Turkey **54** 36.32N 32.02E
Alaşehir Turkey **39** 38.22N 28.29E
Alaska *d.* U.S.A. **94** 65.00N 153.00W
Alaska, G. of U.S.A. **94** 58.45N 145.00W
Alaska Pen. U.S.A. **94** 56.00N 160.00W
Alaska Range *mts.* U.S.A. **94** 62.10N 152.00W
Alazan *r.* U.S.S.R. **55** 41.06N 46.40E
Albacete Spain **37** 39.00N 1.52W
Alba Iulia Romania **39** 46.04N 23.33E
Albania Europe **39** 41.00N 20.00E
Albany Australia **82** 34.57S 117.54E
Albany *r.* Canada **97** 52.10N 82.00W
Albany Ga. U.S.A. **97** 31.37N 84.10W
Albany N.Y. U.S.A. **99** 42.40N 73.49W
Albany Oreg. U.S.A. **96** 44.38N 123.07W
Albemarle Sd. U.S.A. **97** 36.10N 76.00W
Alberche *r.* Spain **37** 40.00N 4.45W
Albert France **36** 50.00N 2.40E
Alberta *d.* Canada **94** 55.00N 115.00W
Albert Canal Belgium **41** 51.00N 5.15E
Albert Nile *r.* Uganda **75** 3.30N 32.00E
Albi France **36** 43.56N 2.08E
Alboran, Isleta de Spain **37** 35.55N 3.10W
Ålborg Denmark **42** 57.03N 9.56E
Albuquerque U.S.A. **96** 35.05N 106.38W
Alburquerque Spain **37** 39.13N 6.59W
Alcácer do Sal Portugal **37** 38.22N 8.30W
Alcalá de Chisvert Spain **37** 40.19N 0.13E
Alcalá de Henares Spain **37** 40.28N 3.22W
Alcalá la Real Spain **37** 37.28N 3.55W
Alcamo Italy **38** 37.59N 12.58E
Alcañiz Spain **37** 41.03N 0.09W
Alcaudete Spain **37** 37.35N 4.05W
Alcazar de San Juan Spain **37** 39.24N 3.12W
Alcazarquiver Morocco **37** 35.01N 5.54W
Alcester England **24** 52.13N 1.52W
Alcira Spain **37** 39.10N 0.27W
Alcoy Spain **37** 38.42N 0.29W
Alcubierre, Sierra de *mts.* Spain **37** 41.40N 0.20W
Alcudia Spain **37** 39.51N 3.09E
Aldabra Is. Indian Oc. **69** 9.00S 47.00E
Aldan U.S.S.R. **45** 58.44N 125.22E
Aldan *r.* U.S.S.R. **45** 63.30N 130.00E
Aldbourne England **24** 51.28N 1.38W
Aldbrough England **29** 53.50N 0.07W
Alde *r.* England **25** 52.02N 1.28E
Aldeburgh England **25** 52.09N 1.35E
Alderney *i.* Channel Is. **27** 49.42N 2.11W
Aldershot England **23** 51.15N 0.47W
Aldridge England **24** 52.36N 1.55W
Aldsworth England **24** 51.48N 1.46W
Alegrete Brazil **110** 29.45S 55.46W
Aleksandrovsk Sakhalinskiy U.S.S.R. **45** 50.55N 142.12E
Alençon France **36** 48.25N 0.05E
Aleppo Syria **54** 36.14N 37.10E
Aleria France **36** 42.05N 9.30E
Alès France **36** 44.08N 4.05E
Alessandria Italy **36** 44.55N 8.37E
Alesund Norway **42** 62.28N 6.11E
Aleutian Is. U.S.A. **52** 57.00N 180.00
Aleutian Range *mts.* U.S.A. **94** 58.00N 156.00W
Aleutian Trench Pacific Oc. **113** 50.00N 178.00E
Alexander Archipelago *is.* U.S.A. **94** 56.30N 134.30W
Alexander Bay *town* R.S.A. **76** 28.40S 16.30E
Alexandra New Zealand **85** 45.14S 169.26E
Alexandria Egypt **54** 31.13N 29.55E
Alexandria Scotland **30** 55.59N 4.35W
Alexandria La. U.S.A. **97** 31.19N 92.29W
Alexandria Va. U.S.A. **99** 38.49N 77.06W

Alexandroúpolis Greece **39** 40.50N 25.53E
Alfaro Spain **37** 42.11N 1.45W
Alfiós r. Greece **39** 37.37N 21.27E
Alford Scotland **33** 57.14N 2.42W
Alfreton England **29** 53.06N 1.22W
Algeciras Spain **37** 36.08N 5.27W
Alger see Algiers Algeria **37**
Algeria Africa **70** 28.00N 2.00E
Al Ghadaf, Wadi r. Iraq **54** 32.54N 43.33E
Alghero Italy **38** 40.33N 8.20E
Algiers Algeria **37** 36.50N 3.00E
Algoa B. R.S.A. **76** 33.56S 26.10E
Al Hamra des. U.A.E. **55** 22.45N 55.10E
Aliákmon r. Greece **39** 40.30N 22.38E
Alicante Spain **37** 38.21N 0.29W
Alice U.S.A. **96** 27.45N 98.06W
Alice Springs town Australia **82** 23.42S 133.52E
Aligarh India **56** 27.54N 78.04E
Aligudarz Iran **55** 33.25N 49.38E
Alima r. Congo **74** 1.36S 16.35E
Alingsås Sweden **42** 57.55N 12.30E
Aliquippa U.S.A. **98** 40.38N 80.16W
Aliwal North R.S.A. **76** 30.42S 26.43E
Al Jaub f. Saudi Arabia **55** 23.00N 50.00E
Al Jauf Saudi Arabia **54** 29.49N 39.52E
Al Jazi des. Iraq **54** 35.00N 41.00E
Al Khamāsīn Saudi Arabia **71** 20.29N 44.49E
Al Khubar Saudi Arabia **55** 26.18N 50.06E
Al Khurr r. Iraq **54** 32.00N 44.15E
Alkmaar Neth. **41** 52.37N 4.44E
Al Kut Iraq **55** 32.30N 45.51E
Allagash r. U.S.A. **99** 47.08N 69.10W
Allahabad India **56** 25.57N 81.50E
Allakaket U.S.A. **94** 66.30N 152.45W
Allaqi, Wadi r. Egypt **54** 22.55N 33.02E
Al Lawz, Jebel mtn. Saudi Arabia **54** 28.40N 35.20E
Allegheny r. U.S.A. **99** 40.26N 80.00W
Allegheny Mts. U.S.A. **99** 40.00N 79.00W
Allen r. England **31** 54.58N 2.18W
Allen, Lough Rep. of Ire. **34** 54.07N 8.04W
Allentown U.S.A. **99** 40.37N 75.30W
Alleppey India **56** 9.30N 76.22E
Aller r. W. Germany **40** 52.43N 9.38E
Alliance Nebr. U.S.A. **96** 42.08N 103.00W
Alliance Ohio U.S.A. **98** 40.56N 81.06W
Allier r. France **36** 46.58N 3.04E
Alloa Scotland **31** 56.07N 3.49W
Alma U.S.A. **98** 43.23N 84.40W
Alma-Ata U.S.S.R. **60** 43.19N 76.55E
Almadén Spain **37** 38.47N 4.50W
Al Maharadh des. Saudi Arabia **55** 20.00N 52.30E
Alma Hill U.S.A. **99** 42.03N 78.01W
Almansa Spain **37** 38.52N 1.06W
Almanzor, Pico de mtn. Spain **37** 40.20N 5.22W
Almanzora r. Spain **37** 37.16N 1.49W
Almazán Spain **37** 41.29N 2.31W
Almeirim Portugal **37** 39.12N 8.37W
Almelo Neth. **41** 52.21N 6.40E
Almeria Spain **37** 36.50N 2.26W
Älmhult Sweden **42** 56.32N 14.10E
Al Mira, Wadi r. Iraq **54** 32.27N 41.21E
Almond r. Scotland **31** 56.25N 3.28W
Almuñécar Spain **37** 36.44N 3.41W
Aln r. England **31** 55.23N 1.36W
Alness Scotland **33** 57.42N 4.15W
Alnwick England **31** 55.25N 1.41W
Alor i. Indonesia **59** 8.20S 124.30E
Alor Setar Malaysia **58** 6.06N 100.23E
Alost Belgium **41** 50.57N 4.03E
Alpena U.S.A. **98** 45.04N 83.27W
Alpes Maritimes mts. France **36** 44.07N 7.08E
Alphen Neth. **41** 52.08N 4.40E
Alpine U.S.A. **96** 30.22N 103.40W
Alps mts. Europe **40** 47.00N 10.00E
Al Qurna Iraq **55** 31.00N 47.26E
Alsager England **28** 53.07N 2.20W
Alsásua Spain **37** 42.54N 2.10W
Alsh, Loch Scotland **32** 57.15N 5.36W
Alston England **28** 54.48N 2.26W
Alta Norway **42** 69.57N 23.10E
Alta r. Norway **42** 70.00N 23.15E
Altagracia Venezuela **101** 10.44N 71.30W
Altai mts. Mongolia **60** 46.30N 93.30E
Altaj Mongolia **60** 46.20N 97.00E
Altamaha r. U.S.A. **97** 31.15N 81.23W
Altamura Italy **39** 40.50N 16.32E
Altay China **60** 47.48N 88.07E
Altea Spain **37** 38.37N 0.03W
Altenburg E. Germany **40** 50.59N 12.27E
Altenkirchen W. Germany **41** 50.41N 7.40E
Al Tihama des. Saudi Arabia **54** 27.50N 35.30E
Altnaharra Scotland **33** 58.16N 4.26W
Alto Araguaia Brazil **110** 17.19S 53.10W
Alto Garcas Brazil **110** 16.57S 53.30W
Alto Molocue Moçambique **75** 15.38S 37.42E
Alton England **24** 51.08N 0.59W

Alton U.S.A. **98** 38.55N 90.10W
Altoona U.S.A. **99** 40.32N 78.23W
Altrincham England **28** 53.25N 2.21W
Altun Shan mts. China **60** 38.10N 87.50E
Al'Ula Saudi Arabia **54** 26.39N 37.58E
Alva Scotland **31** 56.09N 3.49W
Alva U.S.A. **96** 36.48N 98.40W
Alvarado Mexico **100** 18.49N 95.46W
Älvsbyn Sweden **42** 65.41N 21.00E
Al Wajh Saudi Arabia **54** 26.16N 36.28E
Al Wakrah Qatar **55** 25.09N 51.36E
Alwar India **56** 27.32N 76.35E
Alyaty U.S.S.R. **55** 39.59N 49.20E
Alyth Scotland **31** 56.38N 3.14W
Alzette r. Lux. **41** 49.52N 6.07E
Amadeus, L. Australia **82** 24.50S 131.00E
Amadi Sudan **75** 5.32N 30.20E
Amagasaki Japan **64** 34.43N 135.20E
Amami i. Japan **61** 28.20N 129.30E
Amara Iraq **55** 31.52N 47.50E
Amarillo U.S.A. **96** 35.14N 101.50W
Amaro, Monte mtn. Italy **38** 42.06N 14.04E
Amasya Turkey **54** 40.37N 35.50E
Amazon r. Brazil **108** 2.00S 50.00W
Amazon Delta f. Brazil **108** 0.00 50.00W
Ambala India **56** 30.19N 76.49E
Ambarchik U.S.S.R. **45** 69.39N 162.27E
Ambato-Boeni Madagascar **75** 16.30S 46.33E
Amberg W. Germany **40** 49.26N 11.52E
Ambergris Cay i. Belize **100** 18.00N 87.58W
Amberley England **25** 50.54N 0.33W
Amble England **31** 55.20N 1.34W
Ambleside England **28** 54.26N 2.58W
Ambon Indonesia **59** 4.50S 128.10E
Ambriz Angola **74** 7.54S 13.12E
Ameland i. Neth. **41** 53.28N 5.48E
Amersfoort Neth. **41** 52.10N 5.23E
Amersham England **23** 51.40N 0.38W
Amesbury England **24** 51.10N 1.46W
Amga U.S.S.R. **45** 60.51N 131.59E
Amga r. U.S.S.R. **45** 62.40N 135.20E
Amgun r. U.S.S.R. **45** 53.10N 139.47E
Amherst U.S.A. **99** 43.00N 78.45W
Amiata mtn. Italy **38** 42.53N 11.37E
Amiens France **36** 49.54N 2.18E
Amirantes is. Indian Oc. **131** 6.00S 52.00E
Amlwch Wales **26** 53.24N 4.21W
Amman Jordan **54** 31.57N 35.56E
Ammanford Wales **27** 51.48N 4.00W
Amol Iran **55** 36.26N 52.24E
Amorgós i. Greece **39** 36.50N 25.55E
Amos Canada **99** 48.04N 78.08W
Ampala Honduras **100** 13.16N 87.39W
Ampthill England **25** 52.03N 0.30W
Amraoti India **56** 20.58N 77.50E
Amritsar India **56** 31.35N 74.56E
Amroha India **56** 28.54N 78.14E
Amsterdam Neth. **41** 52.22N 4.54E
Amsterdam U.S.A. **99** 42.56N 74.12W
Amsterdam I. Indian Oc. **131** 37.00S 79.00E
Amu Darya r. U.S.S.R. **44** 43.50N 59.00E
Amundsen G. Canada **94** 70.30N 122.00W
Amundsen Sea Antarctica **112** 70.00S 116.00W
Amuntai Indonesia **58** 2.24S 115.14E
Amur r. U.S.S.R. **45** 53.17N 140.00E
Anabar r. U.S.S.R. **45** 72.40N 113.30E
Anadyr U.S.S.R. **45** 64.40N 177.32E
Anadyr r. U.S.S.R. **45** 65.00N 176.00E
Anadyr, G. of U.S.S.R. **45** 64.30N 177.50W
Anaiza Saudi Arabia **55** 26.05N 43.57E
Anambas Is. Indonesia **58** 3.00N 106.10E
Anambra d. Nigeria **73** 6.20N 7.25E
Anan Japan **64** 33.55N 134.39E
Anápolis Brazil **110** 16.19S 48.58W
Anar Iran **55** 30.54N 55.18E
Anatahan i. Asia **59** 16.22N 145.38E
Anatolia f. Turkey **54** 38.00N 35.00E
Anatuya Argentina **110** 28.26S 62.48W
Anchorage U.S.A. **94** 61.10N 150.00W
Ancona Italy **38** 43.37N 13.33E
Ancroft England **31** 55.42N 2.00W
Ancuabe Moçambique **75** 13.00S 39.50E
Anda China **61** 46.25N 125.20E
Andalsnes Norway **42** 62.33N 7.43E
Andaman Is. India **57** 12.00N 93.00E
Andaman Sea Indian Oc. **57** 11.15N 95.30E
Andara Namibia **76** 18.04S 21.29E
Andernach W. Germany **41** 50.25N 7.24E
Anderson r. Canada **94** 69.45N 129.00W
Anderson U.S.A. **98** 40.05N 85.41W
Andes mts. S. America **108** 15.00S 72.00W
And Fjord est. Norway **42** 69.10N 16.20E
Andhra Pradesh d. India **57** 17.00N 79.00E
Andikíthira i. Greece **39** 35.52N 23.18E
Andizhan U.S.S.R. **60** 40.48N 72.23E
Andorra town Andorra **37** 42.29N 1.31E
Andorra **37** 42.30N 1.32E
Andover England **24** 51.13N 1.29W

Andoy i. Norway **42** 69.00N 15.30E
Andreas I.o.M. **28** 54.22N 4.26W
Andreas, C. Cyprus **54** 35.40N 34.35E
Ándros i. Greece **54** 37.50N 24.50E
Andros I. Bahamas **97** 24.30N 78.00W
Andujar Spain **37** 38.02N 4.03W
Andulo Angola **74** 11.28S 16.43E
Anécho Togo **73** 6.17N 1.40E
Anegada i. Virgin Is. **101** 18.46N 64.24W
Aneiza, Jebel mtn. Asia **54** 32.15N 39.19E
Aneto, Pico de mtn. Spain **37** 42.40N 0.19E
Angara r. U.S.S.R. **45** 58.00N 93.00E
Angarsk U.S.S.R. **45** 52.31N 103.55E
Angaston Australia **83** 34.30S 139.03E
Ange Sweden **42** 62.31N 15.40E
Angel de la Guarda i. Mexico **96** 29.10N 113.20W
Angel Falls f. Venezuela **101** 5.55N 62.30W
Ängelholm Sweden **42** 56.15N 12.50E
Ångerman Sweden **42** 62.52N 17.45E
Angers France **36** 47.29N 0.32W
Angkor ruins Cambodia **58** 13.26N 103.50E
Angle Wales **27** 51.40N 5.03W
Anglesey i. Wales **26** 53.16N 4.25W
Angmagssalik Greenland **95** 65.40N 38.00W
Ango Zaire **74** 4.01N 25.52E
Angoche Moçambique **75** 16.10S 39.57E
Angola Africa **74** 11.00S 18.00E
Angoram P.N.G. **59** 4.04S 144.04E
Angoulême France **36** 45.40N 0.10E
Anguilar de Campóo Spain **37** 42.55N 4.15W
Anguilla C. America **101** 18.14N 63.05W
Angumu Zaire **75** 0.10S 27.38E
Anholt W. Germany **41** 51.51N 6.26E
Anhui d. China **63** 32.00N 117.00E
Anhumas Brazil **110** 16.58S 54.43W
Aniak U.S.A. **94** 61.32N 159.40W
Anjouan i. Comoro Is. **75** 12.12S 44.28E
Ankang China **62** 32.38N 109.12E
Ankara Turkey **54** 39.55N 32.50E
Ankober Ethiopia **71** 9.32N 39.43E
Anlu China **63** 31.15N 113.40E
Annaba Algeria **38** 36.55N 7.47E
An Nafud des. Saudi Arabia **54** 28.40N 41.30E
An Najaf Iraq **55** 31.59N 44.19E
Annalee r. Rep. of Ire. **34** 54.02N 7.25W
Annam Highlands mts. Asia **58** 17.40N 105.30E
Annan Scotland **31** 54.59N 3.16W
Annan r. Scotland **31** 54.58N 3.16W
Annandale f. Scotland **31** 55.12N 3.25W
Annapolis U.S.A. **99** 38.59N 76.30W
Annapurna mtn. Nepal **56** 28.34N 83.50E
Ann Arbor U.S.A. **98** 42.18N 83.43W
Annecy France **36** 45.54N 6.07E
Annfield Plain town England **28** 54.42N 1.45W
Annonay France **36** 45.15N 4.40E
Anqing China **63** 30.40N 117.03E
Ansbach W. Germany **40** 49.18N 10.36E
Anshan China **62** 41.06N 122.58E
Anshun China **63** 26.11N 105.50E
Anston England **29** 53.22N 1.13W
Anstruther Scotland **31** 56.14N 2.42W
Antakya Turkey **54** 36.12N 36.10E
Antalya Turkey **54** 36.53N 30.42E
Antalya, G. of Turkey **54** 36.38N 31.00E
Antarctica **111**
Antarctic Pen. Antarctica **109** 65.00S 64.00W
An Teallach mtn. Scotland **32** 57.48N 5.16W
Antequera Spain **37** 37.01N 4.34W
Anticosti I. Canada **95** 49.20N 63.00W
Antigo U.S.A. **98** 45.10N 89.10W
Antigua C. America **101** 17.09N 61.49W
Antigua Guatemala **100** 14.33N 90.42W
Anti-Lebanon mts. Lebanon **54** 34.00N 36.25E
Antofagasta Chile **109** 23.40S 70.23W
Antrim N. Ireland **30** 54.43N 6.14W
Antrim d. N. Ireland **30** 54.58N 6.20W
Antrim, Mts. of N. Ireland **30** 55.00N 6.10W
Antwerp Belgium **41** 51.13N 4.25E
Antwerp d. Belgium **41** 51.16N 4.45E
Anvik U.S.A. **94** 62.38N 160.20W
Anxi China **60** 40.32N 95.57E
Anyang China **62** 36.05N 114.20E
Anzhero-Sudzhensk U.S.S.R. **44** 56.10N 86.10E
Aomori Japan **64** 40.50N 140.43E
Aosta Italy **36** 45.43N 7.19E
Apa r. Paraguay **110** 22.06S 58.00W
Apalachee B. U.S.A. **97** 29.30N 84.00W
Aparri Phil. **59** 18.22N 121.40E
Apatity U.S.S.R. **42** 67.32N 33.21E
Apeldoorn Neth. **41** 52.13N 5.57E
Apennines mts. Italy **38** 42.00N 13.30E
Apolda E. Germany **40** 51.02N 11.31E
Apostle Is. U.S.A. **98** 47.00N 90.30W
Appalachian Mts. U.S.A. **97** 39.30N 78.00W
Appennino Ligure mts. Italy **36** 44.33N 8.45E
Appingedam Neth. **41** 53.18N 6.52E
Appleby England **28** 54.35N 2.29W

Belgrade Yugo. **39** 44.49N 20.28E
Belikh *r.* Syria **54** 35.58N 39.05E
Belitung *i.* Indonesia **58** 3.00S 108.00E
Belize Belize **100** 17.29N 88.20W
Belize C. America **100** 17.00N 88.30W
Bellac France **36** 46.07N 1.04E
Bellary India **56** 15.11N 76.54E
Belleek N. Ireland **34** 54.29N 8.06W
Belle Ile France **36** 47.20N 3.10W
Belle Isle Str. Canada **95** 50.45N 58.00W
Bellerive Australia **83** 42.52S 147.21E
Belleville Canada **99** 44.10N 77.22W
Belleville U.S.A. **98** 38.31N 89.59W
Bellingham England **31** 55.09N 2.15W
Bellingham U.S.A. **96** 48.45N 122.29W
Bellingshausen Sea Antarctica **112** 70.00S 84.00W
Bello Colombia **101** 6.20N 75.41W
Bell Rock *i. see* Inchcape Scotland **31**
Bell Ville Argentina **110** 32.35S 62.41W
Belmopan Belize **100** 17.25N 88.46W
Belmullet Rep. of Ire. **34** 54.14N 10.00W
Belo Horizonte Brazil **110** 19.45S 43.54W
Beloit U.S.A. **98** 42.31N 89.04W
Beloye, L. U.S.S.R. **43** 60.12N 37.45E
Belozersk U.S.S.R. **43** 60.00N 37.49E
Belper England **29** 53.02N 1.29W
Beltra, Lough Rep. of Ire. **34** 53.56N 9.26W
Beltsy U.S.S.R. **43** 47.45N 27.59E
Belturbet Rep. of Ire. **34** 54.06N 7.27W
Belukha, Mt. U.S.S.R. **60** 49.46N 86.40E
Belvedere England **23** 51.30N 0.10E
Bembridge England **24** 50.41N 1.04W
Bemidji U.S.A. **97** 47.29N 94.52W
Ben Alder *mtn.* Scotland **33** 56.49N 4.28W
Benalla Australia **83** 36.35S 145.58E
Benavente Spain **37** 42.00N 5.40W
Ben Avon *mtn.* Scotland **33** 57.06N 3.27W
Benbane Head N. Ireland **30** 55.15N 6.29W
Benbecula *i.* Scotland **32** 57.26N 7.18W
Benbulbin *mtn.* Rep. of Ire. **34** 54.22N 8.28W
Ben Chonzie *mtn.* Scotland **31** 56.27N 4.00W
Ben Cruachan *mtn.* Scotland **30** 56.26N 5.18W
Bend U.S.A. **96** 44.04N 121.20W
Bendel *d.* Nigeria **73** 6.10N 6.00E
Bendigo Australia **83** 36.48S 144.21E
Beneraird *mtn.* Scotland **30** 55.04N 4.56W
Benevento Italy **38** 41.07N 14.46E
Bengal *d.* India **56** 23.00N 88.00E
Bengal, B. of Indian Oc. **57** 17.00N 89.00E
Bengbu China **62** 32.53N 117.26E
Benghazi Libya **70** 32.07N 20.05E
Bengkulu Indonesia **58** 3.46S 102.16E
Ben Griam More *mtn.* Scotland **33** 58.20N 4.02W
Benguela Angola **74** 12.34S 13.24E
Benguela *d.* Angola **74** 12.45S 14.00E
Ben Hee *mtn.* Scotland **33** 58.16N 4.41W
Ben Hiant *mtn.* Scotland **30** 56.42N 6.01W
Ben Hope *mtn.* Scotland **33** 58.24N 4.36W
Ben Horn *mtn.* Scotland **33** 58.07N 4.02W
Ben Hutig *mtn.* Scotland **33** 58.33N 4.31W
Beni *d.* Bolivia **110** 15.50S 65.00W
Beni *r.* Bolivia **108** 10.30S 66.00W
Beni Zaïre **75** 0.29N 29.27E
Benicarló Spain **37** 40.25N 0.25E
Benidorm Spain **37** 38.33N 0.09W
Benin Africa **73** 9.00N 2.30E
Benin, Bight of Africa **73** 5.30N 3.00E
Benin City Nigeria **73** 6.19N 5.41E
Beni-Saf Algeria **37** 35.28N 1.22W
Beni Suef Egypt **54** 29.05N 31.05E
Ben Klibreck *mtn.* Scotland **33** 58.15N 4.22W
Ben Lawers *mtn.* Scotland **30** 56.33N 4.14W
Benllech Wales **26** 53.18N 4.15W
Ben Lomond *mtn.* Australia **83** 30.04S 151.43E
Ben Lomond *mtn.* Scotland **30** 56.12N 4.38W
Ben Loyal *mtn.* Scotland **33** 58.24N 4.26W
Ben Lui *mtn.* Scotland **30** 56.23N 4.49W
Ben Macdhui *mtn.* Scotland **33** 57.04N 3.40W
Ben More *mtn.* Central Scotland **30** 56.23N 4.31W
Ben More *mtn.* Strath. Scotland **30** 56.26N 6.02W
Ben More Assynt *mtn.* Scotland **33** 58.07N 4.52W
Bennane Head Scotland **30** 55.08N 5.00W
Bennettsbridge Rep. of Ire. **35** 52.35N 7.11W
Ben Nevis *mtn.* Scotland **32** 56.48N 5.00W
Benoni R.S.A. **76** 26.12S 28.18E
Ben Rinnes *mtn.* Scotland **33** 57.24N 3.15W
Benton Harbor U.S.A. **98** 42.07N 86.27W
Benue *d.* Nigeria **73** 7.20N 8.00E
Benue *r.* Nigeria **73** 7.52N 6.45E
Ben Vorlich *mtn.* Scotland **30** 56.21N 4.13W
Benwee Head Rep. of Ire. **34** 54.21N 9.48W
Ben Wyvis *mtn.* Scotland **33** 57.40N 4.35W
Benxi China **62** 41.21N 123.47E
Beppu Japan **64** 33.18N 131.30E
Beragh N. Ireland **30** 54.34N 7.10W
Berat Albania **39** 40.42N 19.59E
Berbera Somali Rep. **71** 10.28N 45.02E
Berbérati C.A.E. **73** 4.19N 15.51E

Berchem Belgium **41** 50.48N 3.32E
Berdichev U.S.S.R. **43** 49.54N 28.39E
Berdyansk U.S.S.R. **43** 46.45N 36.47E
Berens *r.* Canada **97** 52.25N 97.00W
Berezniki U.S.S.R. **44** 59.26N 57.00E
Bergama Turkey **39** 39.08N 27.10E
Bergamo Italy **36** 45.42N 9.40E
Bergen Norway **42** 60.23N 5.20E
Bergen op Zoom Neth. **41** 51.30N 4.17E
Bergerac France **36** 44.50N 0.29E
Bergheim W. Germany **41** 50.58N 6.39E
Bergisch Gladbach W. Germany **41** 50.59N 7.10E
Berhampore India **56** 24.06N 88.18E
Berhampur India **57** 19.21N 84.51E
Bering Sea N. America **94** 65.00N 170.00W
Bering Str. U.S.S.R./U.S.A. **94** 65.00N 170.00W
Berkel *r.* Neth. **41** 52.10N 6.12E
Berkhamsted England **23** 51.46N 0.35W
Berkshire *d.* England **24** 51.25N 1.03W
Berkshire Downs *hills* England **24** 51.32N 1.36W
Berlin E. Germany **40** 52.32N 13.25E
Berlin U.S.A. **99** 44.27N 71.13W
Bermagui Australia **83** 36.28S 150.03E
Bermejo *r.* Argentina **110** 26.47S 58.30W
Bermondsey England **23** 51.30N 0.04W
Bermuda Atlantic Oc. **101** 32.18N 64.45W
Bernburg E. Germany **40** 51.49N 11.44E
Berne Switz. **40** 46.57N 7.26E
Berneray *i.* W. Isles Scotland **32** 56.47N 7.38W
Berneray *i.* W. Isles Scotland **32** 57.43N 7.11W
Bernina *mtn.* Italy/Switz. **38** 46.22N 9.57E
Bernkastel W. Germany **41** 49.55N 7.05E
Berri Australia **83** 34.17S 140.36E
Berriedale Scotland **33** 58.11N 3.30W
Berry Head England **27** 50.24N 3.28W
Bertnaghboy B. Rep. of Ire. **34** 53.23N 9.52W
Bertoua Cameroon **73** 4.34N 13.42E
Berwick-upon-Tweed England **31** 55.46N 2.00W
Berwyn *mts.* Wales **26** 52.55N 3.25W
Besalampy Madagascar **75** 16.53S 44.29E
Besançon France **40** 47.14N 6.02E
Bessarabia *f.* U.S.S.R. **43** 46.30N 28.40E
Betanzos Spain **37** 43.17N 8.13W
Bétaré Oya Cameroon **73** 5.34N 14.09E
Bethal R.S.A. **76** 26.27S 29.28E
Bethersden England **25** 51.08N 0.46E
Bethesda Wales **26** 53.11N 4.03W
Bethlehem R.S.A. **76** 28.15S 28.19E
Bethlehem U.S.A. **99** 40.36N 75.22W
Bethnal Green England **23** 51.32N 0.03W
Béthune France **41** 50.32N 2.38E
Bettyhill Scotland **33** 58.30N 4.14W
Betwa *r.* India **56** 25.48N 80.10E
Betws-y-Coed Wales **26** 53.05N 3.48W
Beult *r.* England **23** 51.13N 0.26E
Beverley England **29** 53.52N 0.26W
Beverly U.S.A. **99** 42.35N 70.52W
Beverwijk Neth. **41** 52.29N 4.40E
Bewcastle England **31** 55.03N 2.45W
Bewcastle Fells *hills* England **31** 55.05N 2.50W
Bewdley England **24** 52.23N 2.19W
Bexhill England **25** 50.51N 0.29E
Bexley England **23** 51.26N 0.10E
Beyla Guinea **72** 8.42N 8.39W
Beysehir L. Turkey **54** 37.47N 31.30E
Bezhetsk U.S.S.R. **43** 57.49N 36.40E
Bezhitsa U.S.S.R. **43** 53.19N 34.17E
Béziers France **36** 43.21N 3.13E
Bhagalpur India **56** 25.14N 85.59E
Bhamo Burma **57** 24.15N 97.15E
Bhatpara India **60** 22.51N 88.31E
Bhavnagar India **56** 21.46N 72.14E
Bhima *r.* India **56** 16.30N 77.10E
Bhind India **56** 26.33N 78.47E
Bhopal India **56** 23.17N 77.28E
Bhubaneswar India **57** 20.15N 85.50E
Bhuj India **56** 23.12N 69.54E
Bhutan Asia **56** 27.20N 90.30E
Biak *i.* Asia **59** 0.55S 136.00E
Biak Indonesia **59** 1.10S 136.05E
Białogard Poland **40** 54.00N 16.00E
Białystok Poland **43** 53.09N 23.10E
Biarritz France **36** 43.29N 1.33W
Bicester England **24** 51.53N 1.09W
Bickle Knob *mtn.* U.S.A. **99** 38.56N 79.44W
Bickley England **23** 51.24N 0.03E
Bida Nigeria **73** 9.06N 5.59E
Bidborough England **23** 51.11N 0.14E
Biddeford U.S.A. **99** 43.29N 70.27W
Biddulph England **28** 53.08N 2.11W
Bidean nam Bian *mtn.* Scotland **30** 56.39N 5.02W
Bideford England **27** 51.01N 4.13W
Bideford B. England **27** 51.04N 4.20W
Bié Angola **74** 12.25S 16.58E
Bié *d.* Angola **74** 12.30S 17.30E
Biel Switz. **40** 47.09N 7.16E
Bielefeld W. Germany **40** 52.02N 8.32E
Bié Plateau *f.* Angola **74** 13.00S 16.00E

Big Bald Mtn. Canada **99** 47.12N 66.25W
Bigbury B. England **27** 50.15N 3.56W
Biggar Scotland **31** 55.38N 3.31W
Biggin Hill *town* England **23** 51.19N 0.04E
Biggleswade England **25** 52.06N 0.16W
Big Horn *r.* U.S.A. **96** 46.05N 107.20W
Bignona Senegal **72** 12.48N 16.18W
Big Snowy Mtn. U.S.A. **96** 46.46N 109.31W
Big Spring *town* U.S.A. **96** 32.15N 101.30W
Bihać Yugo. **38** 44.49N 15.53E
Bihar India **56** 25.13N 85.31E
Bihar *d.* India **56** 24.35N 85.40E
Biharamulo Tanzania **75** 2.34S 31.20E
Bihor *mtn.* Romania **43** 46.26N 22.43E
Bijagos Archipelago *is.* Guinea Bissau **72** 11.30N 16.00W
Bijapur India **56** 16.52N 75.47E
Bijar Iran **55** 35.52N 47.39E
Bijawar India **56** 24.36N 79.30E
Bijie China **63** 27.28N 105.20E
Bikaner India **56** 28.01N 73.22E
Bikin U.S.S.R. **61** 46.52N 134.15E
Bikoro Zaïre **74** 0.45S 18.09E
Bilaspur India **56** 22.03N 82.12E
Bilauktaung Range *mts.* Asia **58** 13.20N 99.30E
Bilbao Spain **37** 43.15N 2.56W
Bilecik Turkey **54** 40.10N 29.59E
Billericay England **23** 51.38N 0.25E
Billingham England **29** 54.36N 1.18W
Billings U.S.A. **96** 45.47N 108.30W
Billingshurst England **25** 51.02N 0.28W
Billington England **23** 51.54N 0.39W
Bill of Portland *c.* England **27** 50.32N 2.28W
Bilma Niger **73** 18.46N 12.50E
Biloxi U.S.A. **97** 30.30N 89.00W
Bima *r.* Zaïre **74** 3.24N 25.10E
Bina India **56** 24.09N 78.10E
Binaija *mtn.* Indonesia **59** 3.10S 129.30E
Binche Belgium **41** 50.25N 4.10E
Bindura Zimbabwe **75** 17.20S 31.21E
Binga, Mt. Zimbabwe **76** 19.47S 33.03E
Bingara Australia **83** 29.51S 150.38E
Bingen W. Germany **41** 49.58N 7.55E
Bingerville Ivory Coast **72** 5.20N 3.53W
Bingham England **29** 52.57N 0.57W
Binghamton U.S.A. **99** 42.06N 75.55W
Bingkor Malaysia **58** 5.26N 116.15E
Bingley England **28** 53.51N 1.50W
Bingöl Turkey **54** 38.54N 40.29E
Bingol Dağlari *mtn.* Turkey **54** 39.21N 41.22E
Binhai China **62** 34.00N 119.55E
Binh Dinh Vietnam **58** 13.55N 109.07E
Binjai Indonesia **58** 3.37N 98.25E
Bintan *i.* Indonesia **58** 1.10N 104.30E
Bintulu Malaysia **58** 3.12N 113.01E
Birdum Australia **82** 15.38S 133.12E
Birecik Turkey **54** 37.03N 37.59E
Birhan *mtn.* Ethiopia **71** 11.00N 37.50E
Birjand Iran **55** 32.54N 59.10E
Birkenfeld W. Germany **41** 49.39N 7.10E
Birkenhead England **28** 53.24N 3.01W
Birket Qârûn *l.* Egypt **54** 29.30N 30.40E
Birmingham England **24** 52.30N 1.55W
Birmingham Ala. U.S.A. **97** 33.30N 86.55W
Birmingham Mich. U.S.A. **98** 42.33N 83.12W
Birnin Kebbi Nigeria **73** 12.30N 4.11E
Birni N'Konni Niger **73** 13.49N 5.19E
Birobidzhan U.S.S.R. **61** 48.49N 132.54E
Birq, Wadi *r.* Saudi Arabia **55** 24.08N 47.35E
Birr Rep. of Ire. **35** 53.06N 7.56W
Birreencorragh *mtn.* Rep. of Ire. **34** 53.59N 9.31W
Biscay, B. of France **36** 45.30N 4.00W
Bishop Auckland England **28** 54.40N 1.40W
Bishopbriggs Scotland **30** 55.55N 4.12W
Bishop's Castle England **24** 52.29N 3.00W
Bishop's Lydeard England **24** 51.04N 3.12W
Bishop's Stortford England **23** 51.53N 0.09E
Bishops Waltham England **24** 50.57N 1.13W
Bisina, L. Uganda **75** 1.35N 34.08E
Bisitun Iran **55** 34.22N 47.29E
Biskotasi L. Canada **98** 47.15N 82.15W
Biskra Algeria **38** 34.48N 5.40E
Bisley England **23** 51.20N 0.39W
Bismarck U.S.A. **96** 46.50N 100.48W
Bismarck Range *mts.* P.N.G. **59** 6.00S 145.00E
Bismarck Sea Pacific Oc. **59** 4.00S 146.30E
Bissau Guinea Bissau **72** 11.52N 15.39W
Bistrita *r.* Romania **43** 46.30N 26.54E
Bitburg W. Germany **41** 49.58N 6.31E
Bitlis Turkey **54** 38.23N 42.04E
Bitola Yugo. **39** 41.02N 21.21E
Bitterfontein R.S.A. **76** 31.03S 18.16E
Biu Nigeria **73** 10.36N 12.11E
Biumba Rwanda **75** 1.38S 30.02E
Biwa ko *l.* Japan **64** 35.20N 136.10E
Biysk U.S.S.R. **44** 52.35N 85.16E
Bizerta Tunisia **38** 37.17N 9.51E
Black *r.* Rep. of Ire. **34** 53.50N 7.51W

Black *r.* Ark. U.S.A. **97** 35.30N 91.20W
Black *r.* Wisc. U.S.A. **98** 43.55N 91.20W
Black *r.* Vietnam **58** 21.20N 105.45E
Black Bull Head Rep. of Ire. **35** 51.35N 10.03W
Blackburn England **28** 53.44N 2.30W
Black Combe *mtn.* England **28** 54.15N 3.20W
Blackcraig Hill Scotland **30** 55.19N 4.08W
Black Down Hills England **24** 50.55N 3.10W
Blackford Scotland **31** 56.16N 3.48W
Black Forest *f.* W. Germany **40** 48.00N 7.45E
Black Head N. Ireland **30** 54.46N 5.41W
Black Head Rep. of Ire. **35** 53.09N 9.16W
Black Isle *f.* Scotland **33** 57.35N 4.15W
Blackmoor Vale *f.* England **24** 50.55N 2.25W
Black Mtn. Wales **26** 51.52N 3.50W
Black Mts. Wales **26** 51.52N 3.09W
Blackpool England **28** 53.48N 3.03W
Black River *town* Jamaica **101** 18.02N 77.52W
Blackrock Rep. of Ire. **34** 53.18N 6.13W
Black Rock Desert U.S.A. **96** 41.10N 118.45W
Black Sand Desert U.S.S.R. **55** 37.45N 60.00E
Black Sea Europe **43** 43.00N 35.00E
Blacksod B. Rep. of Ire. **34** 54.04N 10.00W
Black Volta *r.* Ghana/U. Volta **72** 8.14N 2.11W
Blackwater *r.* England **25** 51.43N 0.42E
Blackwater *r.* N. Ireland **34** 54.31N 6.36W
Blackwater Rep. of Ire. **35** 52.26N 6.20W
Blackwater *r.* Meath Rep. of Ire. **34** 53.39N 6.41W
Blackwater *r.* Waterford Rep. of Ire. **35** 51.58N 7.52W
Blackwater Resr. Scotland **30** 56.43N 4.58W
Blackwood Wales **27** 51.38N 3.13W
Bladnoch *r.* Scotland **30** 54.52N 4.26W
Blaenau Ffestiniog Wales **26** 53.00N 3.57W
Blaenavon Wales **27** 51.46N 3.05W
Blagoevgrad Bulgaria **39** 42.02N 23.04E
Blagoveshchensk U.S.S.R. **61** 50.19N 127.30E
Blaina Wales **27** 51.46N 3.10W
Blair Atholl Scotland **33** 56.46N 3.51W
Blairgowrie Scotland **31** 56.36N 3.21W
Blakeney Pt. England **29** 52.58N 0.57E
Blanc, Cap Mauritania **72** 20.44N 17.05W
Blanc, Mont Canada **99** 48.47N 66.51W
Blanc, Mont Europe **36** 45.50N 6.52E
Blanca, Bahía *b.* Argentina **110** 39.15S 61.00W
Blanchardstown Rep. of Ire. **34** 53.24N 6.23W
Blanche, L. Australia **83** 29.15S 139.40E
Blanco, C. Costa Rica **100** 9.36N 85.06W
Blanco, C. U.S.A. **96** 42.50N 124.29W
Blandford Forum England **24** 50.52N 2.10W
Blankenberge Belgium **41** 51.18N 3.08E
Blantyre Malaŵi **75** 15.46S 35.00E
Blarney Rep. of Ire. **35** 51.56N 8.34W
Blavet *r.* France **36** 47.43N 3.18W
Blaydon England **28** 54.58N 1.42W
Blaye France **36** 45.08N 0.40W
Bleaklow Hill England **28** 53.27N 1.50W
Blenheim New Zealand **85** 41.32S 173.58E
Blessington Rep. of Ire. **35** 53.11N 6.33W
Bletchley England **24** 51.59N 0.45W
Blida Algeria **37** 36.30N 2.50E
Blidworth England **29** 53.06N 1.07W
Blindley Heath England **23** 51.12N 0.04W
Blind River *town* Canada **98** 46.12N 82.59W
Blitar Indonesia **58** 8.06S 112.12E
Blitta Togo **73** 8.23N 1.06E
Bloemfontein R.S.A. **76** 29.07S 26.14E
Blois France **36** 47.36N 1.20E
Bloody Foreland *c.* Rep. of Ire. **34** 55.09N 8.17W
Bloomington Ill. U.S.A. **98** 40.29N 89.00W
Bloomington Ind. U.S.A. **98** 39.10N 86.31W
Bloomsburg U.S.A. **99** 41.01N 76.27W
Bluefield U.S.A. **97** 37.14N 81.17W
Bluefields Nicaragua **100** 12.00N 83.49W
Blue Mts. Australia **83** 33.30S 150.15E
Blue Mts. U.S.A. **96** 45.00N 118.00W
Blue Nile *r.* Sudan **71** 15.45N 32.25E
Blue Stack Mts. Rep. of Ire. **34** 54.44N 8.09W
Bluff New Zealand **85** 46.38S 168.21E
Blumenau Brazil **110** 26.55S 49.07W
Blyth England **31** 55.07N 1.29W
Blyth *r.* Northum. England **31** 55.08N 1.29W
Blyth *r.* Suffolk England **25** 52.19N 1.36E
Blyth Bridge *town* Scotland **31** 55.42N 3.23W
Blyth Sands England **23** 51.28N 0.33E
Bo Sierra Leone **72** 7.58N 11.45W
Boardman U.S.A. **98** 41.02N 80.40W
Boa Vista Brazil **108** 2.51N 60.43W
Bobo-Dioulasso U. Volta **72** 11.11N 4.18W
Bobruysk U.S.S.R. **43** 53.08N 29.10E
Bocholt W. Germany **41** 51.49N 6.37E
Bochum W. Germany **41** 51.28N 7.11E
Boddam Scotland **33** 57.28N 1.48W
Bodélé Depression *f.* Chad **73** 16.50N 17.10E
Boden Sweden **42** 65.50N 21.44E
Bodenham England **24** 52.09N 2.41W
Bodmin England **27** 50.28N 4.44W
Bodmin Moor England **27** 50.35N 4.35W
Bodö Norway **42** 67.18N 14.26E
Boende Zaïre **74** 0.15S 20.49E
Boffa Guinea **72** 10.12N 14.02W
Bogan Gate *town* Australia **83** 33.08S 147.50E
Bogenfels Namibia **76** 27.23S 15.22E
Boggabilla Australia **83** 28.36S 150.21E
Boggeragh Mts. Rep. of Ire. **35** 52.03N 8.53W
Boghari Algeria **37** 35.55N 2.47E
Bogia P.N.G. **59** 4.16S 145.00E
Bognor Regis England **24** 50.47N 0.40W
Bog of Allen *f.* Rep. of Ire. **34** 53.17N 7.00W
Bogong, Mt. Australia **83** 36.45S 147.21E
Bogor Indonesia **58** 6.34S 106.45E
Bogotá Colombia **108** 4.38N 74.05W
Bogra Bangla. **56** 24.52N 89.28E
Bogué Mauritania **72** 16.40N 14.10W
Bohai Bay *b.* China **62** 38.30N 117.55E
Bohain France **41** 49.59N 3.28E
Bohemian Forest *mts.* Czech. **40** 49.20N 13.10E
Bohol *i.* Phil. **59** 9.45N 124.10E
Boise U.S.A. **96** 43.38N 116.12W
Bojeador, C. Phil. **59** 18.30N 120.50E
Bojnurd Iran **55** 37.28N 57.20E
Boké Guinea **72** 10.57N 14.13W
Bokn Fjord *est.* Norway **42** 59.15N 5.50E
Bokoro Chad **73** 12.17N 17.04E
Bokungu Zaïre **74** 0.44S 22.28E
Bolamo Guinea Bissau **72** 11.35N 15.30W
Bolangir India **57** 20.41N 83.30E
Bolbec France **36** 49.34N 0.28E
Bole Ghana **72** 9.03N 2.23W
Bolgrad U.S.S.R. **39** 45.42N 28.40E
Bolivar Argentina **110** 36.15S 61.07W
Bolivar *mtn.* Venezuela **101** 7.27N 71.00W
Bolivia S. America **108** 17.00S 65.00W
Bollin *r.* England **28** 53.23N 2.29W
Bollnäs Sweden **42** 61.20N 16.25E
Bolmen *l.* Sweden **42** 57.00N 13.45E
Bolobo Zaïre **74** 2.10S 16.17E
Bologna Italy **38** 44.30N 11.20E
Bologoye U.S.S.R. **43** 57.58N 34.00E
Bolomba Zaïre **74** 0.30N 19.13E
Bolsena, Lago di *l.* Italy **38** 42.36N 11.55E
Bolshevik *i.* U.S.S.R. **45** 78.30N 102.00E
Bolshoi Lyakhovskiy *i.* U.S.S.R. **45** 73.30N 142.00E
Bolsover England **29** 53.14N 1.18W
Bolt Head *c.* England **27** 50.13N 3.48W
Bolton England **28** 53.35N 2.26W
Bolu Turkey **54** 40.45N 31.38E
Bolus Head Rep. of Ire. **35** 51.47N 10.20W
Bolvadin Turkey **54** 38.43N 31.02E
Bolzano Italy **40** 46.30N 11.20E
Boma Zaïre **74** 5.50S 13.03E
Bombala Australia **83** 36.55S 149.16E
Bombay India **56** 18.56N 72.51E
Bom Despacho Brazil **110** 19.46S 45.15W
Bomokandi *r.* Zaïre **75** 3.37N 26.09E
Bomongo Zaïre **74** 1.30N 18.21E
Bomu *r.* C.A.E. **74** 4.08N 22.25E
Bon, C. Tunisia **38** 37.05N 11.02E
Bonaire *i.* Neth. Antilles **101** 12.15N 68.27W
Bonar-Bridge *town* Scotland **33** 57.33N 4.21W
Bonavista Canada **95** 48.38N 53.08W
Bondo Zaïre **74** 3.47N 23.45E
Bondoukou Ivory Coast **72** 8.03N 2.15W
Bone, G. of Indonesia **59** 4.00S 120.50E
Bo'ness Scotland **31** 56.01N 3.36W
Bongandanga Zaïre **74** 1.28N 21.03E
Bonifacio France **38** 41.23N 9.10E
Bonifacio, Str. of Med. Sea **38** 41.18N 9.10E
Bonn W. Germany **41** 50.44N 7.06E
Bonny Nigeria **74** 4.25N 7.15E
Bonny, Bight of Africa **73** 2.58N 7.00E
Bonnyrigg Scotland **31** 55.52N 3.07W
Bontang Indonesia **58** 0.05N 117.31E
Bonthain Indonesia **59** 5.32S 119.58E
Boothia, G. of Canada **95** 70.00N 90.00W
Bootle Cumbria England **28** 54.17N 3.24W
Bootle Mersey. England **28** 53.28N 3.01W
Booué Gabon **74** 0.00 11.58E
Boppard W. Germany **41** 50.13N 7.35E
Borah Peak U.S.A. **96** 44.09N 113.47W
Borås Sweden **42** 57.44N 12.55E
Borazjan Iran **55** 29.14N 51.12E
Bordeaux France **36** 44.50N 0.34W
Borden I. Canada **94** 78.30N 111.00W
Borders *d.* Scotland **31** 55.30N 2.53W
Bordertown Australia **83** 36.18S 140.49E
Bordö *i.* Faroe Is. **42** 62.10N 7.13W
Bordon Camp England **24** 51.06N 0.52W
Borehamwood England **23** 51.40N 0.16W
Boreray *i.* Scotland **32** 57.43N 7.17W
Borgå Finland **42** 60.24N 25.40E
Borgefjell *mtn.* Norway **42** 65.15N 13.50E
Borger U.S.A. **96** 35.39N 101.24W
Borisoglebsk U.S.S.R. **43** 51.23N 42.02E
Borisov U.S.S.R. **43** 54.09N 28.30E
Borken W. Germany **41** 51.50N 6.52E
Borkum W. Germany **41** 53.34N 6.41E
Borkum *i.* W. Germany **41** 53.35N 6.45E
Borlänge Sweden **42** 60.29N 15.25E
Bormida *r.* Italy **36** 45.02N 8.43E
Borneo *i.* Asia **58** 1.00N 114.00E
Bornholm *i.* Denmark **42** 55.02N 15.00E
Borno *d.* Nigeria **73** 12.20N 12.40E
Boroughbridge England **29** 54.06N 1.23W
Borough Green England **23** 51.17N 0.19E
Borris-in-Ossory Rep. of Ire. **35** 52.56N 7.39W
Borrisokane Rep. of Ire. **35** 53.00N 8.08W
Borth Wales **26** 52.29N 4.03W
Borzya U.S.S.R. **61** 50.24N 116.35E
Bosa Italy **38** 40.18N 8.29E
Boscastle England **27** 50.42N 4.42W
Bose China **63** 23.58N 106.32E
Boshan China **62** 36.29N 117.50E
Bosna *r.* Yugo. **39** 45.04N 18.27E
Bosnik Indonesia **59** 1.09S 136.14E
Bosobolo Zaïre **74** 4.11N 19.55E
Boso Hanto *b.* Japan **64** 35.40N 140.50E
Bosporus *str.* Turkey **39** 41.07N 29.04E
Bossangoa C.A.E. **73** 6.27N 17.21E
Bossembelé C.A.E. **74** 5.10N 17.44E
Bosso Niger **73** 13.43N 13.19E
Bosten Hu *l.* China **60** 42.00N 87.00E
Boston England **29** 52.59N 0.02W
Boston U.S.A. **99** 42.20N 71.05W
Botany B. Australia **83** 34.04S 151.08E
Botevgrad Bulgaria **39** 42.55N 23.57E
Bothnia, G. of Europe **42** 63.30N 20.30E
Botletle *r.* Botswana **76** 21.06S 24.47E
Botoşani Romania **43** 47.44N 26.41E
Botrange *mtn.* Belgium **41** 50.30N 6.04E
Botswana Africa **76** 22.00S 24.15E
Bottesford England **29** 52.56N 0.48W
Bottrop W. Germany **41** 51.31N 6.55E
Botucatu Brazil **110** 22.52S 48.30W
Bouaflé Ivory Coast **72** 7.01N 5.47W
Bouaké Ivory Coast **72** 7.42N 5.00W
Bouar C.A.E. **73** 5.58N 15.35E
Bou Craa Western Sahara **70** 26.21N 12.57W
Boufarik Algeria **37** 36.36N 2.54E
Boughton England **29** 53.13N 0.59W
Bougouni Mali **72** 11.25N 7.28W
Bouillon Belgium **36** 49.47N 5.04E
Bouira Algeria **37** 36.22N 3.55E
Boulder Australia **82** 30.55S 121.32E
Boulder U.S.A. **96** 40.02N 105.16W
Boulogne France **36** 50.43N 1.37E
Boumba *r.* Cameroon **73** 2.00N 15.10E
Boumo Chad **73** 9.01N 16.24E
Bouna Ivory Coast **72** 9.19N 2.53W
Boundary Peak *mtn.* U.S.A. **96** 37.51N 118.23W
Boundiali Ivory Coast **72** 9.30N 6.31W
Bourem Mali **72** 16.59N 0.20W
Bourg France **36** 46.12N 5.13E
Bourganeuf France **36** 45.57N 1.44E
Bourges France **36** 47.05N 2.23E
Bourg Madame France **36** 42.26N 1.55E
Bourke Australia **83** 30.09S 145.59E
Bourne England **29** 52.46N 0.23W
Bourne *r.* England **24** 51.04N 1.47W
Bournebridge England **23** 51.37N 0.12E
Bourne End England **23** 51.34N 0.42W
Bournemouth England **24** 50.43N 1.53W
Bovingdon England **23** 51.44N 0.32W
Bowen Australia **82** 20.00S 148.15E
Bowes England **28** 54.31N 2.01W
Bowmore Scotland **30** 55.45N 6.17W
Bowness-on-Solway England **31** 54.57N 3.11W
Bo Xian China **62** 33.50N 115.46E
Boxtel Neth. **41** 51.36N 5.20E
Boyang China **63** 28.59N 116.42E
Boyle Rep. of Ire. **34** 53.58N 8.19W
Boyne *r.* Rep. of Ire. **34** 53.43N 6.17W
Boyoma Falls *f.* Zaïre **74** 0.18N 25.32E
Bozeman U.S.A. **96** 45.40N 111.00W
Braan *r.* Scotland **31** 56.34N 3.36W
Brabant *d.* Belgium **41** 50.47N 4.30E
Brac *i.* Yugo. **39** 43.20N 16.38E
Bracadale, Loch Scotland **32** 57.22N 6.30W
Bräcke Sweden **42** 62.44N 15.30E
Bracknell England **23** 51.26N 0.46W
Brad Romania **39** 46.06N 22.48E
Bradano *r.* Italy **39** 40.23N 16.52E
Bradford England **28** 53.47N 1.45W
Bradford-on-Avon England **24** 51.20N 2.15W
Bradwell-on-Sea England **25** 51.44N 0.55E
Bradworthy England **27** 50.54N 4.22W
Brae Scotland **32** 60.24N 1.21W
Braemar Scotland **33** 57.01N 3.24W
Braemar *f.* Scotland **33** 57.02N 3.24W
Braga Portugal **37** 41.32N 8.26W
Bragado Argentina **110** 35.10S 60.29W
Braganca Portugal **37** 41.47N 6.46W
Brahmaputra *r.* Asia **57** 23.50N 89.45E
Brăila Romania **39** 45.18N 27.58E
Brailsford England **28** 52.58N 1.35W

Brain *r.* England **23** 51.47N 0.40E
Braintree England **23** 51.53N 0.32E
Bramley England **23** 51.11N 0.35W
Brampton Canada **99** 43.41N 79.46W
Brampton England **31** 54.56N 2.43W
Branco *r.* Brazil **108** 1.30S 62.00W
Brandberg *mtn.* Namibia **76** 21.10S 14.33E
Brandenburg E. Germany **40** 52.25N 12.34F
Brandfort R.S.A. **76** 28.42S 26.28E
Brandon Canada **96** 49.50N 99.57W
Brandon Durham England **28** 54.46N 1.37W
Brandon Suffolk England **25** 52.27N 0.37E
Brandon B. Rep. of Ire. **35** 52.16N 10.05W
Brandon Hill Rep. of Ire. **35** 52.30N 7.00W
Brandon Mtn. Rep. of Ire. **35** 52.14N 10.15W
Brandon Pt. Rep. of Ire. **35** 52.17N 10.11W
Brantford Canada **98** 43.09N 80.17W
Brasília Brazil **110** 15.54S 47.50W
Braşov Romania **39** 45.40N 25.35E
Brass Nigeria **73** 4.20N 6.15E
Bratislava Czech. **43** 48.10N 17.10E
Bratsk U.S.S.R. **45** 56.20N 101.15E
Bratsk Resr. U.S.S.R. **45** 54.40N 103.00E
Brattleboro U.S.A. **99** 42.51N 72.36W
Braunschweig W. Germany **40** 52.15N 10.30E
Braunton England **27** 51.06N 4.09W
Brava Somali Rep. **75** 1.02N 44.02E
Brawley U.S.A. **96** 33.10N 115.30W
Bray *r.* England **27** 50.56N 3.54W
Bray Rep. of Ire. **35** 53.12N 6.07W
Bray Head Kerry Rep. of Ire. **35** 51.53N 10.26W
Bray Head Wicklow Rep. of Ire. **35** 53.11N 6.04W
Brazil S. America **110** 19.00S 50.00W
Brazilian Highlands Brazil **110** 17.02S 50.00W
Brazos *r.* U.S.A. **97** 28.55N 95.20W
Brazzaville Congo **74** 4.14S 15.10E
Breadalbane *f.* Scotland **30** 56.30N 4.20W
Breaksea Pt. Wales **27** 51.24N 3.25W
Bream B. New Zealand **85** 36.00S 174.30E
Brechin Scotland **31** 56.44N 2.40W
Breckland *f.* England **25** 52.28N 0.40E
Brecon Wales **26** 51.57N 3.23W
Brecon Beacons *mts.* Wales **26** 51.53N 3.27W
Breda Neth. **41** 51.35N 4.46E
Bredasdorp R.S.A. **76** 34.32S 20.02E
Brede *r.* England **25** 50.57N 0.44E
Bregenz Austria **40** 47.31N 9.46E
Breidha Fjördhur *est.* Iceland **42** 65.15N 23.00W
Bremen W. Germany **40** 53.05N 8.48E
Bremerhaven W. Germany **40** 53.33N 8.35E
Brendon Hills England **24** 51.05N 3.25W
Brenner Pass Austria/Italy **38** 47.00N 11.30E
Brent *d.* England **23** 51.33N 0.16W
Brenta *r.* Italy **38** 45.25N 12.15E
Brentford England **23** 51.30N 0.18W
Brentwood England **23** 51.38N 0.18E
Brescia Italy **38** 45.33N 10.12E
Breskens Neth. **41** 51.24N 3.34E
Bressanone Italy **40** 46.43N 11.40E
Bressay *i.* Scotland **32** 60.08N 1.05W
Bressay Sd. Scotland **32** 60.08N 1.10W
Bressuire France **36** 46.50N 0.28W
Brest France **36** 48.23N 4.30W
Brest U.S.S.R. **43** 52.08N 23.40E
Brest-Nantes Canal France **36** 47.55N 2.30W
Brett, C. New Zealand **85** 35.15S 174.20E
Brewarrina Australia **83** 29.57S 147.54E
Brewer U.S.A. **99** 44.48N 68.44W
Briançon France **36** 44.53N 6.39E
Bricket Wood *town* England **23** 51.42N 0.20W
Bride I.o.M. **28** 54.23N 4.24W
Bride *r.* Rep. of Ire. **35** 52.05N 7.52W
Bridgend Wales **27** 51.30N 3.35W
Bridge of Allan *town* Scotland **31** 56.09N 3.58W
Bridge of Cally *town* Scotland **31** 56.39N 3.25W
Bridge of Earn *town* Scotland **31** 56.24N 3.25W
Bridgeport U.S.A. **99** 41.12N 73.12W
Bridgetown Barbados **101** 13.06N 59.37W
Bridgetown Rep. of Ire. **35** 52.14N 6.33W
Bridgnorth England **24** 52.33N 2.25W
Bridgwater England **24** 51.08N 3.00W
Bridgwater B. England **24** 51.15N 3.10W
Bridlington England **29** 54.06N 0.11W
Bridlington B. England **29** 54.03N 0.10W
Bridport England **24** 50.43N 2.45W
Brienne-le-Chât France **36** 48.24N 4.32E
Brienz Switz. **40** 46.46N 8.02E
Brierfield England **28** 53.49N 2.15W
Brig Switz. **36** 46.19N 8.00E
Brigg England **29** 53.33N 0.30W
Brighouse England **28** 53.42N 1.47W
Bright Australia **83** 36.42S 146.58E
Brightlingsea England **25** 51.49N 1.01E
Brighton England **25** 50.50N 0.09W
Brindisi Italy **39** 40.38N 17.57E
Brisbane Australia **83** 27.30S 153.00E
Bristol England **27** 51.26N 2.35W
Bristol B. U.S.A. **94** 58.00N 158.50W

Bristol Channel England/Wales **27** 51.17N 3.20W
British Antarctic Territory Antarctica **111** 70.00S 50.00W
British Columbia *d.* Canada **94** 55.00N 125.00W
British Isles Europe **112** 54.00N 5.00W
Briton Ferry *town* Wales **27** 51.37N 3.50W
Britstown R.S.A. **76** 30.36S 23.30E
Brive France **36** 45.09N 1.32E
Briviesca Spain **37** 42.33N 3.19W
Brixham England **27** 50.24N 3.31W
Brno Czech. **40** 49.11N 16.39E
Broad B. Scotland **32** 58.15N 6.15W
Broadback *r.* Canada **97** 51.15N 78.55W
Broadford Scotland **32** 57.14N 5.54W
Broad Haven *b.* Rep. of Ire. **34** 54.17N 9.53W
Broad Law *mtn.* Scotland **31** 55.30N 3.21W
Broadstairs England **25** 51.22N 1.27E
Broadstone England **24** 50.45N 2.00W
Broadway England **24** 52.02N 1.51W
Brocken *mtn.* E. Germany **40** 51.50N 10.50E
Brockenhurst England **24** 50.49N 1.34W
Brockham England **23** 51.13N 0.16W
Brockton U.S.A. **99** 42.06N 71.01W
Brockville Canada **99** 44.35N 75.44W
Brod Yugo. **39** 45.09N 18.02E
Brodick Scotland **30** 55.34N 5.09W
Brody U.S.S.R. **43** 50.05N 25.08E
Broken Hill *town* Australia **83** 31.57S 141.30E
Bromley England **23** 51.24N 0.02E
Bromley Common England **23** 51.23N 0.04E
Brompton England **23** 51.24N 0.35E
Bromsgrove England **24** 52.20N 2.03W
Bromyard England **24** 52.12N 2.30W
Brönderslev Denmark **42** 57.16N 9.58E
Brong-Ahafo *d.* Ghana **72** 7.45N 1.30W
Brooke's Point *town* Phil. **58** 8.50N 117.52E
Brookmans Park *town* England **23** 51.43N 0.10W
Brooks Range *mts.* U.S.A. **94** 68.50N 152.00W
Brook Street England **23** 51.37N 0.17E
Broom, Loch Scotland **32** 57.52N 5.07W
Broome Australia **82** 17.58S 122.15E
Brora Scotland **33** 58.01N 3.52W
Brora *r.* Scotland **33** 58.00N 3.51W
Brosna *r.* Rep. of Ire. **35** 53.13N 7.58W
Brotton England **29** 54.34N 0.55W
Brough England **28** 54.32N 2.19W
Brough Head Scotland **33** 59.09N 3.19W
Brough Ness *c.* Scotland **33** 58.44N 2.57W
Broughton England **29** 54.26N 1.08W
Broughton Scotland **31** 55.37N 3.25W
Broughton Wales **28** 53.10N 3.00W
Broughton in Furness England **28** 54.17N 3.12W
Brownhills England **24** 52.38N 1.57W
Brownsville U.S.A. **100** 25.54N 97.30W
Brown Willy *hill* England **27** 50.36N 4.36W
Broxbourne England **23** 51.45N 0.01W
Bruay-en-Artois France **41** 50.29N 2.36E
Bruchsal W. Germany **40** 49.07N 8.35E
Brue *r.* England **24** 51.13N 3.00W
Bruernish Pt. Scotland **32** 56.59N 7.22W
Bruges Belgium **41** 51.13N 3.14E
Brühl W. Germany **41** 50.50N 6.55E
Brunei Asia **58** 4.56N 114.58E
Brunssum Neth. **41** 50.57N 5.59E
Brunswick U.S.A. **97** 31.09N 81.21W
Bruny I. Australia **83** 43.15S 147.16E
Bruree Rep. of Ire. **35** 52.25N 8.40W
Brussels Belgium **41** 50.50N 4.23E
Bruton England **24** 51.06N 2.28W
Bryansk U.S.S.R. **43** 53.15N 34.09E
Bryher *i.* England **27** 49.57N 6.21W
Bryn Brawd *mtn.* Wales **26** 52.08N 3.54W
Brynmawr Wales **27** 51.48N 3.10W
Bua *r.* Malawi **75** 12.42S 34.15E
Bubiyan I. Kuwait **55** 29.45N 48.15E
Bubye *r.* Zimbabwe **76** 22.18S 31.00E
Bucaramanga Colombia **101** 7.08N 73.01W
Buchan *f.* Scotland **33** 57.34N 2.03W
Buchanan Liberia **72** 5.57N 10.02W
Buchan Ness *c.* Scotland **33** 57.28N 1.47W
Bucharest Romania **39** 44.25N 26.06E
Buckfastleigh England **27** 50.28N 3.47W
Buckhaven and Methil Scotland **31** 56.11N 3.03W
Buckhurst Hill England **23** 51.38N 0.03E
Buckie Scotland **33** 57.40N 2.58W
Buckingham England **24** 52.00N 0.59W
Buckinghamshire *d.* England **24** 51.50N 0.48W
Buckley Wales **26** 53.11N 3.04W
Buco Zau Angola **74** 4.46S 12.34E
Budapest Hungary **43** 47.30N 19.03E
Budaun India **56** 28.02N 79.07E
Buddon Ness *c.* Scotland **31** 56.29N 2.42W
Bude England **27** 50.49N 4.33W
Bude B. England **27** 50.50N 4.40W
Budjala Zaïre **74** 2.38N 19.48E
Budleigh Salterton England **24** 50.37N 3.19W
Buea Cameroon **73** 4.09N 9.13E
Buenaventura Colombia **108** 3.54N 77.02W
Buenos Aires Argentina **110** 34.40S 58.25W

Buenos Aires *d.* Argentina **110** 35.00S 61.00W
Buffalo N.Y. U.S.A. **99** 42.52N 78.55W
Buffalo Wyo. U.S.A. **96** 44.21N 106.40W
Bug *r.* Poland **43** 52.29N 21.11E
Bug *r.* U.S.S.R. **43** 46.55N 31.59E
Buggs Island *l.* U.S.A. **97** 36.35N 78.20W
Bugt China **61** 48.45N 121.58E
Bugulma U.S.S.R. **44** 54.32N 52.46E
Buie, Loch Scotland **30** 56.20N 5.53W
Builth Wells Wales **26** 52.09N 3.24W
Buitenpost Neth. **41** 53.15N 6.09E
Bujumbura Burundi **75** 3.22S 29.21E
Bukama Zaïre **74** 9.16S 25.52E
Bukavu Zaïre **75** 2.30S 28.49E
Bukhara U.S.S.R. **55** 39.47N 64.26E
Bukittinggi Indonesia **58** 0.18S 100.20E
Bukoba Tanzania **75** 1.20S 31.49E
Bula Indonesia **59** 3.07S 130.27E
Bulagan Mongolia **60** 48.34N 103.12E
Bulan Phil. **59** 12.40N 123.53E
Bulandshahr India **56** 28.30N 77.49E
Bulawayo Zimbabwe **76** 20.10S 28.43E
Bulgaria Europe **39** 42.30N 25.00E
Bulkington England **24** 52.29N 1.25W
Buller *r.* New Zealand **85** 41.45S 171.35E
Buller, Mt. Australia **83** 37.11S 146.26E
Bulloo *r.* Australia **83** 27.26S 144.06E
Bulolo P.N.G. **59** 7.13S 146.35E
Bultfontein R.S.A. **76** 28.17S 26.10E
Bulu, Gunung *mtn.* Indonesia **58** 3.00N 116.00E
Bulun U.S.S.R. **45** 70.50N 127.20E
Bumba Zaïre **74** 2.15N 22.32E
Bunbury Australia **82** 33.20S 115.34E
Buncrana Rep. of Ire. **34** 55.08N 7.27W
Bundaberg Australia **82** 24.50S 152.21E
Bunde W. Germany **41** 53.12N 7.16E
Bundelkhand *f.* India **56** 24.40N 80.00E
Bundoran Rep. of Ire. **34** 54.28N 8.17W
Bunessan Scotland **30** 56.18N 6.14W
Bungay England **25** 52.27N 1.26E
Bungo suido *str.* Japan **64** 32.52N 132.30E
Bunguran *i.* Indonesia **58** 4.00N 108.20E
Bunguran Selatan *i.* Indonesia **58** 3.00N 108.50E
Buni Nigeria **73** 11.20N 11.59E
Bunia Zaïre **75** 1.30N 30.10E
Buntingford England **25** 51.57N 0.01W
Buol Indonesia **59** 1.12N 121.28E
Buqbuq Egypt **54** 31.30N 25.32E
Bura Coast Kenya **75** 3.30S 38.19E
Buraida Saudi Arabia **55** 26.18N 43.58E
Buraimi U.A.E. **55** 24.15N 55.45E
Burdur Turkey **54** 37.44N 30.17E
Burdwan India **56** 23.15N 87.52E
Bure *r.* England **25** 52.36N 1.44E
Bures England **25** 51.59N 0.46E
Burford England **24** 51.48N 1.38W
Burg E. Germany **40** 52.17N 11.51E
Burgan Kuwait **55** 29.00N 47.53E
Burgas Bulgaria **39** 42.30N 27.29E
Burgess Hill England **25** 50.57N 0.07W
Burghead Scotland **33** 57.42N 3.30W
Burgh Heath England **23** 51.18N 0.12W
Burgh le Marsh England **29** 53.10N 0.15E
Burgos Spain **37** 42.21N 3.41W
Burgsteinfurt W. Germany **41** 52.09N 7.21E
Burgsvik Sweden **42** 57.03N 18.19E
Burhanpur India **56** 21.18N 76.08E
Burias *i.* Phil. **59** 12.50N 123.10E
Burica, Punta Panamá **100** 8.05N 82.50W
Burley U.S.A. **96** 42.32N 113.48W
Burlington Canada **98** 43.19N 79.48W
Burlington Iowa U.S.A. **98** 40.50N 91.07W
Burlington Vt. U.S.A. **99** 44.28N 73.14W
Burma Asia **57** 21.00N 96.30E
Burnham England **23** 51.35N 0.39W
Burnham Beeches England **23** 51.33N 0.39W
Burnham Market England **29** 52.57N 0.43E
Burnham-on-Crouch England **25** 51.37N 0.50E
Burnham-on-Sea England **24** 51.15N 3.00W
Burnie Australia **83** 41.03S 145.55E
Burnley England **28** 53.47N 2.15W
Burntisland Scotland **31** 56.03N 3.15W
Burntwood England **24** 52.42N 1.54W
Burra Australia **83** 33.40S 138.57E
Burravoe Scotland **32** 60.23N 1.20W
Burray *i.* Scotland **33** 58.51N 2.54W
Burren Junction Australia **83** 30.08S 148.59E
Burriana Spain **37** 39.54N 0.05W
Burrinjuck Resr. Australia **83** 35.00S 148.40E
Burrow Head Scotland **30** 54.41N 4.24W
Burry Port Wales **27** 51.41N 4.17W
Bursa Turkey **39** 40.11N 29.04E
Burscough England **28** 53.37N 2.51W
Burton Agnes England **29** 54.04N 0.18W
Burton Latimer England **24** 52.23N 0.41W
Burton upon Trent England **24** 52.58N 1.39W
Buru *i.* Indonesia **59** 3.30S 126.30E
Burujird Iran **55** 33.54N 48.47E

Carmen de Patagones Argentina **110** 40.45S 63.00W
Carmen I. Mexico **100** 18.35N 91.40W
Carmona Spain **37** 37.28N 5.38W
Carmyllie Scotland **31** 56.36N 2.41W
Carnarvon Australia **82** 24.51S 113.45E
Carnarvon R.S.A. **76** 30.59S 22.08E
Carndonagh Rep. of Ire. **30** 55.15N 7.15W
Carnedd y Filiast *mtn.* Wales **26** 52.56N 3.40W
Carnegie, L. Australia **82** 26.15S 123.00E
Carn Eige *mtn.* Scotland **32** 57.17N 5.07W
Carnew Rep. of Ire. **35** 52.43N 6.31W
Carnforth England **28** 54.08N 2.47W
Carnic Alps *mts.* Austria/Italy **38** 46.40N 12.48E
Car Nicobar *i.* India **58** 9.00N 92.30E
Carn Mòr *mtn.* Scotland **33** 57.14N 3.13W
Càrn na Loine *mtn.* Scotland **33** 57.24N 3.33W
Carnot C.A.E. **73** 4.59N 15.56E
Carnoustie Scotland **31** 56.30N 2.44W
Carnsore Pt. Rep. of Ire. **35** 52.10N 6.21W
Carnwath Scotland **31** 55.43N 3.37W
Carolina R.S.A. **76** 26.05S 30.07E
Caroline Is. Pacific Oc. **59** 7.50N 145.00E
Caroní *r.* Venezuela **101** 8.20N 62.45W
Carora Venezuela **101** 10.12N 70.07W
Carpathian Mts. Europe **43** 48.45N 23.45E
Carpentaria, G. of Australia **82** 14.00S 140.00E
Carpentras France **36** 44.03N 5.03E
Carpio Spain **37** 41.13N 5.07W
Carra, Lough Rep. of Ire. **34** 53.41N 9.15W
Carradale Scotland **30** 55.35N 5.28W
Carrara Italy **38** 44.04N 10.06E
Carrauntoohil *mtn.* Rep. of Ire. **35** 52.00N 9.45W
Carrbridge Scotland **33** 57.17N 3.49W
Carriacou *i.* Grenada **101** 12.30N 61.35W
Carrick *f.* Scotland **30** 55.12N 4.38W
Carrickfergus N. Ireland **30** 54.43N 5.49W
Carrick Forest *hills* Scotland **30** 55.11N 4.29W
Carrickmacross Rep. of Ire. **34** 53.58N 6.43W
Carrick-on-Shannon Rep. of Ire. **34** 53.57N 8.06W
Carrick-on-Suir Rep. of Ire. **35** 52.21N 7.26W
Carron *r.* Highland Scotland **32** 57.25N 5.27W
Carron *r.* Highland Scotland **33** 57.54N 4.23W
Carron, Loch Scotland **32** 57.23N 5.30W
Carrowkeel Rep. of Ire. **30** 55.07N 7.12W
Carrowmore Lough Rep. of Ire. **34** 54.11N 9.47W
Çarşamba Turkey **54** 41.13N 36.43E
Çarşamba *r.* Turkey **54** 37.52N 31.48E
Carse of Gowrie *f.* Scotland **31** 56.25N 3.15W
Carshalton England **23** 51.22N 0.10W
Carson City U.S.A. **96** 39.10N 119.46W
Carsphairn Scotland **30** 55.13N 4.15W
Carstairs Scotland **31** 55.42N 3.41W
Cartagena Colombia **101** 10.24N 75.33W
Cartagena Spain **37** 37.36N 0.59W
Cartago Costa Rica **100** 9.50N 83.52W
Carterton New Zealand **85** 41.01S 175.31E
Caruarú Brazil **108** 8.15S 35.55W
Carúpano Venezuela **101** 10.39N 63.14W
Carvin France **41** 50.30N 2.58E
Cary *r.* England **24** 51.10N 3.00W
Casablanca Morocco **70** 33.39N 7.35W
Cascade Range *mts.* U.S.A. **96** 44.00N 144.00W
Cascavel Brazil **110** 24.59S 53.29W
Caserta Italy **38** 41.06N 14.21E
Cashel Rep. of Ire. **35** 52.31N 7.54W
Casino Australia **83** 28.50S 153.02E
Caspe Spain **37** 41.14N 0.03W
Casper U.S.A. **96** 42.50N 106.20W
Caspian Depression *f.* U.S.S.R. **44** 47.00N 48.00E
Caspian Sea U.S.S.R. **44** 42.00N 51.00E
Cassai *r.* Angola **74** 10.38S 22.15E
Cassley *r.* Scotland **33** 57.58N 4.35W
Castaños Mexico **100** 26.48N 101.26W
Casteljaloux France **36** 44.19N 0.06W
Castellón de la Plana Spain **37** 39.59N 0.03W
Castelo Branco Portugal **37** 39.50N 7.30W
Casterton Australia **83** 37.35S 141.25E
Castlebar Rep. of Ire. **34** 53.52N 9.19W
Castlebay *town* Scotland **32** 56.58N 7.30W
Castlebellingham Rep. of Ire. **34** 53.53N 6.24W
Castleblayney Rep. of Ire. **34** 54.08N 6.46W
Castlebridge Rep. of Ire. **35** 52.23N 6.28W
Castle Cary England **24** 51.06N 2.31W
Castlecomer Rep. of Ire. **35** 52.48N 7.14W
Castledawson N. Ireland **30** 54.47N 6.35W
Castlederg N. Ireland **34** 54.42N 7.37W
Castledermot Rep. of Ire. **35** 52.54N 6.52W
Castle Douglas Scotland **31** 54.56N 3.56W
Castlefin Rep. of Ire. **34** 54.48N 7.41W
Castleford England **29** 53.43N 1.21W
Castlegregory Rep. of Ire. **35** 52.16N 10.01W
Castleisland *town* Rep. of Ire. **35** 52.13N 9.28W
Castlemaine Australia **83** 37.05S 144.19E
Castlemaine Rep. of Ire. **35** 52.10N 9.41W
Castlemaine Harbour *est.* Rep. of Ire. **35** 52.08N 9.50W
Castlepollard Rep. of Ire. **34** 53.41N 7.20W
Castlerea Rep. of Ire. **34** 53.45N 8.30W
Castlerock N. Ireland **30** 55.09N 6.47W
Castletown I.o.M. **28** 54.04N 4.38W
Castletownroche Rep. of Ire. **35** 52.10N 8.28W
Castletownshend Rep. of Ire. **35** 51.32N 9.12W
Castlewellan N. Ireland **34** 54.16N 5.57W
Castres France **36** 43.36N 2.14E
Castries St. Lucia **101** 14.01N 60.59W
Catalca Turkey **39** 41.09N 28.29E
Catamarca Argentina **110** 28.28S 65.46W
Catamarca *d.* Argentina **110** 27.40S 67.10W
Catanduanes *i.* Phil. **59** 13.45N 124.20E
Catanduva Brazil **110** 21.03S 49.00W
Catania Italy **38** 37.31N 15.05E
Catanzaro Italy **39** 38.55N 16.35E
Catarman Phil. **59** 12.28N 124.50E
Catbalogan Phil. **59** 11.46N 124.55E
Caterham England **25** 51.17N 0.04W
Catete Angola **74** 9.09S 13.40E
Catford England **23** 51.26N 0.00
Cat I. Bahamas **101** 24.30N 75.30W
Catoche, C. Mexico **100** 21.38N 87.08W
Catonsville U.S.A. **99** 39.17N 76.44W
Catskill Mts. U.S.A. **99** 42.15N 74.15W
Catterick England **28** 54.23N 1.38W
Cauca *r.* Colombia **101** 8.57N 74.30W
Caucasus Mts. U.S.S.R. **43** 43.00N 44.00E
Cauldcleuch Head *mtn.* Scotland **31** 55.18N 2.50W
Caungula Angola **74** 8.26S 18.35E
Caura *r.* Venezuela **101** 7.30N 65.00W
Causeway Rep. of Ire. **35** 52.25N 9.46W
Cavally *r.* Ivory Coast **72** 4.25N 7.39W
Cavan Rep. of Ire. **34** 54.00N 7.22W
Cavan *d.* Rep. of Ire. **34** 53.58N 7.10W
Cavite Phil. **59** 14.30N 120.54E
Cawood England **29** 53.50N 1.07W
Caxias do Sul Brazil **110** 29.14S 51.10W
Caxito Angola **74** 8.32S 13.38E
Cayenne Guiana **108** 4.55N 52.18W
Cayman Brac *i.* Cayman Is. **101** 19.44N 79.48W
Cayman Is. C. America **101** 19.00N 81.00W
Cayuga L. U.S.A. **99** 42.40N 76.40W
Cazombo Angola **74** 11.54S 22.56E
Cebollera, Sierra de *mts.* Spain **37** 41.58N 2.30W
Cebu Phil. **59** 10.17N 123.56E
Cebu *i.* Phil. **59** 10.15N 123.45E
Cecina Italy **38** 43.18N 10.30E
Cedar *r.* U.S.A. **98** 41.10N 91.25W
Cedar City U.S.A. **96** 37.40N 103.04W
Cedar Falls *town* U.S.A. **98** 42.34N 92.26W
Cedar Rapids *town* U.S.A. **98** 41.59N 91.39W
Cedros I. Mexico **96** 28.15N 115.15W
Ceduna Australia **82** 32.07S 133.42E
Cefalù Italy **38** 38.01N 14.03E
Ceiriog *r.* Wales **26** 52.57N 3.01W
Cela Angola **74** 11.26S 15.05E
Celaya Mexico **100** 20.32N 100.48W
Celebes *i.* Indonesia **59** 2.00S 120.30E
Celebes Sea Indonesia **59** 3.00N 122.00E
Celje Yugo. **38** 46.15N 15.16E
Celle W. Germany **40** 52.37N 10.05E
Cemaes Bay *town* Wales **26** 53.24N 4.27W
Cemaes Head Wales **26** 52.08N 4.42W
Central *d.* Ghana **72** 5.30N 1.10W
Central *d.* Kenya **75** 0.30S 37.00E
Central *d.* Scotland **30** 56.10N 4.20W
Central, Cordillera *mts.* Bolivia **110** 19.00S 65.00W
Central, Cordillera *mts.* Colombia **108** 6.00N 75.00W
Central African Empire Africa **70** 6.30N 20.00E
Centralia U.S.A. **98** 38.32N 89.08W
Central Russian Uplands U.S.S.R. **43** 53.00N 37.00E
Central Siberian Plateau *f.* U.S.S.R. **45** 66.00N 108.00E
Ceram *i.* Indonesia **59** 3.10S 129.30E
Ceram Sea Pacific Oc. **59** 2.50S 128.00E
Cerignola Italy **38** 41.17N 15.53E
Cernavodă Romania **39** 44.20N 28.02E
Cerne Abbas England **24** 50.49N 2.29W
Cerro de Pasco Peru **108** 10.43S 76.15W
Cerro Marahuaca *mtn.* Venezuela **108** 4.20N 65.30W
Cervera Spain **37** 41.40N 1.16W
Česke Budějovice Czech. **40** 49.00N 14.30E
Cessnock Australia **83** 32.51S 151.21E
Cetinje Yugo. **39** 42.24N 18.55E
Ceuta Spain **37** 35.53N 5.19W
Cevennes *mts.* France **36** 44.25N 4.05E
Ceyhan *r.* Turkey **54** 36.54N 34.58E
Ceylon *i.* Asia **113** 7.00N 81.00E
Chacabuco Argentina **110** 34.40S 60.27W
Chaco *d.* Argentina **110** 26.30S 61.00W
Chad Africa **73** 15.00N 17.00E
Chad, L. Africa **73** 13.30N 14.00E
Chadwell St. Mary England **23** 51.29N 0.22E
Chagford England **27** 50.40N 3.50W
Chagos Archipelago Indian Oc. **53** 7.00S 72.00E
Chah Bahar Iran **55** 25.17N 60.41E
Chakansur Afghan. **55** 31.10N 62.02E
Chalfont St. Giles England **23** 51.39N 0.35W
Chalfont St. Peter England **23** 51.37N 0.33W
Challans France **36** 46.51N 1.52W
Challenger Depth Pacific Oc. **59** 11.19N 142.15E
Châlons-sur-Marne France **36** 48.58N 4.22E
Chalon-sur-Saône France **36** 46.47N 4.51E
Chamai Thailand **58** 8.10N 99.41E
Chambal *r.* India **56** 26.30N 79.20E
Chambéry France **36** 45.34N 5.55E
Chambeshi *r.* Zambia **75** 11.15S 30.37E
Chamo, L. Ethiopia **75** 4.45N 36.53E
Chamonix France **36** 45.55N 6.52E
Champ Iran **55** 26.40N 60.31E
Champaign U.S.A. **98** 40.07N 88.14W
Champlain, L. U.S.A. **99** 44.45N 73.20W
Chanda India **57** 19.58N 79.21E
Chandeleur Is. U.S.A. **97** 29.50N 88.50W
Chandigarh India **56** 30.44N 76.54E
Changchun China **62** 43.51N 125.15E
Changde China **63** 29.00N 111.35E
Changhua Taiwan **63** 24.05N 120.30E
Changhua Jiang *r.* China **63** 19.20N 108.38E
Changjiang China **63** 25.42N 116.20E
Chang Jiang *r.* China **63** 31.40N 121.15E
Changkwansai Ling *mts.* China **64** 44.30N 128.00E
Changsha China **63** 28.09N 112.59E
Changshan Qundao *is.* China **62** 39.20N 123.00E
Changshou China **63** 29.50N 107.02E
Changshu China **63** 31.48N 120.52E
Changzhi China **62** 36.09N 113.12E
Changzhou Kiangsu China **63** 31.46N 119.58E
Channel Is. U.K. **27** 49.28N 2.13W
Channel Port aux Basques Canada **95** 47.35N 59.10W
Chanthaburi Thailand **57** 12.38N 102.12E
Chao'an China **63** 23.40N 116.32E
Chao Hu *l.* China **63** 31.32N 117.30E
Chao Phraya *r.* Thailand **57** 13.30N 100.25E
Chaoyang China **63** 23.25N 116.31E
Chaoyang China **62** 41.35N 120.20E
Chapala, Lago de Mexico **100** 20.00N 103.00W
Chapayevsk U.S.S.R. **43** 52.58N 49.44E
Chapel en le Frith England **28** 53.19N 1.54W
Chapel St. Leonards England **29** 53.14N 0.20E
Chapleau Canada **98** 47.50N 83.24W
Chapra India **56** 23.31N 88.40E
Chard England **24** 50.52N 2.59W
Chardzhou U.S.S.R. **55** 39.09N 63.34E
Chari *r.* Chad **73** 13.00N 14.30E
Charikar Afghan. **56** 35.02N 69.13E
Charing England **25** 51.12N 0.49E
Charleroi Belgium **41** 50.25N 4.27E
Charleston S.C. U.S.A. **97** 32.48N 79.58W
Charleston W. Va. U.S.A. **97** 38.23N 81.20W
Charlestown Rep. of Ire. **34** 53.57N 8.48W
Charlestown of Aberlour Scotland **33** 57.27N 3.14W
Charleville Australia **82** 26.25S 146.13E
Charleville-Mézières France **41** 49.46N 4.43E
Charlotte U.S.A. **97** 35.05N 80.50W
Charlottenburg W. Germany **40** 52.32N 13.18E
Charlottesville U.S.A. **97** 38.02N 78.29W
Charlottetown Canada **95** 46.14N 63.09W
Charlton Australia **83** 36.18S 143.27E
Charolles France **36** 46.26N 4.17E
Chartres France **36** 48.27N 1.30E
Chascomas Argentina **110** 35.34S 58.00W
Châteaubriant France **36** 47.43N 1.22W
Château du Loir France **36** 47.42N 0.25E
Châteaudun France **36** 48.04N 1.20E
Châteauroux France **36** 46.49N 1.41E
Château Thierry France **36** 49.03N 3.24E
Châtelet Belgium **41** 50.24N 4.32E
Châtellerault France **36** 46.49N 0.33E
Chatham Canada **98** 42.24N 82.11W
Chatham England **23** 51.23N 0.32E
Chatham Is. Pacific Oc. **113** 43.00S 176.00W
Châtillon-s-Seine France **36** 47.52N 4.35E
Chattahoochee *r.* U.S.A. **97** 29.45N 85.00W
Chattanooga U.S.A. **97** 35.01N 85.18W
Chatteris England **25** 52.27N 0.03E
Chauka *r.* India **56** 27.10N 81.28E
Chaumont France **36** 48.07N 5.08E
Chaves Portugal **37** 41.44N 7.28W
Cheadle England **28** 53.24N 2.13W
Cheam England **23** 51.22N 0.13W
Cheb Czech. **40** 50.04N 12.20E
Cheboksary U.S.S.R. **43** 56.08N 47.12E
Cheboygan U.S.A. **98** 45.40N 84.28W
Cheddar England **24** 51.16N 2.47W
Cheju S. Korea **61** 33.31N 126.29E
Cheleken U.S.S.R. **55** 39.26N 53.11E
Chéliff *r.* Algeria **37** 36.15N 2.05E
Chelmer *r.* England **25** 51.43N 0.40E
Chelmsford England **23** 51.44N 0.28E
Cheltenham England **24** 51.53N 2.07W
Chelyabinsk U.S.S.R. **44** 55.10N 61.25E
Chelyuskin, C. U.S.S.R. **45** 77.20N 106.00E
Chemba Moçambique **75** 17.11S 34.53E
Chen, Mt. U.S.S.R. **45** 65.30N 141.20E
Chenab *r.* Asia **56** 29.26N 71.09E
Chengde China **62** 41.00N 117.52E
Chengdu China **63** 30.41N 104.05E
Chenghai China **63** 23.31N 116.43E

Egremont England **28** 54.28N 3.33W
Eğridir Turkey **54** 37.52N 30.51E
Eğridir L. Turkey **54** 38.04N 30.55E
Egypt Africa **54** 27.00N 29.00E
Eibar Spain **37** 43.11N 2.28W
Eifel *f.* W. Germany **41** 50.10N 6.45E
Eigg *i.* Scotland **32** 56.53N 6.09W
Eigg, Sd. of Scotland **32** 56.51N 6.11W
Eighty Mile Beach *f.* Australia **82** 19.00S 121.00E
Eil, Loch Scotland **32** 56.51N 5.12W
Eildon Resr. Australia **83** 37.10S 146.00E
Eindhoven Neth. **41** 51.26N 5.30E
Eisenach E. Germany **40** 50.59N 10.19E
Eisenhut *mtn.* Austria **40** 47.00N 13.45E
Eisenhüttenstadt E. Germany **40** 52.09N 14.41E
Eishort, Loch Scotland **32** 57.09N 5.58W
Eisleben E. Germany **40** 51.32N 11.33E
Eitorf W. Germany **41** 50.46N 7.27E
Ekeia *r.* Congo **74** 1.40N 16.05E
Eksjo Sweden **42** 57.40N 15.00E
El Aaiún W. Sahara **70** 27.10N 13.11W
El Agheila Libya **70** 30.15N 19.12E
El Alamein Egypt **54** 30.50N 28.57E
Elands *r.* Transvaal R.S.A. **76** 24.55S 29.20E
El'Arîsh Egypt **54** 31.08N 33.48E
El'Arîsh, Wâdi *r.* Egypt **54** 31.09N 33.49E
El Asnam Algeria **37** 36.20N 1.30E
Elat Israel **54** 29.33N 34.56E
Elâziğ Turkey **54** 38.41N 39.14E
Elba *i.* Italy **38** 42.47N 10.17E
El Banco Colombia **101** 9.04N 73.59W
Elbasan Albania **39** 41.07N 20.04E
Elbe *r.* W. Germany **40** 53.33N 10.00E
Elbert, Mt. U.S.A. **96** 39.05N 106.27W
Elbeuf France **36** 49.17N 1.01E
Elbistan Turkey **54** 38.14N 37.11E
Elbląg Poland **43** 54.10N 19.25E
Elbrus *mtn.* U.S.S.R. **43** 43.21N 42.29E
Elburg Neth. **41** 52.27N 5.50E
Elburz Mts. Iran **55** 36.00N 52.30E
El Cardon Venezuela **101** 11.24N 70.09W
Elche Spain **37** 38.16N 0.41W
Elde *r.* E. Germany **40** 53.17N 12.40E
Eldorado Argentina **110** 26.28S 54.43W
Eldoret Kenya **75** 0.31N 35.17E
Electrostal U.S.S.R. **43** 55.46N 38.30E
Elephant Butte Resr. U.S.A. **96** 33.25N 107.10W
Elephant I. Atlantic Oc. **109** 61.00S 55.00W
El Escorial Spain **37** 40.34N 4.08W
Eleuthera I. Bahamas **101** 25.00N 76.00W
El Faiyûm Egypt **54** 29.19N 30.50E
El Fasher Sudan **71** 13.37N 25.22E
El Fekka, Wadi *r.* Tunisia **38** 35.25N 9.40E
El Ferrol Spain **37** 43.29N 8.14W
El Galâla, Gebel *mts.* Egypt **54** 29.00N 32.10E
Elgin Scotland **33** 57.39N 3.20W
Elgin U.S.A. **98** 42.03N 88.19W
El Gîza Egypt **54** 30.01N 31.12E
Elgol Scotland **32** 57.09N 6.07W
El Goléa Algeria **70** 30.35N 2.51E
Elgon, Mt. Kenya/Uganda **75** 1.07N 34.35E
El Hamad *des.* Asia **54** 31.45N 39.00E
El Hatob, Wadi *r.* Tunisia **38** 35.25N 9.40E
Elie and Earlsferry Scotland **31** 56.11N 2.50W
Elista U.S.S.R. **43** 46.18N 44.14E
Elizabeth U.S.A. **99** 40.40N 74.13W
El Jauf Libya **71** 24.09N 23.19E
El Khârga Egypt **54** 25.27N 30.32E
Elkhart U.S.A. **98** 41.52N 85.56W
Elkhovo Bulgaria **39** 42.10N 26.35E
Elkins U.S.A. **98** 38.56N 79.53W
Elk Lake *town* Canada **98** 47.44N 80.21W
Elko U.S.A. **96** 40.50N 115.46W
Elland England **28** 53.41N 1.49W
Ellen *r.* England **28** 54.42N 3.30W
Ellen, Mt. U.S.A. **96** 38.06N 110.50W
Ellesmere England **28** 52.55N 2.53W
Ellesmere I. Canada **95** 78.00N 82.00W
Ellesmere Port England **28** 53.17N 2.55W
Ellon Scotland **33** 57.22N 2.05W
Ellsworth U.S.A. **99** 44.34N 68.24W
El Mahalla el Kubra Egypt **54** 30.59N 31.12E
Elmali Turkey **54** 36.43N 29.56E
El Mansûra Egypt **54** 31.03N 31.23E
El Minya Egypt **54** 28.06N 30.45E
Elmira U.S.A. **99** 42.06N 76.50W
Elmshorn W. Germany **40** 53.46N 9.40E
El Muglad Sudan **71** 11.01N 27.50E
El Natrûn, Wâdi *f.* Egypt **54** 30.25N 30.18E
El Obeid Sudan **71** 13.11N 30.10E
Eloy U.S.A. **96** 32.45N 111.33W
El Paso U.S.A. **96** 31.45N 106.30W
Elphin Rep. of Ire. **34** 53.50N 8.11W
El Qantara Egypt **54** 30.52N 32.20E
El Qasr Egypt **54** 25.43N 28.54E
El Qatrun Libya **70** 24.55N 14.38E
El Real Panamá **101** 8.06N 77.42W
El Salvador C. America **100** 13.30N 89.00W
Elstead England **23** 51.11N 0.43W
Elstree England **23** 51.39N 0.18W
El Tarfa, Wâdi *r.* Egypt **54** 28.36N 30.50E
Eltham England **23** 51.27N 0.04E
El Tigre Venezuela **101** 8.44N 64.18W
El Tîh, Gebel *f.* Egypt **54** 28.50N 34.00E
El Tûr Egypt **54** 28.14N 33.37E
Eluru India **57** 16.45N 81.10E
Elvas Portugal **37** 38.53N 7.10W
Elverum Norway **42** 60.54N 11.33E
El Wak Kenya **75** 2.45N 40.52E
Elwy *r.* Wales **26** 53.17N 3.27W
Ely England **25** 52.24N 0.16E
Ely U.S.A. **98** 47.53N 91.52W
Elyria U.S.A. **98** 41.22N 82.06W
Emba *r.* U.S.S.R. **44** 46.40N 53.30E
Embarcación Argentina **110** 23.15S 64.05W
Embleton England **31** 55.30N 1.37W
Embu Kenya **75** 0.32S 37.28E
Emden W. Germany **41** 53.23N 7.13E
Emerson Canada **97** 49.00N 97.11W
Emi Koussi *mtn.* Chad **73** 19.58N 18.30E
Emlagh Pt. Rep. of Ire. **34** 53.46N 9.45W
Emly Rep. of Ire. **35** 52.28N 8.21W
Emmeloord Neth. **41** 52.43N 5.46E
Emmen Neth. **41** 52.48N 6.55E
Emmerich W. Germany **41** 51.49N 6.16E
Emory Peak U.S.A. **96** 29.15N 103.19W
Empangeni R.S.A. **76** 28.45S 31.54E
Empedrado Argentina **110** 27.59S 58.47W
Emporia U.S.A. **97** 38.24N 96.10W
Ems *r.* W. Germany **41** 53.14N 7.25E
Ems-Jade Canal W. Germany **41** 53.28N 7.40E
Emyvale Rep. of Ire. **34** 54.20N 6.59W
Enard B. Scotland **32** 58.05N 5.20W
Encarnación Paraguay **110** 27.20S 55.50W
Enchi Ghana **72** 5.53N 2.48W
Ende Indonesia **59** 8.51S 121.40E
Endicott Mts. U.S.A. **94** 68.00N 152.00W
Enfida Tunisia **38** 36.08N 10.22E
Enfield England **23** 51.40N 0.05W
Enfield Rep. of Ire. **34** 53.25N 6.52W
Engaño, C. Phil. **59** 18.30N 122.20E
Engels U.S.S.R. **43** 51.30N 46.07E
Enggano *i.* Indonesia **58** 5.20S 102.15E
Enghien Belgium **41** 50.42N 4.02E
Englefield Green England **23** 51.26N 0.36W
English Bazar India **56** 25.00N 88.12E
English Channel France/U.K. **36** 50.15N 1.00W
Enkeldoorn Zimbabwe **76** 19.01S 30.53E
Enkhuizen Neth. **41** 52.42N 5.17E
Enköping Sweden **42** 59.38N 17.07E
Enna Italy **38** 37.34N 14.15E
En Nahud Sudan **71** 12.41N 28.28E
Ennell, Lough Rep. of Ire. **34** 53.28N 7.25W
Ennerdale Water *l.* England **28** 54.31N 3.21W
Ennis Rep. of Ire. **35** 52.51N 9.00W
Enniscorthy Rep. of Ire. **35** 52.30N 6.35W
Enniskean Rep. of Ire. **35** 51.45N 8.55W
Enniskerry Rep. of Ire. **35** 53.11N 6.12W
Enniskillen N. Ireland **34** 54.21N 7.40W
Ennistymon Rep. of Ire. **35** 52.56N 9.18W
Enns *r.* Austria **40** 48.14N 14.22E
Enrick *r.* Scotland **33** 57.20N 4.28W
Enschede Neth. **41** 52.13N 6.54E
Ensenada Mexico **96** 31.53N 116.35W
Entebbe Uganda **75** 0.08N 32.29E
Entre Rios *d.* Argentina **110** 31.50S 59.00W
Entre-Rios Moçambique **75** 14.55S 37.09E
Enugu Nigeria **73** 6.20N 7.29E
Epe Neth. **41** 52.21N 5.59E
Epernay France **36** 49.02N 3.58E
Épinal France **40** 48.10N 6.28E
Eport, Loch Scotland **32** 57.30N 7.10W
Epping England **23** 51.42N 0.07E
Epping Forest *f.* England **23** 51.39N 0.03E
Epping Green England **23** 51.43N 0.06E
Epsom England **23** 51.20N 0.16W
Epworth England **29** 53.30N 0.50W
Equateur *d.* Zaïre **74** 0.00 21.00E
Equatorial Guinea Africa **74** 2.00N 10.00E
Erbil Iraq **55** 36.12N 44.01E
Erciyaş, Mt. Turkey **54** 38.33N 35.25E
Erdre *r.* France **36** 47.27N 1.34W
Erebus, Mt. Antarctica **111** 77.40S 167.20E
Ereğli Konya Turkey **54** 37.30N 34.02E
Ereğli Zonguldak Turkey **54** 41.17N 31.26E
Erenhot China **62** 43.48N 112.00E
Erexim Brazil **110** 27.35S 52.15W
Erft *r.* W. Germany **41** 51.12N 6.45E
Erfurt E. Germany **40** 50.58N 11.02E
Ergani Turkey **54** 38.17N 39.44E
Ergene *r.* Turkey **39** 41.02N 26.22E
Eriboll, Loch Scotland **33** 58.28N 4.41W
Ericht, Loch Scotland **33** 56.52N 4.20W
Erie U.S.A. **98** 42.07N 80.05W
Erie, L. Canada/U.S.A. **98** 42.15N 81.00W
Erigavo Somali Rep. **71** 10.40N 47.20E
Erimo saki *c.* Japan **64** 41.55N 143.13E
Eriskay *i.* Scotland **32** 57.04N 7.17W
Erisort, Loch Scotland **32** 58.06N 6.30W
Erith England **23** 51.29N 0.11E
Eritrea *f.* Ethiopia **71** 15.30N 38.00E
Erkelenz W. Germany **41** 51.05N 6.18E
Erlangen W. Germany **40** 49.36N 11.02E
Ermelo Neth. **41** 52.19N 5.38E
Ermelo R.S.A. **76** 26.32S 29.59E
Erne *r.* Rep. of Ire. **34** 54.30N 8.17W
Erode India **56** 11.21N 77.43E
Er Rahad Sudan **71** 12.42N 30.33E
Errigal Mtn. Rep. of Ire. **34** 55.02N 8.08W
Erris Head Rep. of Ire. **34** 54.19N 10.00W
Er Roseires Sudan **71** 11.52N 34.23E
Erskine Scotland **30** 55.53N 4.27W
Ertix He *r.* U.S.S.R. **60** 48.00N 84.20E
Erzincan Turkey **54** 39.44N 39.30E
Erzurum Turkey **54** 39.57N 41.17E
Esbjerg Denmark **42** 55.28N 8.28E
Escanaba U.S.A. **98** 45.47N 87.04W
Esch Lux. **41** 49.31N 5.59E
Eschweiler W. Germany **41** 50.49N 6.16E
Escondido *r.* Nicaragua **100** 11.58N 83.45W
Escuintla Guatemala **100** 14.18N 90.47W
Esha Ness *c.* Scotland **32** 60.29N 1.37W
Esher England **23** 51.23N 0.22W
Eshowe R.S.A. **76** 28.54S 31.28E
Esk *r.* Cumbria England **28** 54.20N 3.24W
Esk *r.* Cumbria England **31** 54.58N 3.02W
Esk *r.* N. Yorks. England **29** 54.29N 0.37W
Eskdale *f.* Scotland **31** 55.13N 3.08W
Eskilstuna Sweden **42** 59.22N 16.31E
Eskimo Point *town* Canada **95** 61.10N 94.15W
Eskişehir Turkey **54** 39.46N 30.30E
Esla *r.* Spain **37** 41.50N 5.48W
Esperance Australia **82** 33.49S 121.52E
Esperanza Argentina **110** 31.29S 61.00W
Espungabera Moçambique **76** 20.28S 32.47E
Esquel Argentina **109** 42.55S 71.20W
Essen W. Germany **41** 51.27N 6.57E
Essendon England **23** 51.46N 0.09W
Essequibo *r.* Guyana **108** 6.48N 58.23W
Essex *d.* England **23** 51.46N 0.30E
Esslingen W. Germany **40** 48.45N 9.19E
Estats, Pic d' *mtn.* Spain **36** 42.40N 1.23E
Estepona Spain **37** 36.26N 5.09W
Estevan Canada **96** 49.09N 103.00W
Eston England **29** 54.34N 1.07W
Estonia Soviet Socialist Republic *d.* U.S.S.R. **42** 58.45N 25.30E
Estrêla, Serra da *mts.* Portugal **37** 40.20N 7.40W
Estremoz Portugal **37** 38.50N 7.35W
Etah India **56** 27.33N 78.39E
Etaples France **36** 50.31N 1.39E
Etawah India **56** 26.40N 79.20E
Ethiopia Africa **71** 10.00N 39.00E
Ethiopian Highlands Ethiopia **71** 10.00N 37.00E
Etive, Loch Scotland **30** 56.27N 5.15W
Etna, Mt. Italy **38** 37.43N 14.59E
Etobicoke Canada **99** 43.38N 79.30W
Eton England **23** 51.31N 0.37W
Etosha Game Res. Namibia **76** 18.45S 14.55E
Etosha Pan *f.* Namibia **76** 18.50S 16.30E
Ettelbrück Lux. **41** 49.51N 6.06E
Ettrick *r.* Scotland **31** 55.36N 2.49W
Ettrick Forest *f.* Scotland **31** 55.30N 3.00W
Ettrick Pen *mtn.* Scotland **31** 55.21N 3.16W
Et Tubeiq, Jebel *mts.* Saudi Arabia **54** 29.30N 37.15E
Euboea *i.* Greece **39** 38.30N 23.50E
Eucla Australia **82** 31.40S 128.51E
Euclid U.S.A. **98** 41.34N 81.33W
Eufaula Resr. U.S.A. **97** 35.15N 95.35W
Eugene U.S.A. **96** 44.03N 123.07W
Eugenia, Punta *c.* Mexico **96** 27.50N 115.50W
Eupen Belgium **41** 50.38N 6.04E
Euphrates *r.* Asia **55** 31.00N 47.27E
Eureka U.S.A. **96** 40.49N 124.10W
Euroa Australia **83** 36.46S 145.35E
Europa, Picos de *mts.* Spain **37** 43.10N 4.40W
Europe 14
Europoort Neth. **41** 51.56N 4.08E
Euskirchen W. Germany **41** 50.40N 6.47E
Evale Angola **74** 16.24S 15.50E
Evans, L. Canada **97** 50.55N 77.00W
Evanston U.S.A. **98** 42.02N 87.41W
Evansville U.S.A. **97** 38.02N 87.24W
Evanton Scotland **33** 57.39N 4.21W
Evenlode *r.* England **24** 51.46N 1.21W
Everard, C. Australia **83** 37.50S 149.16E
Evercreech England **24** 51.08N 2.30W
Everest, Mt. Asia **56** 27.59N 86.56E
Evesham England **24** 52.06N 1.57W
Evje Norway **42** 58.36N 7.51E
Evora Portugal **37** 38.34N 7.54W
Evreux France **36** 49.03N 1.11E
Ewe, Loch Scotland **32** 57.48N 5.38W
Ewell England **23** 51.21N 0.15W

Fort Collins U.S.A. **96** 40.35N 105.05W
Fort Crampel C.A.E. **73** 7.00N 19.10E
Fort-Dauphin Madagascar **69** 25.01S 47.00E
Fort-de-France Martinique **101** 14.36N 61.05W
Fort de Possel C.A.E. **74** 5.03N 19.14E
Fort Frances Canada **98** 48.37N 93.23W
Fort George Canada **95** 53.50N 79.01W
Fort George r. Canada **95** 53.50N 79.00W
Fort Good Hope Canada **94** 66.16N 128.37W
Forth Scotland **31** 55.46N 3.42W
Forth r. Scotland **31** 56.06N 3.48W
Fort Lauderdale U.S.A. **97** 26.08N 80.08W
Fort Liard Canada **94** 60.14N 123.28W
Fort Madison U.S.A. **98** 40.38N 91.21W
Fort Maguire Malaŵi **75** 13.38S 34.59E
Fort McPherson Canada **94** 67.29N 134.50W
Fort Myers U.S.A. **97** 26.39N 81.51W
Fort Nelson Canada **94** 58.48N 122.44W
Fort Norman Canada **94** 64.55N 125.29W
Fort Peck Dam U.S.A. **96** 47.55N 106.15W
Fort Peck Resr. U.S.A. **96** 47.55N 107.00W
Fort Polignac Algeria **70** 26.20N 8.20E
Fort Portal Uganda **75** 0.40N 30.17E
Fort Randall U.S.A. **96** 55.10N 162.47W
Fort Reliance Canada **94** 62.45N 109.08W
Fort Resolution Canada **94** 61.10N 113.39W
Fortrose Scotland **33** 57.34N 4.09W
Fort Rousset Congo **74** 0.30S 15.48E
Fort Rupert Canada **95** 51.30N 79.45W
Fort St. John Canada **94** 56.14N 120.55W
Fort Scott U.S.A. **97** 37.52N 94.43W
Fort Severn Canada **95** 56.00N 87.40W
Fort Shevchenko U.S.S.R. **44** 44.31N 50.15E
Fort Sibut C.A.E. **73** 5.46N 19.06E
Fort Simpson Canada **94** 61.46N 121.15W
Fort Smith U.S.A. **97** 35.22N 94.27W
Fortune i. Bahamas **101** 22.30N 74.15W
Fortuneswell England **24** 50.33N 2.27W
Fort Vermilion Canada **94** 58.22N 115.59W
Fort Victoria Zimbabwe **76** 20.10S 30.49E
Fort Wayne U.S.A. **98** 41.05N 85.08W
Fort William Scotland **32** 56.49N 5.07W
Fort Worth U.S.A. **97** 32.45N 97.20W
Fort Yukon U.S.A. **94** 66.35N 145.20W
Foshan China **63** 23.08N 113.08E
Fostoria U.S.A. **98** 41.10N 83.25W
Fougamou Gabon **74** 1.10S 10.31E
Fougères France **36** 48.21N 1.12W
Foula i. Scotland **32** 60.08N 2.05W
Foulness I. England **25** 51.35N 0.55E
Foulness Pt. England **25** 51.37N 1.00E
Foulwind, C. New Zealand **85** 41.45S 171.30E
Fouman Cameroon **74** 5.43N 10.50E
Four Elms England **23** 51.14N 0.07E
Foveaux Str. New Zealand **85** 46.40S 168.00E
Fowey England **27** 50.20N 4.39W
Fowey r. England **27** 50.22N 4.40W
Fow Kiang r. China **63** 30.02N 106.20E
Fox r. U.S.A. **98** 41.19N 88.59W
Foxe Basin b. Canada **95** 67.30N 79.00W
Foxe Channel Canada **95** 65.00N 80.00W
Foxford Rep. of Ire. **34** 53.58N 9.08W
Foxton New Zealand **85** 40.27S 175.18E
Foyle r. N. Ireland **34** 55.00N 7.20W
Foyle, Lough N. Ireland **30** 55.05N 7.10W
Foz do Iguaçu Brazil **110** 25.33S 54.31W
Framingham U.S.A. **99** 42.18N 71.25W
Framlingham England **25** 52.14N 1.20E
Franca Brazil **110** 20.33S 47.27W
France Europe **36** 47.00N 2.00E
Franceville Gabon **74** 1.38S 13.31E
Francistown Botswana **76** 21.11S 27.32E
Frankfort R.S.A. **76** 27.16S 28.30E
Frankfort U.S.A. **97** 38.11N 84.53W
Frankfurt E. Germany **40** 52.20N 14.32E
Frankfurt W. Germany **40** 50.06N 8.41E
Franklin d. Canada **95** 73.00N 100.00W
Franklin U.S.A. **98** 39.29N 86.02W
Franklin D. Roosevelt L. U.S.A. **96** 47.55N 118.20W
Frank Saale r. W. Germany **36** 50.00N 8.21E
Franz Canada **98** 48.28N 84.25W
Franz Josef Land is. U.S.S.R. **44** 81.00N 54.00E
Fraser r. Canada **96** 49.05N 123.00W
Fraserburg R.S.A. **76** 31.55S 21.31E
Fraserburgh Scotland **33** 57.42N 2.00W
Fray Bentos Uruguay **110** 33.10S 58.20W
Fredericia Denmark **42** 55.34N 9.47E
Frederick U.S.A. **99** 39.25N 77.25W
Fredericksburg U.S.A. **97** 38.18N 77.30W
Fredericton Canada **99** 45.57N 66.40W
Frederikshaab Greenland **95** 62.05N 49.30W
Fredrikshavn Denmark **42** 57.28N 10.33E
Fredrikstad Norway **42** 59.15N 10.55E
Freeport Bahamas **101** 26.40N 78.30W
Freeport U.S.A. **98** 42.17N 89.38W
Freetown Sierra Leone **72** 8.30N 13.17W
Freiburg W. Germany **40** 48.00N 7.52E
Freilingen W. Germany **41** 50.33N 7.50E

Freising W. Germany **40** 48.24N 11.45E
Freital E. Germany **40** 51.00N 13.40E
Fréjus France **36** 43.26N 6.44E
Fremantle Australia **82** 32.07S 115.44E
French Cays is. Bahamas **101** 21.31N 72.14W
Frenchman's Cap mtn. Australia **83** 42.27S 145.54E
Frenda Algeria **37** 35.04N 1.03E
Freshford Rep. of Ire. **35** 52.44N 7.23W
Fresno U.S.A. **96** 36.41N 119.57W
Freycinet Pen. Australia **83** 42.10S 148.18E
Frias Argentina **110** 28.35S 65.06W
Fribourg Switz. **40** 46.50N 7.10E
Friedrichshafen W. Germany **40** 47.39N 9.29E
Friern Barnet England **23** 51.37N 0.09W
Friesland d. Neth. **41** 53.05N 5.45E
Friesoythe W. Germany **41** 53.02N 7.52E
Frimley England **23** 51.19N 0.44W
Frinton England **25** 51.50N 1.16E
Frio, Cabo c. Brazil **109** 22.50S 42.10W
Frisa, Loch Scotland **30** 56.33N 6.05W
Frobisher B. Canada **95** 63.00N 66.00W
Frobisher Bay town Canada **95** 63.45N 68.30W
Frodsham England **28** 53.17N 2.45W
Fro Havet est. Norway **42** 63.55N 9.05E
Frome England **24** 51.16N 2.17W
Frome r. England **24** 50.41N 2.05W
Frome, L. Australia **83** 30.45S 139.45E
Frosinone Italy **38** 41.36N 13.21E
Fröya i. Norway **42** 63.45N 8.30E
Frunze U.S.S.R. **60** 42.53N 74.46E
Fuchun Liang r. China **63** 30.05N 120.00E
Fuday i. Scotland **32** 57.03N 7.23W
Fuerte r. Mexico **96** 25.42N 109.20W
Fuerteventura i. Canary Is. **70** 28.20N 14.10W
Fujairah U.A.E. **55** 25.10N 56.20E
Fujian d. China **63** 26.00N 118.00E
Fujin China **61** 47.15N 131.59E
Fujiyama mtn. Japan **64** 35.23N 138.42E
Fukui Japan **64** 36.04N 136.12E
Fukuoka Japan **64** 33.39N 130.21E
Fukushima Japan **64** 37.44N 140.28E
Fukuyama Japan **64** 34.29N 133.21E
Fulda W. Germany **40** 50.35N 9.41E
Fulham England **23** 51.29N 0.13W
Fuling China **63** 29.40N 107.20E
Fumay France **41** 49.59N 4.42E
Funabashi Japan **64** 35.42N 139.59E
Fundy, B. of N.America **97** 44.30N 66.30W
Funen i. Denmark **42** 55.15N 10.30E
Funiu Shan mts. China **62** 33.40N 112.20E
Funzie Scotland **32** 60.33N 0.48W
Furakawa Japan **64** 38.30N 140.50E
Furancungo Moçambique **75** 14.51S 33.38E
Furg Iran **55** 28.19N 55.10E
Furnas Dam Brazil **109** 20.40S 46.22W
Furnas Resr. Brazil **110** 21.00S 46.00W
Furneaux Group is. Australia **83** 40.15S 148.15E
Furnes Belgium **41** 51.04N 2.40E
Fürstenau W. Germany **41** 52.32N 7.41E
Fürstenwalde E. Germany **40** 52.22N 14.04E
Fürth W. Germany **40** 49.28N 11.00E
Fushun China **62** 41.50N 123.55E
Fussen W. Germany **40** 47.35N 10.43E
Futa Jalon f. Guinea **72** 11.30N 12.30W
Fu Xian China **62** 39.35N 122.07E
Fuxin China **62** 42.08N 121.39E
Fuyang China **62** 32.52N 115.52E
Fuyang He r. China **62** 38.10N 116.08E
Fuyu China **61** 45.12N 124.49E
Fuzhou Fujian China **63** 26.09N 119.21E
Fuzhou Jiangxi China **63** 28.01N 116.13E
Fyfield England **23** 51.45N 0.16E
Fyne, Loch Scotland **30** 55.55N 5.23W
Fyvie Scotland **33** 57.26N 2.24W

G

Gabela Angola **74** 10.52S 14.24E
Gabes Tunisia **70** 33.52N 10.06E
Gabes, G. of Tunisia **70** 34.00N 11.00E
Gabon Africa **74** 0.00 12.00E
Gabon r. Gabon **74** 0.15N 10.00E
Gaborone Botswana **76** 24.45S 25.55E
Gabriel, Mt. Rep. of Ire. **35** 51.34N 9.34W
Gach Saran Iran **55** 30.13N 50.49E
Gadsden U.S.A. **97** 34.00N 86.00W
Gaeta Italy **38** 41.13N 13.35E
Gaeta, G. of Med. Sea **38** 41.05N 13.30E
Gaferut i. Asia **59** 9.14N 145.23E
Gagnoa Ivory Coast **72** 6.04N 5.55W
Gagnon Canada **95** 51.56N 68.16W
Gaillac France **36** 43.54N 1.53E
Gainesville U.S.A. **97** 29.37N 82.31W
Gainford England **28** 54.34N 1.44W
Gainsborough England **29** 53.23N 0.46W
Gairdner, L. Australia **82** 31.30S 136.00E

Gairloch Scotland **32** 57.43N 5.40W
Gairloch, Loch Scotland **32** 57.43N 5.43W
Gairsay i. Scotland **33** 59.05N 2.58W
Gai Xian China **62** 40.25N 122.15E
Galana r. Kenya **75** 3.12S 40.09E
Galangue Angola **74** 13.40S 16.00E
Galapagos Is. Ecuador **107** 0.20S 91.00W
Galashiels Scotland **31** 55.37N 2.49W
Galati Romania **39** 45.27N 27.59E
Galena U.S.A. **98** 40.58N 90.22W
Galena U.S.A. **94** 64.43N 157.00W
Galesburg U.S.A. **98** 40.58N 90.22W
Galey r. Rep. of Ire. **35** 52.26N 9.37W
Galita i. Tunisia **38** 37.31N 8.55E
Gallan Head Scotland **32** 58.14N 7.01W
Galle Sri Lanka **57** 6.01N 80.13E
Gállego r. Spain **37** 41.40N 0.55W
Galley Head Rep. of Ire. **35** 51.32N 8.57W
Gallinas, C. Colombia **108** 12.27N 71.44W
Gallípoli Italy **39** 40.02N 18.01E
Gallipoli Turkey **39** 40.25N 26.31E
Gällivare Sweden **42** 67.10N 20.40E
Galloway f. Scotland **30** 55.00N 4.28W
Gallup U.S.A. **96** 35.32N 108.46W
Galong Australia **83** 34.37S 148.34E
Galston Scotland **30** 55.36N 4.23W
Galt Canada **98** 43.21N 80.19W
Galtby Finland **42** 60.08N 21.33E
Galtymore mtn. Rep. of Ire. **35** 52.22N 8.13W
Galty Mts. Rep. of Ire. **35** 52.20N 8.10W
Galveston U.S.A. **97** 29.17N 94.48W
Galveston B. U.S.A. **97** 29.40N 94.40W
Galvez Argentina **110** 32.03S 61.14W
Galway Rep. of Ire. **34** 53.17N 9.04W
Galway d. Rep. of Ire. **34** 53.25N 9.00W
Galway B. Rep. of Ire. **35** 53.12N 9.07W
Gambia Africa **72** 13.10N 16.00W
Gambia r. Gambia **72** 13.28N 15.55W
Gamboma Congo **74** 1.50S 15.58E
Ganale Dorya r. Ethiopia **75** 4.13N 42.04E
Ganbashao China **63** 26.37N 107.41E
Ganda Angola **74** 12 58S 14.39E
Gandajika Zaïre **74** 6.46S 23.58E
Gandak r. India **56** 25.35N 85.20E
Gander Canada **95** 48.58N 54.34W
Gandia Spain **37** 38.59N 0.11W
Ganges r. India **56** 23.30N 90.25E
Ganges, Mouths of the India/Bangla. **56** 22.00N 89.35E
Gangtok India **56** 27.20N 88.39E
Gangu China **62** 34.30N 105.30E
Gan Jiang r. China **63** 29.10N 116.00E
Gannat France **36** 46.06N 3.11E
Gannett Peak mtn. U.S.A. **96** 43.10N 109.38W
Gansu d. China **62** 36.00N 104.00E
Ganzhou China **63** 25.49N 114.50E
Gao Mali **72** 16.19N 0.09W
Gaoyou China **62** 32.40N 119.30E
Gaoyou Hu l. China **62** 32.50N 119.25E
Gaozhou China **63** 21.58N 110.59E
Gap France **36** 44.33N 6.05E
Gar China **57** 32.10N 79.59E
Gara, Lough Rep. of Ire. **34** 53.57N 8.27W
Gard r. France **36** 43.52N 4.40E
Garda, L. Italy **38** 45.40N 10.40E
Garelochhead Scotland **30** 56.05N 4.49W
Garforth England **29** 53.48N 1.22W
Garies R.S.A. **76** 30.30S 18.00E
Garioch f. Scotland **33** 57.18N 2.30W
Garissa Kenya **75** 0.27S 39.49E
Garlieston Scotland **30** 54.46N 4.22W
Garmisch Partenkirchen W. Germany **40** 47.30N 11.05E
Garmouth Scotland **33** 57.40N 3.07W
Garmsar Iran **55** 35.15N 52.21E
Garo Hills India **56** 25.30N 90.30E
Garonne r. France **36** 45.00N 0.37W
Garoua Cameroon **73** 9.1 /N 13.22E
Garrison Resr. U.S.A. **96** 47.30N 102.20W
Garroch Head Scotland **30** 55.43N 5.02W
Garron Pt. N. Ireland **30** 55.03N 5.57W
Garry, Loch Scotland **33** 57.05N 4.55W
Garry L. Canada **95** 66.00N 100.00W
Garstang England **28** 53.53N 2.47W
Garth Wales **26** 52.08N 3.32W
Garthorpe England **29** 53.40N 0.42W
Garut Indonesia **58** 7.15S 107.55E
Garvagh N. Ireland **30** 54.58N 6.42W
Garvão Portugal **37** 37.42N 8.21W
Garve Scotland **33** 57.37N 4.41W
Garvellachs i. Scotland **30** 56.15N 5.45W
Garvie Mts. New Zealand **85** 45.15S 169.00E
Garwah India **56** 24.11N 83.47E
Gary U.S.A. **98** 41.34N 87.20W
Garyarsa China **60** 32.00N 80.30E
Gascony, G. of France **36** 44.00N 2.40W
Gascoyne r. Australia **82** 25.00S 113.40E
Gaspé Canada **99** 48.30N 64.30W
Gaspé Pen. Canada **99** 48.30N 66.45W
Gata, C. Cyprus **54** 34.33N 33.03E

Gata, Cabo de Spain **37** 36.45N 2.11W
Gata, Sierra de *mts.* Spain **37** 40.20N 6.30W
Gatehouse of Fleet Scotland **30** 54.53N 4.12W
Gateshead England **28** 54.57N 1.35W
Gatineau *r.* Canada **99** 45.25N 75.43W
Gatooma Zimbabwe **76** 18.16S 29.55E
Gatun L. Canal Zone **101** 9.20N 80.00W
Gauhati India **57** 26.05N 91.55E
Gauja *r.* U.S.S.R. **42** 57.10N 24.17E
Gavá Spain **37** 41.18N 2.00E
Gävle Sweden **42** 60.41N 17.10E
Gawler Australia **83** 34.38S 138.44E
Gaya India **56** 24.48N 85.00E
Gaya Niger **73** 11.53N 3.31E
Gaydon England **24** 52.11N 1.27W
Gaza Egypt **54** 31.30N 34.28E
Gaza *d.* Moçambique **76** 23.30S 33.00E
Gaziantep Turkey **54** 37.04N 37.21E
Gcuwa R.S.A. **76** 32.20S 28.09E
Gdańsk Poland **42** 54.22N 18.38E
Gdańsk, G. of Poland **43** 54.45N 19.15E
Gdov U.S.S.R. **42** 58.48N 27.52E
Gdynia Poland **42** 54.31N 18.30E
Geal Chàrn *mtn.* Scotland **33** 57.06N 3.30W
Gebze Turkey **54** 40.48N 29.26E
Gediz *r.* Turkey **39** 38.37N 26.47E
Gedser Denmark **40** 54.35N 11.57E
Geel Belgium **41** 51.10N 5.00E
Geelong Australia **83** 38.10S 144.26E
Geh Iran **55** 26.14N 60.15E
Geidam Nigeria **73** 12.55N 11.55E
Geilenkirchen W. Germany **41** 50.58N 6.08E
Gejiu China **60** 23.25N 103.05E
Gelderland *d.* Neth. **41** 52.05N 6.00E
Geldern W. Germany **41** 51.31N 6.19E
Geleen Neth. **41** 50.58N 5.51E
Gelligaer Wales **27** 51.40N 3.18W
Gelsenkirchen W. Germany **41** 51.30N 7.05E
Gemas Malaysia **58** 2.35N 102.35E
Gembloux Belgium **41** 50.34N 4.42E
Gemena Zaïre **74** 3.14N 19.48E
Gemlik Turkey **54** 40.26N 29.10E
Geneina Sudan **71** 13.27N 22.30E
General Acha Argentina **110** 37.25S 64.38W
General Alvear Argentina **110** 34.59S 67.40W
General Santos Phil. **59** 6.05N 125.15E
Geneva Switz. **40** 46.13N 6.09E
Geneva, L. Switz. **40** 46.30N 6.30E
Genichesk U.S.S.R. **43** 46.10N 34.49E
Genil *r.* Spain **37** 37.42N 5.20W
Genk Belgium **40** 50.58N 5.30E
Genoa Italy **36** 44.24N 8.54E
Genoa, G. of Italy **36** 44.12N 8.55E
Gent Belgium **41** 51.02N 3.42E
George *r.* Canada **95** 58.30N 66.00W
George R.S.A. **76** 33.57S 22.28E
George, L. Australia **83** 35.07S 149.22E
George, L. Uganda **75** 0.00 30.10E
George, L. U.S.A. **99** 43.30N 73.30W
George Town Australia **83** 41.04S 146.48E
Georgetown Cayman Is. **100** 19.20N 81.23W
Georgetown Guyana **108** 6.46N 58.10W
George Town Malaysia **58** 5.30N 100.16E
Georgia *d.* U.S.A. **97** 33.00N 83.00W
Georgia, Str. of Canada **96** 49.15N 123.45W
Georgian B. Canada **98** 45.15N 80.45W
Georgia Soviet Socialist Republic *f.* U.S.S.R. **54** 42.00N 43.30E
Gera E. Germany **40** 50.51N 12.11E
Geraardsbergen Belgium **41** 50.47N 3.53E
Geraldton Australia **82** 28.49S 114.36E
Germiston R.S.A. **76** 26.15S 28.10E
Gerona Spain **37** 41.59N 2.49E
Gerrards Cross England **23** 51.35N 0.34W
Getafe Spain **37** 40.18N 3.44W
Gete *r.* Belgium **41** 50.58N 5.07E
Geyve Turkey **54** 40.32N 30.18E
Gezira *f.* Sudan **71** 14.30N 33.00E
Ghadames Libya **70** 30.10N 9.30E
Ghaghara *r.* India **56** 25.45N 84.50E
Ghana Africa **72** 8.00N 1.00W
Ghanzi Botswana **76** 21.34S 21.42E
Ghardaïa Algeria **70** 32.20N 3.40E
Ghat Libya **70** 24.59N 10.11E
Ghazaouet Algeria **37** 35.10N 1.50W
Ghaziabad India **56** 28.37N 77.30E
Ghazipur India **56** 25.36N 83.36E
Ghazni Afghan. **56** 33.33N 68.28E
Ghurian Afghan. **55** 34.20N 61.25E
Gia Dinh Vietnam **58** 10.48N 106.43E
Gialo Libya **71** 29.00N 21.30E
Giant's Causeway *f.* N. Ireland **30** 55.14N 6.32W
Gibraltar Europe **37** 36.07N 5.22W
Gibraltar, Str. of Africa/Europe **37** 36.00N 5.25W
Gibraltar Pt. England **29** 53.05N 0.20E
Gibson Desert Australia **82** 24.30S 124.00E
Giessen W. Germany **40** 50.35N 8.42E
Gieten Neth. **41** 53.01N 6.45E

Gifford Scotland **31** 55.55N 2.45W
Gifu Japan **64** 35.27N 136.50E
Gigha *i.* Scotland **30** 55.41N 5.44W
Gigha, Sd. of Scotland **30** 55.40N 5.41W
Giglio *i.* Italy **38** 42.21N 10.53E
Gijón Spain **37** 43.32N 5.40W
Gila *r.* U.S.A. **96** 32.45N 114.30W
Gilbert Is. Pacific Oc. **113** 2.00S 175.00E
Gilé Moçambique **75** 16.10S 38.17E
Gilehdar Iran **55** 27.36N 52.42E
Gilgandra Australia **83** 31.42S 148.40E
Gilgil Kenya **75** 0.29S 36.19E
Gilgit Jammu and Kashmir **56** 35.54N 74.20E
Gilgunnia Australia **83** 32.25S 146.04E
Gill, Lough Rep. of Ire. **34** 54.15N 8.14W
Gillingham Dorset England **24** 51.02N 2.17W
Gillingham Kent England **23** 51.24N 0.33E
Gilsland England **31** 54.59N 2.34W
Gimbala, Jebel *mtn.* Sudan **71** 13.00N 24.20E
Ginz *r.* W. Germany **40** 48.28N 10.18E
Gippsland *f.* Australia **83** 37.40S 147.00E
Giresun Turkey **54** 40.55N 38.25E
Giri *r.* Zaïre **74** 0.30N 17.58E
Gironde *r.* France **36** 45.35N 1.00W
Girvan Scotland **30** 55.15N 4.51W
Gisborne New Zealand **85** 38.41S 178.02E
Gitega Burundi **75** 3.25S 29.58E
Giurgiu Romania **39** 43.52N 25.58E
Givet France **41** 50.08N 4.49E
Gizhiga U.S.S.R. **45** 62.00N 160.34E
Gizhiga G. U.S.S.R. **45** 61.00N 158.00E
Gjøvik Norway **42** 60.47N 10.41E
Glacier Peak *mtn.* U.S.A. **96** 48.07N 121.06W
Gladstone Australia **82** 23.52S 151.16E
Glamis Scotland **31** 56.37N 3.01W
Glan *r.* W. Germany **41** 49.46N 7.43E
Glanamman Wales **27** 51.49N 3.54W
Glanaruddery Mts. Rep. of Ire. **35** 52.19N 9.27W
Glandorf W. Germany **41** 52.05N 8.00E
Glanton England **31** 55.25N 1.53W
Glasgow Scotland **30** 55.52N 4.15W
Glasgow U.S.A. **96** 48.12N 106.37W
Glas Maol *mtn.* Scotland **33** 56.52N 3.22W
Glass, Loch Scotland **33** 57.43N 4.30W
Glasson England **28** 54.00N 2.49W
Glastonbury England **24** 51.09N 2.42W
Glazov U.S.S.R. **43** 58.09N 52.42E
Glen *r.* England **25** 52.50N 0.06W
Glen Affric *f.* Scotland **32** 57.15N 5.03W
Glen Almond *f.* Scotland **31** 56.28N 3.48W
Glenanane Rep. of Ire. **34** 53.37N 9.40W
Glénans, Îles de France **36** 47.43N 3.57W
Glenarm N. Ireland **30** 54.57N 5.58W
Glen Cannich *f.* Scotland **32** 57.19N 5.03W
Glen Clova *f.* Scotland **33** 56.48N 3.01W
Glen Coe *f.* Scotland **30** 56.40N 5.03W
Glendive U.S.A. **96** 47.08N 104.42W
Glen Dochart *f.* Scotland **30** 56.25N 4.30W
Glen Dye *f.* Scotland **33** 56.58N 2.34W
Glenelg Scotland **32** 57.13N 5.37W
Glenelly *r.* N. Ireland **30** 54.45N 7.19W
Glen Esk *f.* Scotland **33** 56.53N 2.46W
Glen Etive *f.* Scotland **30** 56.37N 5.01W
Glenfinnan Scotland **32** 56.53N 5.27W
Glengarriff Rep. of Ire. **35** 51.45N 9.33W
Glen Garry *f.* Highland Scotland **32** 57.03N 5.04W
Glen Garry *f.* Tayside Scotland **33** 56.47N 4.02W
Glengormley N. Ireland **30** 54.40N 5.59W
Glen Head Rep. of Ire. **34** 54.44N 8.46W
Glen Innes Australia **83** 29.42S 151.45E
Glen Kinglass *f.* Scotland **30** 56.29N 5.03W
Glenluce Scotland **30** 54.53N 4.48W
Glen Lyon *f.* Scotland **30** 56.36N 4.15W
Glen Mòr *f.* Scotland **33** 57.15N 4.30W
Glen More *f.* Scotland **33** 57.08N 3.40W
Glennagalliagh *mtn.* Rep. of Ire. **35** 52.49N 8.32W
Glen Orchy *f.* Scotland **30** 56.28N 4.50W
Glen Orrin *f.* Scotland **33** 57.30N 4.45W
Glen Prosen *f.* Scotland **33** 56.45N 3.05W
Glenrothes Scotland **31** 56.12N 3.10W
Glen Roy *f.* Scotland **33** 56.58N 4.47W
Glens Falls *town* U.S.A. **99** 43.17N 73.41W
Glenshaw U.S.A. **98** 40.31N 79.57W
Glenshee *f.* Scotland **33** 56.45N 3.25W
Glen Spean *f.* Scotland **33** 56.53N 4.40W
Glenties Rep. of Ire. **34** 54.47N 8.17W
Glen Tilt *f.* Scotland **33** 56.50N 3.45W
Glenwhappen Rig *mtn.* Scotland **31** 55.33N 3.30W
Glin Rep. of Ire. **35** 52.34N 9.17W
Glittertind *mtn.* Norway **42** 61.30N 8.20E
Głogów Poland **40** 51.40N 16.06E
Glomma *r.* Norway **42** 59.15N 10.55E
Glossop England **28** 53.27N 1.56W
Gloucester England **24** 51.52N 2.15W
Gloucester U.S.A. **99** 42.37N 70.41W
Gloucestershire *d.* England **24** 51.45N 2.00W
Glyncorrwg Wales **27** 51.40N 3.39W
Glyn Neath Wales **27** 51.45N 3.37W

Gmünd Austria **40** 48.47N 14.59E
Gmunden Austria **40** 47.56N 13.48E
Gniezno Poland **43** 52.32N 17.32E
Goa *d.* India **56** 15.30N 74.00E
Goalpara India **56** 26.10N 90.38E
Goat Fell *mtn.* Scotland **30** 55.37N 5.12W
Gobabis Namibia **76** 22.30S 18.58E
Gobi *des.* Asia **62** 45.00N 108.00E
Godalming England **23** 51.11N 0.37W
Godavari *r.* India **57** 16.40N 82.15E
Goderich Canada **98** 43.43N 81.43W
Godhavn Greenland **95** 69.20N 53.30W
Godhra India **56** 22.49N 73.40E
Godmanchester England **25** 52.19N 0.11W
Godrevy Pt. England **27** 50.15N 5.25W
Godstone England **23** 51.15N 0.04W
Godthaab Greenland **95** 64.10N 51.40W
Gogra *r.* see Ghaghara India **56**
Goiandira Brazil **110** 18.06S 48.07W
Goiânia Brazil **110** 16.43S 49.18W
Goiás Brazil **110** 15.57S 50.07W
Goiás *d.* Brazil **110** 16.00S 50.10W
Göksun Turkey **54** 38.03N 36.30E
Gol Norway **42** 60.43N 8.55E
Gola I. Rep. of Ire. **34** 55.05N 8.21W
Golden Canada **96** 51.19N 116.58W
Golden Rep. of Ire. **35** 52.30N 7.59W
Golden B. New Zealand **85** 40.45S 172.50E
Golden Vale *f.* Rep. of Ire. **35** 52.30N 8.07W
Golders Green England **23** 51.35N 0.12W
Golfito Costa Rica **100** 8.42N 83.10W
Golspie Scotland **33** 57.58N 3.58W
Golyshi U.S.S.R. **43** 58.26N 45.28E
Goma Zaïre **75** 1.37S 29.10E
Gombe Nigeria **73** 10.17N 11.20E
Gombe *r.* Tanzania **75** 4.43S 31.30E
Gomel U.S.S.R. **43** 52.25N 31.00E
Gómez Palacio Mexico **100** 25.39N 103.30W
Gomshall England **23** 51.13N 0.25W
Gonaives Haiti **101** 19.29N 72.42W
Gonâve, G. of Haiti **101** 19.20N 73.00W
Gonâve I. Haiti **101** 18.50N 73.00W
Gonbad-e-Kavus Iran **55** 37.15N 55.11E
Gonda India **56** 27.08N 81.58E
Gondar Ethiopia **71** 12.39N 37.29E
Gongga Shan *mtn.* China **60** 29.30N 101.30E
Gongola *d.* Nigeria **73** 8.40N 11.30E
Gongola *r.* Nigeria **73** 9.30N 12.06E
Good Hope, C. of R.S.A. **76** 34.20S 18.25E
Goodooga Australia **83** 29.08S 147.30E
Goodwin Sands *f.* England **25** 51.16N 1.31E
Goole England **29** 53.42N 0.52W
Goondiwindi Australia **83** 28.30S 150.17E
Goose L. U.S.A. **96** 41.55N 120.25W
Göppingen W. Germany **40** 48.43N 9.39E
Gorakhpur India **56** 26.45N 83.23E
Gordon Scotland **31** 55.41N 2.34W
Gore New Zealand **85** 46.06S 168.58E
Gorebridge Scotland **31** 55.51N 3.02W
Gorey Rep. of Ire. **35** 52.40N 6.19W
Gorgan Iran **55** 36.50N 54.29E
Gorgan *r.* Iran **55** 37.00N 54.00E
Gori U.S.S.R. **55** 41.59N 44.05E
Gorinchem Neth. **41** 51.50N 4.59E
Goring England **24** 51.32N 1.08W
Gorizia Italy **38** 45.58N 13.37E
Gorki U.S.S.R. **43** 56.20N 44.00E
Görlitz E. Germany **40** 51.09N 15.00E
Gorlovka U.S.S.R. **43** 48.17N 38.05E
Gorm, Loch Scotland **30** 55.48N 6.25W
Goroka P.N.G. **59** 6.02S 145.22E
Gorongosa *r.* Moçambique **76** 20.29S 34.36E
Gorontalo Indonesia **59** 0.33N 123.05E
Gorseinon Wales **27** 51.40N 4.03W
Gort Rep. of Ire. **35** 53.04N 8.49W
Gortin N. Ireland **34** 54.43N 7.15W
Gorzów Wielkopolski Poland **40** 52.42N 15.12E
Gosford Australia **83** 33.25S 151.18E
Gosforth England **31** 55.02N 1.35W
Goslar W. Germany **40** 51.54N 10.25E
Gospić Yugo. **38** 4.34N 15.23E
Gosport England **24** 50.48N 1.08W
Göta Canal Sweden **42** 57.50N 11.50E
Göteborg Sweden **42** 57.45N 12.00E
Gotha E. Germany **40** 50.57N 10.43E
Gotland *i.* Sweden **42** 57.30N 18.30E
Gottingen W. Germany **40** 51.32N 9.57E
Gouda Neth. **41** 52.01N 4.43E
Gough I. Atlantic Oc. **130** 41.00S 10.00W
Gouin Resr. Canada **99** 48.00N 74.45W
Goulburn Australia **83** 34.47S 149.43E
Goundam Mali **72** 17.27N 3.39W
Gourdon France **36** 44.45N 1.22E
Gouré Niger **73** 13.59N 10.15E
Gourma-Rarous Mali **72** 16.58N 1.50W
Gournay France **36** 49.29N 1.44E
Gourock Scotland **30** 55.58N 4.49W
Gourock Range *mts.* Australia **83** 35.45S 149.25E

Governador Valadares Brazil **109** 18.51S 42.00W
Gower *pen.* Wales **27** 51.37N 4.10W
Gowna, Lough Rep. of Ire. **34** 53.50N 7.34W
Gowran Rep. of Ire. **35** 52.38N 7.04W
Gozo *i.* Malta **38** 36.03N 14.16E
Gracias á Dios, Cabo *c.* Honduras/Nicaragua **100** 15.00N 83.10W
Grafton Australia **83** 29.40S 152.56E
Grafton U.S.A. **97** 48.28N 97.25W
Grahamstown R.S.A. **76** 33.19S 26.32E
Graiguenamanagh Rep. of Ire. **35** 52.33N 6.57W
Grain England **25** 51.28N 0.43E
Grampian *d.* Scotland **33** 57.22N 2.35W
Grampian Highlands Scotland **33** 56.55N 4.00W
Grampound England **27** 50.18N 4.54W
Granada Nicaragua **100** 11.58N 85.59W
Granada Spain **37** 37.10N 3.35W
Granard Rep. of Ire. **34** 53.47N 7.30W
Granby Canada **99** 45.23N 72.44W
Gran Canaria *i.* Canary Is. **70** 28.00N 15.30W
Gran Chaco *f.* S. America **110** 23.20S 60.00W
Grand *r.* Canada **98** 42.53N 79.35W
Grand Bahama I. Bahamas **101** 26.35N 78.00W
Grand Bassam Ivory Coast **72** 5.14N 3.45W
Grand Canal China **62** 34.00N 118.25E
Grand Canal Rep. of Ire. **34** 53.21N 6.14W
Grand Canyon *f.* U.S.A. **96** 36.15N 113.00W
Grand Canyon *town* U.S.A. **96** 36.04N 112.07W
Grand Cayman *i.* Cayman Is. **100** 19.20N 81.30W
Grande *r.* Brazil **110** 20.00S 51.00W
Grande Comore *i.* Comoro Is. **75** 11.35S 43.20E
Grande I. Brazil **110** 23.15S 44.30W
Grande Prairie *town* Canada **94** 55.10N 118.52W
Grand Falls *town* New Brunswick Canada **99** 47.02N 67.46W
Grand Falls *town* Newfoundland Canada **95** 48.57N 55.40W
Grand Forks U.S.A. **97** 47.57N 97.05W
Grand Fort Philippe France **25** 51.00N 2.06E
Grand Island *town* U.S.A. **96** 40.56N 98.21W
Grand Junction U.S.A. **96** 39.04N 108.33W
Grand Manan I. Canada **99** 44.45N 66.45W
Grand Marais U.S.A. **98** 47.45N 90.20W
Grândola Portugal **37** 38.10N 8.34W
Grand Rapids *town* Mich. U.S.A. **98** 42.57N 85.40W
Grand Rapids *town* Minn. U.S.A. **98** 47.13N 93.31W
Grand Teton *mtn.* U.S.A. **96** 43.45N 110.50W
Grand Union Canal England **23** 52.37N 0.30W
Graney, Lough Rep. of Ire. **35** 52.59N 8.40W
Grangemouth Scotland **31** 56.01N 3.44W
Grange-over-Sands England **28** 54.12N 2.55W
Granite Peak *mtn.* U.S.A. **96** 45.10N 109.50W
Grankulla Finland **42** 60.12N 24.45E
Granóllers Spain **37** 41.37N 2.18E
Gran Paradiso *mtn.* Italy **38** 45.31N 7.15E
Gran Pilastro *mtn.* Italy **40** 46.58N 11.44E
Grantham England **29** 52.55N 0.39W
Grantown-on-Spey Scotland **33** 57.20N 3.38W
Grants Pass *town* U.S.A. **96** 42.26N 123.20W
Granville France **36** 48.50N 1.35W
Graskop R.S.A. **76** 24.55S 30.50E
Grasse France **36** 43.40N 6.56E
Grave Neth. **41** 51.45N 5.45E
Grave, Pointe de France **36** 45.35N 1.04W
Gravelines France **25** 50.59N 2.08E
Gravesend England **23** 51.27N 0.24E
Gravir Scotland **32** 58.03N 6.26W
Gray France **36** 47.27N 5.35E
Grayling U.S.A. **98** 44.40N 84.43W
Grays England **23** 51.29N 0.20E
Graz Austria **40** 47.05N 15.22E
Great Abaco I. Bahamas **101** 26.30N 77.00W
Great Artesian Basin *f.* Australia **82** 26.30S 143.02E
Great Australian Bight Australia **82** 33.20S 130.00E
Great Baddow England **23** 51.43N 0.29E
Great Bardfield England **25** 51.57N 0.26E
Great Barrier I. New Zealand **85** 36.15S 175.30E
Great Barrier Reef *f.* Australia **82** 16.30S 146.30E
Great Basin *f.* U.S.A. **96** 39.00N 115.30W
Great Bear L. Canada **94** 66.00N 120.00W
Great Bend *town* U.S.A. **96** 38.22N 98.47W
Great Bernera *i.* Scotland **32** 58.13N 6.50W
Great Bitter L. Egypt **54** 30.20N 32.50E
Great Blasket I. Rep. of Ire. **35** 52.05N 10.32W
Great Bookham England **23** 51.16N 0.20W
Great Chesterford England **25** 52.04N 0.11E
Great Coates England **29** 53.34N 0.05W
Great Coco *i.* Burma **58** 14.10N 93.25E
Great Dividing Range *mts.* Australia **83** 33.00S 151.00E
Great Driffield England **29** 54.01N 0.26W
Great Dunmow England **23** 51.53N 0.22E
Great Eccleston England **28** 53.51N 2.52W
Greater Antilles *is.* C. America **101** 17.00N 70.00W
Greater London *d.* England **23** 51.31N 0.06W
Greater Manchester *d.* England **28** 53.30N 2.18W
Great Exuma I. Bahamas **101** 23.00N 76.00W
Great Falls *town* U.S.A. **96** 47.30N 111.16W
Great Fish *r.* Namibia **76** 28.07S 17.10E
Great Harwood England **28** 53.48N 2.24W
Great Inagua I. Bahamas **101** 21.00N 73.20W
Great Irgiz *r.* U.S.S.R. **43** 52.00N 47.20E
Great Karas Mts. Namibia **76** 27.30S 18.45E
Great Karroo *f.* R.S.A. **76** 32.50S 22.30E
Great L. Australia **83** 41.50S 146.43E
Great Lakes N. America **112** 47.00N 83.00W
Great Malvern England **24** 52.07N 2.19W
Great Missenden England **23** 51.43N 0.43W
Great Nama Land *f.* Namibia **76** 25.30S 17.30E
Great Nicobar *i.* India **57** 7.00N 93.50E
Great Ormes Head Wales **26** 53.20N 3.52W
Great Ouse *r.* England **29** 52.47N 0.23E
Great Plains *f.* N. America **112** 45.00N 107.00W
Great Rift Valley *f.* Africa **113** 7.00S 33.00E
Great Ruaha *r.* Tanzania **75** 7.55S 37.52E
Great St. Bernard Pass Italy/Switz. **36** 45.52N 7.11E
Great Salt L. U.S.A. **96** 41.10N 112.40W
Great Sandy Desert Australia **82** 22.00S 125.00E
Great Sandy Desert Saudi Arabia **54** 28.40N 41.30E
Great Shelford England **25** 52.09N 0.08E
Great Shunner Fell *mtn.* England **28** 54.22N 2.12W
Great Skellig *i.* Rep. of Ire. **35** 51.46N 10.33W
Great Slave L. Canada **94** 61.30N 114.20W
Great Stour *r.* England **25** 51.19N 1.15E
Great Torrington England **27** 50.57N 4.09W
Great Victoria Desert Australia **82** 29.00S 127.30E
Great Whale *r.* Canada **95** 55.28N 77.45W
Great Whernside *mtn.* England **28** 54.09N 1.59W
Great Yarmouth England **25** 52.40N 1.45E
Great Zab *r.* Iraq **55** 35.37N 43.20E
Gredos, Sierra de *mts.* Spain **37** 40.18N 5.20W
Greece Europe **39** 39.00N 22.00E
Greece U.S.A. **99** 43.14N 77.38W
Greeley U.S.A. **96** 40.26N 104.43W
Green *r.* U.S.A. **96** 38.20N 109.53W
Green B. U.S.A. **98** 45.00N 87.30W
Green Bay *town* U.S.A. **98** 44.32N 88.00W
Greencastle Rep. of Ire. **30** 55.12N 6.59W
Greenhithe England **23** 51.28N 0.17E
Greenland N. America **95** 68.00N 45.00W
Greenlaw Scotland **31** 55.43N 2.28W
Green Lowther *mtn.* Scotland **31** 55.23N 3.45W
Green Mts. U.S.A. **99** 43.30N 73.00W
Greenock Scotland **30** 55.57N 4.45W
Greenore Pt. Rep. of Ire. **35** 52.14N 6.19W
Greensboro U.S.A. **97** 36.03N 79.50W
Greenstone Pt. Scotland **32** 57.55N 5.37W
Greenville Liberia **72** 5.01N 9.03W
Greenville Maine U.S.A. **99** 45.28N 69.36W
Greenville Miss. U.S.A. **97** 33.23N 91.03W
Greenville S.C. U.S.A. **97** 34.52N 82.25W
Greenwich *d.* England **23** 51.28N 0.00
Greenwich U.S.A. **99** 41.02N 73.37W
Gregory, L. Australia **83** 28.55S 139.00E
Greifswald E. Germany **40** 54.06N 13.24E
Greiz E. Germany **40** 50.40N 12.11E
Grenå Denmark **42** 56.25N 10.53E
Grenada C. America **101** 12.15N 61.45W
Grenade France **36** 43.47N 1.10E
Grenoble France **36** 45.11N 5.43E
Greta *r.* England **28** 54.09N 2.37W
Gretna Scotland **31** 55.00N 3.04W
Grey *r.* New Zealand **85** 42.28S 171.13E
Greyabbey N. Ireland **30** 54.32N 5.35W
Greymouth New Zealand **85** 42.28S 171.12E
Grey Range *mts.* Australia **83** 28.30S 142.15E
Greystones Rep. of Ire. **35** 53.09N 6.04W
Gribbin Head England **27** 50.19N 4.41W
Griffith Australia **83** 34.18S 146.04E
Grim, C. Australia **83** 40.45S 144.45E
Griminish Pt. Scotland **32** 57.40N 7.29W
Grimsay *i.* Scotland **32** 57.29N 7.14W
Grimsby England **29** 53.35N 0.05W
Grimsvötn *mtn.* Iceland **42** 64.30N 17.10W
Griqualand East *f.* R.S.A. **76** 30.30S 29.00E
Griqualand West *f.* R.S.A. **76** 28.55S 22.50E
Gris Nez, Cap France **25** 50.52N 1.35E
Grodno U.S.S.R. **43** 53.40N 23.50E
Groenlo Neth. **41** 52.02N 6.36E
Groix, Île de France **36** 47.38N 3.26N
Gröningen Neth. **41** 53.13N 6.35E
Gröningen *d.* Neth. **41** 53.15N 6.45E
Groomsport N. Ireland **30** 54.41N 5.37W
Groot *r.* Cape Province R.S.A. **76** 33.57S 25.00E
Groote Eylandt *i.* Australia **82** 14.00S 136.30E
Grootfontein Namibia **76** 19.32S 18.05E
Grootlaagte *r.* Botswana **76** 20.50S 22.05E
Grosnez Pt. Channel Is. **27** 49.15N 2.15W
Grossenbrode W. Germany **40** 54.23N 11.07E
Grosseto Italy **38** 42.46N 11.08E
Gross Glockner *mtn.* Austria **40** 47.05N 12.50E
Grote Nete *r.* Belgium **41** 51.07N 4.20E
Groundhog *r.* Canada **98** 48.45N 82.00W
Grove Park England **23** 51.24N 0.03E
Groznyy U.S.S.R. **43** 43.21N 45.42E
Grumeti *r.* Tanzania **75** 2.05S 33.45E
Gruting Voe *b.* Scotland **32** 60.12N 1.32W
Guadalajara Mexico **100** 20.30N 103.20W
Guadalajara Spain **37** 40.37N 3.10W
Guadalete *r.* Spain **37** 36.37N 6.15W
Guadalmena *r.* Spain **37** 38.00N 3.50W
Guadalquivir *r.* Spain **37** 36.50N 6.20W
Guadalupe Mexico **100** 25.41N 100.15W
Guadalupe, Sierra de *mts.* Spain **37** 39.30N 5.25W
Guadalupe I. Mexico **96** 29.00N 118.25W
Guadarrama *r.* Spain **37** 39.55N 4.10W
Guadarrama, Sierra de *mts.* Spain **37** 41.00N 3.50W
Guadeloupe C. America **101** 16.20N 61.40W
Guadiana *r.* Spain **37** 37.10N 8.36W
Guadix Spain **37** 37.19N 3.08W
Guaira Falls *f.* Brazil **110** 24.00S 54.10W
Guajará Mirim Brazil **108** 10.50S 65.21W
Guajira Pen. Colombia **101** 12.00N 72.00W
Gualeguay Argentina **110** 33.10S 59.14W
Guam *i.* Pacific Oc. **59** 13.30N 144.40E
Guanajuato Mexico **100** 21.00N 101.16W
Guanajuato *d.* Mexico **100** 21.01N 101.00W
Guanare *r.* Venezuela **101** 8.20N 67.50W
Guane Cuba **100** 22.13N 84.07W
Guang'an China **63** 30.30N 106.35E
Guanghan China **63** 30.59N 104.15E
Guanghua China **62** 32.26N 111.41E
Guangji China **63** 29.42N 115.39E
Guangxi Zhuangzu *d.* China **63** 23.30N 109.00E
Guangze China **63** 27.27N 117.23E
Guangzhou *see* Canton China **61**
Guantánamo Cuba **101** 20.09N 75.14W
Guan Xian China **57** 30.59N 103.40E
Guaporé *r.* Brazil **108** 12.00S 65.15W
Guarapuava Brazil **110** 25.22S 51.28W
Guaratingueta Brazil **110** 22.49S 45.09W
Guarda Portugal **37** 40.32N 7.17W
Guardafui, C. Somali Rep. **71** 12.00N 51.30E
Guardo Spain **37** 42.47N 4.50W
Guatemala C. America **100** 15.40N 90.00W
Guatemala City Guatemala **100** 14.38N 90.22W
Guaviare *r.* Venezuela **108** 4.30N 77.40W
Guaxupe Brazil **110** 21.17S 46.44W
Guayaquil Ecuador **108** 2.13S 79.54W
Guayaquil, G. of Ecuador **108** 2.30S 80.00W
Guaymas Mexico **96** 27.59N 110.54W
Gubin Poland **40** 51.59N 14.42E
Gudermes U.S.S.R. **43** 43.22N 46.06E
Guebwiller France **40** 47.55N 7.13E
Guecho Spain **37** 43.21N 3.01W
Guelph Canada **98** 43.34N 80.16W
Guéret France **36** 46.10N 1.52E
Guernsey *i.* Channel Is. **27** 49.27N 2.35W
Guerrero *d.* Mexico **100** 18.00N 100.00W
Guguan *i.* Asia **59** 17.20N 145.51E
Guiana S. America **108** 4.00N 53.00W
Guiana Highlands S. America **108** 4.00N 60.00W
Guiding China **63** 26.32N 107.15E
Gui Jiang *r.* China **63** 23.25N 111.20E
Guildford England **23** 51.14N 0.35W
Guildtown Scotland **31** 56.28N 3.25W
Guilherne Capelo Ihe Angola **74** 5.11S 12.10E
Guilin China **63** 25.20N 110.10E
Guinea Africa **72** 10.30N 11.30W
Guinea, G. of Africa **73** 3.00N 3.00E
Guinea Bissau Africa **72** 11.30N 15.00W
Güines Cuba **100** 22.50N 82.02W
Guînes France **25** 50.51N 1.52E
Guingamp France **36** 48.34N 3.09W
Guiping China **63** 23.20N 110.02E
Güiria Venezuela **108** 10.37N 62.21W
Guisborough England **29** 54.32N 1.02W
Guise France **41** 49.54N 3.39E
Guiseley England **28** 53.53N 1.42W
Guiuan Phil. **59** 11.02N 125.44E
Guixi China **63** 28.12N 117.10E
Gui Xian China **63** 23.02N 109.40E
Guiyang China **63** 26.31N 106.39E
Guizhou *d.* China **63** 27.00N 107.00E
Gujarat *d.* India **56** 22.45N 71.30E
Gujranwala Pakistan **56** 32.06N 74.11E
Gujrat Pakistan **56** 32.35N 74.06E
Gulbarga India **56** 17.22N 76.47E
Gulbin Ka *r.* Nigeria **73** 11.35N 4.10E
Gulgong Australia **83** 32.20S 149.49E
Gulja China **60** 43.57N 81.23E
Gullane Scotland **31** 56.02N 2.49W
Gulpaigan Iran **55** 33.23N 50.18E
Gulu Uganda **75** 2.46N 32.21E
Gümüşane Turkey **54** 40.26N 39.26E
Guna India **56** 24.39N 77.18E
Gundagai Australia **83** 35.07S 148.05E
Gungu Zaïre **74** 5.43S 19.20E
Gunnedah Australia **83** 30.59S 150.15E
Guntersville L. U.S.A. **97** 34.35N 86.00W
Guntur India **57** 16.20N 80.27E
Gurnard's Head *c.* England **27** 50.12N 5.35W
Gürün Turkey **54** 38.44N 37.15E
Guryev U.S.S.R. **44** 47.00N 52.00E
Gusau Nigeria **73** 12.12N 6.40E

154

Güstrow E. Germany 40 53.48N 12.11E
Gutcher Scotland 32 60.40N 1.00W
Gütersloh W. Germany 40 51.54N 8.22E
Guyana S. America 108 5.00N 59.00W
Guyhirn England 25 52.37N 0.05E
Guyuan China 62 36.00N 106.25E
Gwabegar Australia 83 30.34S 149.00E
Gwadar Pakistan 55 25.09N 62.21E
Gwai Zimbabwe 76 19.15S 27.42E
Gwai r. Zimbabwe 76 18.00S 26.47E
Gwalior India 56 26.12N 78.09E
Gwanda Zimbabwe 76 20.59S 29.00E
Gwatar Iran 55 25.10N 61.31E
Gweebarra B. Rep. of Ire. 34 54.52N 8.28W
Gwelo Zimbabwe 76 19.25S 29.50E
Gwent d. Wales 27 51.44N 3.00W
Gwynedd d. Wales 26 53.00N 4.00W
Gyangzê China 56 29.00N 89.40E
Gydanskiy Pen. U.S.S.R. 44 70.00N 78.30E
Györ Hungary 43 47.41N 17.40E

H

Haapajärvi Finland 42 63.45N 25.20E
Haapamäki Finland 42 62.15N 24.25E
Haapsalu U.S.S.R. 42 58.58N 23.32E
Haarlem Neth. 41 52.22N 4.38E
Habbaniya Iraq 54 33.22N 43.35E
Hachinohe Japan 64 40.30N 141.30E
Hacketstown Rep. of Ire. 35 52.52N 6.35W
Hackney d. England 23 51.33N 0.03W
Haddington Scotland 31 55.57N 2.47W
Hadejia Nigeria 73 12.30N 10.03E
Hadejia r. Nigeria 73 12.47N 10.44E
Haderslev Denmark 42 55.15N 9.30E
Hadfield England 28 53.28N 1.59W
Hadhramaut d. S. Yemen 71 16.30N 49.30E
Hadleigh England 25 52.03N 0.58E
Hadong Vietnam 63 20.40N 105.58E
Haeju N. Korea 61 38.04N 125.40E
Hafar Saudi Arabia 55 28.28N 46.00E
Hafnarfjördhur Iceland 42 64.04N 21.58W
Haft Kel Iran 55 31.28N 49.35E
Hagen W. Germany 41 51.22N 7.27E
Hagerstown U.S.A. 99 33.39N 77.44W
Hagi Japan 64 34.25N 131.22E
Ha Giang Vietnam 63 22.50N 105.00E
Hags Head Rep. of Ire. 35 52.56N 9.29W
Hai'an Shan mts. China 63 23.00N 115.30E
Haicheng China 62 40.52N 122.48E
Hai Dong Vietnam 63 20.52N 106.28E
Hai Duong Vietnam 58 20.56N 106.21E
Haifa Israel 54 32.49N 34.59E
Haikou China 63 20.03N 110.27E
Hail Saudi Arabia 54 27.31N 41.45E
Hailar China 61 49.15N 119.41E
Hailsham England 25 50.52N 0.17E
Hailun China 61 47.29N 126.58E
Hailuoto i. Finland 42 65.00N 24.50E
Haimen China 63 28.41N 121.30E
Hainan i. China 63 19.00N 109.30E
Hainan Str. China 63 20.09N 110.20E
Hainaut d. Belgium 41 50.30N 3.45E
Haines U.S.A. 94 59.11N 135.23W
Haining China 63 30.30N 120.35E
Haiphong Vietnam 63 20.48N 106.40E
Haiti C. America 101 19.00N 73.00W
Hajiki saki c. Japan 64 38.25N 138.32E
Hakari Turkey 55 37.36N 43.45E
Hakodate Japan 64 41.46N 140.44E
Halberstadt E. Germany 40 51.54N 11.04E
Halden Norway 42 59.08N 11.13E
Halesowen England 24 52.27N 2.02W
Halesworth England 25 52.21N 1.30E
Haliburton Highlands Canada 99 45.10N 78.30W
Halifax Canada 95 44.38N 63.35W
Halifax England 28 53.43N 1.51W
Halil r. Iran 56 27.35N 58.44E
Halkett, C. U.S.A. 94 71.00N 152.00W
Halkirk Scotland 33 58.30N 3.30W
Halladale r. Scotland 33 58.34N 3.54W
Halle Belgium 41 50.45N 4.14E
Halle E. Germany 40 51.28N 11.58E
Hallow England 24 52.14N 2.15W
Hallsberg Sweden 42 59.05N 15.07E
Hall's Creek town Australia 82 18.17S 127.44E
Hallstavik Sweden 42 60.06N 18.42E
Halmahera i. Indonesia 59 0.45N 128.00E
Halmstad Sweden 42 56.41N 12.55E
Hälsingborg Sweden 42 56.05N 12.45E
Halstead England 25 51.57N 0.39E
Haltern W. Germany 41 51.45N 7.10E
Haltia Tunturi mtn. Norway 42 69.20N 21.10E
Haltwhistle England 31 54.58N 2.27W
Ham Scotland 32 6.08N 2.04W
Hama Syria 54 35.09N 36.44E

Hamadān Iran 55 34.47N 48.33E
Hamamatsu Japan 64 34.42N 137.42E
Hamar Norway 42 60.47N 10.55E
Hamata, Gebel mtn. Egypt 54 24.11N 35.01E
Hamble England 24 50.52N 1.19W
Hambleton England 29 53.46N 1.11W
Hambleton Hills England 29 54.15N 1.11W
Hamborn W. Germany 41 51.29N 6.46E
Hamburg W. Germany 40 53.33N 10.00E
Hamdh, Wadi r. Saudi Arabia 54 25.49N 36.37E
Hämeenlinna Finland 42 61.00N 24.25E
Hameln W. Germany 40 52.06N 9.21E
Hamersley Range mts. Australia 82 22.00S 118.00E
Hamhung N. Korea 61 39.54N 127.35E
Hami China 60 42.40N 93.30E
Hamilton Australia 83 37.45S 142.04E
Hamilton Bermuda 101 32.18N 64.48W
Hamilton Canada 98 43.15N 79.50W
Hamilton New Zealand 85 37.46S 175.18E
Hamilton Scotland 31 55.46N 4.10W
Hamilton U.S.A. 98 39.23N 84.33W
Hamina Finland 42 60.33N 27.15E
Hamirpur India 56 25.57N 80.08E
Hamm W. Germany 41 51.40N 7.49E
Hammerfest Norway 42 70.40N 23.44E
Hammersmith d. England 23 51.30N 0.14W
Hammond U.S.A. 98 39.48N 88.37W
Hamoir Belgium 41 50.25N 5.32E
Hampreston England 24 50.47N 1.56W
Hampshire d. England 24 51.03N 1.20W
Hampshire Downs hills England 24 51.18N 1.25W
Hampstead England 23 51.33N 0.11W
Hampton England 23 51.25N 0.23W
Hamrin, Jabal mts. Iraq 55 34.40N 44.10E
Hamun-i-Sabari l. Iran 55 31.24N 61.16E
Hanakiya Saudi Arabia 54 24.53N 40.30E
Hanamaki Japan 64 39.23N 141.07E
Hanang mtn. Tanzania 75 4.30S 35.21E
Hanau W. Germany 40 50.08N 8.56E
Hancheng China 62 35.29N 110.30E
Hancock U.S.A. 98 47.08N 88.34W
Handa i. Scotland 32 58.23N 5.12W
Handan China 62 36.37N 114.26E
Handeni Tanzania 75 5.25S 38.04E
Hanggin Houqi China 62 40.50N 107.06E
Hangö Finland 42 59.50N 23.00E
Hangu China 62 39.11N 117.45E
Hangzhou China 63 30.14N 120.08E
Hangzhou Bay b. China 63 30.30N 121.30E
Hanjiang China 63 25.30N 119.14E
Hannibal U.S.A. 98 39.41N 91.20W
Hanningfield Water England 23 51.38N 0.28E
Hannover W. Germany 40 52.23N 9.44E
Hannut Belgium 41 50.40N 5.05E
Hanoi Vietnam 63 21.01N 105.53E
Hanover R.S.A. 76 31.05S 24.27E
Han Shui r. China 63 30.32N 114.20E
Hantengri Feng mtn. China 60 42.09N 80.12E
Hanworth England 23 51.26N 0.23W
Hanyang China 63 30.42N 113.50E
Hanzhong China 62 33.08N 107.04E
Haparanda Sweden 42 65.50N 24.10E
Haradh Saudi Arabia 55 24.12N 49.08E
Harar Ethiopia 71 9.20N 42.10E
Harbin China 61 45.45N 126.41E
Harburg W. Germany 40 53.27N 9.58E
Hardanger Fjord est. Norway 42 60.15N 6.25E
Hardanger Vidda f. Norway 42 60.20N 8.00E
Harderwijk Neth. 41 52.21N 5.37E
Harding R.S.A. 76 30.36S 29.55E
Hardoi India 56 27.23N 80.06E
Harefield England 23 51.36N 0.28W
Haren W. Germany 41 52.48N 7.15E
Hargeisa Somali Rep. 71 9.31N 44.02E
Har Hu l. China 60 38.20N 97.40E
Hari r. Afghan. 55 35.42N 61.12E
Hari r. Indonesia 58 1.00S 104.15E
Harima nada str. Japan 64 34.30N 134.30E
Haringey d. England 23 51.36N 0.06W
Harlech Wales 26 52.52N 4.08W
Harleston England 25 52.25N 1.18E
Harlingen Neth. 41 53.10N 5.25E
Harlington England 23 51.29N 0.25W
Harlow England 23 51.47N 0.08E
Harmerhill England 28 52.48N 2.45W
Harney Basin f. U.S.A. 96 43.20N 119.00W
Härnösand Sweden 42 62.37N 17.55E
Harold Hill England 23 51.36N 0.12E
Haroldswick Scotland 32 60.47N 0.50W
Harold Wood England 23 51.35N 0.12E
Harpenden England 23 51.49N 0.22W
Harricanaw r. Canada 97 51.05N 79.45W
Harris i. Scotland 32 57.50N 6.55W
Harris, Sd. of Scotland 32 57.43N 7.05W
Harrisburg U.S.A. 99 40.17N 76.54W
Harrismith R.S.A. 76 28.16S 29.08E
Harrison, C. Canada 95 55.00N 58.00W

Harrogate England 29 53.59N 1.32W
Harrow England 23 51.35N 0.21W
Harrow on the Hill England 23 51.34N 0.21W
Harstad Norway 42 68.48N 16.30E
Hartford U.S.A. 99 41.45N 72.42W
Hartington England 28 53.08N 1.49W
Hartland England 27 50.59N 4.29W
Hartland Pt. England 27 51.01N 4.32W
Hartlepool England 29 54.42N 1.11W
Hartley England 23 51.23N 0.18E
Hartley Zimbabwe 76 18.04S 30.06E
Harud r. Afghan. 55 31.36N 61.12E
Harvey U.S.A. 98 41.38N 87.40W
Harwich England 25 51.56N 1.18E
Haryana d. India 56 29.15N 76.00E
Harz Mts. E. Germany/W. Germany 40 51.40N 10.55E
Hasa Oasis Saudi Arabia 55 25.37N 49.40E
Hase r. W. Germany 41 52.42N 7.17E
Hashtrud Iran 55 37.29N 47.05E
Haslemere England 24 51.05N 0.41W
Haslingden England 28 53.43N 2.20W
Hasselt Belgium 41 50.56N 5.20E
Hassi Messaoud Algeria 70 31.53N 5.43E
Hässleholm Sweden 42 56.09N 13.45E
Hastings England 25 50.51N 0.36E
Hastings New Zealand 85 39.39S 176.52E
Hastings U.S.A. 98 44.43N 92.50W
Hatfield Australia 83 33.53S 143.47E
Hatfield England 23 51.46N 0.13W
Hatherleigh England 27 50.49N 4.04W
Hathersage England 28 53.20N 1.39W
Hathras India 56 27.36N 78.02E
Ha Tinh Vietnam 63 18.28N 106.58E
Ha Tinh Vietnam 58 18.21N 105.55E
Hatteras, C. U.S.A. 97 35.14N 75.31W
Hattiesburg U.S.A. 97 31.25N 89.19W
Hatton England 28 52.52N 1.40W
Haugesund Norway 42 59.25N 5.16E
Hauki Vesi l. Finland 42 62.10N 28.30E
Hauraki G. New Zealand 85 36.30S 175.00E
Hauran, Wadi r. Iraq 54 33.57N 42.35E
Haut Zaïre d. Zaïre 75 2.00N 27.00E
Havana Cuba 100 23.07N 82.25W
Havana d. Cuba 100 23.07N 82.25W
Havant England 24 50.51N 0.59W
Havel r. E. Germany 40 52.51N 11.57E
Haverfordwest Wales 27 51.48N 4.59W
Haverhill England 25 52.06N 0.27E
Haverhill U.S.A. 99 42.47N 71.07W
Havering England 23 51.34N 0.14E
Havlickuv Brod Czech. 40 49.38N 15.35E
Havre U.S.A. 96 48.34N 109.45W
Havre de Grace U.S.A. 99 39.33N 76.06W
Hawaii d. U.S.A. 96 21.00N 156.00W
Hawaii i. Hawaii U.S.A. 96 19.30N 155.30W
Hawaiian Is. U.S.A. 96 21.00N 157.00W
Hawea, L. New Zealand 85 44.30S 169.15E
Hawera New Zealand 85 39.35S 174.19E
Hawes England 28 54.18N 2.12W
Hawes Water l. England 28 54.30N 2.45W
Hawick Scotland 31 55.25N 2.47W
Hawke, C. Australia 83 32.12S 152.33E
Hawke B. New Zealand 85 39.18S 177.15E
Hawkhurst England 25 51.02N 0.31E
Hawthorne U.S.A. 96 38.13N 118.37W
Hay Australia 83 34.31S 144.31E
Haydon Bridge England 31 54.58N 2.14W
Hayes r. Canada 95 57.00N 92.30W
Hayes England 23 51.31N 0.25W
Hayle England 27 50.12N 5.25W
Hay-on-Wye Wales 26 52.04N 3.09W
Hay River town Canada 94 60.51N 115.42W
Haywards Heath f. England 25 51.00N 0.05W
Hazaribagh India 56 24.00N 85.23E
Hazelton Canada 94 55.16N 127.18W
Hazlemere England 23 51.39N 0.42W
Hazleton U.S.A. 99 40.58N 75.59W
Heacham England 29 52.55N 0.30E
Headcorn England 23 51.11N 0.37E
Headford Rep. of Ire. 34 53.28N 9.08W
Heads of Ayr c. Scotland 30 55.26N 4.42W
Heanor England 29 53.01N 1.20W
Heard I. Indian Oc. 131 53.07S 73.20E
Hearst Canada 98 49.42N 83.40W
Heath End England 24 51.21N 1.08W
Heathfield England 25 50.58N 0.18E
Hebden Bridge town England 28 53.45N 2.00W
Hebei d. China 62 39.00N 116.00E
Hebel Australia 83 28.55S 147.49E
Hebi China 62 35.57N 114.08E
Hebrides is. U.K. 14 58.00N 7.00W
Hebron Jordan 54 31.32N 35.06E
Hecate Str. Canada 94 53.00N 131.00W
Hechtel Belgium 41 51.07N 5.22E
Hechuan China 63 30.05N 106.14E
Heckington England 29 52.59N 0.18W
Hedon England 29 53.44N 0.11W
Heemstede Neth. 41 52.21N 4.38E

Hualien Taiwan **63** 24.00N 121.39E
Huambo Angola **74** 12.47S 15.44E
Huambo *d.* Angola **74** 12.30S 15.45E
Huancayo Peru **108** 12.15S 75.12W
Huanggang China **63** 30.33N 114.59E
Huang He *r.* China **62** 38.00N 118.40E
Huangshi China **63** 30.10N 115.04E
Huangyan China **63** 28.42N 121.25E
Huan Jiang *r.* China **62** 35.13N 108.00E
Huánuco Peru **108** 10.00S 76.11W
Huascaran *mtn.* Peru **108** 9.20S 77.36W
Hubei *d.* China **63** 31.00N 112.00E
Hubli India **56** 15.20N 75.14E
Hucknall England **29** 53.03N 1.12W
Hucqueliers France **25** 50.34N 1.55E
Huddersfield England **28** 53.38N 1.49W
Hudiksvall Sweden **42** 61.45N 17.10E
Hudson *r.* U.S.A. **99** 40.45N 74.00W
Hudson B. Canada **95** 58.00N 86.00W
Hudson Str. Canada **95** 62.00N 70.00W
Hué Vietnam **58** 16.28N 107.35E
Huelva Spain **37** 37.15N 6.56W
Huelva *r.* Spain **37** 37.25N 6.00W
Huércal Overa Spain **37** 37.23N 1.56W
Huesca Spain **37** 42.02N 0.25W
Hughenden Australia **82** 20.50S 144.10E
Hugh Town England **27** 49.55N 6.19W
Huiarau Range *mts.* New Zealand **85** 38.20S 177.15E
Huila *d.* Angola **74** 15.30S 15.30E
Huimin China **62** 37.30N 117.29E
Huixtla Mexico **100** 15.09N 92.30W
Huizhou China **63** 23.05N 114.29E
Hull Canada **99** 45.26N 75.45W
Hull *r.* England **29** 53.44N 0.23W
Hullbridge England **23** 51.37N 0.36E
Hultsfred Sweden **42** 57.30N 15.50E
Hulun Chih *l.* China **61** 49.00N 117.20E
Humansdorp R.S.A. **76** 34.01S 24.45E
Humber *r.* England **29** 53.40N 0.12W
Humberside *d.* England **29** 53.48N 0.35W
Hume, L. Australia **83** 36.05S 147.10E
Humphreys Peak *mtn.* U.S.A. **96** 35.21N 111.41W
Hun Libya **70** 29.06N 15.57E
Húna Flói *b.* Iceland **42** 65.45N 20.50W
Hunan *d.* China **63** 27.30N 111.30E
Hunchun Ho *r.* China **64** 42.19N 130.24E
Hungary Europe **43** 47.30N 19.00E
Hungerford Australia **83** 29.00S 144.26E
Hungerford England **24** 51.25N 1.30W
Hungnam N. Korea **61** 39.49N 127.40E
Hunse *r.* Neth. **41** 53.20N 6.18E
Hunsrück *mts.* W. Germany **41** 49.44N 7.05E
Hunstanton England **29** 52.57N 0.30E
Hunte *r.* W. Germany **40** 52.30N 8.19E
Hunter Mtn. U.S.A. **99** 42.10N 74.14W
Huntingdon England **25** 52.20N 0.11W
Huntly New Zealand **85** 37.35S 175.10E
Huntly Scotland **33** 57.27N 2.47W
Huntsville Canada **99** 45.20N 79.14W
Huntsville U.S.A. **97** 30.43N 95.34W
Hunyani *r.* Moçambique **76** 15.35S 30.30E
Hunyuan China **62** 39.45N 113.35E
Huon Pen. P.N.G. **59** 6.00S 147.00E
Huo Shan *mts.* China **62** 36.40N 112.00E
Hurd, C. Canada **98** 45.14N 81.44W
Hurghada Egypt **54** 27.17N 33.47E
Hurliness Scotland **33** 58.47N 3.13W
Huron U.S.A. **96** 44.22N 98.12W
Huron, L. Canada/U.S.A. **98** 45.00N 82.30W
Hursley England **24** 51.01N 1.23W
Hurst Green England **23** 51.14N 0.00
Hurstpierpoint England **25** 50.56N 0.11W
Husavik Iceland **42** 66.03N 17.17W
Husbands Bosworth England **24** 52.27N 1.03W
Huskvarna Sweden **42** 57.47N 14.15E
Husum W. Germany **40** 54.29N 9.04E
Hutchinson U.S.A. **96** 38.03N 97.56W
Hutton Cranswick England **29** 53.57N 0.27W
Hutur He *r.* China **62** 39.10N 117.12E
Huy Belgium **41** 50.31N 5.14E
Hvar *i.* Yugo. **39** 43.10N 16.45E
Hvita *r.* Iceland **42** 64.33N 21.45W
Hyde England **28** 53.26N 2.06W
Hyde Park *f.* England **23** 51.31N 0.12W
Hyderabad India **57** 17.22N 78.26E
Hyderabad Pakistan **56** 25.23N 68.24E
Hyères France **36** 43.07N 6.08E
Hyères, Îles d' France **36** 43.01N 6.25E
Hyndman Peak U.S.A. **96** 43.46N 113.55W
Hynish Scotland **30** 56.26N 6.55W
Hynish B. Scotland **30** 56.28N 6.52W
Hythe Hants. England **24** 50.51N 1.24W
Hythe Kent England **25** 51.04N 1.05E
Hyvinkää Finland **42** 60.37N 24.50E

I

Ialomita *r.* Romania **39** 44.41N 27.52E
Iar Connacht *f.* Rep. of Ire. **34** 53.21N 9.22W
Iaşi Romania **43** 47.09N 27.38E
Ibadan Nigeria **73** 7.23N 3.56E
Ibagué Colombia **108** 4.35N 75.30W
Ibar *r.* Yugo. **39** 43.44N 20.44E
Ibarra Ecuador **108** 0.23N 77.50W
Ibbenbüren W. Germany **41** 52.17N 7.44E
Ibi Nigeria **73** 8.11N 9.44E
Ibina *r.* Zaïre **75** 1.00N 28.40E
Ibiza Spain **37** 38.55N 1.30E
Ibiza *i. see* Iviza Spain **37**
Ibstock England **24** 52.42N 1.23W
Iceland Europe **42** 64.45N 18.00W
Ichinomiya Japan **64** 35.18N 136.48E
Ickenham England **23** 51.34N 0.26W
Idah Nigeria **73** 7.05N 6.45E
Idaho *d.* U.S.A. **96** 45.00N 115.00W
Idaho Falls *town* U.S.A. **96** 43.30N 112.01W
Idar W. Germany **41** 49.43N 7.19E
Idfu Egypt **54** 24.58N 32.50E
Ídhi *mtn.* Greece **39** 35.13N 24.45E
Idi Amin Dada, L. Uganda/Zaïre **75** 0.30S 29.30E
Idiofa Zaïre **74** 4.58S 19.38E
Idrigill Pt. Scotland **32** 57.20N 6.35W
Iesi Italy **38** 43.32N 13.15E
Ifalik *is.* Asia **59** 7.15N 144.27E
Ife Western Nigeria **73** 7.33N 4.34E
Ighil Izane Algeria **37** 35.45N 0.30E
Iglésias Italy **38** 39.18N 8.32E
Iğneada, C. Turkey **39** 41.50N 28.05E
Igoumenitsa Greece **39** 39.32N 20.14E
Iguaçu *r.* Brazil **110** 25.33S 54.35W
Iguala Mexico **100** 18.21N 99.31W
Igualada Spain **37** 41.35N 1.37E
Iguape Brazil **110** 24.44S 47.31W
Ii *r.* Finland **42** 65.17N 25.15E
Iide yama *mtn.* Japan **64** 37.50N 139.42E
Iisalmi Finland **42** 63.34N 27.08E
Ijebu Ode Nigeria **73** 6.47N 3.54E
IJmuiden Neth. **41** 52.28N 4.37E
IJssel *r.* South Holland Neth. **41** 51.54N 4.32E
IJssel *r.* Overijssel Neth. **41** 52.34N 5.50E
IJsselmeer *l.* Neth. **41** 52.45N 5.20E
Ijzer *r.* Belgium **41** 51.09N 2.44E
Ikaría *i.* Greece **39** 37.35N 26.10E
Ikela Zaïre **74** 1.06S 23.04E
Ikelemba Congo **74** 1.15N 16.38E
Ikelemba *r.* Zaïre **74** 0.08N 18.19E
Iki shima *i.* Japan **64** 33.47N 129.43E
Ikomba Tanzania **75** 9.09S 32.20E
Ikopa *r.* Madagascar **75** 16.00S 46.22E
Ilagan Phil. **59** 17.07N 121.53E
Ilam Iran **55** 33.27N 46.27E
Ilaro Nigeria **73** 6.53N 3.03E
Ilchester England **24** 51.00N 2.41W
Ilebo Zaïre **74** 4.20S 20.35E
Ilen *r.* Rep. of Ire. **35** 51.53N 9.20W
Ilesha Western Nigeria **73** 7.39N 4.38E
Ilford England **23** 51.33N 0.06E
Ilfracombe England **27** 51.13N 4.08W
Ili *r.* U.S.S.R. **60** 45.00N 74.20E
Iligan Phil. **59** 8.12N 124.13E
Ilkeston England **29** 52.59N 1.19W
Ilkley England **28** 53.56N 1.49W
Iller *r.* W. Germany **36** 48.29N 10.03E
Illescas Uruguay **110** 33.34S 55.20W
Illinois *d.* U.S.A. **98** 40.15N 89.15W
Illinois *r.* U.S.A. **98** 38.56N 90.27W
Ilminster England **24** 50.55N 2.56W
Iloilo Phil. **59** 10.45N 122.33E
Ilorin Nigeria **73** 8.32N 4.34E
Imabari Japan **64** 34.04N 132.59E
Imala Moçambique **75** 14.39S 39.34E
Imandra, L. U.S.S.R. **42** 67.30N 32.45E
Imatra Finland **42** 61.14N 28.50E
Immingham England **29** 53.37N 0.12W
Imo *d.* Nigeria **73** 5.30N 7.20E
Imperia Italy **36** 43.53N 8.00E
Imperial Dam U.S.A. **96** 33.01N 114.25W
Impfondo Congo **74** 1.36N 17.58E
Imphal India **57** 24.47N 93.55E
Imroz *i.* Turkey **39** 40.10N 25.51E
Ina *r.* Poland **40** 53.32N 14.38E
Inari *l.* Finland **42** 69.00N 28.00E
Inca Spain **37** 39.43N 2.54E
Incesu Turkey **54** 38.39N 35.12E
Inchard, Loch Scotland **32** 58.27N 5.05W
Inchcape *i.* Scotland **31** 56.27N 2.24W
Inchfree B. Rep. of Ire. **34** 55.03N 8.23W
Inchkeith *i.* Scotland **31** 56.02N 3.08W
Inchnadamph Scotland **32** 58.08N 4.58W
Inchon S. Korea **61** 37.30N 126.38E
Indaal, Loch Scotland **30** 55.45N 6.20W
Indals *r.* Sweden **42** 62.30N 17.20E
Inderagiri *r.* Indonesia **58** 0.30S 103.08E
India Asia **57** 23.00N 78.30E
Indiana *d.* U.S.A. **98** 40.00N 86.05W
Indianapolis U.S.A. **98** 39.45N 86.10W
Indian Harbour Canada **95** 54.25N 57.20W
Indian Ocean **113**
Indigirka *r.* U.S.S.R. **45** 71.00N 148.45E
Indonesia Asia **58** 6.00S 118.00E
Indore India **56** 22.42N 75.54E
Indravati *r.* India **57** 18.45N 80.16E
Indre *r.* France **36** 47.16N 0.06W
Indus *r.* Pakistan **56** 24.00N 67.33E
Inebolu Turkey **54** 41.57N 33.45E
Infiesto Spain **37** 43.21N 5.21W
Ingatestone England **23** 51.41N 0.22E
Ingende Zaïre **74** 0.17S 18.58E
Ingham Australia **82** 18.35S 146.12E
Ingleborough *mtn.* England **28** 54.10N 2.23W
Ingleton England **28** 54.09N 2.29W
Ingolstadt W. Germany **40** 48.46N 11.27E
Inhambane Moçambique **76** 23.51S 35.29E
Inhambane *d.* Moçambique **76** 22.20S 34.00E
Inharrime Moçambique **76** 24.29S 35.01E
Inishark *i.* Rep. of Ire. **34** 53.37N 10.18W
Inishbofin *i.* Donegal Rep. of Ire. **34** 55.10N 8.10W
Inishbofin *i.* Galway Rep. of Ire. **34** 53.38N 10.14W
Inisheer *i.* Rep. of Ire. **35** 53.04N 9.32W
Inishkea *i.* Rep. of Ire. **34** 54.08N 10.13W
Inishmaan *i.* Rep. of Ire. **35** 53.06N 9.36W
Inishmore *i.* Rep. of Ire. **35** 53.08N 9.43W
Inishmurray *i.* Rep. of Ire. **34** 54.26N 8.40W
Inishowen Head Rep. of Ire. **30** 55.09N 6.56W
Inishowen Pen. Rep. of Ire. **30** 55.08N 7.20W
Inishturk *i.* Rep. of Ire. **34** 53.43N 10.08W
Inishvickillane *i.* Rep. of Ire. **35** 52.02N 10.36W
Inn *r.* Europe **40** 48.33N 13.26E
Innellan Scotland **30** 55.54N 4.58W
Inner Hebrides *is.* Scotland **32** 56.50N 6.45W
Innerleithen Scotland **31** 55.37N 3.04W
Inner Mongolia *d.* China **62** 42.00N 112.00E
Inner Sd. Scotland **32** 57.30N 5.55W
Innsbruck Austria **40** 46.17N 11.25E
Inny *r.* England **27** 50.35N 4.17W
Inny *r.* Rep. of Ire. **35** 51.51N 10.10W
Inongo Zaïre **74** 1.55S 18.20E
Inoucdjouac Canada **95** 58.25N 78.18W
Inowrocław Poland **43** 52.49N 18.12E
Insch Scotland **33** 57.21N 2.36W
Insein Burma **58** 16.54N 96.08E
Interlaken Switz. **40** 46.42N 7.52E
International Falls *town* U.S.A. **98** 48.38N 93.26W
Inubo saki *c.* Japan **64** 35.41N 140.52E
Inuvik Canada **94** 68.16N 133.40W
Inveraray Scotland **30** 56.24N 5.05W
Inver B. Rep. of Ire. **34** 54.36N 8.20W
Inverbervie Scotland **33** 56.51N 2.17W
Invercargill New Zealand **85** 46.26S 168.21E
Inverell Australia **83** 29.46S 151.10E
Invergordon Scotland **33** 57.42N 4.10W
Inverie Scotland **32** 57.03N 5.41W
Inverkeithing Scotland **31** 56.02N 3.25W
Invermoriston Scotland **33** 57.13N 4.38W
Inverness Scotland **33** 57.27N 4.15W
Inverurie Scotland **33** 57.17N 2.23W
Inyangani *mtn.* Zimbabwe **76** 18.18S 32.54E
Inyonga Tanzania **75** 6.43S 32.02E
Inzia *r.* Zaïre **74** 3.47S 17.57E
Ioánnina Greece **39** 39.39N 20.49E
Iona *i.* Scotland **30** 56.20N 6.25W
Iona, Sd. of Scotland **30** 56.19N 6.24W
Ionian Is. Greece **39** 38.45N 20.00E
Ionian Sea Med. Sea **39** 38.30N 18.45E
Ios *i.* Greece **39** 36.42N 25.20E
Iowa *d.* U.S.A. **97** 42.00N 93.00W
Iowa City U.S.A. **98** 41.39N 91.31W
Ipoh Malaysia **58** 4.36N 101.02E
Ipswich Australia **83** 27.38S 152.40E
Ipswich England **25** 52.04N 1.09E
Iquique Chile **109** 20.15S 70.08W
Iquitos Peru **108** 3.51S 73.13W
Iráklion Greece **39** 35.20N 25.08E
Iran Asia **55** 32.00N 54.30E
Iran, Pegunungan *mts.* Indonesia/Malaysia **58** 3.20N 115.00E
Iranian Plateau *f.* Asia **113** 33.00N 55.00E
Iranshar Iran **55** 27.14N 60.42E
Irapuato Mexico **100** 20.40N 101.40W
Iraq Asia **54** 33.00N 44.00E
Irazu *mtn.* Costa Rica **100** 9.59N 83.52W
Ireland's Eye *i.* Rep. of Ire. **34** 53.25N 6.05W
Irian Jaya *d.* Indonesia **59** 4.00S 138.00E
Iringa Tanzania **75** 7.49S 35.39E
Iringa *d.* Tanzania **75** 8.30S 35.00E
Iriomote *i.* Japan **61** 24.30N 124.00E
Irish Sea U.K./Rep. of Ire. **34** 53.30N 5.40W
Irkutsk U.S.S.R. **60** 52.18N 104.15E
Iron-Bridge England **24** 52.38N 2.30W
Irondequoit U.S.A. **99** 43.12N 77.36W

Joyce's Country *f.* Rep. of Ire. **34** 53.33N 9.36W
Juan Fernandez Is. Chile **109** 34.20S 80.00W
Juárez Argentina **110** 37.40S 59.48W
Juba *r.* Somali Rep. **75** 0.20S 42.40E
Juba Sudan **75** 4.50N 31.35E
Jubail Saudi Arabia **55** 27.59N 49.40E
Júcar *r.* Spain **37** 39.10N 0.15W
Juchitán Mexico **100** 20.04N 104.06W
Juist *i.* W. Germany **41** 53.43N 7.00E
Juiz de Fora Brazil **110** 21.47S 43.23W
Jujuy *d.* Argentina **110** 23.00S 66.00W
Julfa Iran **55** 32.40N 51.39E
Juliana Canal Neth. **41** 51.00N 5.48E
Julianehaab Greenland **95** 60.45N 46.00W
Jülich W. Germany **41** 50.55N 6.21E
Julio de Castilhos Brazil **110** 29.13S 53.40W
Jullundur India **56** 31.18N 75.40E
Jumet Belgium **41** 50.27N 4.27E
Jumla Nepal **57** 29.17N 82.10E
Jumna *r. see* Yamuna India **56**
Junagadh India **56** 21.32N 70.32E
Junction City U.S.A **97** 39.02N 96.51W
Jundiaí Brazil **110** 23.10S 46.54W
Juneau U.S.A. **94** 58.20N 134.20W
Junee Australia **83** 34.51S 147.40E
Jungfrau *mtn.* Switz. **40** 46.30N 8.00E
Junggar Pendi *f.* Asia **60** 44.20N 86.30E
Junin Argentina **110** 34.34S 60.55W
Jun Xian China **62** 32.40N 111.18E
Jura *i.* Scotland **30** 55.58N 5.55W
Jura, Sd. of Scotland **30** 56.00N 5.45W
Jura Mts. Europe **40** 46.55N 6.45E
Jurby Head I.o.M. **28** 54.22N 4.33W
Juruá *r.* Brazil **108** 2.30S 65.40W
Juticalpa Honduras **100** 14.45N 86.12W
Juwain Afghan. **55** 31.43N 61.39E
Jyväskylä Finland **42** 62.16N 25.50E

K

K2 *mtn.* Asia **60** 35.53N 76.32E
Kabaena *i.* Indonesia **59** 5.25S 122.00E
Kabala Sierra Leone **72** 9.40N 11.36W
Kabale Uganda **75** 1.13S 30.00E
Kabalega Falls *f.* Uganda **75** 2.17N 31.46E
Kabalega Falls Nat. Park Uganda **75** 2.15N 31.45E
Kabalo Zaïre **75** 6.02S 27.00E
Kabambare Zaïre **75** 4.40S 27.41E
Kabba Nigeria **73** 7.50N 6.07E
Kabia *i.* Indonesia **59** 6.07S 120.28E
Kabinda Zaïre **74** 6.10S 24.29E
Kabir Kuh *mts.* Iran **55** 33.00N 47.00E
Kabompo *r.* Zambia **74** 14.17S 23.15E
Kabongo Zaïre **74** 7.22S 25.34E
Kabul Afghan. **56** 34.30N 69.10E
Kabunda Zaïre **75** 12.27S 29.15E
Kabwe Zambia **75** 14.27S 28.25E
Kacha Kuh *mts.* Iran **55** 29.30N 61.20E
Kachin State *d.* Burma **57** 25.30N 96.30E
Kade Ghana **72** 6.08N 0.51W
Kadei *r.* C.A.E. **73** 3.28N 16.05E
Kadiyevka U.S.S.R. **43** 48.34N 38.40E
Kaduna Nigeria **73** 10.28N 7.25E
Kaduna *d.* Nigeria **73** 11.00N 7.35E
Kaduna *r.* Nigeria **73** 8.45N 5.45E
Kadusam *mtn.* China **57** 28.30N 96.45E
Kaedi Mauritania **72** 16.12N 13.32W
Kafanchan Nigeria **73** 9.38N 8.20E
Kafirévs, C. Greece **39** 38.11N 24.30E
Kafo *r.* Uganda **75** 1.40N 32.07E
Kafue Zambia **75** 15.40S 28.13E
Kafue *r.* Zambia **75** 15.53S 28.55E
Kafue Dam Zambia **75** 15.40S 27.10E
Kafue Nat. Park Zambia **74** 15.30S 25.35E
Kağizman Turkey **54** 40.08N 43.07E
Kagoshima Japan **64** 31.37N 130.32E
Kagoshima wan *b.* Japan **64** 31.00N 131.00E
Kahama Tanzania **75** 3.48S 32.38E
Kahemba Zaïre **74** 7.20S 19.00E
Kaiama Nigeria **73** 9.37N 4.03E
Kaiapoi New Zealand **85** 43.23S 172.39E
Kaifeng China **62** 34.46N 114.22E
Kai Is. Indonesia **59** 5.45S 132.55E
Kaikohe New Zealand **85** 35.25S 173.49E
Kaikoura New Zealand **85** 42.24S 173.41E
Kaikoura Range *mts.* New Zealand **85** 42.00S 173.40E
Kaimana Asia **59** 3.39S 133.44E
Kaimanawa Mts. New Zealand **85** 37.10S 176.15E
Kainantu P.N.G. **59** 6.16S 145.50E
Kaipara Harbour New Zealand **85** 36.30S 174.00E
Kairouan Tunisia **38** 35.40N 10.04E
Kaiserslautern W. Germany **41** 49.27N 7.47E
Kaitaia New Zealand **85** 35.08S 173.18E
Kaitum *r.* Sweden **42** 67.30N 21.00E
Kaiyuan China **62** 42.45N 123.50E
Kajaani Finland **42** 64.14N 27.37E

Kajo Kaji Sudan **75** 3.56N 31.40E
Kakamas R.S.A. **76** 28.45S 20.33E
Kakamega Kenya **75** 0.21N 34.47E
Kakhovskoye Resr. U.S.S.R. **43** 47.30N 34.00E
Kakinada India **57** 16.59N 82.20E
Kalahari Desert Botswana **76** 23.30S 22.00E
Kalahari Gemsbok Nat. Park R.S.A. **76** 25.30S 20.30E
Kala-i-Fath Afghan. **55** 30.32N 61.52E
Kalámai Greece **39** 37.02N 22.05E
Kalamazoo U.S.A. **98** 42.17N 85.36W
Kalat Iran **55** 37.02N 59.46E
Kalat Pakistan **56** 29.01N 66.38E
Kalecik Turkey **54** 40.06N 33.22E
Kalehe Zaïre **75** 2.05S 28.53E
Kalemie Zaïre **75** 5.57S 29.10E
Kalgoorlie Australia **82** 30.49S 121.29E
Kaliakra, C. Bulgaria **39** 43.23N 28.29E
Kalima Zaïre **75** 2.35S 26.34E
Kalimantan *d.* Indonesia **58** 1.00S 113.00E
Kalinin U.S.S.R. **43** 56.47N 35.57E
Kaliningrad U.S.S.R. **42** 54.40N 20.30E
Kalispell U.S.A. **96** 48.12N 114.19W
Kalisz Poland **43** 51.46N 18.02E
Kaliua Tanzania **75** 5.08S 31.50E
Kalix *r.* Sweden **42** 65.50N 23.10E
Kalkfontein Botswana **76** 22.08S 20.53E
Kalla Vesi *l.* Finland **42** 62.45N 28.00E
Kallsjön *l.* Sweden **42** 63.30N 13.00E
Kalmar Sweden **42** 56.39N 16.20E
Kalomo Zambia **75** 16.55S 26.29E
Kaluga U.S.S.R. **43** 54.31N 36.16E
Kalundborg Denmark **42** 55.42N 11.06E
Kama *r.* U.S.S.R. **44** 55.30N 52.00E
Kamaishi Japan **64** 39.16N 141.53E
Kamchatka Pen. U.S.S.R. **45** 56.00N 160.00E
Kamen *mtn.* U.S.S.R. **45** 68.40N 94.20E
Kamenskoye U.S.S.R. **45** 62.31N 165.15E
Kamensk-Shakhtinskiy U.S.S.R. **43** 48.20N 40.16E
Kamensk-Ural'skiy U.S.S.R. **44** 56.29N 61.49E
Kames Scotland **30** 55.54N 5.15W
Kamet *mtn.* China **57** 31.03N 79.25E
Kamina Zaïre **74** 8.46S 24.58E
Kamloops Canada **96** 50.39N 120.24W
Kampala Uganda **75** 0.19N 32.35E
Kampar *r.* Indonesia **58** 0.20N 102.55E
Kampen Neth. **41** 52.33N 5.55E
Kampot Cambodia **57** 10.37N 104.11E
Kamyshin U.S.S.R. **43** 50.05N 45.24E
Kana *r.* Zimbabwe **76** 18.28S 27.03E
Kananga Zaïre **74** 5.53S 22.26E
Kanazawa Japan **64** 36.35N 136.40E
Kanchanaburi Thailand **57** 14.08N 99.31E
Kanchenjunga *mtn.* Asia **56** 27.44N 88.11E
Kanchipuram India **57** 12.50N 79.44E
Kandahar Afghan. **56** 31.36N 65.47E
Kandalaksha U.S.S.R. **42** 67.09N 32.31E
Kandalakskaya G. U.S.S.R. **42** 66.30N 34.00E
Kandangan Indonesia **58** 2.50S 115.15E
Kandi Benin **73** 11.05N 2.59E
Kandira Turkey **54** 41.05N 30.08E
Kandos Australia **83** 32.53S 149.59E
Kandreho Madagascar **75** 17.33S 46.00E
Kandy Sri Lanka **57** 7.18N 80.43E
Kane U.S.A. **99** 41.40N 78.48W
Kangan Iran **55** 27.50N 52.07E
Kangar Malaysia **57** 6.27N 100.12E
Kangaroo I. Australia **83** 35.45S 137.30E
Kangding China **60** 30.05N 102.04E
Kangean Is. Indonesia **58** 7.00S 115.45E
Kangnŭng S. Korea **61** 37.30N 129.02E
Kango Gabon **74** 0.15N 10.14E
Kaniama Zaïre **74** 7.32S 24.11E
Kanin, C. U.S.S.R. **44** 68.50N 43.30E
Kanin Pen. U.S.S.R. **44** 68.00N 45.00E
Kankakee U.S.A. **98** 41.08N 87.52W
Kankan Guinea **72** 10.22N 9.11W
Kanker India **57** 20.17N 81.30E
Kano Nigeria **73** 12.00N 8.31E
Kano *d.* Nigeria **73** 12.00N 9.00E
Kanoya Japan **64** 31.22N 130.50E
Kanpur India **56** 26.27N 80.14E
Kansas *d.* U.S.A. **96** 38.00N 99.00W
Kansas City U.S.A. **97** 39.02N 94.33W
Kansk U.S.S.R. **45** 56.11N 95.20E
Kanto *d.* Japan **64** 37.00N 140.00E
Kanturk Rep. of Ire. **35** 52.10N 8.54W
Kanye Botswana **76** 24.59S 25.19E
Kaohsiung Taiwan **63** 22.40N 120.18E
Kaoko Veld *f.* Namibia **76** 18.30S 13.30E
Kaolack Senegal **72** 14.09N 16.08W
Kaoma Zambia **74** 14.55S 24.58E
Kapanga Zaïre **74** 8.22S 22.37E
Kapfenberg Austria **44** 47.27N 15.18E
Kapiri Mposhi Zambia **75** 13.59S 28.40E
Kapiti I. New Zealand **85** 40.50S 174.50E
Kapoeta Sudan **75** 4.50N 33.35E
Kaposvár Hungary **39** 46.22N 17.47E
Kapsabet Kenya **75** 0.12N 35.05E

Kapuas *r.* Indonesia **58** 0.05N 111.25E
Kapuskasing Canada **98** 49.25N 82.26W
Kara U.S.S.R. **44** 69.12N 65.00E
Kara Bogaz Gol B. U.S.S.R. **55** 41.20N 53.40E
Karabuk Turkey **54** 41.12N 32.36E
Karachi Pakistan **56** 24.51N 67.02E
Karaganda U.S.S.R. **44** 49.53N 73.07E
Karak Jordan **54** 31.11N 35.42E
Karakelong *i.* Indonesia **59** 4.20N 126.50E
Karakoram Pass Asia **57** 35.53N 77.51E
Karakoram Range *mts.* Jammu and Kashmir **56** 35.30N 76.30E
Kara Kum *des.* U.S.S.R. **55** 37.45N 60.00E
Kara-Kum Canal U.S.S.R. **55** 37.30N 65.48E
Karaman Turkey **54** 37.11N 33.13E
Karamea Bight *b.* New Zealand **85** 41.15S 171.30E
Karamürsel Turkey **54** 40.42N 29.37E
Karand Iran **55** 34.16N 46.15E
Kara Nur *l.* Mongolia **60** 48.10N 93.30E
Karasburg Namibia **76** 28.00S 18.43E
Kara Sea U.S.S.R. **44** 73.00N 65.00E
Karasjok Norway **42** 69.27N 25.30E
Kara-Su *r.* Iran **55** 35.58N 56.25E
Karauli India **56** 26.30N 77.00E
Kara Usa Nor *l.* Mongolia **60** 48.10N 92.10E
Karawa Zaïre **74** 3.12N 20.20E
Karawanken *mts.* Austria **40** 46.20N 14.50E
Karbala Iraq **55** 32.37N 44.03E
Kardhítsa Greece **39** 39.22N 21.59E
Karema Tanzania **75** 6.50S 30.25E
Karhula Finland **42** 60.31N 26.50E
Kariba Zimbabwe **76** 16.32S 28.50E
Kariba, L. Zimbabwe/Zambia **76** 16.50S 28.00E
Kariba Dam Zimbabwe/Zambia **75** 16.15S 28.55E
Karibib Namibia **76** 21.59S 15.51E
Karikal India **57** 10.58N 79.50E
Karima Sudan **71** 18.32N 31.48E
Karis Finland **42** 60.05N 23.40E
Karisimbi, Mt. Zaïre/Rwanda **75** 1.31S 29.25E
Karkheh *r.* Iran **55** 31.45N 47.52E
Karkinitskiy, G. of U.S.S.R. **43** 45.50N 32.45E
Karkkila Finland **42** 60.32N 24.10E
Kar Kuh *mtn.* Iran **55** 31.37N 53.47E
Karl Marx Stadt E. Germany **40** 50.50N 12.55E
Karlovac Yugo. **38** 45.30N 15.34E
Karlovy Vary Czech. **40** 50.14N 12.53E
Karlsborg Sweden **42** 58.32N 14.32E
Karlshamn Sweden **42** 56.10N 14.50E
Karlskoga Sweden **42** 59.19N 14.33E
Karlskrona Sweden **42** 56.10N 15.35E
Karlsruhe W. Germany **40** 49.00N 8.24E
Karlstad Sweden **42** 59.24N 13.32E
Karmöy *i.* Norway **42** 59.15N 5.05E
Karnafuli Resr. Bangla. **57** 22.40N 92.05E
Karnataka *d.* India **56** 14.45N 76.00E
Karnobat Bulgaria **39** 42.40N 27.00E
Karonga Malaŵi **75** 9.54S 33.55E
Kárpathos *i.* Greece **39** 35.35N 27.08E
Kars Turkey **54** 40.35N 43.05E
Karsakpay U.S.S.R. **44** 47.47N 66.43E
Karun *r.* Iran **55** 30.25N 48.12E
Kasai *r.* Zaïre **74** 3.10S 16.13E
Kasai Occidental *d.* Zaïre **74** 5.00S 21.30E
Kasai Oriental *d.* Zaïre **74** 5.00S 24.00E
Kasama Zambia **75** 10.10S 31.11E
Kasane Botswana **76** 17.50S 25.05E
Kasanga Tanzania **75** 8.27S 31.10E
Kasempa Zambia **74** 13.28S 25.48E
Kasese Uganda **75** 0.07N 30.06E
Kashan Iran **55** 33.59N 51.31E
Kashi China **60** 39.29N 76.02E
Kashmar Iran **55** 35.12N 58.26E
Kaskaskia U.S.A. **98** 38.30N 89.15W
Kasongo Zaïre **75** 4.32S 26.33E
Kasongo-Lunda Zaïre **74** 6.30S 16.47E
Kásos *i.* Greece **54** 35.22N 26.57E
Kassala Sudan **71** 15.24N 36.30E
Kassel W. Germany **40** 51.18N 9.30E
Kasserine Tunisia **38** 35.15N 8.44E
Kastamonu Turkey **54** 41.22N 33.47E
Kastellorizon *i.* Greece **54** 36.08N 29.32E
Kastoria Greece **39** 40.32N 21.15E
Kasungu Malaŵi **75** 13.04S 33.29E
Kasur Pakistan **56** 31.07N 74.30E
Kataba Zambia **74** 16.12S 25.05E
Katahdin, Mt. U.S.A. **99** 45.55N 68.57W
Katako Kombe Zaïre **74** 3.27S 24.21E
Katete Zambia **75** 14.08S 31.50E
Katha Burma **57** 24.11N 96.20E
Katherina, Gebel *mtn.* Egypt **54** 28.30N 33.57E
Katherine Australia **82** 14.29S 132.20E
Kati Mali **72** 12.41N 8.04W
Katihar India **56** 25.33N 87.34E
Katima Rapids *f.* Zambia **74** 17.15S 24.20E
Katmandu Nepal **56** 27.42N 85.19E
Katonga *r.* Uganda **75** 0.03N 30.15E
Katoomba Australia **83** 33.42S 150.23E
Katowice Poland **43** 50.15N 18.59E

Katrine, Loch Scotland 30 56.15N 4.30W
Katrineholm Sweden 42 58.59N 16.15E
Katsina Nigeria 73 13.00N 7.32E
Katsina Ala Nigeria 73 7.10N 9.30E
Katsina Ala r. Nigeria 73 7.50N 8.58E
Kattegat str. Denmark/Sweden 42 57.00N 11.20E
Katwijk aan Zee Neth. 41 52.13N 4.27E
Kauai i. Hawaii U.S.A. 96 22.05N 159.30W
Kaufbeuren W. Germany 40 47.53N 10.37E
Kauhajoki Finland 42 62.26N 21.10E
Kauhava Finland 42 63.06N 23.05E
Kaunas U.S.S.R. 42 54.52N 23.55E
Kaura Namoda Nigeria 73 12.39N 6.38E
Kavali India 57 14.55N 80.01E
Kaválla Greece 39 40.56N 24.24E
Kawagoe Japan 64 35.58N 139.30E
Kawaguchi Japan 64 35.55N 139.50E
Kawambwa Zambia 75 9.47S 29.10E
Kawasaki Japan 64 35.30N 139.45E
Kawerau New Zealand 85 38.05S 176.42E
Kawimbe Zambia 75 8.50S 31.31E
Kawthoolei d. Burma 57 19.00N 96.30E
Kayah Burma 60 18.20N 97.00E
Kayan r. Indonesia 58 2.47N 117.46E
Kayes Mali 72 14.26N 11.28W
Kayseri Turkey 54 38.42N 35.28E
Kazachye U.S.S.R. 45 70.46N 136.15E
Kazakhstan Soviet Socialist Republic d. U.S.S.R. 43 48.00N 48.00E
Kazan U.S.S.R. 43 55.45N 49.10E
Kazanlŭk Bulgaria 39 42.38N 25.26E
Kazarun Iran 55 29.35N 51.39E
Kazbek mtn. U.S.S.R. 43 42.42N 44.30E
Kazumba Zaïre 74 6.30S 22.02E
Kéa i. Greece 39 37.36N 24.20E
Keady N. Ireland 34 54.15N 6.43W
Keal, Loch na Scotland 30 56.28N 6.04W
Kearney U.S.A. 96 40.42N 99.04W
Kebbi r. Nigeria 70 11.22N 4.10E
Kebnekaise mtn. Sweden 42 67.55N 18.30E
Kebock Head Scotland 32 58.02N 6.22W
Kecskemet Hungary 43 46.56N 19.43E
Kediri Indonesia 58 7.55S 112.01E
Kédougou Senegal 72 12.35N 12.09W
Keele Peak mtn. Canada 94 63.15N 129.50W
Keen, Mt. Scotland 33 56.58N 2.56W
Keene U.S.A. 99 42.55N 72.17W
Keeper Hill Rep. of Ire. 35 52.45N 8.17W
Keetmanshoop Namibia 76 26.36S 18.08E
Keewatin Canada 97 49.46N 94.30W
Keewatin d. Canada 95 67.00N 90.00W
Kefallinía i. Greece 39 38.15N 20.33E
Keflavik Iceland 42 64.01N 22.35W
Kei r. R.S.A. 76 32.40S 28.22E
Keighley England 28 53.52N 1.54W
Keitele l. Finland 42 62.59N 26.00E
Keith Scotland 33 57.32N 2.57W
Kelberg W. Germany 41 50.17N 6.56E
Kelkit r. Turkey 54 40.46N 36.32E
Kelloselkä Finland 42 66.55N 28.50E
Kells Kilkenny Rep. of Ire. 35 52.32N 7.18W
Kells Meath Rep. of Ire. 34 53.44N 6.53W
Kelowna Canada 96 49.50N 119.29W
Kelsall England 28 53.14N 2.44W
Kelso Scotland 31 55.36N 2.26W
Kelvedon England 25 51.50N 0.43E
Kelvedon Hatch England 23 51.40N 0.16E
Kemaliye Turkey 54 39.16N 38.29E
Kemerovo U.S.S.R. 44 55.25N 86.10E
Kemi Finland 42 65.45N 24.12E
Kemi r. Finland 42 55.47N 24.28E
Kemijärvi Finland 42 66.40N 27.21E
Kempsey Australia 83 31.05S 152.50E
Kempston England 25 52.07N 0.30W
Kempt, L. Canada 99 47.30N 74.15W
Kempten W. Germany 40 47.44N 10.19E
Kemsing England 23 51.18N 0.14E
Ken, Loch Scotland 31 55.02N 4.04W
Kendal Australia 83 31.28S 152.40E
Kendal England 28 54.19N 2.44W
Kendari Indonesia 59 3.57S 122.36E
Kenema Sierra Leone 72 7.57N 11.11W
Kenge Zaïre 74 4.56S 17.04E
Kengtung Burma 57 21.16N 99.39E
Kenhardt R.S.A. 76 29.19S 21.08E
Kenilworth England 24 52.22N 1.35W
Kenitra Morocco 70 34.20N 6.34W
Kenmare Rep. of Ire. 35 51.53N 9.36W
Kenmare r. Rep. of Ire. 35 51.47N 9.52W
Kenmore Scotland 31 56.35N 4.00W
Kennebec r. U.S.A. 99 43.55N 69.49W
Kennet r. England 24 51.28N 0.57W
Kennington England 25 51.10N 0.54E
Kenogamissi L. Canada 98 48.10N 81.35W
Keno Hill town Canada 94 63.58N 135.22W
Kenora Canada 97 49.47N 94.26W
Kenosha U.S.A. 98 42.34N 87.50W
Kensington and Chelsea d. England 23 51.29N 0.12W

Kent d. England 25 51.12N 0.40E
Kentford England 25 52.16N 0.30E
Kentucky d. U.S.A. 97 38.00N 85.00W
Kentucky L. U.S.A. 97 36.15N 88.00W
Kenya Africa 75 1.00N 38.00E
Kenya, Mt. Kenya 75 0.10S 37.19E
Kerala d. India 56 10.30N 76.30E
Kerang Australia 83 35.42S 143.59E
Kerch U.S.S.R. 43 45.22N 36.27E
Kerch Str. U.S.S.R. 43 45.15N 36.35E
Kerema P.N.G. 59 7.59S 145.46E
Kerguelen i. Indian Oc. 131 49.30S 69.30E
Kericho Kenya 75 0.22S 35.19E
Kerinci, Gunung mtn. Indonesia 58 1.45S 101.20E
Kerkrade Neth. 41 50.52N 6.02E
Kerloch mtn. Scotland 33 56.59N 2.30W
Kermān Iran 55 30.18N 57.05E
Kermānshāhān Iran 55 34.19N 47.04E
Kerme, G. of Turkey 39 36.52N 27.53E
Kerpen W. Germany 41 50.52N 6.42E
Kerrera i. Scotland 30 56.24N 5.33W
Kerry d. Rep. of Ire. 35 52.07N 9.35W
Kerry Head Rep. of Ire. 35 52.24N 9.56W
Kerulen r. Mongolia 61 48.45N 117.00E
Keşan Turkey 39 40.50N 26.39E
Kessingland England 25 52.25N 1.41E
Keswick England 28 54.35N 3.09W
Ketapang Kalimantan Indonesia 58 1.50S 110.02E
Ketchikan U.S.A. 94 55.25N 131.40W
Kete Krachi Ghana 72 7.50N 0.03W
Kettering England 24 52.24N 0.44W
Kettering U.S.A. 98 39.42N 84.11W
Kew England 23 51.29N 0.18W
Keweenaw B. U.S.A. 98 47.00N 88.15W
Keweenaw Pt. U.S.A. 98 47.23N 87.42W
Key, Lough Rep. of Ire. 34 54.00N 8.15W
Keyingham England 29 53.42N 0.07W
Keynsham England 24 51.25N 2.30W
Key West U.S.A. 100 24.34N 81.48W
Keyworth England 29 52.52N 1.08W
Khabarovsk U.S.S.R. 61 48.32N 135.08E
Khabur r. Syria 54 35.07N 40.30E
Khaburah Oman 55 23.58N 57.10E
Khairpur Pakistan 56 27.30N 68.50E
Khalkidhiki pen. Greece 54 40.30N 23.25E
Khalkis Greece 39 38.27N 23.36E
Khanaqin Iraq 55 34.22N 45.22E
Khandwa India 56 21.49N 76.23E
Khanka, L. U.S.S.R. 64 45.00N 132.30E
Khanty-Mansiysk U.S.S.R. 44 61.00N 69.00E
Khanu Iran 55 27.55N 57.45E
Kharagpur India 56 22.23N 87.22E
Kharan r. Iran 55 27.37N 58.48E
Kharga Oasis Egypt 54 25.00N 30.40E
Kharkov U.S.S.R. 43 50.00N 36.15E
Kharovsk U.S.S.R. 43 59.67N 40.07E
Khartoum Sudan 71 15.33N 32.35E
Khartoum North Sudan 71 15.39N 32.34E
Khash r. Afghan. 55 31.12N 62.00E
Khaskovo Bulgaria 39 41.56N 25.33E
Khatanga U.S.S.R. 45 71.50N 102.31E
Khatangskiy G. U.S.S.R. 45 75.00N 112.10E
Khemmarat Thailand 57 16.04N 105.10E
Khenifra Morocco 70 33.00N 5.40W
Kherson U.S.S.R. 43 46.39N 32.38E
Khíos Greece 54 38.23N 26.07E
Khíos i. Greece 39 38.23N 26.04E
Khirsan r. Iran 55 31.29N 48.53E
Khiva U.S.S.R. 55 41.25N 60.49E
Khmelnitskiy U.S.S.R. 43 49.25N 26.49E
Khöbsögöl Dalai l. Mongolia 60 51.00N 100.30E
Khoi Iran 55 38.32N 45.02E
Khomas-Hochland mts. Namibia 76 22.45S 16.20E
Khoper r. U.S.S.R. 43 49.35N 42.17E
Khor Qatar 55 25.39N 51.32E
Khorramabad Iran 55 33.29N 48.21E
Khorramshahr Iran 55 30.26N 48.09E
Khotin U.S.S.R. 43 48.30N 26.31E
Khulna Bangla. 56 22.49N 89.34E
Khunsar Iran 55 33.12N 50.20E
Khur Iran 55 33.47N 55.06E
Khurmuj Iran 55 28.40N 51.20E
Khwash Iran 55 28.14N 61.15E
Khyber Pass Asia 56 34.06N 71.05E
Kibali r. Zaïre 75 3.37N 28.38E
Kibombo Zaïre 74 3.58S 25.57E
Kibondo Tanzania 75 3.35S 30.41E
Kibungu Rwanda 75 2.10S 30.31E
Kibwezi Kenya 75 2.28S 37.57E
Kicking Horse Pass Canada 96 51.28N 116.23W
Kidal Mali 73 18.27N 1.25E
Kidan des. Saudi Arabia 55 22.20N 54.20E
Kidderminster England 24 52.24N 2.13W
Kidsgrove England 28 53.06N 2.15W
Kidwelly Wales 27 51.44N 4.20W
Kiel W. Germany 40 54.20N 10.08E
Kiel B. W. Germany 40 54.30N 10.30E

Kiel Canal W. Germany 40 53.54N 9.12E
Kielder Forest hills England 31 55.15N 2.30W
Kielder Resr. England 31 55.14N 2.30W
Kiev U.S.S.R. 43 50.28N 30.29E
Kiffa Mauritania 72 16.38N 11.28W
Kigali Rwanda 75 1.59S 30.05E
Kigoma Tanzania 75 4.52S 29.36E
Kigoma d. Tanzania 75 4.45S 30.00E
Kigosi r. Tanzania 75 4.37S 31.29E
Kii sanchi mts. Japan 64 34.00N 135.20E
Kii suido str. Japan 64 34.00N 135.00E
Kikinda Yugo. 39 45.51N 20.30E
Kikori P.N.G. 82 7.25S 144.13E
Kikwit Zaïre 74 5.02S 18.51E
Kil Sweden 42 59.30N 13.20E
Kila Kila P.N.G. 59 9.31S 147.10E
Kilbaha Rep. of Ire. 35 52.35N 9.52W
Kilbeggan Rep. of Ire. 34 53.22N 7.31W
Kilberry Head Scotland 30 55.47N 5.38W
Kilbirnie Scotland 30 55.45N 4.41W
Kilbrannan Sd. Scotland 30 55.37N 5.25W
Kilchrenan Scotland 30 56.21N 5.11W
Kilchu N. Korea 64 40.58N 129.21E
Kilcock Rep. of Ire. 34 53.25N 6.43W
Kilcreggan Scotland 30 55.59N 4.50W
Kilcrohane Rep. of Ire. 35 51.35N 9.42W
Kilcullen Rep. of Ire. 35 53.08N 6.46W
Kildare Rep. of Ire. 35 53.10N 6.55W
Kildare d. Rep. of Ire. 35 53.10N 6.50W
Kildonan Zimbabwe 76 17.15S 30.44E
Kildorrery Rep. of Ire. 35 52.14N 8.26W
Kilfinan Scotland 30 55.58N 5.18W
Kilfinane Rep. of Ire. 35 52.21N 8.28W
Kilgarvan Rep. of Ire. 35 51.54N 9.28W
Kilifi Kenya 75 3.30S 39.50E
Kilimanjaro d. Tanzania 75 3.45S 37.40E
Kilimanjaro mtn. Tanzania 75 3.02S 37.20E
Kilis Turkey 54 36.43N 37.07E
Kilkee Rep. of Ire. 35 52.41N 9.40W
Kilkeel N. Ireland 34 54.04N 6.00W
Kilkelly Rep. of Ire. 34 53.52N 8.52W
Kilkenny Rep. of Ire. 35 52.39N 7.16W
Kilkenny d. Rep. of Ire. 35 52.35N 7.15W
Kilkhampton England 27 50.53N 4.29W
Kilkieran B. Rep. of Ire. 34 53.20N 9.42W
Kilkis Greece 39 40.59N 22.51E
Killala Rep. of Ire. 34 54.13N 9.14W
Killala B. Rep. of Ire. 34 54.15N 9.10W
Killaloe Rep. of Ire. 35 52.47N 8.28W
Killamarsh England 29 53.19N 1.19W
Killard Pt. N. Ireland 34 54.41N 5.31W
Killarney Rep. of Ire. 35 52.04N 9.32W
Killary Harbour est. Rep. of Ire. 34 53.38N 9.56W
Killchianaig Scotland 30 56.01N 5.47W
Killeagh Rep. of Ire. 35 51.56N 8.00W
Killearn Scotland 30 56.03N 4.22W
Killeshandra Rep. of Ire. 34 54.01N 7.33W
Killin Scotland 30 56.29N 4.19W
Killington Mtn. U.S.A. 99 43.36N 72.49W
Killingworth England 31 55.02N 1.32W
Killíni mtn. Greece 39 37.56N 22.22E
Killorglin Rep. of Ire. 35 52.07N 9.45W
Killucan Rep. of Ire. 34 53.30N 7.09W
Killybegs Rep. of Ire. 34 54.38N 8.27W
Killyleagh N. Ireland 34 54.24N 5.39W
Kilmacolm Scotland 30 55.55N 4.38W
Kilmacthomas Rep. of Ire. 35 52.12N 7.26W
Kilmaganny Rep. of Ire. 35 52.26N 7.21W
Kilmallock Rep. of Ire. 35 52.24N 8.35W
Kilmaluag Scotland 32 57.41N 6.19W
Kilmarnock Scotland 30 55.37N 4.30W
Kilmartin Scotland 30 56.18N 5.28W
Kilmar Tor hill England 27 50.34N 4.29W
Kilmichael Pt. Rep. of Ire. 35 52.44N 6.09W
Kilmore Australia 83 37.18S 144.58E
Kilmore Quay Rep. of Ire. 35 52.11N 6.34W
Kilnaleck Rep. of Ire. 34 53.51N 7.20W
Kilninver Scotland 30 56.21N 5.30W
Kilombero r. Tanzania 75 8.30S 37.28E
Kilosa Tanzania 75 6.49S 37.00E
Kilrane Rep. of Ire. 35 52.15N 6.21W
Kilrea N. Ireland 34 54.57N 6.35W
Kilronan Rep. of Ire. 35 53.08N 9.41W
Kilrush Rep. of Ire. 35 52.39N 9.30W
Kilsyth Scotland 31 55.59N 4.04W
Kiltimagh Rep. of Ire. 34 53.51N 9.00W
Kilwa Kivinje Tanzania 75 8.45S 39.21E
Kilwa Masoko Tanzania 75 8.55S 39.31E
Kilwinning Scotland 30 55.40N 4.41W
Kilworth Mts. Rep. of Ire. 35 52.14N 8.12W
Kimberley R.S.A. 76 28.45S 24.46E
Kimberly Plateau Australia 82 17.20S 127.20E
Kimbolton England 25 52.17N 0.23W
Kimito i. Finland 42 60.05N 22.30E
Kimpton England 23 51.52N 0.18W
Kinabalu mtn. Malaysia 58 6.10N 116.40E
Kinbrace Scotland 33 58.15N 3.56W
Kincardine Scotland 31 56.04N 3.44W

Magangué Colombia **101** 9.14N 74.46W
Magas Iran **55** 27.08N 61.36E
Magburaka Sierra Leone **72** 8.44N 11.57W
Magdalena r. Colombia **101** 10.56N 74.58W
Magdalena Mexico **96** 30.38N 110.59W
Magdeburg E. Germany **40** 52.08N 11.36E
Magelang Indonesia **58** 7.28S 110.11E
Magellan's Str. Chile **109** 53.00S 71.00W
Mageröya i. Norway **42** 71.00N 25.50E
Maggiore, L. Italy **36** 45.57N 8.37E
Maghera N. Ireland **30** 54.51N 6.41W
Magherafelt N. Ireland **30** 54.45N 6.38W
Maghull England **28** 53.31N 2.56W
Magnitogorsk U.S.S.R. **44** 53.28N 59.06E
Magude Moçambique **76** 25.02S 32.40E
Magué Moçambique **75** 15.46S 31.42E
Magwe Burma **57** 20.10N 95.00E
Mahabad Iran **55** 36.44N 45.44E
Mahaddei Wen Somali Rep. **75** 2.58N 45.32E
Mahagi Zaïre **75** 2.16N 30.59E
Mahalapye Botswana **76** 23.05S 26.51E
Mahallat Iran **55** 33.54N 50.28E
Mahanadi r. India **57** 20.17N 86.43E
Maharashtra d. India **56** 20.00N 77.00E
Mahdia Tunisia **38** 35.28N 11.01E
Mahenge Tanzania **75** 8.46S 36.38E
Mahia Pen. New Zealand **85** 37.10S 178.30E
Mahón Spain **37** 39.55N 4.18E
Maidenhead England **23** 51.32N 0.44W
Maiden Newton England **24** 50.46N 2.35W
Maidens Scotland **30** 55.20N 4.49W
Maidstone England **23** 51.17N 0.32E
Maiduguri Nigeria **73** 11.53N 13.16E
Maihar India **56** 24.14N 80.50E
Maiko r. Zaïre **74** 0.15N 25.35E
Maimana Afghan. **56** 35.54N 64.43E
Main r. N. Ireland **30** 54.43N 6.19W
Main r. W. Germany **40** 50.00N 8.19E
Main Barrier Range mts. Australia **83** 31.25S 141.25E
Mai Ndombe l. Zaïre **74** 2.00S 18.20E
Maine r. Rep. of Ire. **35** 52.09N 9.44W
Maine d. U.S.A. **99** 45.00N 69.00W
Mainland i. Shetland Is. Scotland **33** 60.15N 1.22W
Mainland i. Orkney Is. Scotland **33** 59.00N 3.10W
Mainpuri India **56** 27.14N 79.01E
Mainz W. Germany **40** 50.00N 8.16E
Maipu Argentina **110** 36.52S 57.52W
Maitland Australia **83** 32.33S 151.33E
Maizuru Japan **64** 35.30N 135.20E
Maja i. Indonesia **58** 1.05S 109.25E
Majene Indonesia **58** 3.33S 118.59E
Majma'a Saudi Arabia **55** 25.52N 45.25E
Majorca i. Spain **37** 39.35N 3.00E
Majuba Hill R.S.A. **76** 27.30S 29.50E
Majunga Madagascar **75** 15.50S 46.20E
Makale Indonesia **58** 3.06S 119.53E
Makarikari Salt Pan f. Botswana **76** 20.50S 25.45E
Makassar Str. Indonesia **58** 3.00S 118.00E
Makeni Sierra Leone **72** 8.57N 12.02W
Makeyevka U.S.S.R. **43** 48.01N 38.00E
Makhachkala U.S.S.R. **44** 42.59N 47.30E
Makó Hungary **39** 46.13N 20.30E
Makokou Gabon **74** 0.38N 12.47E
Makoua Congo **74** 0.01S 15.40E
Makran f. Asia **55** 26.30N 61.20E
Makurdi Nigeria **73** 7.44N 8.35E
Malabo Equat. Guinea **73** 3.45N 8.48E
Malacca, Straits of Indian Oc. **58** 3.00N 100.30E
Málaga Colombia **101** 6.44N 72.45W
Málaga Spain **37** 36.43N 4.25W
Malahide Rep. of Ire. **34** 53.27N 6.10W
Malakal Sudan **71** 9.31N 31.40E
Malakand Pakistan **56** 34.34N 71.57E
Malang Indonesia **58** 7.59S 112.45E
Malange Angola **74** 9.36S 16.21E
Malange d. Angola **74** 9.00S 17.00E
Mälaren l. Sweden **42** 59.30N 17.00E
Malatya Turkey **54** 38.22N 38.18E
Malawi Africa **75** 12.00S 34.00E
Malawi, L. Africa **75** 12.00S 34.30E
Malayer Iran **55** 34.19N 48.51E
Malaysia Asia **58** 5.00N 110.00E
Malbork Poland **43** 54.02N 19.01E
Malden England **23** 51.23N 0.15W
Malden U.S.A. **99** 42.24N 71.04W
Maldive Is. Indian Oc. **56** 6.20N 73.00E
Maldon England **25** 51.43N 0.41E
Maldonado Uruguay **110** 34.57S 54.59W
Maléa, C. Greece **39** 36.27N 23.11E
Malebo Pool f. Zaïre **74** 4.15S 15.25E
Malegaon India **56** 20.32N 74.38E
Mali Africa **72** 17.30N 2.30E
Malili Indonesia **59** 2.38S 121.06E
Malin Rep. of Ire. **30** 55.18N 7.15W
Malindi Kenya **75** 3.14S 40.08E
Malines Belgium **41** 51.01N 4.28E
Malin Head Rep. of Ire. **34** 55.23N 7.24W
Malin More Rep. of Ire. **34** 54.42N 8.48W

Malipo China **63** 23.11N 104.41E
Mallacoota Australia **83** 37.34S 149.43E
Mallaig Scotland **32** 57.00N 5.50W
Mallawi Egypt **54** 27.44N 30.50E
Mallorca i. see MajorcaSpain **37**
Mallow Rep. of Ire. **35** 52.08N 8.39W
Malmédy Belgium **41** 50.25N 6.02E
Malmesbury England **24** 51.35N 2.05W
Malmesbury R.S.A. **76** 33.28S 18.43E
Malmö Sweden **42** 55.35N 13.00E
Malone U.S.A. **99** 44.52N 74.19W
Malonga Zaïre **74** 10.26S 23.10E
Måløy Norway **42** 61.57N 5.06E
Malta Europe **38** 35.55N 14.25E
Malta i. Malta **38** 35.55N 14.25E
Malta Channel Med. Sea **38** 36.20N 14.45E
Maltby England **29** 53.25N 1.12W
Malton England **29** 54.09N 0.48W
Maluku d. Indonesia **59** 4.00S 129.00E
Malvern Hills England **24** 52.05N 2.16W
Mambasa Zaïre **75** 1.20N 29.05E
Mamberamo r. Asia **59** 1.45S 137.25E
Mambéré r. C.A.E. **73** 3.30N 16.08E
Mambilima Falls town Zambia **75** 10.32S 28.45E
Mamfe Cameroon **73** 5.46N 9.18E
Mamore r. Bolivia **108** 12.00S 65.15W
Mamou Guinea **72** 10.24N 12.05W
Mamudju Indonesia **58** 2.41S 118.55E
Man Ivory Coast **72** 7.31N 7.37W
Manacle Pt. England **24** 50.04N 5.05W
Manacor Spain **37** 39.32N 3.12E
Manado Indonesia **59** 1.30N 124.58E
Managua Nicaragua **100** 12.06N 86.18W
Managua, L. Nicaragua **100** 12.10N 86.30W
Manama Bahrain **55** 26.12N 50.36E
Manapouri, L. New Zealand **85** 45.30S 167.00E
Manastir Turkey **54** 37.33N 31.37E
Manaus Brazil **108** 3.06S 60.00W
Manchester England **28** 53.30N 2.15W
Manchester Conn. U.S.A. **99** 41.47N 72.31W
Manchester N.H. U.S.A. **99** 42.59N 71.28W
Manchuria f. China **62** 42.30N 123.00E
Manchurian Plain f. Asia **113** 42.00N 122.00E
Mand r. Iran **55** 28.09N 51.16E
Manda i. Tanzania **75** 10.30S 34.37E
Mandal Norway **42** 58.02N 7.30E
Mandala Peak Asia **59** 4.45S 140.15E
Mandalay Burma **57** 21.57N 96.04E
Mandalgovi Mongolia **62** 45.40N 106.10E
Mandara Mts. Nigeria/Cameroon **73** 10.30N 13.30E
Mandla India **56** 22.35N 80.28E
Manfredonia Italy **38** 41.38N 15.54E
Mangalia Romania **39** 43.48N 28.30E
Mangalore India **56** 12.54N 74.51E
Mangerton Mtn. Rep. of Ire. **35** 51.58N 9.30W
Mangnai China **60** 37.52N 91.26E
Mangochi Malawi **75** 14.29S 35.15E
Mangotsfield England **24** 51.29N 2.29W
Mangueira L. Brazil **110** 33.15S 52.50W
Mangyshlak Pen. U.S.S.R. **44** 44.00N 52.30E
Manhiça Moçambique **76** 25.23S 32.49E
Maniamba Moçambique **75** 12.30S 35.05E
Manica Moçambique **76** 19.04S 33.29E
Manicouagan r. Canada **95** 49.00N 68.13W
Manila Phil. **59** 14.36N 120.59E
Maninga r. Zambia **74** 13.28S 24.25E
Manipur d. India **57** 25.00N 93.40E
Manisa Turkey **39** 38.37N 27.28E
Manistee r. U.S.A. **98** 44.17N 85.45W
Manistique U.S.A. **98** 45.58N 86.17W
Manitoba d. Canada **95** 54.00N 96.00W
Manitoba, L. Canada **95** 51.35N 99.00W
Manitou Is. U.S.A. **98** 45.05N 86.05W
Manitoulin I. Canada **98** 45.50N 82.15W
Manitowoc U.S.A. **98** 44.04N 87.40W
Maniwaki Canada **99** 46.22N 75.58W
Manizales Colombia **108** 5.03N 75.32W
Manjil Iran **55** 36.44N 49.29E
Mankono Ivory Coast **72** 8.01N 6.09W
Manly Australia **83** 33.47S 151.17E
Mannar, G. of India/Sri Lanka **57** 8.20N 79.00E
Mannheim W. Germany **40** 49.30N 8.28E
Mannin B. Rep. of Ire. **34** 53.28N 10.06W
Manningtree England **25** 51.56N 1.03E
Mannu r. Italy **38** 39.16N 9.00E
Manokwari Asia **59** 0.53S 134.05E
Manono Zaïre **75** 7.18S 27.24E
Manorhamilton Rep. of Ire. **34** 54.18N 8.10W
Manosque France **36** 43.50N 5.47E
Manresa Spain **37** 41.43N 1.50E
Mansa Zambia **75** 11.10S 28.52E
Mansel I. Canada **95** 62.00N 80.00W
Mansfield Australia **83** 37.04S 146.04E
Mansfield England **29** 53.08N 1.12W
Mansfield U.S.A. **98** 40.46N 82.31W
Mänttä Finland **42** 62.00N 24.40E
Mantua Italy **38** 45.09N 10.47E
Manukau Harbour New Zealand **85** 37.10S 174.00E

Manus i. Pacific Oc. **59** 2.00S 147.00E
Manyara, L. Tanzania **75** 3.40S 35.50E
Manych r. U.S.S.R. **43** 47.14N 40.20E
Manych Gudilo, L. U.S.S.R. **43** 46.20N 42.45E
Manyoni Tanzania **75** 5.46S 34.50E
Manzala, L. Egypt **54** 31.20N 32.00F
Manzanares Spain **37** 39.00N 3.23W
Manzanillo Cuba **101** 20.21N 77.21W
Manzhouli China **61** 49.36N 117.28E
Manzini Swaziland **76** 26.30S 31.22E
Maoke Range mts. Indonesia **59** 4.00S 137.30E
Maoming China **63** 21.50N 110.56E
Maoniu Shan mtn. China **62** 33.00N 103.56E
Maopi Tou c. Taiwan **63** 22.00N 120.45E
Mapai Moçambique **76** 22.51S 32.00E
Mapia Is. Asia **59** 1.00N 134.15E
Mappi Indonesia **59** 7.06S 139.23E
Maprik P.N.G. **59** 3.38S 143.02E
Maputo Moçambique **76** 25.58S 32.35E
Maputo d. Moçambique **76** 26.00S 32.30E
Ma'qala Saudi Arabia **55** 26.29N 47.20E
Maquela do Zombo Angola **74** 6.06S 15.12E
Maquinchao Argentina **110** 41.19S 68.47W
Mar f. Scotland **33** 57.07N 3.03W
Mar, Serra do mts. Brazil **110** 28.00S 49.30W
Mara d. Tanzania **75** 1.45S 34.30E
Mara r. Tanzania **75** 1.30S 33.52E
Maracaibo Venezuela **101** 10.44N 71.37W
Maracaibo, L. Venezuela **101** 10.00N 71.30W
Maracaju Brazil **110** 21.38S 55.10W
Maracaju, Serra de mts. Brazil **110** 21.00S 55.05W
Maracay Venezuela **101** 10.20N 67.28W
Maradi Niger **73** 13.29N 7.10E
Maragheh Iran **55** 37.25N 46.13E
Marajó I. Brazil **108** 1.00S 49.30W
Maralal Kenya **75** 1.15N 36.48E
Marand Iran **55** 38.25N 45.50E
Marandellas Zimbabwe **76** 18.05S 31.42E
Marañón r. Peru **108** 4.00S 73.30W
Marapi mtn. Indonesia **58** 0.20S 100.45E
Maraş Turkey **54** 37.34N 36.54E
Marathon Greece **39** 38.10N 23.59E
Marazion England **27** 50.08N 5.29W
Marbella Spain **37** 36.31N 4.53W
Marble Bar Australia **82** 21.16S 119.45E
Marburg W. Germany **40** 50.49N 8.36E
March England **25** 52.33N 0.05E
Marche Belgium **41** 50.13N 5.21E
Marchena Spain **37** 37.20N 5.24W
Marcy, Mt. U.S.A. **99** 44.07N 73.56W
Mardan Pakistan **56** 34.14N 72.05E
Mar del Plata Argentina **110** 38.00S 57.32W
Marden England **23** 51.11N 0.30E
Mardin Turkey **54** 37.19N 40.43E
Maree, Loch Scotland **32** 57.41N 5.28W
Marettimo i. Italy **38** 37.58N 12.05E
Margarita I. Venezuela **101** 11.00N 64.00W
Margate England **25** 51.23N 1.24E
Mariana Is. Pacific Oc. **59** 15.00N 145.00E
Marianao Cuba **100** 23.03N 82.29W
Marianas Trench Pacific Oc. **113** 19.00N 146.00E
Maribor Yugo. **40** 46.35N 15.40E
Marico r. R.S.A. **76** 24.15S 26.48E
Maricourt Canada **95** 61.30N 72.00W
Maridi Sudan **75** 4.55N 29.30E
Marie Galante i. Guadeloupe **101** 16.00N 61.15W
Mariehamn Finland **42** 60.05N 19.55E
Mariental Namibia **76** 24.36S 17.59E
Mariestad Sweden **42** 58.44N 13.50E
Mariga r. Nigeria **73** 9.37N 5.55E
Marília Brazil **109** 22.13S 50.20W
Marinette U.S.A. **98** 45.06N 87.38W
Maringá Brazil **110** 23.36S 52.02W
Maringa r. Zaïre **74** 1.13N 19.50E
Maringue Moçambique **76** 17.55S 34.24E
Marinha Grande Portugal **37** 39.45N 8.55W
Marion Ind. U.S.A. **98** 40.33N 85.40W
Marion Ohio U.S.A. **98** 40.35N 83.08W
Mariscal Estigarribia Paraguay **110** 22.03S 60.35W
Maritsa r. Turkey **39** 41.00N 26.15E
Markaryd Sweden **42** 56.26N 13.35E
Markerwaard f. Neth. **41** 52.30N 5.15E
Market Deeping England **25** 52.40N 0.20W
Market Drayton England **28** 52.55N 2.30W
Market Harborough England **24** 52.29N 0.55W
Market Rasen England **29** 53.24N 0.20W
Market Weighton England **29** 53.52N 0.04W
Markha r. U.S.S.R. **45** 63.37N 119.00E
Markinch Scotland **31** 56.12N 3.09W
Markyate England **23** 51.51N 0.28W
Marlborough England **24** 51.26N 1.44W
Marlborough Downs hills England **24** 51.28N 1.48W
Marle France **41** 49.44N 3.47E
Marlow England **23** 51.35N 0.48W
Marlpit Hill town England **23** 51.13N 0.04E
Marmagao India **56** 15.26N 73.50E
Marmara i. Turkey **39** 40.38N 27.37E
Marmara, Sea of Turkey **39** 40.45N 28.15E

Marmaris Turkey **39** 36.50N 28.17E
Marne *r.* France **36** 48.50N 2.25E
Maroua Cameroon **73** 10.35N 14.20E
Marovoay Madagascar **75** 16.05S 46.35E
Marple England **28** 53.23N 2.05W
Marquesas Is. Pacific Oc. **112** 9.00S 139.00W
Marquette U.S.A. **98** 46.33N 87.23W
Marquise France **25** 50.48N 1.42E
Marrakesh Morocco **70** 31.49N 8.00W
Marrawah Australia **83** 40.57S 144.44E
Marrupa Moçambique **75** 13.10S 37.30E
Marsabit Kenya **75** 2.20N 37.59E
Marsala Italy **38** 37.48N 12.27E
Marsden England **28** 53.36N 1.55W
Marseille France **36** 43.18N 5.22E
Marshall Is. Pacific Oc. **113** 8.00N 172.00E
Marshfield England **24** 51.28N 2.19W
Marshfield U.S.A. **98** 44.40N 90.11W
Marshland Fen *f.* England **25** 52.40N 0.18E
Marske-by-the-Sea England **29** 54.35N 1.00W
Martaban Burma **57** 16.30N 97.35E
Martaban, G. of Burma **57** 15.10N 96.30E
Martelange Belgium **41** 49.50N 5.44E
Martés, Sierra *mts.* Spain **37** 39.10N 1.00W
Martha's Vineyard *i.* U.S.A. **99** 41.25N 70.35W
Martigny Switz. **40** 46.07N 7.05E
Martinique C. America **101** 14.40N 61.00W
Martin Pt. U.S.A. **94** 70.10N 143.50W
Martinsburg U.S.A. **99** 39.28N 77.59W
Marton New Zealand **85** 40.04S 175.25E
Maruchak Afghan. **55** 35.50N 63.08E
Marudi Malaysia **58** 4.15N 114.19E
Marum Neth. **41** 53.06N 6.16E
Marvejols France **36** 44.33N 3.18E
Mary U.S.S.R. **71** 37.42N 61.54E
Maryborough Qld. Australia **82** 25.32S 152.36E
Maryborough Vic. Australia **83** 37.05S 143.47E
Maryland *d.* U.S.A. **97** 39.00N 76.30W
Maryport England **28** 54.43N 3.30W
Masai Steppe *f.* Tanzania **75** 4.30S 37.00E
Masaka Uganda **75** 0.20S 31.46E
Masan S. Korea **61** 35.10N 128.35E
Masasi Tanzania **75** 10.43S 38.48E
Masbate *i.* Phil. **59** 12.00N 123.30E
Mascara Algeria **37** 35.20N 0.09E
Maseru Lesotho **76** 29.19S 27.29E
Masham England **28** 54.15N 1.40W
Mashhad Iran **55** 36.16N 59.34E
Mashonaland *f.* Zimbabwe **76** 18.20S 32.00E
Masi-Manimba Zaïre **74** 4.47S 17.54E
Masindi Uganda **75** 1.41N 31.45E
Masira I. Oman **56** 20.30N 58.50E
Masjid-i-Sulaiman Iran **55** 31.59N 49.18E
Mask, Lough Rep. of Ire. **34** 53.38N 9.22W
Mason City U.S.A. **97** 43.10N 93.10W
Massa Italy **38** 44.02N 10.09E
Massachusetts *d.* U.S.A. **99** 43.00N 72.25W
Massangena Moçambique **76** 21.31S 33.03E
Massawa Ethiopia **71** 15.36N 39.29E
Massif Central *mts.* France **36** 45.00N 3.30E
Massif de l'Ouarsenis *mts.* Algeria **37** 35.55N 1.40E
Massillon U.S.A. **98** 40.48N 81.32W
Massinga Moçambique **76** 23.20S 35.25E
Masterton New Zealand **85** 40.57S 175.39E
Masurian Lakes Poland **43** 54.00N 21.45E
Matabeleland *f.* Zimbabwe **76** 19.30S 28.15E
Matadi Zaïre **74** 5.50S 13.36E
Matagorda B. U.S.A. **97** 28.30N 96.20W
Matakana I. New Zealand **85** 37.35S 176.15E
Matam Senegal **72** 15.40N 13.18W
Matamata New Zealand **85** 37.49S 175.46E
Matamoros Mexico **100** 25.33N 103.15W
Matandu *r.* Tanzania **75** 8.44S 39.22E
Matane Canada **99** 48.50N 67.13W
Matanzas Cuba **100** 23.04N 81.35W
Matanzas *d.* Cuba **100** 23.04N 81.35W
Matapan, C. Greece **39** 36.22N 22.28E
Mataram Indonesia **58** 8.36S 116.07E
Mataró Spain **37** 41.32N 2.72E
Matatiele R.S.A. **76** 30.20S 28.49E
Mataura *r.* New Zealand **85** 46.34S 168.45E
Matawin *r.* Canada **99** 46.56N 72.55W
Matehuala Mexico **100** 23.40N 100.40W
Matera Italy **39** 40.41N 16.36E
Mateur Tunisia **38** 37.02N 9.39E
Mathews Peak *mtn.* Kenya **75** 1.18N 37.20E
Mathura India **56** 27.30N 77.42E
Matlock England **29** 53.08N 1.32W
Mato Grosso *d.* Brazil **110** 19.00S 55.00W
Mato Grosso *f.* Brazil **108** 15.00S 55.00W
Matope Malaŵi **75** 15.20S 34.57E
Matopo Hills Zimbabwe **76** 20.45S 28.30E
Matrah Oman **55** 23.37N 58.33E
Matruh Egypt **54** 31.21N 27.15E
Matsue Japan **64** 35.29N 133.00E
Matsu Is. Taiwan **63** 26.12N 120.00E
Matsumoto Japan **64** 36.18N 137.58E
Matsusaka Japan **64** 34.34N 136.32E
Matsuyama Japan **64** 33.50N 132.47E
Mattagami *r.* Canada **98** 49.45N 82.00W
Mattawa Canada **99** 46.19N 58.42W
Matterhorn *mtn.* Switz. **36** 45.58N 7.38E
Maturín Venezuela **101** 9.45N 61.16W
Maubeuge France **41** 50.17N 3.58E
Mauchline Scotland **30** 55.31N 4.23W
Maude Australia **83** 34.27S 144.21E
Mau-é-ele Moçambique **76** 24.21S 34.07E
Mauganj India **56** 24.40N 81.53E
Maughold Head I.o.M. **28** 54.18N 4.19W
Maui *i.* Hawaii U.S.A. **96** 20.45N 156.15W
Maumee *r.* U.S.A. **98** 41.34N 83.41W
Maumere Indonesia **59** 8.35S 122.13E
Maun Botswana **76** 19.52S 23.40E
Mauritania Africa **72** 20.00N 10.00E
Mauritius Indian Oc. **131** 20.10S 58.00E
Mavinga Angola **74** 15.47S 20.21E
Mavuradonha Mts. Zimbabwe **76** 16.30S 31.30E
Mawlaik Burma **57** 23.40N 94.26E
May, C. U.S.A. **99** 38.55N 74.55W
May, Isle of Scotland **31** 56.12N 2.32W
Maya Spain **37** 43.12N 1.29W
Mayaguana I. Bahamas **101** 22.30N 73.00W
Mayaguez Puerto Rico **101** 18.13N 67.09W
Mayamey Iran **55** 36.27N 55.40E
Maya Mts. Belize **100** 16.30N 89.00W
Maybole Scotland **30** 55.21N 4.41W
Maydena Australia **83** 42.48S 146.30E
Mayen W. Germany **41** 50.19N 7.14E
Mayenne France **36** 48.18N 0.37W
Mayenne *r.* France **36** 48.18N 0.37W
Mayfield England **25** 51.01N 0.17E
Maykop U.S.S.R. **43** 44.37N 40.48E
Maymyo Burma **57** 22.05N 96.33E
Maynooth Rep. of Ire. **34** 53.23N 6.37W
Mayo *d.* Rep. of Ire. **34** 53.47N 9.07W
Mayo Daga Nigeria **73** 6.59N 11.25E
Mayo Landing Canada **94** 63.45N 135.45W
Mayor I. New Zealand **85** 37.15S 176.15E
Mayotte, Île *i.* Comoro Is. **75** 12.50S 45.10E
Mayoumba Gabon **74** 3.23S 10.38E
Mazabuka Zambia **75** 15.50S 27.47E
Mazatenango Guatemala **100** 14.31N 91.30W
Mažeikiai U.S.S.R. **42** 56.06N 23.06E
Mazoe *r.* Moçambique **75** 16.22S 33.38E
Mazoe Zimbabwe **76** 17.30S 31.03E
Mbabane Swaziland **76** 26.20S 31.08E
M'Baere *r.* C.A.E. **74** 3.45N 17.35E
M'Baiki C.A.E. **73** 3.53N 18.01E
Mbala Zambia **75** 8.50S 31.24E
Mbale Uganda **75** 1.04N 34.12E
Mbamba Bay *town* Tanzania **75** 11.18S 34.50E
Mbandaka Zaïre **74** 0.03N 18.21E
M'Bangé Cameroon **74** 4.32N 9.31E
Mbanza Congo Angola **74** 6.18S 14.16E
Mbarara Uganda **75** 0.36S 30.40E
Mbeya Tanzania **75** 8.54S 33.29E
Mbeya *d.* Tanzania **75** 8.30S 32.30E
Mbinda Congo **74** 2.11S 12.55E
M'bridge *r.* Angola **74** 7.12S 12.55E
Mbuji Mayi Zaïre **74** 6.08S 23.39E
Mbulamuti Uganda **75** 0.50N 33.05E
McClintock Channel Canada **95** 71.20N 102.00W
McClure Str. Canada **94** 74.30N 116.00W
McConaughy, L. U.S.A. **96** 41.20N 102.00W
McCook U.S.A **96** 40.15N 100.45W
McGrath U.S.A. **94** 62.58N 155.40W
Mchinja Tanzania **75** 9.44S 39.45E
Mchinji Malaŵi **75** 13.48S 32.55E
McKeesport U.S.A. **98** 40.21N 79.52W
McKinley, Mt. U.S.A. **94** 63.00N 151.00W
McMurray Canada **94** 56.45N 111.27W
McSwyne's B. Rep. of Ire. **34** 54.36N 8.26W
Mead, L. U.S.A. **96** 36.10N 114.25W
Meadville U.S.A. **98** 41.38N 80.10W
Mealasta *i.* Scotland **32** 58.05N 7.07W
Meath *d.* Rep. of Ire. **34** 53.32N 6.40W
Meaux France **36** 48.58N 2.54E
Mecca Saudi Arabia **71** 21.26N 39.49E
Meconta Moçambique **75** 15.00S 39.50E
Medan Indonesia **58** 3.35N 98.39E
Médéa Algeria **37** 36.15N 2.48E
Mededsiz *mtn.* Turkey **54** 37.33N 34.38E
Medellín Colombia **101** 6.15N 75.36W
Medenine Tunisia **70** 33.24N 10.25E
Méderdra Mauritania **72** 17.02N 15.41W
Medford U.S.A. **99** 42.25N 71.05W
Medicine Hat Canada **96** 50.03N 110.41W
Medina Saudi Arabia **54** 24.30N 39.35E
Medina del Campo Spain **37** 41.20N 4.55W
Medina de Rioseco Spain **37** 41.53N 5.03W
Mediterranean Sea 38 36.00N 16.00E
Mediterranean Sea 70 37.00N 15.00E
Medjerda, Wadi *r.* Algeria **38** 37.07N 10.12E
Medjerda Mts. Algeria **38** 36.35N 8.20E
Medveditsa *r.* U.S.S.R. **43** 49.35N 42.45E
Medway *r.* England **23** 51.24N 0.31E
Meekatharra Australia **82** 26.35S 118.30E
Meerut India **56** 29.00N 77.42E
Mega Ethiopia **71** 4.02N 38.19E
Megantic Canada **99** 45.34N 70.53W
Megantic Mtn. Canada **99** 45.27N 71.09W
Mégara Greece **39** 38.00N 23.21E
Meghalaya *d.* India **56** 25.30N 91.00E
Meiktila Burma **57** 20.53N 95.54E
Meiningen E. Germany **40** 50.34N 10.25E
Meishan China **63** 30.02N 103.50E
Meissala Chad **73** 8.20N 17.40E
Meissen E. Germany **40** 51.10N 13.28E
Mei Xian China **63** 24.19N 116.13E
Meknès Morocco **70** 33.53N 5.37W
Mekong *r.* Asia **58** 10.00N 106.20E
Mekong Delta Vietnam **58** 10.00N 106.20E
Mekongga *mtn.* Indonesia **59** 3.39S 121.15E
Mékrou *r.* Benin **73** 12.20N 2.47E
Melaka Malaysia **58** 2.11N 102.16E
Melbourn England **25** 52.05N 0.01E
Melbourne Australia **83** 37.45S 144.58E
Melbourne England **29** 52.50N 1.25W
Melfi Chad **73** 11.04N 18.03E
Melfi Italy **38** 40.59N 15.39E
Melilla Spain **37** 35.17N 2.57W
Melitopol U.S.S.R. **43** 46.51N 35.22E
Melksham England **24** 51.22N 2.09W
Mellerud Sweden **42** 58.42N 12.27E
Melmore Pt. Rep. of Ire. **34** 55.15N 7.49W
Melo Uruguay **110** 32.22S 54.10W
Melrose Scotland **31** 55.36N 2.43W
Melsetter Zimbabwe **76** 19.48S 32.50E
Meltham England **28** 53.36N 1.52W
Melton Mowbray England **24** 52.46N 0.53W
Melun France **36** 48.32N 2.40E
Melvaig Scotland **32** 57.48N 5.49W
Melville Canada **96** 50.57N 102.49W
Melville, C. Australia **82** 14.02S 144.30E
Melville I. Australia **82** 11.30S 131.00E
Melville I. Canada **94** 75.30N 110.00W
Melville Pen. Canada **95** 68.00N 84.00W
Melvin, Lough N. Ireland **34** 54.26N 8.12W
Memba Moçambique **75** 14.16S 40.30E
Memel *see* Klaipeda U.S.S.R. **43**
Memmingen W. Germany **40** 47.59N 10.11E
Memphis *ruins* Egypt **54** 29.52N 31.12E
Memphis U.S.A. **97** 35.05N 90.00W
Menai Bridge *town* Wales **26** 53.14N 4.11W
Menai Str. Wales **26** 53.17N 4.20W
Mendawai *r.* Indonesia **58** 3.17S 113.20E
Mende France **36** 44.32N 3.30E
Menderes *r.* Turkey **39** 37.30N 27.05E
Mendi P.N.G. **59** 6.13S 143.39E
Mendip Hills England **24** 51.15N 2.40W
Mendocino, C. U.S.A. **96** 40.26N 124.24W
Mendoza Argentina **109** 33.00S 68.52W
Mendoza *d.* Argentina **110** 34.00S 67.40W
Mengzi China **57** 23.20N 103.21E
Menin Belgium **41** 50.48N 3.07E
Menindee Australia **83** 32.23S 142.30E
Menongue Angola **74** 14.40S 17.41E
Menorca *i. see* MinorcaSpain **37**
Mentawai Is. Indonesia **58** 2.50S 99.00E
Menteith, L. of Scotland **30** 56.10N 4.18W
Menton France **36** 43.47N 7.30E
Mentor U.S.A. **98** 41.42N 81.22W
Menyapa, Gunung *mtn.* Indonesia **58** 1.00N 116.20E
Meon *r.* England **24** 50.49N 1.15W
Meopham Station England **23** 51.23N 0.22E
Meppel Neth. **41** 52.42N 6.12E
Meppen W. Germany **41** 52.42N 7.17E
Merano Italy **40** 46.41N 11.10E
Merauke Indonesia **59** 8.30S 140.22E
Merca Somali Rep. **75** 1.42N 44.47E
Merced U.S.A. **96** 37.17N 120.29W
Mercedes Buenos Aires Argentina **110** 34.42S 59.30W
Mercedes Corrientes Argentina **110** 29.15S 58.05W
Mercedes San Luis Argentina **110** 33.43S 65.29W
Mercedes Uruguay **110** 33.16S 58.05W
Mere England **24** 51.05N 2.16W
Mergui Burma **57** 12.26N 98.34E
Mergui Archipelago *is.* Burma **57** 11.30N 98.15E
Meribah Australia **83** 34.42S 140.53E
Mérida Mexico **100** 20.59N 89.39W
Mérida Spain **37** 38.55N 6.20W
Mérida Venezuela **101** 8.24N 71.08W
Mérida, Cordillera de *mts.* Venezuela **101** 8.00N 71.30W
Meriden U.S.A. **99** 41.32N 72.48W
Meridian U.S.A. **97** 32.21N 88.42W
Merir *i.* Asia **59** 4.19N 132.18E
Merksem Belgium **41** 51.14N 4.25E
Merowe Sudan **71** 18.30N 31.49E
Merrick *mtn.* Scotland **30** 55.08N 4.29W
Merrygoen Australia **83** 31.51S 149.16E
Merse *f.* Scotland **31** 55.45N 2.15W
Mersea I. England **25** 51.47N 0.58E
Merseburg E. Germany **40** 51.22N 12.00E
Mersey *r.* England **28** 53.22N 2.37W

Muskingum *r.* U.S.A. **98** 39.25N 81.25W
Muskogee U.S.A. **97** 35.45N 95.21W
Musoma Tanzania **75** 1.31S 33.48E
Musselburgh Scotland **31** 55.57N 3.04W
Mussende Angola **74** 10.33S 16.02E
Mustang Nepal **57** 29.10N 83.55E
Muutjala U.S.S.R. **42** 58.30N 22.10E
Muswellbrook Australia **83** 32.17S 150.55E
Mut Turkey **54** 36.38N 33.27E
Mutsu wan *b.* Japan **64** 41.10N 141.05E
Muwai Hakran Saudi Arabia **54** 22.41N 41.37E
Muxima Angola **74** 9.33S 13.58E
Muyinga Burundi **75** 2.48S 30.21E
Muzaffarnagar India **56** 29.28N 77.42E
Muzaffarpur India **56** 26.07N 85.23E
Mwanza Tanzania **75** 2.30S 32.54E
Mwanza *d.* Tanzania **75** 3.00S 32.30E
Mwanza Zaïre **75** 7.51S 26.43E
Mwaya Mbeya Tanzania **75** 9.33S 33.56E
Mweelrea Mts. Rep. of Ire. **34** 53.40N 9.52W
Mweka Zaïre **74** 4.51S 21.34E
Mwene Ditu Zaïre **74** 7.04S 23.27E
Mweru, L. Zaïre/Zambia **75** 9.00S 28.40E
Mwinilunga Zambia **74** 11.44S 24.24E
Myanaung Burma **57** 18.25N 95.10E
Myingyan Burma **57** 21.25N 95.20E
Myitkyina Burma **57** 25.24N 97.25E
Mymensingh Bangla. **56** 24.45N 90.23E
Mynydd Bach *mts.* Wales **26** 52:18N 4.03W
Mynydd Eppynt *mts.* Wales **26** 52.06N 3.30W
Mynydd Preselly *mts.* Wales **26** 51.58N 4.47W
Myrdal Norway **42** 60.44N 7.08E
Mysen Norway **42** 59.33N 11.20E
Mysore India **56** 12.18N 76.37E
My Tho Vietnam **58** 10.21N 106.21E
Mytishchi U.S.S.R. **43** 55.54N 37.47E
Mzimba Malaŵi **75** 12.00S 33.39E

N

Naas Rep. of Ire. **35** 53.13N 6.41W
Naberezhnyye Chelny U.S.S.R. **44** 55.42N 52.20E
Nabeul Tunisia **38** 36.28N 10.44E
Nacala Moçambique **75** 14.30S 40.37E
Nachingwea Tanzania **75** 10.21S 38.46E
Nadder *r.* England **24** 51.05N 1.52W
Nadiad India **56** 22.42N 72.55E
Naestved Denmark **42** 55.14N 11.47E
Naft Safid Iran **55** 31.38N 49.20E
Naga Phil. **59** 13.36N 123.12E
Nagaland *d.* India **57** 26.10N 94.30E
Nagano Japan **64** 36.39N 138.10E
Nagaoka Japan **64** 37.30N 138.50E
Nagappattinam India **57** 10.45N 79.50E
Nagasaki Japan **64** 32.45N 129.52E
Nagercoil India **56** 8.11N 77.30E
Nag' Hammadi Egypt **54** 26.04N 32.13E
Nagishot Sudan **75** 4.18N 33.32E
Nagles Mts. Rep. of Ire. **35** 52.06N 8.26W
Nagoya Japan **64** 35.08N 136.53E
Nagpur India **57** 21.10N 79.12E
Nagykanizsa Hungary **39** 46.27N 17.01E
Naha Japan **61** 26.10N 127.40E
Nahavand Iran **55** 34.13N 48.23E
Nahe *r.* W. Germany **41** 49.58N 7.54E
Nahr Ouassel *r.* Algeria **37** 35.30N 2.03E
Nailsworth England **24** 51.41N 2.12W
Nain Canada **95** 56.30N 61.45W
Nain Iran **55** 32.52N 53.05E
Nairn Scotland **33** 57.35N 3.52W
Nairn *r.* Scotland **33** 57.35N 3.51W
Nairobi Kenya **75** 1.17S 36.50E
Naivasha Kenya **75** 0.44S 36.26E
Najin N. Korea **64** 42.10N 130.20E
Nakaminato Japan **64** 36.21N 140.36E
Nakano shima *i.* Japan **64** 29.55N 129.55E
Nakatsu Japan **64** 33.37N 131.11E
Nakhichevan U.S.S.R. **55** 39.12N 45.24E
Nakhodka U.S.S.R. **64** 42.53N 132.54E
Nakhon Pathom Thailand **57** 13.59N 100.01E
Nakhon Phanom Thailand **58** 17.22N 104.45E
Nakhon Ratchasima Thailand **57** 14.59N 102.12E
Nakhon Sawan Thailand **57** 15.35N 100.10E
Nakhon Si Thammarat Thailand **57** 8.29N 100.00E
Naknek U.S.A. **94** 58.45N 157.00W
Nakskov Denmark **40** 54.50N 11.10E
Nakuru Kenya **75** 0.16S 36.04E
Nakusimi *r.* Canada **98** 49.55N 82.00W
Nalchik U.S.S.R. **43** 43.31N 43.38E
Nalon *r.* Spain **37** 43.35N 6.06W
Nalut Libya **70** 31.53N 10.59E
Namaki *r.* Iran **55** 31.02N 55.20E
Namanga Kenya **75** 2.33S 36.48E
Namangan U.S.S.R. **60** 40.59N 71.41E
Namapa Moçambique **75** 13.48S 39.44E
Namaponda Moçambique **75** 15.51S 39.52E

Namarroi Moçambique **75** 15.58S 36.55E
Nam Co *l.* China **57** 30.40N 90.30E
Nam Dinh Vietnam **63** 20.21N 106.09E
Nametil Moçambique **75** 15.41S 39.30E
Namib Desert Namibia **76** 23.30S 15.00E
Namibia Africa **76** 22.30S 17.00E
Namlea Indonesia **59** 3.15S 127.07E
Nampo N. Korea **61** 38.40N 125.30E
Nampula Moçambique **75** 15.09S 39.14E
Nampula *d.* Moçambique **75** 15.00S 39.00E
Namsos Norway **42** 64.28N 11.30E
Namuchabawashan *mtn.* China **57** 29.30N 95.10E
Namur Belgium **41** 50.28N 4.52E
Namur *d.* Belgium **41** 50.20N 4.45E
Namurro Moçambique **75** 16.57S 39.06E
Namutoni Namibia **76** 18.49S 16.55E
Namwala Zambia **75** 15.44S 26.25E
Nana Candundo Angola **74** 11.28S 23.01E
Nanaimo Canada **96** 49.08N 123.58W
Nanao Japan **64** 37.03N 136.58E
Nanchang China **63** 28.37N 115.57E
Nancheng China **63** 27.35N 116.33E
Nanchong China **63** 30.53N 106.05E
Nanchuan China **63** 29.12N 107.30E
Nancy France **40** 48.42N 6.12E
Nanda Devi *mtn.* India **57** 30.21N 79.50E
Nander India **56** 19.11N 77.21E
Nandewar Range *mts.* Australia **83** 30.20S 150.45E
Nandu Jiang *r.* China **63** 20.04N 110.20E
Nanga Parbat *mtn.* Jammu & Kashmir **56** 35.10N 74.35E
Nanjing China **63** 32.02N 118.52E
Nan Ling *mts.* China **63** 25.10N 110.00E
Nanning China **63** 22.48N 108.18E
Nanping China **63** 26.38N 118.10E
Nanpu Xi *r.* China **63** 26.38N 118.10E
Nanshan Is. Asia **58** 10.30N 116.00E
Nantaise *r.* France **36** 47.12N 1.35W
Nantes France **36** 47.14N 1.35W
Nantong China **62** 32.02N 120.55E
Nantucket I. U.S.A. **99** 41.16N 70.00W
Nantucket Sd. U.S.A. **99** 41.30N 70.15W
Nantwich England **28** 53.05N 2.31W
Nanwan Resr. China **63** 32.05N 113.55E
Nanxi China **63** 28.52N 104.59E
Nanxiong China **63** 25.10N 114.16E
Nanyang China **62** 33.07N 112.30E
Nanyuki Kenya **75** 0.01N 37.03E
Napier New Zealand **85** 39.29S 176.58E
Naples Italy **38** 40.50N 14.14E
Naples, G. of Med. Sea **38** 40.42N 14.15E
Nar *r.* England **25** 52.45N 0.24E
Nara Mali **72** 15.13N 7.20W
Naracoorte Australia **83** 36.58S 140.46E
Narayanganj Bangla. **56** 23.36N 90.28E
Narbada *r. see* NarmadaIndia **56**
Narberth Wales **27** 51.48N 4.45W
Narbonne France **36** 43.11N 3.00E
Nare Head England **27** 50.12N 4.55W
Nares Str. Canada **95** 78.30N 75.00W
Narmada *r.* India **56** 21.40N 73.00E
Narodnaya *mtn.* U.S.S.R. **44** 65.00N 61.00E
Narok Kenya **75** 1.04S 35.54E
Narooma Australia **83** 36.15S 150.06E
Narrabri Australia **83** 30.20S 149.49E
Narrandera Australia **83** 34.36S 146.34E
Narran L. Australia **83** 29.40S 147.25E
Narrogin Australia **82** 32.58S 117.10E
Narromine Australia **83** 32.17S 148.20E
Narsimhapur India **56** 22.58N 79.15E
Narva U.S.S.R. **42** 59.22N 28.17E
Narva *r.* U.S.S.R. **42** 59.30N 28.00E
Narvik Norway **42** 68.26N 17.25E
Naryan Mar U.S.S.R. **44** 67.37N 53.02E
Nasarawa Nigeria **73** 8.35N 7.44E
Nash Pt. Wales **27** 51.25N 3.35W
Nashua U.S.A. **99** 42.44N 71.28W
Nashville U.S.A. **97** 36.10N 86.50W
Nasik India **56** 20.00N 73.52E
Nasratabad Iran **55** 29.54N 59.58E
Nassau Bahamas **101** 25.03N 77.20W
Nasser, L. Egypt **54** 22.40N 32.00E
Nässjö Sweden **42** 57.39N 14.40E
Natal Brazil **108** 5.46S 35.15W
Natal Indonesia **58** 0.35N 99.07E
Natal *d.* R.S.A. **76** 28.30S 31.00E
Natanz Iran **55** 33.30N 51.57E
Natchez U.S.A. **97** 31.22N 91.24W
Natitingou Benin **73** 10.17N 1.19E
Natron, L. Tanzania **75** 2.18S 36.05E
Naumburg E. Germany **40** 51.09N 11.48E
Nava *r.* Zaïre **75** 1.45N 27.06E
Navalmoral de la Mata Spain **37** 39.54N 5.33W
Navan Rep. of Ire. **34** 53.39N 6.42W
Nave *i.* Scotland **30** 55.55N 6.20W
Navenby England **29** 53.07N 0.32W
Naver *r.* Scotland **33** 58.32N 4.14W
Naver, Loch Scotland **33** 58.17N 4.20W
Návpaktos Greece **39** 38.24N 21.49E

Návplion Greece **39** 37.33N 22.47E
Navrongo Ghana **72** 10.51N 1.03W
Nawabshah Pakistan **56** 26.15N 68.26E
Náxos *i.* Greece **39** 37.03N 25.30E
Nayarit *d.* Mexico **100** 21.30N 104.00W
Nayland England **25** 51.59N 0.52E
Nazareth Israel **54** 32.41N 35.16E
Nazas *r.* Mexico **100** 25.34N 103.25W
Nazilli Turkey **54** 37.55N 28.20E
Ndalatando Angola **74** 9.12S 14.54E
N'Dendé Gabon **74** 2.20S 11.23E
N'Djamena Chad **73** 12.10N 14.59E
Ndjolé Gabon **74** 0.07S 10.45E
Ndola Zambia **75** 13.00S 28.35E
Neagh, Lough N. Ireland **30** 54.36N 6.25W
Neath Wales **27** 51.39N 3.49W
Neath *r.* Wales **27** 51.39N 3.50W
Nebit Dag U.S.S.R. **55** 39.31N 54.24E
Nebraska *d.* U.S.A. **96** 41.30N 100.00W
Nebrodi Mts. Italy **38** 37.53N 14.32E
Neches *r.* U.S.A. **97** 29.55N 93.50W
Neckar *r.* W. Germany **40** 49.32N 8.26E
Necochea Argentina **110** 38.31S 58.46W
Necuto Angola **74** 4.55S 12.38E
Needham Market England **25** 52.09N 1.02E
Needles U.S.A. **96** 34.51N 114.36W
Neerpelt Belgium **41** 51.13N 5.28E
Nefyn Wales **26** 52.55N 4.31W
Negaunee U.S.A. **98** 46.31N 87.37W
Negev *des.* Israel **54** 30.42N 34.55E
Negoiu *mtn.* Romania **39** 45.36N 24.32E
Negotin Yugo. **39** 44.14N 22.33E
Negra, C. Peru **108** 6.06S 81.09W
Negrais, C. Burma **57** 16.00N 94.30E
Negro *r.* Argentina **110** 41.00S 62.48W
Negro *r.* Brazil **108** 3.30S 60.00W
Negro *r.* Uruguay **110** 33.27S 58.20W
Negros *i.* Phil. **59** 10.00N 123.00E
Neijiang China **63** 29.29N 105.03E
Nei Monggol *d. see* Inner Mongolia *d.* China **61**
Neisse *r.* Poland/E. Germany **40** 52.05N 14.42E
Neiva Colombia **108** 2.58N 75.15W
Nejd *d.* Saudi Arabia **54** 25.00N 45.00E
Nekső Denmark **42** 55.04N 15.09E
Nellore India **57** 14.29N 80.00E
Nelson Canada **96** 49.29N 117.17W
Nelson *r.* Canada **95** 57.00N 93.20W
Nelson England **28** 53.50N 2.14W
Nelson New Zealand **85** 41.18S 173.17E
Nelson U.S.A. **96** 35.30N 113.16W
Nelson, C. Australia **83** 38.27S 141.35E
Nelspruit R.S.A. **76** 25.30S 30.58E
Néma Mauritania **72** 16.32N 7.12W
Neman *r.* U.S.S.R. **42** 55.23N 21.15E
Nemours France **36** 48.16N 2.41E
Nemuro Japan **64** 43.22N 145.36E
Nemuro kaikyo *str.* Japan **64** 44.00N 145.50E
Nenagh Rep. of Ire. **35** 52.52N 8.13W
Nenana U.S.A. **94** 64.35N 149.20W
Nene *r.* England **29** 52.49N 0.12E
Nenjiang China **61** 49.10N 125.15E
Nepal Asia **56** 28.00N 84.30E
Nephin *mtn.* Rep. of Ire. **34** 54.01N 9.23W
Nephin Beg *mtn.* Rep. of Ire. **34** 54.02N 9.38W
Nephin Beg Range *mts.* Rep. of Ire. **34** 54.00N 9.37W
Nera *r.* Italy **38** 42.33N 12.43E
Neretva *r.* Yugo. **39** 43.02N 17.28E
Neriquinha Angola **74** 15.50S 21.40E
Nero Deep Pacific Oc. **59** 12.40N 145.50E
Nes Neth. **41** 53.27N 5.46E
Ness *f.* Scotland **32** 58.26N 6.15W
Ness, Loch Scotland **33** 57.16N 4.30W
Neston England **28** 53.17N 3.03W
Netherlands Europe **41** 52.00N 5.30E
Nether Stowey England **24** 51.10N 3.10W
Neto *r.* Italy **39** 39.12N 17.08E
Neubrandenburg E. Germany **40** 53.33N 13.16E
Neuchâtel Switz. **40** 47.00N 6.56E
Neuchâtel, Lac de Switz. **40** 46.50N 6.55E
Neuenhaus W. Germany **41** 52.30N 6.58E
Neufchâteau Belgium **41** 49.51N 5.26E
Neufchâtel France **36** 49.44N 1.26E
Neumünster W. Germany **40** 54.06N 9.59E
Neuquén Argentina **110** 38.55S 68.55W
Neuse *r.* U.S.A. **97** 35.04N 77.04W
Neusiedler, L. Austria **40** 47.52N 16.45E
Neuss W. Germany **41** 51.12N 6.42E
Neustrelitz E. Germany **40** 53.22N 13.05E
Neutral Territory Asia **55** 29.05N 45.40E
Neuwied W. Germany **41** 50.26N 7.28E
Nevada *d.* U.S.A. **96** 39.00N 117.00W
Nevada, Sierra *mts.* Spain **37** 37.04N 3.20W
Nevada, Sierra *mts.* U.S.A. **96** 37.30N 119.00W
Nevada de Cocuy, Sierra *mts.* Colombia **101**
6.15N 72.00W
Nevada de Santa Marta, Sierra *mts.* Colombia **101**
11.00N 73.30W
Nevel U.S.S.R. **43** 56.00N 29.59E

North Korea Asia 61 40.00N 128.00E
North Kyme England 29 53.04N 0.17W
Northleach England 24 51.49N 1.50W
North Platte U.S.A. 96 41.09N 100.45W
North Platte *r.* U.S.A. 96 41.09N 100.55W
North Pt. U.S.A. 98 45.02N 83.17W
North Ronaldsay *i.* Scotland 33 59.23N 2.26W
North Ronaldsay Firth *est.* Scotland 33 59.20N 2.25W
North Sd. Rep. of Ire. 35 53.11N 9.34W
North Sea Europe 14 56.00N 5.00E
North Somercotes England 29 53.28N 0.08E
North Sporades *is.* Greece 39 39.00N 24.00E
North Taranaki Bight *b.* New Zealand 85 38.45S 174.15E
North Tawton England 27 50.48N 3.55W
North Tidworth England 24 51.14N 1.40W
North Tolsta Scotland 32 58.20N 6.13W
North Truchas Peak *mtn.* U.S.A. 96 35.58N 105.48W
North Tyne *r.* England 31 54.59N 2.08W
North Uist *i.* Scotland 32 57.35N 7.20W
Northumberland *d.* England 31 55.12N 2.00W
North Walsham England 25 52.49N 1.22E
Northway U.S.A. 94 62.58N 142.00W
North Weald Bassett England 23 51.42N 0.12E
North West Highlands Scotland 32 57.30N 5.15W
North West River *town* Canada 95 53.30N 60.10W
Northwest Territories *d.* Canada 95 66.00N 95.00W
Northwich England 28 53.16N 2.30W
Northwood England 23 51.36N 0.25W
North York Canada 99 43.44N 79.26W
North York Moors *hills* England 29 54.21N 0.50W
North Yorkshire *d.* England 29 54.14N 1.14W
Norton England 29 54.08N 0.47W
Norton Sound *b.* U.S.A. 94 63.50N 164.00W
Norwalk U.S.A. 99 41.07N 73.25W
Norway Europe 42 65.00N 13.00E
Norway House *town* Canada 95 53.59N 97.50W
Norwegian Sea Europe 52 65.00N 5.00E
Norwich England 25 52.38N 1.17E
Norwich U.S.A. 99 41.32N 72.05W
Noss, I. of Scotland 32 60.08N 1.01W
Noss Head Scotland 33 58.28N 3.03W
Nossob *r.* R.S.A./Botswana 76 26.54S 20.39E
Noteć *r.* Poland 40 52.44N 15.26E
Nottingham England 29 52.57N 1.10W
Nottinghamshire *d.* England 29 53.10N 1.00W
Notwani *r.* Botswana 76 23.14S 27.30E
Nouadhibou Mauritania 72 20.54N 17.01W
Nouakchott Mauritania 70 18.09N 15.58W
Noup Head Scotland 33 59.20N 3.04W
Nouvelle Anvers Zaïre 74 1.38N 19.10E
Nova Gaia Angola 74 10.09S 17.35E
Nova Lima Brazil 110 20.00S 43.51W
Novara Italy 36 45.27N 8.37E
Nova Scotia *d.* Canada 95 45.00N 64.00W
Nova Sofala Moçambique 76 20.09S 34.42E
Novaya Ladoga U.S.S.R. 43 60.09N 32.15E
Novaya Siberia *i.* U.S.S.R. 45 75.20N 148.00E
Novaya Zemlya *i.* U.S.S.R. 44 74.00N 56.00E
Novelda Spain 37 38.24N 0.45W
Novgorod U.S.S.R. 43 58.30N 31.20E
Novi-Ligure Italy 36 44.46N 8.47E
Novi Pazar Yugo. 39 43.08N 20.28E
Novi Sad Yugo. 39 45.16N 19.52E
Novocherkassk U.S.S.R. 43 47.25N 40.05E
Novograd Volynskiy U.S.S.R. 43 50.34N 27.32E
Novogrudok U.S.S.R. 43 53.35N 25.50E
Novo Hamburgo Brazil 110 29.37S 51.07W
Novokazalinsk U.S.S.R. 44 45.48N 62.06E
Novokuznetsk U.S.S.R. 44 53.45N 87.12E
Novomoskovsk U.S.S.R. 43 54.06N 38.15E
Novorossiysk U.S.S.R. 43 44.44N 37.46E
Novoshakhtinsk U.S.S.R. 43 47.46N 39.55E
Novosibirsk U.S.S.R. 44 55.04N 82.55E
Novy Port U.S.S.R. 44 67.38N 72.33E
Nowa Ruda Poland 40 50.34N 16.30E
Nowa Sól Poland 40 51.49N 15.41E
Nowgong India 57 26.20N 92.41E
Nowra Australia 83 34.54S 150.36E
Nowy Sącz Poland 43 49.39N 20.40E
Noyon France 41 49.35N 3.00E
Nsanje Malaŵi 75 16.55S 35.12E
Nsukka Nigeria 73 6.51N 7.29E
Ntcheu Malaŵi 75 14.50S 34.45E
Nuanetsi *r.* Moçambique 76 22.42S 31.45E
Nuanetsi Zimbabwe 76 21.22S 30.45E
Nubian Desert Sudan 71 21.00N 34.00E
Nudushan Iran 55 32.03N 53.33E
Nueces *r.* U.S.A. 97 27.55N 97.30W
Nueva Gerona Cuba 100 21.53N 82.49W
Nuevitas Cuba 101 21.34N 77.18W
Nuevo Laredo Mexico 96 27.30N 99.30W
Nuevo Leon *d.* Mexico 100 26.00N 99.00W
Nu Jiang *r. see* Salween *r.* China 57
Nukha U.S.S.R. 55 41.12N 47.10E
Nullarbor Plain *f.* Australia 82 31.30S 128.00E
Numazu Japan 64 35.08N 138.50E
Nuneaton England 24 52.32N 1.29W
Nungo Moçambique 75 13.25S 37.45E
Nunivak I. U.S.A. 94 60.00N 166.30W
Nuqra Saudi Arabia 54 25.35N 41.28E
Nure *r.* Italy 36 45.06N 9.50E
Nurmes Finland 42 63.32N 29.10E
Nürnberg W. Germany 40 49.27N 11.05E
Nusaybin Turkey 54 37.05N 41.11E
Nuweveld Mts. R.S.A. 76 32.00S 21.50E
Nyahururu Kenya 75 0.04N 36.22E
Nyakanazi Tanzania 75 3.05S 31.16E
Nyala Sudan 71 12.01N 24.50E
Nyamandhlovu Zimbabwe 76 19.50S 28.15E
Nyanga *r.* Gabon 74 3.00S 10.17E
Nyanza *d.* Kenya 75 0.30S 34.30E
Nyanza Rwanda 75 2.20S 29.42E
Nybro Sweden 42 56.44N 15.55E
Nyeri Kenya 75 0.22S 36.56E
Nyika Plateau *f.* Malaŵi 75 10.25S 33.50E
Nyiru, Mt. Kenya 75 2.06N 36.44E
Nyköbing Falster Denmark 40 54.47N 11.53E
Nyköbing Thisted Denmark 42 56.49N 8.50E
Nyköping Sweden 42 58.45N 17.03E
Nylstroom R.S.A. 76 24.42S 28.20E
Nymagee Australia 83 32.05S 146.20E
Nynäshamn Sweden 42 58.54N 17.55E
Nyngan Australia 83 31.34S 147.14E
Nyong *r.* Cameroon 73 3.15N 9.55E
Nyons France 36 44.22N 5.08E
Nyunzu Zaïre 75 5.55S 28.00E
Nzega Tanzania 75 4.13S 33.09E
N'zérékoré Guinea 72 7.49N 8.48W
Nzeto Angola 74 7.13S 12.56E

O

Oadby England 24 52.37N 1.07W
Oahe Resr. U.S.A. 96 45.45N 100.20W
Oahu *i.* Hawaii U.S.A. 96 21.30N 158.00W
Oakengates England 24 52.42N 2.29W
Oakham England 24 52.40N 0.43W
Oakland U.S.A. 96 37.50N 122.15W
Oak Lawn U.S.A. 98 41.42N 87.45W
Oak Park *town* U.S.A. 98 41.52N 87.47W
Oakville Canada 99 43.27N 79.41W
Oamaru New Zealand 85 45.07S 170.58E
Oasis *d.* Algeria 73 22.00N 6.00E
Oaxaca Mexico 100 17.05N 96.41W
Oaxaca *d.* Mexico 100 17.30N 97.00W
Ob *r.* U.S.S.R. 44 66.50N 69.00E
Ob, G. of U.S.S.R. 44 68.30N 74.00E
Oba Canada 98 49.04N 84.07W
Oban Scotland 30 56.26N 5.28W
Obbia Somali Rep. 71 5.20N 48.30E
Oberhausen W. Germany 41 51.28N 6.51E
Obi *i.* Indonesia 59 1.45S 127.30E
Obihoro Japan 64 42.55N 143.00E
Obo C.A.E. 75 5.18N 26.28E
Obuasi Ghana 72 6.15N 1.36W
Ocaña Spain 37 39.57N 3.30W
Occidental, Cordillera *mts.* Colombia 108 6.00N 76.15W
Ochil Hills Scotland 31 56.16N 3.25W
Ock *r.* England 24 51.40N 1.18W
Ocotlán Mexico 100 20.21N 102.42W
October Revolution *i.* U.S.S.R. 45 79.30N 96.00E
Ocua Moçambique 75 13.37S 39.42E
Oda Ghana 72 5.55N 0.56W
Odádhahraun *mts.* Iceland 42 65.00N 17.30W
Odate Japan 64 40.16N 140.34E
Odawara Japan 64 35.20N 139.08E
Odda Norway 42 60.03N 6.45E
Oddur Somali Rep. 75 4.11N 43.52E
Ödemis Turkey 39 38.12N 28.00E
Odense Denmark 42 55.24N 10.25E
Odenwald *mts.* W. Germany 40 49.40N 9.20E
Oder *r.* Europe 40 53.30N 14.36E
Odessa U.S.A. 96 31.50N 102.23W
Odessa U.S.S.R. 43 46.30N 30.46E
Odienné Ivory Coast 72 9.36N 7.32W
Odorhei Romania 39 46.18N 25.18E
Odzi *r.* Zimbabwe 76 19.49S 32.15E
Ofanto *r.* Italy 38 41.22N 16.12E
Offaly *d.* Rep. of Ire. 35 53.15N 7.30W
Offenbach W. Germany 40 50.06N 8.46E
Offenburg W. Germany 40 48.29N 7.57E
Ogaki Japan 64 35.25N 136.36E
Ogbomosho Nigeria 73 8.05N 4.11E
Ogden U.S.A. 96 41.14N 111.59W
Ogdensburg U.S.A. 99 44.42N 75.31W
Ogeechee *r.* U.S.A. 97 32.54N 81.05W
Ognon *r.* France 36 47.20N 5.37E
Ogoja Nigeria 73 6.40N 8.45E
Ogoki *r.* Canada 97 51.00N 84.30W
Ogosta *r.* Bulgaria 39 43.44N 23.51E
Ogowe *r.* Gabon 74 1.00S 9.05E
Ogulin Yugo. 38 45.17N 15.14E
Ogun *d.* Nigeria 73 6.50N 3.20E
Ohio *d.* U.S.A. 98 40.10N 82.20W
Ohio *r.* U.S.A. 98 37.07N 89.10W
Ohře *r.* Czech. 40 50.32N 14.08E
Ohrid Yugo. 39 41.06N 20.48E
Ohridsko, L. Albania/Yugo. 39 41.00N 20.43E
Oich *r.* Scotland 33 57.04N 4.46W
Oich, Loch Scotland 33 57.04N 4.46W
Oil City U.S.A. 99 41.26N 79.44W
Oise *r.* France 36 49.00N 2.10E
Oita Japan 64 33.15N 131.40E
Ojocaliente Mexico 100 22.35N 102.18W
Ojo de Agua Argentina 110 29.30S 63.44W
Oka *r.* U.S.S.R. 43 56.09N 43.00E
Okaba Indonesia 59 8.06S 139.46E
Okahandja Namibia 76 21.59S 16.58E
Okanogan *r.* U.S.A. 96 47.45N 120.05W
Okavango *r.* Botswana 76 18.30S 22.04E
Okavango Basin *f.* Botswana 76 19.30S 23.00E
Okayama Japan 64 34.40N 133.54E
Okazaki Japan 64 34.58N 137.10E
Okeechobee, L. U.S.A. 97 27.00N 80.45W
Okeefenoke Swamp *f.* U.S.A. 97 30.40N 82.40W
Okehampton England 27 50.44N 4.01W
Okement *r.* England 27 50.50N 4.04W
Okere *r.* Uganda 75 1.37N 33.53E
Okha India 56 22.29N 69.09E
Okha U.S.S.R. 45 53.35N 142.50E
Okhotsk U.S.S.R. 45 59.20N 143.15E
Okhotsk, Sea of U.S.S.R. 45 55.00N 150.00E
Oki gunto *is.* Japan 64 36.10N 133.10E
Okinawa *i.* Japan 61 26.30N 128.00E
Okino Torishima *i.* Pacific Oc. 59 20.24N 136.02E
Okipoko *r.* Namibia 76 18.40S 16.03E
Okitipupa Nigeria 73 6.31N 4.50E
Oklahoma *d.* U.S.A. 97 35.00N 97.00W
Oklahoma City U.S.A. 97 35.28N 97.33W
Okushiri shima *i.* Japan 64 42.00N 139.50E
Öland *i.* Sweden 42 56.50N 16.50E
Olary Australia 83 32.18S 140.19E
Olavarria Argentina 110 36.57S 60.20W
Olbia Italy 38 40.55N 9.29E
Old Crow Canada 94 67.34N 139.43W
Oldenburg Niedersachsen West W. Germany 41 53.08N 8.13E
Oldenburg Schleswig Holstein W. Germany 40 54.17N 10.52E
Oldenzaal Neth. 41 52.19N 6.55E
Old Fletton England 25 52.34N 0.14W
Oldham England 28 53.33N 2.08W
Old Head of Kinsale *c.* Rep. of Ire. 35 51.37N 8.33W
Oldmeldrum Scotland 33 57.20N 2.20W
Old Rhine *r.* Neth. 41 52.14N 4.26E
Old Windsor England 23 51.28N 0.35W
Olean U.S.A. 99 42.05N 78.26W
Olekma *r.* U.S.S.R. 45 60.20N 120.30E
Olekminsk U.S.S.R. 45 60.25N 120.00E
Olenek U.S.S.R. 45 68.38N 112.15E
Olenek *r.* U.S.S.R. 45 73.00N 120.00E
Olenekskiy G. U.S.S.R. 45 74.00N 120.00E
Oléron, Île d' *i.* France 36 45.55N 1.16W
Olga U.S.S.R. 64 43.48N 135.17E
Olhão Portugal 37 37.01N 7.50W
Olifants *r.* Cape Province R.S.A. 76 31.43S 18.10E
Olifants *r.* Namibia 76 25.28S 19.23E
Olifants *r.* Transvaal R.S.A. 76 24.08S 32.40E
Olivares Spain 37 39.45N 2.21W
Olney England 24 52.09N 0.42W
Ölögey Mongolia 60 48.54N 90.00E
Olomouc Czech. 43 49.38N 17.15E
Oloron France 36 43.12N 0.35W
Olot Spain 37 42.11N 2.30E
Olpe W. Germany 41 51.02N 7.52E
Olsztyn Poland 43 53.48N 20.29E
Oltenița Romania 39 44.05N 26.31E
Oltet *r.* Romania 39 44.13N 24.28E
Olympus, Mt. Cyprus 54 34.55N 32.52E
Olympus, Mt. Greece 39 40.04N 22.20E
Omagh N. Ireland 34 54.36N 7.20W
Omaha U.S.A. 97 41.15N 96.00W
Oman Asia 56 22.30N 57.30E
Oman, G. of Asia 55 25.00N 58.00E
Omaruru Namibia 76 21.28S 15.56E
Ombrone *r.* Italy 38 42.40N 11.00E
Omdurman Sudan 71 15.37N 32.59E
Ommen Neth. 41 52.32N 6.25E
Ömnögovĭ *d.* Mongolia 62 43.00N 105.00E
Omolon *r.* U.S.S.R. 45 68.50N 158.30E
Omono *r.* Japan 64 39.44N 140.05E
Omsk U.S.S.R. 44 55.00N 73.22E
Omuramba Omatako *r.* Namibia 76 17.59S 20.32E
Omuta Japan 64 33.02N 130.26E
Oña Spain 37 42.44N 3.25W
Onda Spain 37 39.58N 0.16W
Ondangua Namibia 76 17.59S 16.02E
Ondo *d.* Nigeria 72 7.10N 5.20E
Onega, L. U.S.S.R. 44 62.00N 35.30E
Oneida L. U.S.A. 99 43.13N 75.55W
Oneonta U.S.A. 99 42.28N 75.04W
Onitsha Nigeria 73 6.10N 6.47E

Papenburg W. Germany **41** 53.05N 7.25E
Paphos Cyprus **54** 34.45N 32.25E
Paps of Jura *mts.* Scotland **30** 55.55N 6.00W
Papua, G. of P.N.G. **59** 8.50S 145.00E
Papua New Guinea Austa. **59** 6.00S 143.00E
Papun Burma **58** 18.05N 97.26E
Paracatu Brazil **110** 17.14S 46.52W
Paracatu *r.* Brazil **110** 16.30S 45.10W
Paracel Is. Asia **58** 16.20N 112.00E
Paragua *r.* Venezuela **101** 6.45N 63.00W
Paraguaná Pen. Venezuela **101** 12.00N 70.00W
Paraguarí Paraguay **110** 25.36S 57.06W
Paraguay *r.* Argentina **110** 27.30S 58.50W
Paraguay S. America **110** 23.00S 57.00W
Parakou Benin **73** 9.23N 2.40E
Paramaribo Surinam **108** 5.50N 55.14W
Paraná Argentina **110** 31.45S 60.30W
Paraná *r.* Argentina **110** 34.00S 58.30W
Paraná *d.* Brazil **110** 24.30S 52.00W
Paranaguá Brazil **110** 25.32S 48.36W
Paranaiba *r.* Brazil **110** 20.00S 51.00W
Paranapanema *r.* Brazil **110** 22.30S 53.03W
Paranapiacaba, Serra *mts.* Brazil **110** 24.30S 49.15W
Parana Plateau Paraguay **110** 24.32S 55.00W
Paraparaumu New Zealand **85** 40.55S 175.00E
Pardo *r.* Brazil **110** 20.10S 48.30W
Pardubice Czech. **40** 50.03N 15.45E
Parepare Indonesia **58** 4.03S 119.40E
Paria, G. of Venezuela **101** 10.30N 62.00W
Pariaman Indonesia **58** 0.36S 100.09E
Paria Pen. Venezuela **101** 10.45N 62.30W
Parigi Indonesia **59** 0.49S 120.10E
Paris France **36** 48.52N 2.20E
Park *f.* Scotland **32** 58.05N 6.32W
Parkano Finland **42** 62.03N 23.00E
Parker Dam U.S.A. **96** 34.25N 114.05W
Parkersburg U.S.A. **98** 39.17N 81.33W
Parkes Australia **83** 33.10S 148.13E
Park Falls *town* U.S.A. **98** 45.57N 90.28W
Park Forest *town* U.S.A. **98** 41.28N 87.40W
Parkville U.S.A. **99** 39.23N 76.32W
Parma Italy **38** 44.48N 10.18E
Parma U.S.A. **98** 41.24N 81.44W
Parnaíba *r.* Brazil **108** 3.00S 42.00W
Parnassos *mtn.* Greece **39** 38.33N 22.35E
Pärnu U.S.S.R. **42** 58.28N 24.30E
Pärnu *r.* U.S.S.R. **42** 58.23N 24.32E
Paroo *r.* Australia **83** 31.30S 143.34E
Paropamisus Mts. Afghan. **55** 34.30N 63.30E
Páros *i.* Greece **39** 37.04N 25.11E
Parral Mexico **96** 26.58N 105.40W
Parramatta Australia **83** 33.50S 150.57E
Parrett *r.* England **24** 51.10N 3.00W
Parry, C. Greenland **95** 76.50N 71.00W
Parry Is. Canada **95** 76.00N 102.00W
Parry Sound *town* Canada **98** 45.21N 80.03W
Parseta *r.* Poland **40** 54.12N 15.33E
Partabpur India **56** 23.28N 83.15E
Parthenay France **36** 46.39N 0.14W
Partry Mts. Rep. of Ire. **34** 53.40N 9.30W
Parys R.S.A. **76** 26.55S 27.28E
Pasadena U.S.A. **96** 34.10N 118.09W
Pas de Calais *d.* France **25** 50.30N 2.30E
Paso de Bermejo *f.* Argentina **109** 32.50S 70.00W
Paso de los Toros *town* Uruguay **110** 32.45S 56.47W
Paso Socompa *f.* Chile **109** 24.27S 68.18W
Passage East *town* Rep. of Ire. **35** 52.14N 7.00W
Passage West *town* Rep. of Ire. **35** 51.52N 8.20W
Passau W. Germany **40** 48.35N 13.28E
Passero, C. Italy **38** 36.40N 15.08E
Pass of Thermopylae Greece **39** 38.47N 22.34E
Passo Fundo Brazil **110** 28.16S 52.20W
Pasto Colombia **108** 1.12N 77.17W
Pasuruan Indonesia **58** 7.38S 112.44E
Pasvik *r.* Norway **42** 69.45N 30.00E
Patagonia *f.* Argentina **110** 40.20S 67.00W
Pate I. Kenya **75** 2.08S 41.02E
Pateley Bridge *town* England **28** 54.05N 1.45W
Paterson U.S.A. **99** 40.55N 74.10W
Pathari India **56** 23.56N 78.12E
Pathfinder Resr. U.S.A. **96** 42.25N 106.55W
Patiala India **56** 30.21N 76.27E
Patkai Hills Burma **57** 26.30N 95.40E
Patna India **56** 25.37N 85.12E
Patna Scotland **30** 55.22N 4.30W
Patos, L. Brazil **110** 31.00S 51.10W
Pátras Greece **39** 38.15N 21.45E
Patras, G. of Med. Sea **39** 38.15N 21.35E
Patrickswell Rep. of Ire. **35** 52.36N 8.43W
Patrington England **29** 53.41N 0.02W
Patuca *r.* Honduras **100** 30.48N 84.25W
Pau France **36** 43.18N 0.22W
Pauillac France **36** 45.12N 0.44W
Pavia Italy **36** 45.12N 9.09E
Pavlodar U.S.S.R. **44** 52.21N 76.59E
Pavlograd U.S.S.R. **43** 48.34N 35.50E
Pawtucket U.S.A. **99** 41.53N 71.23W
Payne *r.* Canada **95** 60.00N 69.45W
Paysandú Uruguay **110** 32.21S 58.05W
Peace *r.* Canada **94** 59.00N 111.26W
Peace River *town* Canada **94** 56.15N 117.18W
Peace River Resr. Canada **94** 55.00N 126.00W
Peaked Mtn. Canada **99** 46.34N 68.49W
Peak Hill *town* Australia **83** 32.47S 148.13E
Peale, Mt. U.S.A. **96** 38.26N 109.14W
Pearl *r.* U.S.A. **97** 30.15N 89.25W
Pebane Moçambique **75** 17.14S 38.10E
Pec Yugo. **39** 42.40N 20.17E
Pechenga U.S.S.R. **42** 69.28N 31.04E
Pechora *r.* U.S.S.R. **44** 68.10N 54.00E
Pechora G. U.S.S.R. **44** 69.00N 56.00E
Pecos U.S.A. **100** 31.25N 103.30W
Pecos *r.* U.S.A. **96** 29.45N 101.25W
Pécs Hungary **39** 46.05N 18.14E
Pedro J. Caballero Paraguay **110** 22.30S 55.44W
Peebinga Australia **83** 34.55S 140.57E
Peebles Scotland **31** 55.39N 3.12W
Peel *r.* Canada **94** 68.13N 135.00W
Peel I.o.M. **28** 54.14N 4.42W
Peel *f.* Neth. **41** 51.30N 5.50E
Peel Fell *mtn.* England/Scotland **31** 55.17N 2.35W
Peene *r.* E. Germany **40** 53.53N 13.49E
Pegasus B. New Zealand **85** 43.15S 173.00E
Pegu Burma **57** 17.18N 96.31E
Pegu Yoma *mts.* Burma **57** 18.40N 96.00E
Pegwell B. England **25** 51.18N 1.25E
Pehuajó Argentina **110** 35.50S 61.50W
Peipus, L. U.S.S.R. **42** 58.30N 27.30E
Pekalongan Indonesia **58** 6.54S 109.37E
Pekin U.S.A. **98** 40.34N 89.40W
Peking China **62** 39.52N 116.20E
Pelabuhan Kelang Malaysia **58** 2.57N 101.24E
Pelat, Mont *mtn.* France **36** 44.17N 6.41E
Pelee, Pt. Canada **98** 41.45N 82.09W
Peleng *i.* Indonesia **59** 1.30S 123.10E
Pelly *r.* Canada **94** 62.50N 137.35W
Pelotas Brazil **110** 31.45S 52.20W
Pematangsiantar Indonesia **58** 2.59N 99.01E
Pemba Moçambique **75** 13.02S 40.30E
Pemba I. Tanzania **75** 5.10S 39.45E
Pembridge England **24** 52.13N 2.54W
Pembroke Canada **99** 45.49N 77.08W
Pembroke Wales **27** 51.41N 4.57W
Peñaranda de Bracamonte Spain **37** 40.54N 5.13W
Penarth Wales **27** 51.26N 3.11W
Peñas, Cabo de Spain **37** 43.42N 5.52W
Pende *r.* Chad **73** 7.30N 16.20E
Pendembu Eastern Sierra Leone **72** 8.09N 10.42W
Pendine Wales **27** 51.44N 4.33W
Pendle Hill England **28** 53.52N 2.18W
Penganga *r.* India **57** 18.52N 79.56E
Penge England **23** 51.25N 0.04W
Penghu Liehtao *is.* Taiwan **63** 23.35N 119.32E
Penicuik Scotland **31** 55.49N 3.13W
Penistone England **28** 53.31N 1.38W
Penmaenmawr Wales **26** 53.16N 3.54W
Pennsylvania *d.* U.S.A. **99** 41.00N 75.45W
Penny Highland Canada **95** 67.10N 66.50W
Penobscot *r.* U.S.A. **99** 44.34N 68.48W
Penola Australia **83** 37.23S 140.21E
Penonomé Panamá **101** 8.30N 80.20W
Penrhyndeudraeth Wales **26** 52.56N 4.04W
Penrith Australia **83** 33.47S 150.44E
Penrith England **28** 54.40N 2.45W
Penryn England **27** 50.10N 5.07W
Pensacola U.S.A. **97** 30.30N 87.12W
Penticton Canada **96** 49.29N 119.38W
Pentire Pt. England **27** 50.35N 4.55W
Pentland Firth *str.* Scotland **33** 58.40N 3.00W
Pentland Hills Scotland **31** 55.50N 3.20W
Pen-y-ghent *mtn.* England **28** 54.10N 2.14W
Pen-y-groes Wales **26** 53.03N 4.18W
Penza U.S.S.R. **43** 53.11N 45.00E
Penzance England **27** 50.07N 5.32W
Penzhina, G. of U.S.S.R. **45** 61.00N 163.00E
Peoria U.S.A. **98** 40.43N 89.38W
Perabumulih Indonesia **58** 3.29S 104.14E
Pereira Colombia **108** 4.47N 75.46W
Perekop U.S.S.R. **43** 46.10N 33.42E
Pergamino Argentina **110** 33.55S 60.32W
Peribonca *r.* Canada **97** 48.50N 72.00W
Périgueux France **36** 45.12N 0.44E
Perija, Sierra de *mts.* Venezuela **101** 9.00N 73.00W
Perim *i.* Asia **71** 12.40N 43.24E
Perito Moreno Argentina **109** 46.35S 71.00W
Perm U.S.S.R. **44** 58.01N 56.10E
Pernik *see* Dimitrovo Bulgaria **39**
Péronne France **41** 49.56N 2.57E
Perpignan France **36** 42.42N 2.54E
Perranporth England **27** 50.21N 5.09W
Persepolis *ruins* Iran **55** 29.55N 53.00E
Pershore England **24** 52.07N 2.04W
Persian G. Asia **55** 27.00N 50.00E
Perth Australia **82** 31.58S 115.49E
Perth Scotland **31** 56.24N 3.28W
Perth Amboy U.S.A. **99** 40.32N 74.17W
Peru S. America **108** 10.00S 75.00W
Peru U.S.A. **98** 40.45N 86.04W
Peru-Chile Trench Pacific Oc. **109** 23.00S 71.30W
Perugia Italy **38** 43.06N 12.24E
Péruwelz Belgium **41** 50.32N 3.36E
Pésaro Italy **38** 43.54N 12.54E
Pescara Italy **38** 42.27N 14.13E
Pescara *r.* Italy **38** 42.28N 14.13E
Peshawar Pakistan **56** 34.01N 71.40E
Petatlán Mexico **100** 17.31N 101.16W
Petauke Zambia **75** 14.16S 31.21E
Peterborough Australia **83** 33.00S 138.51E
Peterborough Canada **99** 44.19N 78.20W
Peterborough England **25** 52.35N 0.14W
Peterhead Scotland **33** 57.30N 1.46W
Peterlee England **31** 54.45N 1.18W
Petersfield England **24** 51.00N 0.56W
Petra *ruins* Jordan **54** 30.19N 35.26E
Petrich Bulgaria **39** 41.25N 23.13E
Petropavlovsk U.S.S.R. **44** 54.53N 69.13E
Petropavlovsk Kamchatskiy U.S.S.R. **45** 53.03N 158.43E
Petrópolis Brazil **110** 22.30S 43.06W
Petrovsk Zabaykal'skiy U.S.S.R. **45** 51.20N 108.55E
Petrozavodsk U.S.S.R. **44** 61.46N 34.19E
Petworth England **24** 50.59N 0.37W
Pewsey England **24** 51.20N 1.46W
Pézenas France **36** 43.28N 3.25E
Pforzheim W. Germany **40** 48.53N 8.41E
Phangnga Thailand **57** 8.29N 98.31E
Phan Rang Vietnam **58** 11.35N 109.00E
Phet Buri Thailand **57** 13.01N 99.55E
Philadelphia U.S.A. **99** 40.00N 75.10W
Philippeville Belgium **41** 50.12N 4.32E
Philippine Is. Asia **113** 10.00N 124.00E
Philippines Asia **59** 13.00N 123.00E
Philippine Trench Pacific Oc. **59** 8.45N 127.20E
Philipstown R.S.A. **76** 30.26S 24.28E
Phnom Penh Cambodia **57** 11.35N 104.55E
Phoenix U.S.A. **96** 33.30N 111.55W
Phong Saly Laos **58** 21.40N 102.06E
Phu Dien Vietnam **63** 19.00N 105.35E
Phukao Miang *mtn.* Thailand **57** 16.50N 101.00E
Phuket Thailand **57** 8.00N 98.28E
Phuket *i.* Thailand **58** 8.10N 98.20E
Phu Ly Vietnam **63** 20.30N 105.58E
Phu Quoc *i.* Cambodia **58** 10.10N 104.00E
Phu Tho Vietnam **63** 21.28N 105.12E
Piacenza Italy **38** 45.03N 9.42E
Piangil Australia **83** 35.04S 143.20E
Pianosa *i.* Italy **38** 42.35N 10.05E
Piave *r.* Italy **38** 45.33N 12.45E
Pic *r.* Canada **98** 48.35N 86.17W
Picardy *f.* France **41** 49.47N 2.45E
Pickering England **29** 54.15N 0.46W
Pickwick L. U.S.A. **97** 35.00N 88.10W
Picton Canada **99** 44.01N 77.09W
Picton New Zealand **85** 41.17S 174.02E
Picton, Mt. Australia **83** 43.10S 146.30E
Piedras Negras Mexico **96** 28.40N 100.32W
Pieksämäki Finland **42** 62.18N 27.10E
Pielinen *l.* Finland **42** 63.20N 29.50E
Pierowall Scotland **33** 59.19N 3.00W
Pierre U.S.A. **96** 44.23N 100.20W
Pietermaritzburg R.S.A. **76** 29.36S 30.24E
Pietersburg R.S.A. **76** 23.54S 29.23E
Piet Retief R.S.A. **76** 27.00S 30.49E
Pigailoe *i.* Asia **59** 8.08N 146.40E
Pikes Peak U.S.A. **96** 38.50N 105.03W
Piketberg R.S.A. **76** 32.55S 18.45E
Pila Poland **40** 53.09N 16.44E
Pilcomayo *r.* Argentina/Paraguay **110** 25.15S 57.43W
Pilgrim's Hatch England **23** 51.37N 0.16E
Pilibhit India **56** 28.37N 79.48E
Pílos Greece **39** 36.55N 21.40E
Pinang, Pulau *i.* Malaysia **57** 5.30N 100.10E
Pinarbaşi Turkey **54** 38.43N 36.23E
Pinar del Rio Cuba **100** 22.24N 83.42W
Pinar del Rio *d.* Cuba **100** 22.30N 83.30W
Pindus Mts. Albania/Greece **39** 39.40N 21.00E
Pine Bluff U.S.A. **97** 34.13N 92.00W
Pines, I. of Cuba **100** 21.40N 82.40W
Ping *r.* Thailand **57** 15.45N 100.10E
Pingdingshan Henan China **62** 33.38N 113.30E
Pingdingshan Liaoning China **62** 41.26N 124.46E
Pingliang China **62** 35.21N 107.12E
Pingtan Dao *i.* China **63** 25.36N 119.48E
Pingtung Taiwan **63** 22.44N 120.30E
Pingxiang China **63** 27.36N 113.48E
Pingxiang China **58** 22.06N 106.44E
Pingyao China **62** 37.12N 112.08E
Pini *i.* Indonesia **58** 0.10N 98.30E
Pinios *r.* Greece **39** 37.51N 22.37E
Pinnaroo Australia **83** 35.18S 140.54E
Pinner England **23** 51.36N 0.23W
Pinrang Indonesia **58** 3.48S 119.41E
Pinsk U.S.S.R. **43** 52.08N 26.01E
Pinto Argentina **110** 29.09S 62.38W
Piombino Italy **38** 42.56N 10.30E

Piqua U.S.A. **98** 40.08N 84.14W
Piquiri *r.* Brazil **110** 24.00S 54.00W
Piracicaba Brazil **109** 22.20S 47.40W
Piraeus Greece **39** 37.56N 23.38E
Pirapora Brazil **110** 17.20S 44.54W
Pirbright England **23** 51.18N 0.39W
Pírgos Greece **39** 37.42N 21.27E
Pirmasens W. Germany **40** 49.12N 7.37E
Pirna E. Germany **40** 50.58N 13.58E
Pirot Yugo. **39** 43.10N 22.32E
Pisa Italy **38** 43.43N 10.24E
Pisciotta Italy **38** 40.08N 15.12E
Pisek Czech. **40** 49.19N 14.10E
Pishan China **60** 37.30N 78.20E
Pisuerga *r.* Spain **37** 41.35N 5.40W
Pita Guinea **72** 11.05N 12.15W
Pitea Sweden **42** 65.19N 21.30E
Piteşti Romania **39** 44.52N 24.51E
Pitlochry Scotland **33** 56.43N 3.45W
Pittenweem Scotland **31** 56.13N 2.44W
Pittsburgh U.S.A. **98** 40.26N 80.00W
Pittsfield U.S.A. **99** 42.27N 73.15W
Piura Peru **108** 5.15S 80.38W
Plain of Bornu *f.* Nigeria **73** 12.30N 13.00E
Plains of Ellertrin *f.* Rep. of Ire. **34** 53.37N 9.11W
Plains of Mayo *f.* Rep. of Ire. **34** 53.46N 9.05W
Plasencia Spain **37** 40.02N 6.05W
Platani *r.* Italy **38** 37.24N 13.15E
Plate, R. *see* la Plata, Rio de Argentina **110**
Plateau *d.* Nigeria **73** 8.50N 9.00E
Platí, C. Greece **39** 40.26N 23.59E
Platinum U.S.A. **94** 59.00N 161.50W
Platte *r.* U.S.A. **97** 41.05N 96.50W
Plattsburgh U.S.A. **99** 44.42N 73.29W
Plauen E. Germany **40** 50.29N 12.08E
Pleiku Vietnam **58** 13.57N 108.01E
Plenty, B. of New Zealand **85** 37.40S 176.50E
Pleven Bulgaria **39** 43.25N 24.39E
Pljevlja Yugo. **39** 43.22N 19.22E
Ploieşti Romania **39** 44.57N 26.02E
Plomb du Cantal *mtn.* France **36** 45.04N 2.45E
Plombières France **40** 47.58N 6.28E
Ploudalmézeau France **36** 48.33N 4.39W
Plovdiv Bulgaria **39** 42.09N 24.45E
Plumtree Zimbabwe **76** 20.30S 27.50E
Plym *r.* England **27** 50.21N 4.06W
Plymouth England **27** 50.23N 4.09W
Plymouth Ind. U.S.A. **98** 41.20N 86.19W
Plymouth Mass. U.S.A. **99** 41.58N 70.40W
Plympton England **27** 50.24N 4.02W
Plzeň Czech. **40** 49.45N 13.22E
Po *r.* Italy **38** 44.51N 12.30E
Pô U. Volta **72** 11.11N 1.10W
Pobé Benin **73** 7.00N 2.56E
Pobeda, Mt. U.S.S.R. **45** 65.20N 145.50E
Pobla de Segur Spain **37** 42.15N 0.58E
Pocatello U.S.A. **96** 42.53N 112.26W
Pocklington England **29** 53.56N 0.48W
Podolsk U.S.S.R. **43** 55.23N 37.32E
Podor Senegal **72** 16.35N 15.02W
Pods Brook *r.* England **23** 51.52N 0.33E
Pofadder R.S.A. **76** 29.09S 19.25E
Poh Indonesia **59** 1.00S 122.50E
Pohang S. Korea **64** 36.10N 129.26E
Pointe-à-Pitre Guadeloupe **101** 16.14N 61.32W
Pointe Noire *town* Congo **74** 4.46S 11.53E
Poitiers France **36** 46.35N 0.20E
Pokhara Nepal **56** 28.14N 83.58E
Poko Zaïre **75** 3.08N 26.51E
Poland Europe **43** 52.30N 19.00E
Polatli Turkey **54** 39.34N 32.08E
Polden Hills England **24** 51.07N 2.50W
Polegate England **25** 50.49N 0.15E
Policastro, G. of Med. Sea **38** 40.00N 15.35E
Poligny France **36** 46.50N 4.42E
Pollina *mtn.* Italy **38** 39.53N 16.11E
Pollnalaght *mtn.* N. Ireland **34** 54.34N 7.27W
Polperro England **27** 50.19N 4.31W
Poltava U.S.S.R. **43** 49.35N 34.35E
Pombal Portugal **37** 39.55N 8.38W
Ponce Puerto Rico **101** 18.00N 66.40W
Pondicherry India **57** 11.59N 79.50E
Pond Inlet *str.* Canada **95** 72.30N 75.00W
Ponferrada Spain **37** 42.32N 6.31W
Pongola *r.* Moçambique **76** 26.13S 32.38E
Ponta Grossa Brazil **110** 25.00S 50.09W
Pont-à-Mousson France **40** 48.55N 6.03E
Ponta Pora Brazil **110** 22.27S 55.39W
Pontardawe Wales **27** 51.44N 3.51W
Pontardulais Wales **27** 51.42N 4.03W
Pontchartrain, L. U.S.A. **100** 30.50N 90.00W
Pontefract England **29** 53.42N 1.19W
Ponteland England **31** 55.03N 1.43W
Ponterwyd Wales **26** 52.25N 3.50W
Pontevedra Spain **37** 42.25N 8.39W
Pontiac U.S.A. **98** 42.39N 83.18W
Pontianak Indonesia **58** 0.05S 109.16E
Pontine Is. Italy **38** 40.56N 12.58E
Pontine Mts. Turkey **54** 40.32N 38.00E
Pontoise France **36** 49.03N 2.05E
Pontrilas England **24** 51.56N 2.53W
Pontypool Wales **27** 51.42N 3.01W
Pontypridd Wales **24** 51.36N 3.21W
Poole England **24** 50.42N 2.02W
Poole B. England **24** 50.40N 1.55W
Poolewe Scotland **32** 57.45N 5.37W
Pooley Bridge *town* England **28** 54.37N 2.49W
Poopó, L. Bolivia **109** 19.00S 67.00W
Poperinge Belgium **41** 50.51N 2.44E
Poplar England **23** 51.31N 0.01E
Poplar Bluff U.S.A. **97** 36.40N 90.25W
Popocatépetl *mtn.* Mexico **100** 19.02N 98.38W
Popokabaka Zaïre **74** 5.41S 16.40E
Popondetta P.N.G. **59** 8.45S 148.15E
Porahat India **56** 22.35N 85.27E
Porbandar India **56** 21.40N 69.40E
Porcupine *r.* U.S.A. **94** 66.25N 145.20W
Pori Finland **42** 61.28N 21.45E
Porirua New Zealand **85** 41.08S 174.50E
Porkkala Finland **42** 60.00N 24.25E
Porlamar Venezuela **101** 11.01N 63.54W
Porlock England **27** 51.14N 3.36W
Pornic France **36** 47.07N 2.05W
Pornivir Colombia **108** 4.45N 71.24W
Poronaysk U.S.S.R. **45** 49.13N 142.55E
Porsanger *est.* Norway **42** 70.30N 25.45E
Porsgrunn Norway **42** 59.10N 9.40E
Porsuk *r.* Turkey **54** 39.41N 31.56E
Port Adelaide Australia **83** 34.52S 138.30E
Portadown N. Ireland **34** 54.25N 6.27W
Portaferry N. Ireland **34** 54.23N 5.33W
Portage U.S.A. **98** 43.33N 89.29W
Portage la Prairie *town* Canada **96** 50.01N 98.20W
Portalegre Portugal **37** 39.17N 7.25W
Port Alfred R.S.A. **76** 33.36S 26.54E
Port Angeles U.S.A. **96** 48.06N 123.26W
Port Antonio Jamaica **101** 18.10N 76.27W
Portarlington Rep. of Ire. **35** 53.10N 7.12W
Port Arthur Australia **83** 43.08S 147.50E
Port Arthur U.S.A. **97** 29.55N 93.56W
Port Askaig Scotland **30** 55.51N 6.07W
Port Augusta Australia **82** 32.30S 137.46E
Port-au-Prince Haiti **101** 18.33N 72.20W
Port Austin U.S.A. **98** 44.04N 82.59W
Port Bannatyne Scotland **30** 55.52N 5.04W
Port Blair India **57** 11.40N 92.30E
Port Bou Spain **37** 42.25N 3.09E
Port Bouet Ivory Coast **72** 5.14N 3.58W
Port Burwell Canada **98** 42.39N 80.47W
Port Cartier Canada **95** 50.03N 66.46W
Port Chalmers New Zealand **85** 45.49S 170.37E
Port Charlotte Scotland **30** 55.45N 6.23W
Port Dinorwic Wales **26** 53.11N 4.12W
Port Elizabeth R.S.A. **76** 33.58S 25.36E
Port Ellen Scotland **30** 55.38N 6.12W
Port Erin I.o.M. **28** 54.05N 4.45W
Port-Eynon Wales **27** 51.33N 4.13W
Port Gentil Gabon **74** 0.40S 8.46E
Port Glasgow Scotland **30** 55.56N 4.40W
Portglenone N. Ireland **30** 54.52N 6.30W
Port Harcourt Nigeria **73** 4.43N 7.05E
Porthcawl Wales **27** 51.28N 3.42W
Port Hedland Australia **82** 20.24S 118.36E
Porthmadog Wales **26** 52.55N 4.08W
Port Huron U.S.A. **98** 42.59N 82.28W
Portimão Portugal **37** 37.08N 8.32W
Port Isaac B. England **27** 50.36N 4.50W
Portishead England **24** 51.29N 2.46W
Portiţei Mouth *f.* Romania **39** 44.40N 29.00E
Port Kembla Australia **83** 34.30S 150.54E
Portknockie Scotland **33** 57.42N 2.52W
Portland Australia **83** 38.21S 141.38E
Portland Ind. U.S.A. **98** 40.25N 84.58W
Portland Maine U.S.A. **99** 43.41N 70.18W
Portland Oreg. U.S.A. **96** 45.32N 122.40W
Portland, C. Australia **83** 40.43S 148.08E
Portland, I. of England **27** 50.32N 2.25W
Port Laoise Rep. of Ire. **35** 53.03N 7.20W
Port Lincoln Australia **82** 34.43S 135.49E
Port Logan Scotland **30** 54.43N 4.57W
Port Loko Sierra Leone **72** 8.50N 12.50W
Port Macquarie Australia **83** 31.28S 152.25E
Portmahomack Scotland **33** 57.49N 3.50W
Portmarnock Rep. of Ire. **34** 53.25N 6.09W
Port Moresby P.N.G. **59** 9.30S 147.07E
Portnacroish Scotland **32** 56.25N 5.22W
Portnaguiran Scotland **32** 58.15N 6.10W
Portnahaven Scotland **30** 55.41N 6.31W
Port Nelson Canada **95** 57.10N 92.35W
Port Nolloth R.S.A. **76** 29.17S 16.51E
Port-Nouveau Québec Canada **95** 58.35N 65.59W
Pôrto *see* Oporto Portugal **37**
Pôrto Alegre Brazil **110** 30.03S 51.10W
Porto Alexandre Angola **74** 15.55S 11.51E
Porto Amboim Angola **74** 10.45S 13.43E
Port of Ness Scotland **32** 58.30N 6.13W
Port of Spain Trinidad **101** 10.38N 61.31W
Pörtom Finland **42** 62.44N 21.35E
Porton England **24** 51.08N 1.44W
Porto-Novo Benin **73** 6.30N 2.47E
Porto Torres Italy **38** 40.49N 8.24E
Porto Vecchio France **36** 41.35N 9.16E
Pôrto Velho Brazil **108** 8.45S 63.54W
Portpatrick Scotland **30** 54.51N 5.07W
Port Phillip B. Australia **83** 38.05S 144.50E
Port Pirie Australia **83** 33.11S 138.01E
Portreath England **27** 50.15N 5.17W
Portree Scotland **32** 57.24N 6.12W
Portrush N. Ireland **30** 55.12N 6.40W
Port Safâga Egypt **54** 26.45N 33.55E
Port Said Egypt **54** 31.17N 32.18E
Port St. Louis France **36** 43.25N 4.40E
Port Shepstone R.S.A. **76** 30.44S 30.28E
Portskerra Scotland **33** 58.33N 3.55W
Portsmouth England **24** 50.48N 1.06W
Portsmouth N.H. U.S.A. **99** 43.03N 70.47W
Portsmouth Ohio U.S.A. **98** 38.45N 82.59W
Portsoy Scotland **33** 57.41N 2.41W
Portstewart N. Ireland **30** 55.11N 6.43W
Port Sudan Sudan **71** 19.39N 37.01E
Port Talbot Wales **27** 51.35N 3.48W
Portugal Europe **37** 39.30N 8.05W
Portumna Rep. of Ire. **35** 53.06N 8.14W
Port Vendres France **36** 42.31N 3.06E
Port Victoria Kenya **75** 0.07N 34.00E
Port William Scotland **30** 54.46N 4.35W
Porz W. Germany **41** 50.53N 7.05E
Posadas Argentina **110** 27.25S 55.48W
Poso Indonesia **59** 1.23S 120.45E
Postmasburg R.S.A. **76** 28.20S 23.05E
Potchefstroom R.S.A. **76** 26.42S 27.06E
Potenza Italy **38** 40.40N 15.47E
Potgietersrus R.S.A. **76** 24.15S 28.55E
Poti U.S.S.R. **43** 42.11N 41.41E
Potiskum Nigeria **73** 11.40N 11.03E
Potomac *r.* U.S.A. **99** 38.35N 77.00W
Potosí Bolivia **110** 19.34S 65.45W
Potosi *d.* Bolivia **110** 21.50S 66.00W
Potsdam E. Germany **40** 52.24N 13.04E
Potters Bar England **23** 51.42N 0.11W
Potter Street England **23** 51.46N 0.08E
Pottstown U.S.A. **99** 40.15N 75.38W
Pottsville U.S.A. **99** 40.42N 76.13W
Poughkeepsie U.S.A. **99** 41.43N 73.56W
Póvoa de Varzim Portugal **37** 41.22N 8.46W
Povorino U.S.S.R. **43** 51.12N 42.15E
Powder *r.* U.S.A. **96** 46.40N 105.15W
Powell, L. U.S.A. **96** 37.30N 110.45W
Powys *d.* Wales **26** 52.26N 3.26W
Poyang Hu *l.* China **63** 29.10N 116.20E
Poyntz Pass N. Ireland **34** 54.16N 6.23W
Požarevac Yugo. **39** 44.38N 21.12E
Poza Rica Mexico **100** 20.34N 97.26W
Poznań Poland **40** 52.25N 16.53E
Pozoblanco Spain **37** 38.23N 4.51W
Prachuap Khiri Khan Thailand **57** 11.50N 99.49E
Prades France **36** 42.38N 2.25E
Prague Czech. **40** 50.05N 14.25E
Praha *see* Prague Czech. **40**
Prato Italy **38** 43.52N 10.50E
Pratt's Bottom England **23** 51.21N 0.06E
Prawle Pt. England **27** 50.12N 3.43W
Preesall England **28** 53.55N 2.58W
Preparis *i.* Burma **58** 14.40N 93.40E
Prescot England **28** 53.27N 2.49W
Prescott U.S.A. **96** 34.34N 112.28W
Presidente Epitácio Brazil **110** 21.56S 52.07W
Presidente Prudente Brazil **110** 22.09S 51.24W
Prespa, L. Albania/Greece/Yugo. **39** 40.53N 21.02E
Presque Isle *town* U.S.A. **99** 46.42N 68.01W
Prestatyn Wales **26** 53.20N 3.24W
Prestea Ghana **72** 5.26N 2.07W
Presteigne Wales **26** 52.17N 3.00W
Preston England **28** 53.46N 2.42W
Prestonpans Scotland **31** 55.57N 3.00W
Prestwick Scotland **30** 55.30N 4.36W
Prestwood England **23** 51.42N 0.43W
Pretoria R.S.A. **76** 25.45S 28.12E
Préveza Greece **39** 38.58N 20.43E
Příbram Czech. **40** 49.42N 14.00E
Prieska R.S.A. **76** 29.40S 22.45E
Prikumsk U.S.S.R. **43** 44.46N 44.10E
Prilep Yugo. **39** 41.20N 21.32E
Priluki U.S.S.R. **43** 50.35N 32.24E
Primorsk U.S.S.R. **42** 60.18N 28.35E
Prince Albert Canada **94** 53.13N 105.45W
Prince Albert R.S.A. **76** 33.15S 22.03E
Prince Alfred C. Canada **94** 74.30N 125.00W
Prince Charles I. Canada **95** 67.50N 76.00W
Prince Edward I. Canada **97** 46.15N 64.00W
Prince Edward Is. Indian Oc. **113** 47.00S 37.00E
Prince Edward Island *d.* Canada **95** 46.15N 63.10W
Prince George Canada **94** 53.55N 122.49W
Prince of Wales, C. U.S.A. **94** 66.00N 168.30W

Ramsar Iran **55** 36.54N 50.41E
Ramsbottom England **28** 53.38N 2.20W
Ramsey England **25** 52.27N 0.06W
Ramsey I.o.M. **28** 54.19N 4.23W
Ramsey *i.* Wales **26** 51.53N 5.21W
Ramsey B. I.o.M. **28** 54.20N 4.20W
Ramsgate England **25** 51.20N 1.25E
Rancagua Chile **109** 34.10S 70.45W
Ranchi India **56** 23.22N 85.20E
Randalstown N. Ireland **30** 54.45N 6.20W
Randers Denmark **42** 56.28N 10.03E
Rangiora New Zealand **85** 43.18S 172.38E
Rangitaiki *r.* New Zealand **85** 37.55S 176.50E
Rangoon Burma **57** 16.45N 96.20E
Rangpur Bangla. **56** 25.45N 89.21E
Rannoch, Loch Scotland **33** 56.41N 4.20W
Rannoch Moor *f.* Scotland **33** 56.38N 4.40W
Rann of Kutch *f.* India **56** 23.50N 69.50E
Ranobe *r.* Madagascar **75** 17.20S 44.05E
Rantauparapat Indonesia **58** 2.05N 99.46E
Rantekombola *mtn.* Indonesia **58** 3.30S 119.58E
Raoping China **63** 23.45N 117.05E
Rapallo Italy **36** 44.20N 9.14E
Rapid City U.S.A. **96** 44.06N 103.14W
Raqqa Syria **54** 35.57N 39.03E
Ras al Hadd *c.* Oman **55** 22.32N 59.49E
Ras al Khaimah U.A.E. **55** 25.48N 55.56E
Ras Banas *c.* Egypt **54** 23.54N 35.48E
Ras Dashan *mtn.* Ethiopia **71** 13.20N 38.10E
Rashid Egypt **54** 31.25N 30.25E
Ras Madraka *c.* Oman **56** 19.00N 57.55E
Râs Muhammad *c.* Egypt **54** 27.42N 34.13E
Rass Saudi Arabia **54** 25.54N 43.30E
Ras Tanura *c.* Saudi Arabia **55** 26.40N 50.10E
Rastatt W. Germany **40** 48.51N 8.13E
Rat Buri Thailand **58** 13.30N 99.50E
Rathangan Rep. of Ire. **35** 53.13N 7.00W
Rathcoole Rep. of Ire. **34** 53.17N 6.30W
Rathcormack Rep. of Ire. **35** 52.05N 8.18W
Rathdowney Rep. of Ire. **35** 52.51N 7.36W
Rathdrum Rep. of Ire. **35** 52.56N 6.15W
Rathenow E. Germany **40** 52.37N 12.21E
Rathfriland N. Ireland **34** 54.14N 6.10W
Rathkeale Rep. of Ire. **35** 52.30N 8.57W
Rathlin I. N. Ireland **30** 55.17N 6.15W
Rathlin Sd. N. Ireland **30** 55.15N 6.15W
Rath Luirc Rep. of Ire. **35** 52.21N 8.41W
Rathmore Rep. of Ire. **35** 52.05N 9.12W
Rathmullen Rep. of Ire. **34** 55.06N 7.32W
Rathnew Rep. of Ire. **35** 53.01N 6.07W
Rathvilly Rep. of Ire. **35** 52.52N 6.43W
Ratlam India **56** 23.18N 75.06E
Raton U.S.A. **96** 36.54N 104.27W
Rattray Head Scotland **33** 57.37N 1.50W
Rättvik Sweden **42** 60.56N 15.10E
Rauch Argentina **110** 36.45S 59.05W
Rauma Finland **42** 61.09N 21.30E
Raunds England **25** 52.21N 0.33W
Ravar Iran **55** 31.14N 56.51E
Ravenna Italy **38** 44.25N 12.12E
Ravensburg W. Germany **40** 47.47N 9.37E
Ravi *r.* Pakistan **56** 30.30N 72.13E
Rawalpindi Pakistan **56** 33.40N 73.08E
Rawlinna Australia **82** 31.00S 125.21E
Rawlins U.S.A. **96** 41.46N 107.16W
Rawmarsh England **29** 53.27N 1.20W
Rawtenstall England **28** 53.42N 2.18W
Rayen Iran **55** 29.34N 57.26E
Rayleigh England **23** 51.36N 0.36E
Razan Iran **55** 35.22N 49.02E
Razgrad Bulgaria **39** 43.32N 26.30E
Ré, Ile de *i.* France **36** 46.10N 1.26W
Reading England **24** 51.27N 0.57W
Reading U.S.A. **99** 40.20N 75.55W
Reay Forest *f.* Scotland **33** 58.17N 4.48W
Rebun jima *i.* Japan **64** 45.25N 141.04E
Recife Brazil **108** 8.06S 34.53W
Recklinghausen W. Germany **41** 51.36N 7.11E
Reconquista Argentina **110** 29.08S 59.38W
Recreo Argentina **110** 29.18S 65.05W
Red *r.* Canada **97** 50.30N 96.50W
Red *r.* U.S.A. **97** 31.10N 92.00W
Red *r.* Vietnam **63** 20.15N 106.36E
Red B. N. Ireland **30** 55.04N 6.02W
Red Basin *f.* China **63** 31.00N 106.00E
Red Bluff U.S.A. **96** 40.11N 122.16W
Redbourn England **23** 51.48N 0.24W
Redbridge England **23** 51.35N 0.06E
Redcar England **29** 54.37N 1.04W
Red Deer Canada **94** 52.15N 113.48W
Red Deer *r.* Canada **96** 50.55N 110.00W
Redding U.S.A. **96** 40.35N 122.24W
Redditch England **24** 52.18N 1.57W
Rede *r.* England **31** 55.08N 2.13W
Redhill England **23** 51.14N 0.11W
Red L. U.S.A. **97** 48.00N 95.00W
Red Lake *town* Canada **97** 50.59N 93.40W

Redpoint Scotland **32** 57.39N 5.49W
Redruth England **27** 50.14N 5.14W
Red Sea Africa/Asia **71** 20.00N 39.00E
Red Tower Pass Romania **39** 45.37N 24.17E
Red Volta *r.* Ghana **72** 10.32N 0.31W
Red Wharf B. Wales **26** 53.20N 4.10W
Ree, Lough Rep. of Ire. **34** 53.31N 7.58W
Reedham England **25** 52.34N 1.33E
Rega *r.* Poland **40** 54.10N 15.18E
Regen *r.* W. Germany **40** 49.02N 12.03E
Regensburg W. Germany **40** 49.01N 12.07E
Reggane Algeria **70** 26.30N 0.30E
Reggio Calabria Italy **38** 38.07N 15.38E
Reggio Emilia-Romagna Italy **38** 44.40N 10.37E
Regina Canada **96** 50.30N 104.38W
Rehoboth Namibia **76** 23.18S 17.03E
Reigate England **23** 51.14N 0.13W
Reims France **36** 49.15N 4.02E
Reindeer L. Canada **94** 57.00N 102.20W
Reinosa Mexico **100** 26.09N 97.10W
Reinosa Spain **37** 43.01N 4.09W
Reiss Scotland **33** 58.28N 3.09W
Rembang Indonesia **58** 6.45S 111.22E
Remich Lux. **41** 49.34N 6.23E
Remscheid W. Germany **41** 51.10N 7.11E
Renaix Belgium **41** 50.45N 3.36E
Rendsburg W. Germany **40** 54.19N 9.39E
Renfrew Canada **99** 45.28N 76.44W
Renfrew Scotland **30** 55.52N 4.23W
Rengat Indonesia **58** 0.26S 102.35E
Reni U.S.S.R. **39** 45.28N 28.17E
Renish Pt. Scotland **32** 57.43N 6.58W
Renkum Neth. **41** 51.59N 5.46E
Renmark Australia **83** 34.10S 140.45E
Rennes France **36** 48.06N 1.40W
Reno *r.* Italy **38** 44.36N 12.17E
Reno U.S.A. **96** 39.32N 119.49W
Renvyle Pt. Rep. of Ire. **34** 53.37N 10.04W
Republican *r.* U.S.A. **97** 39.05N 94.50W
Republic of Ireland Europe **35** 53.00N 8.00W
Republic of South Africa Africa **76** 28.30S 24.50E
Requena Spain **37** 39.29N 1.08W
Resistencia Argentina **110** 27.28S 59.00W
Resolute Canada **95** 74.40N 95.00W
Resolution I. New Zealand **85** 45.40S 166.30E
Resort, Loch Scotland **32** 58.03N 6.56W
Rethel France **41** 49.31N 4.22E
Réthimnon Greece **39** 35.22N 24.29E
Réunion *i.* Indian Oc. **113** 22.00S 55.00E
Reus Spain **37** 41.10N 1.06E
Reutlingen W. Germany **40** 48.30N 9.13E
Revelstoke Canada **96** 51.00N 118.12W
Revilla Gigedo Is. Mexico **93** 19.00N 111.00W
Revue *r.* Moçambique **76** 19.58S 34.40E
Rewa India **56** 24.32N 81.18E
Reykjavik Iceland **42** 64.09N 21.58W
Rezaiyeh Iran **55** 37.32N 45.02E
Rēzekne U.S.S.R. **42** 56.30N 27.22E
Rhayader Wales **26** 52.19N 3.30W
Rheden Neth. **41** 52.01N 6.02E
Rheine W. Germany **41** 52.17N 7.26E
Rhenen Neth. **41** 51.58N 5.34E
Rheydt W. Germany **41** 51.10N 6.25E
Rhine *r.* Europe **41** 51.53N 6.03E
Rhinelander U.S.A. **98** 45.39N 89.23W
Rhinns of Kells *hills* Scotland **30** 55.08N 4.21W
Rhinns Pt. Scotland **30** 55.40N 6.29W
Rhino Camp *town* Uganda **75** 2.58N 31.20E
Rhode Island *d.* U.S.A. **99** 43.30N 71.35W
Rhodes Greece **39** 36.24N 28.15E
Rhodes *i.* Greece **39** 36.12N 28.00E
Rhodesia *see* Zimbabwe Africa **76**
Rhodope Mts. Bulgaria **39** 41.35N 24.35E
Rhondda Wales **27** 51.39N 3.30W
Rhondda Valley *f.* Wales **27** 51.38N 3.29W
Rhône *r.* France **36** 43.25N 4.45E
Rhosllanerchrugog Wales **26** 53.03N 3.04W
Rhosneigr Wales **26** 53.14N 4.31W
Rhum *i.* Scotland **32** 57.00N 6.20W
Rhum, Sd. of *str.* Scotland **32** 56.57N 6.15W
Rhyddhywel *mtn.* Wales **26** 52.25N 3.27W
Rhyl Wales **26** 53.19N 3.29W
Riau Is. Indonesia **58** 0.50N 104.00E
Rib *r.* England **23** 51.48N 0.04W
Ribadeo Spain **37** 43.32N 7.04W
Ribauè Moçambique **75** 14.57S 38.27E
Ribble *r.* England **28** 53.45N 2.44W
Ribblesdale *f.* England **28** 54.03N 2.17W
Ribeirão Prêto Brazil **110** 21.09S 47.48W
Riberac France **36** 45.14N 0.22E
Riccall England **29** 53.50N 1.04W
Richelieu *r.* Canada **99** 46.02N 73.03W
Richfield U.S.A. **96** 44.51N 93.17W
Richland U.S.A. **96** 46.20N 119.17W
Richmond England **28** 54.24N 1.43W
Richmond New Zealand **85** 45.01S 171.03E
Richmond Cape Province R.S.A. **76** 31.25S 23.57E
Richmond Ind. U.S.A. **98** 39.50N 84.51W

Richmond Va. U.S.A. **97** 37.34N 77.27W
Richmond Park *f.* England **23** 51.26N 0.13W
Richmond-upon-Thames England **23** 51.26N 0.17W
Rickmansworth England **23** 51.39N 0.29W
Ridderkirk Neth. **41** 51.53N 4.39E
Riesa E. Germany **40** 51.18N 13.18E
Rieti Italy **38** 42.24N 12.53E
Rift Valley *d.* Kenya **75** 1.00N 36.00E
Riga U.S.S.R. **42** 56.53N 24.08E
Riga, G. of U.S.S.R. **42** 57.30N 23.50E
Rigan Iran **55** 28.40N 58.58E
Rigmati Iran **55** 27.40N 58.11E
Rihand Dam India **56** 24.09N 83.02E
Riihimaki Finland **42** 60.45N 24.45E
Rijeka Yugo. **38** 45.20N 14.25E
Rijswijk Neth. **41** 52.03N 4.22E
Rima, Wadi *r.* Saudi Arabia **54** 26.10N 44.00E
Rimini Italy **38** 44.01N 12.34E
Rimouski Canada **99** 48.27N 68.32W
Ringköbing Denmark **42** 56.06N 8.15E
Ringvassöy *i.* Norway **42** 70.00N 19.00E
Ringwood England **24** 50.50N 1.48W
Rinrawros Pt. Rep. of Ire. **34** 55.01N 8.34W
Riobamba Ecuador **108** 1.44S 78.40W
Rio Branco *town* Brazil **108** 10.00S 67.49W
Rio Claro *town* Brazil **110** 22.19S 47.35W
Rio de Janeiro *town* Brazil **110** 22.53S 43.17W
Rio Gallegos *town* Argentina **109** 51.35S 69.15W
Rio Grande *town* Brazil **110** 32.03S 52.08W
Rio Grande *r.* Mexico/U.S.A. **100** 25.55N 97.08W
Río Grande *r.* Nicaragua **100** 12.48N 83.30W
Rio Grande do Sul *d.* Brazil **110** 30.15S 53.30W
Ríohacha Colombia **101** 11.34N 72.58W
Rio Negro *d.* Argentina **110** 41.15S 67.15W
Riosucio Colombia **101** 7.25N 77.05W
Rio Verde *town* Brazil **110** 17.50S 50.55W
Ripley Derbys. England **29** 53.03N 1.24W
Ripley Surrey England **23** 51.18N 0.29W
Ripon England **29** 54.08N 1.31W
Risca Wales **27** 51.36N 3.06W
Risha, Wadi *r.* Saudi Arabia **55** 25.40N 44.08E
Rishiri jima *i.* Japan **64** 45.11N 141.15E
Risor Norway **42** 58.44N 9.15E
Ristikent U.S.S.R. **42** 68.40N 31.47E
Rivas Nicaragua **100** 11.26N 85.50W
Riverhead England **23** 51.17N 0.11E
Riverina *f.* Australia **83** 35.00S 146.00E
Rivers *d.* Nigeria **73** 4.45N 6.35E
Riversdale R.S.A. **76** 34.05S 21.14E
Riverton New Zealand **85** 46.21S 168.01E
Rivière-du-Loup *town* Canada **99** 47.49N 69.32W
Riyadh Saudi Arabia **55** 24.39N 46.44E
Rize Turkey **54** 41.03N 40.31E
Rizzuto, C. Italy **39** 38.53N 17.06E
Rjukan Norway **42** 59.54N 8.33E
Roanne France **36** 46.02N 4.05E
Roanoke *r.* U.S.A. **97** 36.00N 76.35W
Roaringwater B. Rep. of Ire. **35** 51.32N 9.26W
Robertson R.S.A. **76** 33.48S 19.53E
Roberval Canada **99** 48.31N 72.16W
Robin Hood's Bay *town* England **29** 54.26N 0.31W
Robinvale Australia **83** 34.37S 142.50E
Roboré Bolivia **110** 18.20S 59.45W
Robson, Mt. Canada **94** 53.00N 121.00W
Roca, Cabo de Portugal **37** 38.40N 9.31W
Roccella Italy **39** 38.19N 16.24E
Rocha Uruguay **110** 34.30S 54.22W
Rochdale England **28** 53.36N 2.10W
Rochechouart France **36** 45.49N 0.50E
Rochefort Belgium **41** 50.10N 5.13E
Rochefort France **36** 45.57N 0.58W
Rochester Kent England **23** 51.22N 0.30E
Rochester Northum. England **31** 55.16N 2.16W
Rochester Minn. U.S.A. **98** 44.01N 92.27W
Rochester N.Y. U.S.A. **99** 43.12N 77.37W
Rochfort Bridge Rep. of Ire. **34** 53.25N 7.19W
Rock *r.* U.S.A. **98** 41.30N 90.35W
Rockford U.S.A. **98** 42.16N 89.06W
Rockhampton Australia **82** 23.22S 150.32E
Rockingham Forest *f.* England **24** 52.30N 0.35W
Rock Island *town* U.S.A. **98** 41.30N 90.34W
Rockland U.S.A. **99** 44.06N 69.08W
Rocklands Resr. Australia **83** 37.13S 141.52E
Rock Springs *town* U.S.A. **96** 41.35N 109.13W
Rockville U.S.A. **99** 39.05N 77.10W
Rocky Mts. N. America **94** 50.00N 114.00W
Rocroi France **41** 49.56N 4.31E
Rodel Scotland **32** 57.44N 6.58W
Roden *r.* England **28** 52.42N 2.36W
Rodez France **36** 44.21N 2.34E
Roding *r.* England **23** 51.31N 0.05E
Rodonit, C. Albania **39** 41.34N 19.25E
Roe *r.* N. Ireland **30** 55.06N 7.00W
Roermond Neth. **41** 51.12N 6.00E
Rogan's Seat *mtn.* England **28** 54.25N 2.05W
Rogers City U.S.A. **98** 45.24N 83.50W
Rohtak India **56** 28.54N 76.35E
Rokan *r.* Indonesia **58** 2.00N 101.00E

178

St. Dié France **40** 48.17N 6.57E
St. Dizier France **36** 48.38N 4.58E
St. Elias, Mt. U.S.A. **94** 60.20N 139.00W
Saintes France **36** 45.44N 0.38W
Saintfield N. Ireland **34** 54.28N 5.50W
St. Fillans Scotland **30** 56.24N 4.07W
St. Finan's B. Rep. of Ire. **35** 51.49N 10.21W
St. Flour France **36** 45.02N 3.05E
St. Gallen Switz. **40** 47.25N 9.23E
St. Gaudens France **36** 43.07N 0.44E
St. George Australia **83** 28.03S 148.30E
St. George's Grenada **101** 12.04N 61.44W
St. George's Channel Rep. of Ire./U.K. **35** 51.30N 6.20W
St. Germain France **36** 48.53N 2.04E
St. Gheorghe's Mouth est. Romania **39** 44.51N 29.37E
St. Gilles-sur-Vie France **36** 46.42N 1.56W
St. Girons France **36** 42.59N 1.08E
St. Gotthard Pass Switz. **40** 46.30N 8.55E
St. Govan's Head Wales **27** 51.36N 4.55W
St. Helena i. Atlantic Oc. **130** 16.00S 6.00W
St. Helena B. R.S.A. **76** 32.35S 18.00E
St. Helens England **26** 53.28N 2.43W
St. Helier Channel Is. **27** 49.12N 2.07W
St. Hubert Belgium **41** 50.02N 5.22E
St. Hyacinthe Canada **99** 45.38N 72.57W
St. Ives Cambs. England **25** 52.20N 0.05W
St. Ives Cornwall England **27** 50.13N 5.29W
St. Ives B. England **27** 50.14N 5.26W
St. Jean Pied de Port France **36** 43.10N 1.14W
St. Jérôme Canada **99** 45.47N 74.01W
St. John Canada **97** 45.16N 66.03W
St. John r. Canada **95** 45.30N 66.05W
St. John, L. Canada **99** 48.40N 72.00W
St. John's Antigua **101** 17.07N 61.51W
St. John's Canada **95** 47.34N 52.41W
St. John's Pt. N. Ireland **34** 54.14N 5.39W
St. John's Pt. Rep. of Ire. **34** 54.34N 8.28W
St. Joseph U.S.A. **97** 39.45N 94.51W
St. Joseph, L. Canada **97** 51.00N 91.05W
St. Just England **27** 50.07N 5.41W
St. Keverne England **27** 50.03N 5.05W
St. Kitts i. C. America **101** 17.25N 62.45W
St. Lawrence r. Canada **99** 48.45N 68.30W
St. Lawrence, G. of Canada **95** 48.00N 52.00W
St. Lawrence I. U.S.A. **94** 63.00N 170.00W
St. Leonard Canada **99** 47.10N 67.55W
St. Lô France **36** 49.07N 1.05W
St. Louis Senegal **72** 16.01N 16.30W
St. Louis U.S.A. **98** 38.40N 90.15W
St. Lucia C. America **101** 14.05N 61.00W
St. Magnus B. Scotland **32** 60.25N 1.35W
St. Maixent France **36** 46.25N 0.12W
St. Malo France **36** 48.39N 2.00W
St. Malo, Golfe de France **36** 49.20N 2.00W
St. Marc Haiti **101** 19.08N 72.41W
St. Margaret's at Cliffe England **25** 51.10N 1.23E
St. Margaret's Hope Scotland **33** 58.49N 2.57W
St. Martin C. America **101** 18.05N 63.05W
St. Martin Channel Is. **27** 49.27N 2.34W
St. Martin's i. England **27** 49.57N 6.16W
St. Mary Channel Is. **27** 49.14N 2.10W
St. Marys Australia **83** 41.33S 148.12E
St. Mary's i. England **27** 49.55N 6.16W
St. Mary's Scotland **33** 58.54N 2.55W
St. Mary's Loch Scotland **31** 55.29N 3.12W
St. Maurice r. Canada **99** 46.20N 72.30W
St. Mawes England **27** 50.10N 5.01W
St. Moritz Switz. **40** 46.30N 9.51E
St. Nazaire France **36** 47.17N 2.12W
St. Neots England **25** 52.14N 0.16W
St. Nicolas Belgium **41** 51.10N 4.09E
St. Ninian's I. Scotland **32** 59.58N 1.21W
St. Omer France **25** 50.45N 2.15E
St. Pancras England **23** 51.32N 0.08W
St. Paul France **36** 42.49N 2.29E
St. Paul i. Indian Oc. **131** 38.44S 77.30E
St. Paul U.S.A. **98** 45.00N 93.10W
St. Paul's Cray England **23** 51.24N 0.06E
St. Peter Port Channel Is. **27** 49.27N 2.32W
St. Petersburg U.S.A. **97** 27.45N 82.40W
St. Pierre-Miquelon i. N. America **95** 47.00N 56.15W
St. Pölten Austria **40** 48.13N 15.37E
St. Quentin France **41** 49.51N 3.17E
St. Sampson Channel Is. **27** 49.29N 2.31W
St. Stephen Canada **99** 45.12N 67.18W
St. Thomas Canada **98** 42.46N 81.12W
St. Thomas i. Virgin Is. **101** 18.22N 64.57W
St. Trond Belgium **41** 50.49N 5.11E
St. Tropez France **36** 43.16N 6.39E
St. Vallier France **36** 45.11N 4.49E
St. Vincent C. America **101** 13.10N 61.15W
St. Vincent, C. Portugal **37** 37.01N 8.59W
St. Vith Belgium **41** 50.15N 6.08E
St. Wendel W. Germany **41** 49.27N 7.10E
St. Yrieix France **36** 45.31N 1.12E
Saipen i. Asia **59** 15.12N 145.43E
Sakai Japan **64** 34.37N 135.28E

Sakaka Saudi Arabia **54** 29.59N 40.12E
Sakania Zaïre **75** 12.44S 28.34E
Sakarya r. Turkey **54** 41.08N 30.36E
Sakata Japan **64** 38.55N 139.51E
Sakété Benin **73** 6.45N 2.45E
Sakhalin i. U.S.S.R. **61** 50.00N 143.00E
Sakrivier R.S.A. **76** 30.50S 20.26E
Sakti India **56** 22.02N 82.56E
Sal r. U.S.S.R. **43** 47.33N 40.40E
Sala Sweden **42** 59.55N 16.38E
Salado r. La Pampa Argentina **110** 36.15S 66.45W
Salado r. Santa Fé Argentina **110** 32.30S 61.00W
Salado r. Mexico **100** 26.46N 98.55W
Salala Oman **56** 17.00N 54.04E
Salamanca Spain **37** 40.58N 5.40W
Salar de Uyuni l. Bolivia **109** 20.30S 67.45W
Salatiga Indonesia **58** 7.15S 110.34E
Salbris France **36** 47.26N 2.03E
Salcombe England **27** 50.14N 3.47W
Saldanha B. R.S.A. **76** 33.00S 17.56E
Sale Australia **83** 38.06S 147.06E
Sale England **28** 53.26N 2.19W
Salekhard U.S.S.R. **44** 66.33N 66.35E
Salem India **57** 11.38N 78.08E
Salem U.S.A. **98** 38.37N 88.58W
Salen Highland Scotland **30** 56.43N 5.46W
Salen Strath. Scotland **30** 56.31N 5.56W
Salerno Italy **38** 40.41N 14.45E
Salerno, G. of Med. Sea **38** 40.30N 14.45E
Salford England **28** 53.30N 2.17W
Salfords England **23** 51.12N 0.12W
Salima Malaŵi **75** 13.45S 34.29E
Salina Cruz Mexico **100** 16.11N 95.12W
Salins France **36** 46.56N 4.53E
Salisbury England **24** 51.04N 1.48W
Salisbury U.S.A. **97** 38.22N 75.37W
Salisbury Zimbabwe **76** 17.43S 31.05E
Salisbury Plain f. England **24** 51.15N 1.55W
Salmon r. U.S.A. **96** 45.50N 116.50W
Salmon River Mts. U.S.A. **96** 44.30N 114.30W
Salo Finland **42** 60.23N 23.10E
Salobreña Spain **37** 36.45N 3.35W
Salon France **36** 43.38N 5.06E
Salonga r. Zaïre **74** 0.09S 19.52E
Salop d. England **24** 52.35N 2.40W
Salsk U.S.S.R. **43** 46.30N 41.33E
Salso r. Italy **38** 37.07N 13.57E
Salt Jordan **54** 32.03N 35.44E
Salta Argentina **110** 24.46S 65.28W
Salta d. Argentina **110** 25.05S 65.00W
Saltash England **27** 50.25N 4.13W
Saltburn-by-the-Sea England **29** 54.35N 0.58W
Saltcoats Scotland **30** 55.37N 4.47W
Saltee Is. Rep. of Ire. **35** 52.08N 6.36W
Saltfleet England **29** 53.25N 0.11E
Saltillo Mexico **100** 25.30N 101.00W
Salt Lake City U.S.A. **96** 40.45N 111.55W
Salto Uruguay **110** 31.27S 57.50W
Salton Sea l. U.S.A. **96** 33.25N 115.45W
Salûm Egypt **54** 31.31N 25.09E
Salvador Brazil **108** 12.58S 38.20W
Salwa Qatar **55** 24.44N 50.50E
Salween r. Burma **57** 16.30N 97.33E
Salyany U.S.S.R. **55** 39.36N 48.59E
Salzach r. Austria **40** 48.35N 13.30E
Salzburg Austria **40** 47.54N 13.03E
Salzgitter W. Germany **40** 52.02N 10.22E
Samana Dom. Rep. **101** 19.14N 69.20W
Samana Cay i. Bahamas **101** 23.05N 73.45W
Samar i. Phil. **59** 11.45N 125.15E
Samarinda Indonesia **58** 0.30S 117.09E
Samarkand U.S.S.R. **44** 39.40N 66.57E
Samarra Iraq **55** 34.13N 43.52E
Samawa Iraq **55** 31.18N 45.18E
Sambalpur India **57** 21.28N 84.04E
Samborombon Bay Argentina **110** 36.00S 56.50W
Sambre r. Belgium **41** 50.29N 4.52E
Samchok S. Korea **64** 37.30N 129.10E
Same Tanzania **75** 4.10S 37.43E
Samer France **25** 50.38N 1.45E
Samirum Iran **55** 31.31N 52.10E
Sam Neua Laos **58** 20.25N 104.04E
Samoa Is. Pacific Oc. **113** 13.00S 171.00W
Sámos i. Greece **39** 37.44N 26.45E
Samothráki i. Greece **39** 40.26N 25.35E
Sampit Indonesia **58** 2.34S 112.59E
Samrong Cambodia **58** 14.12N 103.31E
Samsun Turkey **54** 41.17N 36.22E
San Mali **72** 13.21N 4.57W
Sana Yemen **71** 16.02N 49.44E
Sana r. Yugo. **38** 45.03N 16.22E
Sanaga r. Cameroon **73** 3.35N 9.40E
San Ambrosio i. Pacific Oc. **109** 26.28S 79.53W
Sanandaj Iran **55** 35.18N 47.01E
San Antonio U.S.A. **96** 29.25N 98.30W
San Antonio i. Cuba **101** 21.50N 84.57W
San Antonio, Punta c. Mexico **96** 29.45N 115.41W
San Antonio Oeste Argentina **110** 40.45S 65.05W

San Bernardino U.S.A. **96** 34.07N 117.18W
San Blas, C. U.S.A. **97** 29.40N 85.25W
San Carlos Argentina **109** 41.11S 71.23W
San Carlos Phil. **59** 15.59N 120.22E
Sancha He r. China **63** 26.50N 106.04E
San Cristóbal Argentina **110** 30.20S 61.14W
San Cristóbal Dom. Rep. **101** 18.27N 70.07W
San Cristóbal Venezuela **101** 7.46N 72.15W
Sancti Spíritus Cuba **101** 21.55N 79.28W
Sanda i. Scotland **30** 55.17N 5.34W
Sandakan Malaysia **58** 5.52N 118.04E
Sanday i. Scotland **33** 59.15N 2.33W
Sanday Sd. Scotland **33** 59.11N 2.35W
Sandbach England **28** 53.09N 2.23W
Sandbank Scotland **30** 55.59N 4.58W
Sanderstead England **23** 51.21N 0.05W
Sandgate Australia **83** 27.18S 153.00E
Sandgate England **25** 51.05N 1.09E
San Diego U.S.A. **96** 32.45N 117.10W
Sandling England **23** 51.18N 0.33E
Sandnes Norway **42** 58.51N 5.45E
Sandness Scotland **32** 60.18N 1.38W
Sandö i. Faroe Is. **42** 61.50N 6.45W
Sandoa Zaïre **74** 9.41S 22.56E
Sandoway Burma **57** 18.28N 94.20E
Sandown England **24** 50.39N 1.09W
Sandpoint U.S.A. **96** 48.17N 116.34W
Sandray i. Scotland **32** 56.53N 7.31W
Sandringham England **29** 52.50N 0.30E
Sandusky U.S.A. **98** 41.27N 82.42W
Sandviken Sweden **42** 60.38N 16.50E
Sandwich England **25** 51.16N 1.21E
Sandwick Scotland **32** 60.00N 1.14W
Sandy England **25** 52.08N 0.18W
Sandy L. Canada **97** 53.00N 93.00W
San Felipe Mexico **96** 31.03N 114.52W
San Felipe Venezuela **101** 10.25N 68.40W
San Felíu de Guixols Spain **37** 41.47N 3.02E
San Felix i. Pacific Oc. **109** 26.23S 80.05W
San Félix Venezuela **101** 8.22N 62.37W
San Fernando Phil. **59** 16.39N 120.19E
San Fernando Spain **37** 36.28N 6.12W
San Fernando Trinidad **101** 10.16N 61.28W
San Fernando Venezuela **101** 7.53N 67.15W
San Francisco Argentina **110** 31.29S 62.06W
San Francisco U.S.A. **96** 37.45N 122.27W
San Francisco, C. Ecuador **108** 0.38N 80.08W
San Francisco de Macorís Dom. Rep. **101** 19.19N 70.15W
Sangerhausen E. Germany **40** 51.29N 11.18E
Sanggan He r. China **62** 40.23N 115.18E
Sangha r. Congo **74** 1.10S 16.47E
Sangi i. Indonesia **59** 3.30N 125.30E
Sangihe Is. Indonesia **59** 2.45N 125.20E
Sangli India **56** 16.55N 74.37E
Sangonera r. Spain **37** 37.58N 1.04W
San Javier Bolivia **110** 16.22S 62.38W
San Jorge r. Colombia **101** 9.10N 74.40W
San Jorge, G. of Argentina **109** 46.00S 66.00W
San Jorge, G. of Spain **37** 40.50N 1.10E
San José Costa Rica **100** 9.59N 84.04W
San José Guatemala **100** 13.58N 90.50W
San José Uruguay **110** 34.20S 56.42W
San Jose U.S.A. **96** 37.20N 121.55W
San José de Chiquitos Bolivia **110** 17.53S 60.45W
San Juan Argentina **109** 31.33S 68.31W
San Juan r. Costa Rica **100** 10.50N 83.40W
San Juan Puerto Rico **101** 18.29N 66.08W
San Juan r. U.S.A. **96** 37.20N 110.05W
San Juan del Norte Nicaragua **100** 10.58N 83.40W
San Juan de los Morros Venezuela **101** 9.53N 67.23W
San Juan Mts. U.S.A. **96** 37.30N 107.00W
Sankuru r. Zaïre **74** 4.20S 20.27E
San Leonardo Spain **37** 41.49N 3.04W
Sanlúcar de Barrameda Spain **37** 36.46N 6.21W
San Lucas, C. N. America **112** 22.50N 110.00W
San Luis Argentina **110** 33.20S 66.23W
San Luis d. Argentina **110** 33.00S 66.10W
San Luis Cuba **101** 20.13N 75.50W
San Luis Obispo U.S.A. **96** 35.16N 120.40W
San Luis Potosi Mexico **100** 22.10N 101.00W
San Luis Potosi d. Mexico **100** 23.00N 100.00W
San Marino Europe **38** 43.55N 12.27E
San Marino town San Marino **38** 43.55N 12.27E
San Matias, G. of Argentina **110** 41.30S 64.00W
Sanmenxia China **62** 34.46N 111.17E
Sanmenxia Resr. China **62** 34.38N 111.05E
San Miguel El Salvador **100** 13.28N 88.10W
San Miguel de Tucumán Argentina **110** 26.47S 65.15W
Sanming China **63** 26.25N 117.35E
San Nicolás Argentina **110** 33.25S 60.15W
San Pablo Phil. **59** 13.58N 121.10E
San Pedro Argentina **110** 24.30S 65.00W
San Pedro Dom. Rep. **101** 18.30N 69.18W
San Pedro Mexico **100** 24.50N 102.59W
San Pedro Paraguay **110** 24.08S 57.08W
San Pedro, Punta c. Costa Rica **100** 8.30N 83.30W

Sesheke Zambia **74** 17.14S 24.22E
Sesimbra Portugal **37** 38.26N 9.06W
Sète France **36** 43.25N 3.43E
Sete Lagoas Brazil **110** 19.29S 44.15W
Sétif Algeria **38** 36.10N 5.26E
Setté Cama Gabon **74** 2.32S 9.46E
Settle England **28** 54.05N 2.18W
Setúbal Portugal **37** 38.31N 8.54W
Setúbal, B. of Portugal **37** 38.20N 9.00W
Seul, Lac *l.* Canada **97** 50.25N 92.15W
Sevan, L. U.S.S.R. **55** 40.22N 45.20E
Sevastopol' U.S.S.R. **43** 44.36N 33.31E
Seven Heads *c.* Rep. of Ire. **35** 51.34N 8.43W
Seven Kings England **23** 51.34N 0.06E
Sevenoaks England **23** 51.16N 0.12E
Séverac France **36** 44.20N 3.05E
Severn *r.* Canada **95** 56.00N 87.40W
Severn *r.* England **24** 51.50N 2.21W
Severnaya Zemlya *is.* U.S.S.R. **45** 80.00N 96.00E
Seville Spain **37** 37.24N 5.59W
Sèvre Niortaise *r.* France **36** 46.35N 1.05W
Sewa *r.* Sierra Leone **72** 7.15N 12.08W
Seward U.S.A. **94** 60.05N 149.34W
Seward Pen. U.S.A. **94** 65.00N 164.10W
Seychelles Indian Oc. **53** 5.00S 55.00E
Seychelles *is.* Indian Oc. **113** 5.00S 55.00E
Seydhisfjördhur Iceland **42** 65.16N 14.02W
Seymour U.S.A. **98** 38.57N 85.55W
Sézanne France **36** 48.44N 3.44E
Sfântu Gheorghe Romania **39** 45.52N 25.50E
Sfax Tunisia **70** 34.45N 10.43E
'sGravenhage *see* The Hague Neth. **41**
Sgurr Mòr *mtn.* Scotland **32** 57.41N 5.01W
Sgurr na Lapaich *mtn.* Scotland **32** 57.22N 5.04W
Shaanxi *d.* China **62** 35.00N 108.30E
Shaba *d.* Zaïre **75** 8.00S 27.00E
Shabani Zimbabwe **76** 20.20S 30.05E
Shabunda Zaïre **75** 2.42S 27.20E
Shache China **60** 38.27N 77.16E
Shaftesbury England **24** 51.00N 2.12W
Shahabad Iran **55** 34.08N 46.35E
Shah Dad Iran **55** 30.27N 57.44E
Shahdol India **56** 23.10N 81.26E
Shahjahanpur India **56** 27.53N 79.55E
Shahpur Iran **55** 38.13N 44.50E
Shahreza Iran **55** 32.00N 51.52E
Shahr-i-Babak Iran **55** 30.08N 55.04E
Shahr Kord Iran **55** 32.40N 50.52E
Shahr Rey Iran **55** 35.35N 51.27E
Shahrud Iran **55** 36.25N 55.00E
Shahsawar Iran **55** 36.49N 50.54E
Shaib al Qur *r.* Saudi Arabia **54** 31.02N 42.00E
Shakhty U.S.S.R. **43** 47.43N 40.16E
Shakotan misaki *c.* Japan **64** 43.30N 140.15E
Shalford England **23** 51.13N 0.35W
Sham, Jebel *mtn.* Oman **55** 23.14N 57.17E
Shamiya Desert Iraq **55** 30.30N 45.30E
Shamley Green England **23** 51.11N 0.30W
Shamva Zimbabwe **76** 17.20S 31.38E
Shanchung Taiwan **59** 23.47N 120.41E
Shandong *d.* China **62** 36.00N 119.00E
Shandong Peninsula *pen.* China **62** 37.00N 121.30E
Shangchuan Dao *i.* China **63** 21.40N 112.47E
Shanghai China **63** 31.18N 121.50E
Shangqiu China **62** 34.21N 115.40E
Shangrao China **63** 28.28N 117.54E
Shangshui China **62** 33.31N 114.39E
Shanhaiguan China **62** 39.58N 119.45E
Shanklin England **24** 50.39N 1.09W
Shannon *r.* Rep. of Ire. **34** 52.39N 8.43W
Shannon, Mouth of the *est.* Rep. of Ire. **35** 52.29N 9.57W
Shan State *d.* Burma **57** 21.30N 98.00E
Shantar Is. U.S.S.R. **45** 55.00N 138.00E
Shantou China **63** 23.22N 116.39E
Shanxi *d.* China **62** 37.00N 112.00E
Shanyin China **62** 39.30N 112.50E
Shaoguan China **63** 24.53N 113.31E
Shaoxing China **63** 30.01N 120.40E
Shaoyang China **63** 27.10N 111.14E
Shap England **28** 54.32N 2.40W
Shapinsay *i.* Scotland **33** 59.03N 2.51W
Shapinsay Sd. Scotland **33** 59.01N 2.55W
Shapur *ruins* Iran **55** 29.42N 51.30E
Shaqra Saudi Arabia **55** 25.17N 45.14E
Sharjah U.A.E. **55** 25.20N 55.26E
Sharon U.S.A. **98** 41.16N 80.30W
Shashi *r.* Botswana **76** 22.10S 29.15E
Shashi China **63** 30.18N 112.20E
Shasta, Mt. U.S.A. **96** 41.35N 122.12W
Shatt al Arab *r.* Iraq **55** 30.00N 48.30E
Shau Xian China **62** 32.30N 116.35E
Shawano U.S.A. **98** 44.46N 88.38W
Shawinigan Canada **99** 46.33N 72.45W
Sha Xi *r.* China **63** 26.38N 118.10E
Sha Xian China **63** 26.27N 117.42E
Shebelle *r.* Somali Rep. **75** 0.30N 43.10E
Sheboygan U.S.A. **98** 43.46N 87.44W
Shebshi Mts. Nigeria **73** 8.30N 11.45E
Sheeffry Hills Rep. of Ire. **34** 53.41N 9.42W
Sheelin, Lough Rep. of Ire. **34** 53.48N 7.20W
Sheep Haven *b.* Rep. of Ire. **34** 55.12N 7.52W
Sheep's Head Rep. of Ire. **35** 51.33N 9.52W
Sheerness England **25** 51.26N 0.47E
Sheffield England **29** 53.23N 1.28W
Shefford England **25** 52.02N 0.20W
Shehy Mts. Rep. of Ire. **35** 51.47N 9.15W
Shelag *r.* Afghan. **55** 30.18N 61.02E
Shelby U.S.A. **96** 48.30N 111.52W
Shelikof Str. U.S.A. **94** 58.00N 153.45W
Shellharbour Australia **83** 34.35S 150.52E
Shëngjin Albania **39** 41.49N 19.33E
Shengze China **63** 30.53N 120.40E
Shenley England **23** 51.43N 0.17W
Shenyang China **62** 41.48N 123.27E
Shepparton Australia **83** 36.25S 145.26E
Shepperton England **23** 51.23N 0.28W
Sheppey, Isle of England **25** 51.24N 0.50E
Shepshed England **29** 52.46N 1.17W
Shepton Mallet England **24** 51.11N 2.31W
Shepway England **23** 51.15N 0.33E
Sherborne England **24** 50.56N 2.31W
Sherbro I. Sierra Leone **72** 7.30N 12.50W
Sherbrooke Canada **99** 45.24N 71.54W
Shere England **23** 51.13N 0.28W
Sheridan U.S.A. **96** 44.48N 107.05W
Sheringham England **29** 52.56N 1.11E
Sherkin I. Rep. of Ire. **35** 51.28N 9.25W
Sherman U.S.A. **97** 33.39N 96.35W
Sherridon Canada **95** 57.07N 101.05W
'sHertogenbosch Neth. **41** 51.42N 5.19E
Sherwood Forest *f.* England **29** 53.10N 1.05W
Shetland Is. *d.* Scotland **32** 60.20N 1.15W
Shevchenko U.S.S.R. **44** 43.40N 51.20E
Shiant Is. Scotland **32** 57.54N 6.20W
Shiel, Loch Scotland **32** 56.48N 5.33W
Shiel Bridge *town* Scotland **32** 57.12N 5.26W
Shieldaig Scotland **32** 57.31N 5.40W
Shifnal England **24** 52.40N 2.23W
Shihpai Hu *l.* China **63** 31.20N 118.48E
Shihpao Shan *mts.* China **63** 30.00N 112.00E
Shijiazhuang China **62** 38.03N 114.26E
Shikarpur Pakistan **56** 27.58N 68.42E
Shikoku *d.* Japan **64** 33.30N 133.00E
Shikoku *i.* Japan **64** 33.30N 133.00E
Shikoku sanchi *mts.* Japan **64** 34.00N 134.00E
Shikotsu ko *l.* Japan **64** 43.50N 141.26E
Shilbottle England **31** 55.22N 1.43W
Shildon England **28** 54.37N 1.39W
Shilka U.S.S.R. **61** 51.55N 116.01E
Shilka *r.* U.S.S.R. **61** 53.20N 121.10E
Shillong India **57** 25.34N 91.53E
Shilong China **63** 23.02N 113.50E
Shimizu Japan **64** 35.08N 138.38E
Shimoga India **56** 13.56N 75.31E
Shimo jima *i.* Japan **64** 32.10N 130.30E
Shimo Koshiki jima *i.* Japan **64** 31.50N 130.00E
Shimonoseki Japan **64** 34.02N 130.58E
Shin, Loch Scotland **33** 58.06N 4.32W
Shinano *r.* Japan **64** 37.58N 139.02E
Shingu Japan **64** 33.44N 135.59E
Shinyanga Tanzania **75** 3.40S 33.20E
Shinyanga *d.* Tanzania **75** 3.30S 33.00E
Shiono misaki *c.* Japan **64** 33.28N 135.47E
Shipka Pass Bulgaria **39** 42.45N 25.25E
Shipley England **28** 53.50N 1.47W
Shipston on Stour England **24** 52.04N 1.38W
Shipton England **29** 54.01N 1.09W
Shiqian China **63** 27.20N 108.10E
Shirakawa Japan **64** 37.10N 140.15E
Shirak Steppe *f.* U.S.S.R. **55** 41.40N 46.20E
Shirane san *mtn.* Japan **64** 35.42N 138.12E
Shiraz Iran **55** 29.36N 52.33E
Shire *r.* Moçambique **75** 17.46S 35.20E
Shirebrook England **29** 53.14N 1.16W
Shiriya saki *c.* Japan **64** 41.24N 141.30E
Shir Kuh *mtn.* Iran **55** 31.38N 54.07E
Shivpuri India **56** 25.26N 77.39E
Shiwan Dashan *mts.* China **63** 21.48N 107.50E
Shizuishan China **62** 39.17N 106.52E
Shizuoka Japan **64** 35.02N 138.28E
Shkodër Albania **39** 42.03N 19.30E
Shkoder, L. Albania/Yugo. **39** 42.10N 19.18E
Shoeburyness England **25** 51.31N 0.49E
Sholapur India **56** 17.43N 75.56E
Shoreditch England **23** 51.32N 0.05W
Shoreham-by-Sea England **25** 50.50N 0.17W
Shostka U.S.S.R. **43** 51.53N 33.30E
Shotts Scotland **31** 55.49N 3.48W
Shou Xian China **62** 32.30N 116.35E
Shreveport U.S.A. **97** 32.30N 93.46W
Shrewsbury England **24** 52.42N 2.45W
Shrewton England **24** 51.11N 1.55W
Shu'aiba Iraq **55** 30.30N 47.40E
Shuangliao China **62** 43.30N 123.29E
Shuangyashan China **61** 46.37N 131.22E
Shumagin Is. U.S.A. **94** 55.00N 160.00W
Shunde China **63** 22.40N 113.20E
Shur *r.* Iran **55** 28.00N 55.45E
Shurab *r.* Iran **55** 31.30N 55.18E
Shushtar Iran **55** 32.04N 48.53E
Shwebo Burma **57** 22.35N 95.42E
Sialkot Pakistan **56** 32.29N 74.35E
Siam, G. of Asia **57** 10.30N 101.00E
Siargao *i.* Phil. **59** 9.55N 126.05E
Siauliai U.S.S.R. **42** 55.51N 23.20E
Šibenik Yugo. **38** 43.45N 15.55E
Siberia *d.* Asia **113** 62.00N 104.00E
Siberut *i.* Indonesia **58** 1.30S 99.00E
Sibi Pakistan **56** 29.31N 67.54E
Sibiti Congo **74** 3.40S 13.24E
Sibiti *r.* Tanzania **75** 3.47S 34.45E
Sibiu Romania **39** 45.47N 24.09E
Sibolga Indonesia **58** 1.42N 98.48E
Sibu Malaysia **58** 2.18N 111.49E
Sichuan *d.* China **63** 30.00N 106.00E
Sicily *i.* Italy **38** 37.30N 14.00E
Sidcup England **23** 51.26N 0.07E
Sidi Barrani Egypt **54** 31.38N 25.58E
Sidi-bel-Abbès Algeria **37** 35.15N 0.39W
Sidlaw Hills Scotland **31** 56.31N 3.10W
Sidmouth England **24** 50.40N 3.13W
Siedlce Poland **43** 52.10N 22.18E
Sieg *r.* W. Germany **41** 50.49N 7.11E
Siegburg W. Germany **41** 50.48N 7.13E
Siegen W. Germany **41** 50.52N 8.02E
Siena Italy **38** 43.19N 11.20E
Sierra Blanca *mtn.* U.S.A. **96** 33.23N 105.49W
Sierra Leone Africa **72** 9.00N 12.00W
Sighişoara Romania **39** 46.13N 24.49E
Sighty Crag *mtn.* England **31** 55.07N 2.38W
Siglufjördhur Iceland **42** 66.09N 18.55W
Signy France **41** 49.42N 4.25E
Sigüenza Spain **37** 41.04N 2.38W
Siguiri Guinea **72** 11.28N 9.07W
Siirt Turkey **54** 37.56N 41.56E
Sikar India **56** 27.33N 75.12E
Sikasso Mali **72** 11.18N 5.38W
Sikhote-Alin Range *mts.* U.S.S.R. **64** 44.00N 135.00E
Sikkim *d.* India **56** 27.30N 88.30E
Sil *r.* Spain **37** 42.24N 7.15W
Silchar India **57** 24.49N 92.47E
Sileby England **24** 52.44N 1.06W
Silesian Plateau *f.* Poland **43** 50.30N 20.00E
Silgarhi Nepal **57** 29.14N 80.58E
Silifke Turkey **54** 36.22N 33.57E
Siliguri India **56** 26.42N 88.30E
Siling Co *l.* China **57** 31.40N 88.30E
Silistra Bulgaria **39** 44.07N 27.17E
Siljan *l.* Sweden **42** 60.50N 14.40E
Silkeborg Denmark **42** 56.10N 9.39E
Silloth England **31** 54.53N 3.25W
Silsden England **28** 53.55N 1.55W
Silver City U.S.A. **96** 32.47N 108.16W
Silver End England **23** 51.51N 0.38E
Silvermines Rep. of Ire. **35** 52.48N 8.15W
Silvermines Mts. Rep. of Ire. **35** 52.46N 8.17W
Silver Spring *town* U.S.A. **99** 39.00N 77.01W
Silverstone England **24** 52.05N 1.03W
Silverton England **24** 50.49N 3.29W
Simanggang Malaysia **58** 1.10N 111.32E
Simao China **57** 22.50N 101.00E
Simard, L. Canada **99** 47.37N 78.40W
Simav *r.* Turkey **39** 40.24N 28.31E
Simcoe, L. Canada **99** 44.25N 79.20W
Simeulue *i.* Indonesia **58** 2.30N 96.00E
Simferopol' U.S.S.R. **43** 44.57N 34.05E
Simiyu *r.* Tanzania **75** 2.32S 33.25E
Simla India **56** 31.07N 77.09E
Simmern W. Germany **41** 49.59N 7.32E
Simo *r.* Finland **42** 65.38N 24.57E
Simonsbath England **27** 51.07N 3.45W
Simonstown R.S.A. **76** 34.12S 18.26E
Simplon Pass Switz. **36** 46.15N 8.03E
Simplon Tunnel Italy/Switz. **40** 46.20N 8.05E
Simpson Desert Australia **82** 25.00S 136.50E
Simrishamn Sweden **42** 55.35N 14.20E
Sinai *pen.* Egypt **54** 29.00N 34.00E
Sinan China **63** 27.51N 108.24E
Sinclair's B. Scotland **33** 58.30N 3.07W
Sines Portugal **37** 37.58N 8.52W
Singapore Asia **58** 1.20N 103.45E
Singapore *town* Singapore **58** 1.20N 103.45E
Singaraja Indonesia **58** 8.06S 115.07E
Singen W. Germany **40** 47.45N 8.50E
Singida Tanzania **75** 4.45S 34.42E
Singida *d.* Tanzania **75** 6.00S 34.30E
Singitikos G. Med. Sea **39** 40.12N 24.00E
Singkawang Indonesia **58** 0.57N 108.57E
Singkep *i.* Indonesia **58** 0.30S 104.20E
Sinj Yugo. **39** 43.42N 16.38E
Sinoia Zimbabwe **76** 17.21S 30.13E
Sinop Turkey **54** 42.02N 35.09E
Sintang Indonesia **58** 0.03N 111.31E
Sint Eustatius *i.* Neth. Antilles **101** 17.33N 63.00W

Sinu *r.* Colombia **101** 9.25N 76.00W
Sinuiju N. Korea **61** 40.04N 124.25E
Sioux City U.S.A. **97** 42.30N 96.28W
Sioux Falls *town* U.S.A. **97** 43.34N 96.42W
Sioux Lookout *town* Canada **97** 50.07N 91.54W
Siping China **62** 43.15N 124.25E
Sipolilo Zimbabwe **76** 16.43S 30.43E
Sipora *i.* Indonesia **58** 2.10S 99.40E
Sira *r.* Norway **42** 58.13N 6.13E
Siracusa Italy **38** 37.05N 15.17E
Siret *r.* Romania **39** 45.28N 27.56E
Sirhan, Wadi *f.* Saudi Arabia **54** 31.00N 37.30E
Sirra, Wadi *r.* Saudi Arabia **55** 23.10N 44.22E
Sirte Libya **70** 31.10N 16.39E
Sirte, G. of Libya **70** 31.45N 17.50E
Sisak Yugo. **38** 45.30N 16.21E
Sishen R.S.A. **76** 27.47S 23.00E
Sisophon Cambodia **57** 13.37N 102.58E
Sisteron France **36** 44.16N 5.56E
Sitapur India **56** 27.33N 80.40E
Sitka U.S.A. **94** 57.05N 135.20W
Sittang *r.* Burma **57** 17.30N 96.53E
Sittard Neth. **41** 51.00N 5.52E
Sittingbourne England **25** 51.20N 0.43E
Sivas Turkey **54** 39.44N 37.01E
Sivrihisar Turkey **54** 39.29N 31.32E
Siwa Egypt **54** 29.11N 25.31E
Siwa Oasis Egypt **54** 29.10N 25.45E
Sixmilebridge *town* Rep. of Ire. **35** 52.45N 8.47W
Sixmilecross N. Ireland **30** 54.34N 7.08W
Skagen Denmark **42** 57.44N 10.37E
Skagerrak *str.* Denmark/Norway **42** 57.45N 8.55E
Skagway U.S.A. **94** 59.23N 135.20W
Skaill Scotland **33** 58.56N 2.43W
Skalintyy *mtn.* U.S.S.R. **45** 56.00N 130.40E
Skara Sweden **42** 58.23N 13.25E
Skaw Taing *c.* Scotland **32** 60.23N 0.56W
Skeena *r.* Canada **94** 54.10N 129.08W
Skegness England **29** 53.09N 0.20E
Skellefte *r.* Sweden **42** 64.44N 21.07E
Skellefteå Sweden **42** 64.45N 21.00E
Skelmersdale England **28** 53.34N 2.49W
Skelmorlie Scotland **30** 55.51N 4.52W
Skene Sweden **42** 57.30N 12.35E
Skerries Rep. of Ire. **34** 53.35N 6.07W
Skerryvore *i.* Scotland **30** 56.20N 7.05W
Skewen Wales **27** 51.40N 3.51W
Skhiza *i.* Greece **39** 36.42N 21.45E
Ski Norway **42** 59.43N 10.52E
Skibbereen Rep. of Ire. **35** 51.34N 9.16W
Skiddaw *mtn.* England **28** 54.40N 3.09W
Skien Norway **42** 59.14N 9.37E
Skikda Algeria **38** 36.53N 6.54E
Skipness Scotland **30** 56.45N 5.22W
Skipton England **28** 53.57N 2.01W
Skíros *i.* Greece **39** 38.50N 24.33E
Skjálfanda Fljót *r.* Iceland **42** 65.55N 17.30W
Skokholm *i.* Wales **27** 51.42N 5.17W
Skokie U.S.A. **98** 42.01N 87.45W
Skomer *i.* Wales **27** 51.45N 5.18W
Skopje Yugo. **39** 41.58N 21.27E
Skövde Sweden **42** 58.24N 13.52E
Skovorodino U.S.S.R. **45** 54.00N 123.53E
Skreia Norway **42** 60.38N 10.57E
Skull Rep. of Ire. **35** 51.32N 9.33W
Skye *i.* Scotland **32** 57.20N 6.15W
Slagelse Denmark **42** 55.24N 11.23E
Slaidburn England **28** 53.57N 2.28W
Slamat *mtn.* Indonesia **58** 7.10S 109.10E
Slane Rep. of Ire. **34** 53.43N 6.33W
Slaney *r.* Rep. of Ire. **35** 52.21N 6.30W
Slantsy U.S.S.R. **42** 59.09N 28.09E
Slapin, Loch Scotland **32** 57.10N 6.01W
Slatina Romania **39** 44.26N 24.23E
Slave *r.* Canada **94** 51.10N 113.30W
Slavgorod R.S.F.S.R. U.S.S.R. **44** 53.01N 78.37E
Slavgorod W.R.S.S.R. U.S.S.R. **43** 53.25N 31.00E
Slavyansk U.S.S.R. **43** 48.51N 37.36E
Sleaford England **29** 53.00N 0.22W
Slea Head Rep. of Ire. **35** 52.05N 10.27W
Sleat, Pt. of Scotland **32** 57.01N 6.01W
Sleat, Sd. of *str.* Scotland **32** 57.05N 5.48W
Sledmere England **29** 54.04N 0.35W
Sleetmute U.S.A. **94** 61.40N 157.11W
Sleights England **29** 54.26N 0.40W
Sliabh Gaoil *mtn.* Scotland **30** 55.54N 5.30W
Slide Mtn. U.S.A. **99** 42.00N 74.23W
Sliedrecht Neth. **41** 51.48N 4.46E
Slieveardagh Hills Rep. of Ire. **35** 52.39N 7.32W
Slieve Aughty *mtn.* Rep. of Ire. **35** 53.05N 8.37W
Slieve Aughty Mts. Rep. of Ire. **35** 53.05N 8.31W
Slieve Bernagh *mts.* Rep. of Ire. **35** 52.48N 8.35W
Slieve Bloom Mts. Rep. of Ire. **35** 53.03N 7.35W
Slieve Callan *mtn.* Rep. of Ire. **35** 52.51N 9.18W
Slieve Donard *mtn.* N. Ireland **34** 54.11N 5.56W
Slieve Felim Mts. Rep. of Ire. **35** 52.40N 8.16W
Slieve Fyagh *mtn.* Rep. of Ire. **34** 54.12N 9.42W
Slieve Gamph *mts.* Rep. of Ire. **34** 54.06N 8.52W
Slievekimalta *mtn.* Rep. of Ire. **35** 52.45N 8.17W
Slieve Mish *mts.* Rep. of Ire. **35** 52.48N 9.48W
Slieve Miskish *mts.* Rep. of Ire. **35** 51.41N 9.56W
Slievemore *mtn.* Rep. of Ire. **34** 54.01N 10.04W
Slieve Na Calliagh *mtn.* Rep. of Ire. **34** 53.45N 7.06W
Slievenamon *mtn.* Rep. of Ire. **35** 52.25N 7.34W
Slieve Snaght *mtn.* Donegal Rep. of Ire. **34** 55.12N 7.20W
Sligachan Scotland **32** 57.17N 6.10W
Sligo Rep. of Ire. **34** 54.17N 8.28W
Sligo *d.* Rep. of Ire. **34** 54.10N 8.35W
Sligo B. Rep. of Ire. **34** 54.18N 8.40W
Slioch *mtn.* Scotland **32** 57.40N 5.20W
Sliven Bulgaria **39** 42.41N 26.19E
Slobodskoy U.S.S.R. **43** 58.42N 50.10E
Slough England **23** 51.30N 0.35W
Sluch *r.* U.S.S.R. **43** 52.05N 27.52E
Sluis Neth. **41** 51.18N 3.23E
Słupsk Poland **40** 54.28N 17.00E
Slyne Head Rep. of Ire. **34** 53.25N 10.12W
Slyudyanka U.S.S.R. **60** 51.40N 103.40E
Smithfield R.S.A. **76** 30.13S 26.32E
Smith's Falls *town* Canada **99** 44.54N 76.01W
Smöla *i.* Norway **42** 63.20N 8.00E
Smolensk U.S.S.R. **43** 54.49N 32.04E
Smólikas *mtn.* Greece **39** 40.06N 20.55E
Smolyan Bulgaria **39** 41.34N 24.45E
Smorgon U.S.S.R. **43** 54.28N 27.20E
Snaefell *mtn.* I.o.M. **28** 54.16N 4.28W
Snaith England **29** 53.42N 1.01W
Snake *r.* Idaho U.S.A. **96** 43.50N 117.05W
Snake *r.* Wash. U.S.A. **96** 46.15N 119.00W
Snåsa Norway **42** 64.15N 12.23E
Snåsavatn *l.* Norway **42** 64.10N 12.00E
Sneek Neth. **41** 53.03N 5.40E
Sneem Rep. of Ire. **35** 51.50N 9.54W
Sneeuwberg *mtn.* R.S.A. **76** 32.20S 19.10E
Snizort, Loch Scotland **32** 57.35N 6.30W
Snodland England **23** 51.20N 0.27E
Snöhetta *mtn.* Norway **42** 62.15N 9.05E
Snook Pt. England **31** 55.31N 1.35W
Snowdon *mtn.* Wales **26** 53.05N 4.05W
Snowy *r.* Australia **83** 37.49S 148.30E
Snowy Mtn. U.S.A. **99** 43.42N 74.23W
Snowy Mts. Australia **83** 36.25S 145.15E
Soalala Madagascar **75** 16.08S 45.21E
Soar *r.* England **29** 52.52N 1.17W
Soasiu Indonesia **59** 0.40N 127.25E
Soay *i.* Scotland **32** 57.09N 6.13W
Soay Sd. *str.* Scotland **32** 57.09N 6.16W
Sobat *r.* Sudan/Ethiopia **71** 9.30N 31.30E
Sobernheim W. Germany **41** 49.47N 7.40E
Sobral Brazil **108** 3.45S 40.20W
Sochi U.S.S.R. **43** 43.35N 39.46E
Society Is. Pacific Oc. **112** 17.00S 150.00W
Socotra *i.* Indian Oc. **71** 12.30N 54.00E
Sodankylä Finland **42** 67.21N 26.31E
Söderhamn Sweden **42** 61.19N 17.10E
Södertälje Sweden **42** 59.11N 17.39E
Soest W. Germany **41** 51.34N 8.06E
Sofala *d.* Moçambique **75** 17.30S 34.00E
Sofia Bulgaria **39** 42.41N 23.19E
Sogne Fjord *est.* Norway **42** 61.10N 5.50E
Söğüt Turkey **54** 40.02N 30.10E
Sohag Egypt **54** 26.33N 31.42E
Soham England **25** 52.20N 0.20E
Sohar Oman **55** 24.23N 56.43E
Soignies Belgium **41** 50.35N 4.04E
Soissons France **36** 49.23N 3.20E
Söke Turkey **39** 37.46N 27.26E
Sokodé Togo **73** 8.59N 1.11E
Sokol U.S.S.R. **43** 59.28N 40.04E
Sokolo Mali **72** 14.53N 6.11W
Sokoto Nigeria **73** 13.02N 5.15E
Sokoto *d.* Nigeria **73** 11.50N 5.05E
Sokoto *r.* Nigeria **73** 13.05N 5.13E
Soledad Colombia **101** 10.54N 74.58W
Solihull England **24** 52.26N 1.47W
Solingen W. Germany **41** 51.10N 7.05E
Sollas Scotland **32** 57.39N 7.22W
Sollefteå Sweden **42** 63.09N 17.15E
Soller Spain **37** 39.47N 2.41E
Solling *mtn.* W. Germany **40** 51.45N 9.30E
Solomon Is. Austa. **131** 10.00S 160.00E
Solomon Sea Austa. **82** 7.00S 150.00E
Solta *i.* Yugo. **38** 43.23N 16.17E
Solway Firth *est.* England/Scotland **28** 54.50N 3.30W
Solwezi Zambia **75** 12.11S 26.23E
Soma Turkey **39** 39.11N 27.36E
Somabula Zimbabwe **76** 19.40S 29.38E
Somali Republic Africa **71** 5.30N 47.00E
Sombor Yugo. **39** 45.48N 19.08E
Somerset *d.* England **24** 51.09N 3.00W
Somerset East R.S.A. **76** 32.44S 25.35E
Somerset I. Canada **95** 73.00N 93.30W
Somerton England **24** 51.03N 2.44W
Somes *r.* Hungary **43** 48.40N 22.30E
Somme *r.* France **36** 50.01N 1.40E
Son *r.* India **56** 25.55N 84.55E
Sönderborg Denmark **40** 54.55N 9.48E
Sondrio Italy **40** 46.11N 9.52E
Song Ca *r.* Vietnam **63** 18.47N 105.40E
Songea Tanzania **75** 10.42S 35.39E
Song Gam *r.* Vietnam **63** 21.12N 105.23E
Songhua Jiang *r.* China **61** 47.46N 132.30E
Songjiang China **63** 31.01N 121.20E
Songkhla Thailand **57** 7.13N 100.37E
Song Ma *r.* Vietnam **63** 19.48N 105.55E
Songololo Zaïre **74** 5.40S 14.05E
Son La Vietnam **58** 21.20N 103.55E
Sonneberg E. Germany **40** 50.22N 11.10E
Sonora *r.* Mexico **96** 28.45N 111.55W
Sonsorol *i.* Asia **59** 5.20N 132.13E
Son Tay Vietnam **63** 21.15N 105.17E
Sorel Canada **99** 46.03N 73.06W
Soria Spain **37** 41.46N 2.28W
Sorisdale Scotland **30** 56.40N 6.28W
Sor Kvalöy *i.* Norway **42** 69.45N 18.20E
Sorocaba Brazil **110** 23.30S 47.32W
Sorol *i.* Asia **59** 8.09N 140.25E
Sorong Asia **59** 0.50S 131.17E
Soroti Uganda **75** 1.40N 33.37E
Söröya *i.* Norway **42** 70.30N 22.30E
Sorraia *r.* Portugal **37** 39.00N 8.51W
Sorsele Sweden **42** 65.32N 17.34E
Sortavala U.S.S.R. **42** 61.40N 30.40E
Sotik Kenya **75** 0.40S 35.08E
Sotra *i.* Norway **42** 60.20N 5.00E
Souk Ahras Algeria **38** 36.14N 7.59E
Soure Portugal **37** 40.04N 8.38W
Souris *r.* U.S.A. **96** 49.38N 99.35W
Sousse Tunisia **38** 35.48N 10.38E
Soustons France **36** 43.45N 1.19W
Southall England **23** 51.31N 0.23W
Southam England **24** 52.16N 1.24W
South America 108
Southampton England **24** 50.54N 1.23W
Southampton I. Canada **95** 64.30N 84.00W
Southampton Water *est.* England **24** 50.52N 1.21W
South Atlantic Ocean 109
South Australia *d.* Australia **82** 29.00S 135.00E
South Barrule *mtn.* I.o.M. **28** 54.09N 4.41W
South Bend U.S.A. **98** 41.40N 86.15W
South Benfleet England **23** 51.33N 0.34E
South Beveland *f.* Neth. **41** 51.30N 3.50E
Southborough England **25** 51.10N 0.15E
South Brent England **27** 50.26N 3.50W
South Carolina *d.* U.S.A. **97** 34.00N 81.00W
South Cave England **29** 53.46N 0.37W
South Cerney England **24** 51.40N 1.55W
South China Sea Asia **58** 12.30N 115.00E
South Dakota *d.* U.S.A. **96** 44.30N 100.00W
South Dorset Downs *hills* England **24** 50.40N 2.25W
South Downs *hills* England **24** 50.04N 0.34W
South East C. Australia **83** 43.38S 146.48E
Southend Scotland **30** 55.19N 5.38W
Southend-on-Sea England **25** 51.32N 0.43E
Southern Alps *mts.* New Zealand **85** 43.20S 170.45E
Southern Cross Australia **82** 31.14S 119.16E
Southern Lueti *r.* Zambia **76** 16.16S 23.15E
Southern Uplands *hills* Scotland **31** 55.30N 3.30W
Southern Yemen Asia **71** 16.00N 49.30E
South Esk *r.* Scotland **31** 56.43N 2.32W
South Flevoland *f.* Neth. **41** 52.22N 5.22E
South Foreland *c.* England **25** 51.08N 1.24E
Southgate England **23** 51.38N 0.07W
South Georgia *i.* Atlantic Oc. **109** 54.00S 37.00W
South Glamorgan *d.* Wales **27** 51.27N 3.22W
South-haa Scotland **32** 60.34N 1.17W
South Harris *f.* Scotland **32** 57.49N 6.55W
South Haven U.S.A. **98** 42.25N 86.16W
South Hayling England **24** 50.47N 0.56W
South Holland *d.* Neth. **41** 52.00N 4.30E
South Hornchurch England **23** 51.32N 0.13E
South Horr Kenya **75** 2.10N 36.45E
South I. New Zealand **85** 43.00S 171.00E
South Kirby England **29** 53.35N 1.25W
South Korea Asia **61** 36.00N 128.00E
Southland *f.* New Zealand **85** 45.40S 167.15E
Southminster England **25** 51.40N 0.51E
South Molton England **27** 51.01N 3.50W
South Nahanni *r.* Canada **94** 61.00N 123.20W
South Norwood England **23** 51.24N 0.04W
South Nutfield England **23** 51.14N 0.06W
South Ockendon England **23** 51.32N 0.18E
South Orkney Is. Atlantic Oc. **109** 63.00S 45.00W
South Oxhey England **23** 51.38N 0.24W
Southport Australia **83** 27.58S 153.20E
Southport England **28** 53.38N 3.01W
South Ronaldsay *i.* Scotland **33** 58.47N 2.56W
South Sandwich Is. Atlantic Oc. **109** 58.00S 27.00W
South Sandwich Trench Atlantic Oc. **109** 57.00S 25.00W
South Saskatchewan *r.* Canada **96** 50.45N 108.30W
South Sd. Rep. of Ire. **35** 53.03N 9.28W
South Shetland Is. Antarctica **112** 62.00S 60.00W
South Shields England **29** 55.00N 1.24W
South Tyne *r.* England **31** 54.59N 2.08W

Sunagawa Japan **64** 43.30N 141.55E
Sunart f. Scotland **32** 56.44N 5.35W
Sunart, Loch Scotland **32** 56.43N 5.45W
Sunbury England **23** 51.24N 0.25W
Sunbury U.S.A. **99** 40.52N 76.47W
Sundarbans f. India/Bangla. **56** 22.00N 89.00E
Sundargarh India **56** 22 04N 84.08E
Sunda Str. Indonesia **58** 6.00S 105.50E
Sundays r. R.S.A. **76** 33.49S 25.46E
Sunderland England **31** 54.55N 1.22W
Sundsvall Sweden **42** 62.22N 17.20E
Sungaipenuh Indonesia **58** 2.00S 101.28E
Sungguminasa Indonesia **58** 5.14S 119.27E
Sungurlu Turkey **54** 40.10N 34.23E
Sunninghill town England **23** 51.24N 0.39W
Sunwu r. China **61** 53.30N 121.48E
Sunyani Ghana **72** 7.22N 2.18W
Suomussalmi Finland **42** 64.52N 29.10E
Suo nada str. Japan **64** 33.45N 131.30E
Suonenjoki Finland **42** 62.40N 27.06E
Supaul India **56** 26.57N 86.15E
Superior U.S.A. **98** 46.42N 92.05W
Superior, L. N. America **98** 48.00N 88.00W
Süphan Dağlari mtn. Turkey **54** 38.55N 42.55E
Sur Oman **55** 22.23N 59.32E
Sura U.S.S.R. **43** 53.52N 45.45E
Sura r. U.S.S.R. **43** 56.13N 46.00E
Surabaya Indonesia **58** 7.14S 112.45E
Surakarta Indonesia **58** 7.32S 110.50E
Surat Australia **83** 27.10S 149.05E
Surat India **56** 21.10N 72.54E
Surat Thani Thailand **57** 9.03N 99.28E
Surbiton England **23** 51.24N 0.19W
Sûre r. Lux. **41** 49.43N 6.31E
Surigao Phil. **59** 9.47N 125.29E
Surin Thailand **57** 14.50N 103.34E
Surinam S. America **108** 4.30N 56.00W
Surrey d. England **25** 51.16N 0.30W
Surrey Hill England **23** 51.23N 0.43W
Surtsey i. Iceland **42** 63.18N 20.37W
Susquehanna r. U.S.A. **99** 39.33N 76.05W
Sutherland R.S.A. **76** 32.24S 20.40E
Sutlej r. Pakistan **56** 29.26N 71.09E
Sutton G.L. England **23** 51.22N 0.12W
Sutton Surrey England **23** 51.12N 0.26W
Sutton Bridge England **29** 52.46N 0.12E
Sutton Coldfield England **24** 52.33N 1.50W
Sutton in Ashfield England **29** 53.08N 1.16W
Sutton on Sea England **29** 53.18N 0.18E
Suwanee r. U.S.A. **100** 29.15N 82.50W
Suwon S. Korea **61** 37.16N 126.59E
Su Xian China **62** 33.38N 117.02E
Suzhou China **63** 31.22N 120.45E
Suzu misaki c. Japan **64** 37.30N 137.21E
Svartisen mtn. Norway **42** 66.30N 14.00E
Sveg Sweden **42** 62.02N 14.20E
Svendborg Denmark **42** 55.04N 10.38E
Sverdlovsk U.S.S.R. **44** 56.52N 60.35E
Svetogorsk U.S.S.R. **42** 61.07N 28.50E
Svishtov Bulgaria **39** 43.36N 25.23E
Svobodnyy U.S.S.R. **61** 51.24N 128.05E
Svolvaer Norway **42** 68.15N 14.40E
Swabian Jura mts. W. Germany **40** 48.20N 9.20E
Swadlincote England **29** 52.47N 1.34W
Swaffham England **25** 52.38N 0.42E
Swakop r. Namibia **76** 22.38S 14.30E
Swakopmund Namibia **76** 22.40S 14.34E
Swale r. England **29** 54.05N 1.20W
Swanage England **24** 50.36N 1.59W
Swan Hill town Australia **83** 35.23S 143.37E
Swanley England **23** 51.24N 0.12E
Swanlinbar Rep. of Ire. **34** 54.12N 7.44W
Swan River town Canada **96** 52.06N 101.17W
Swanscombe England **23** 51.26N 0.19E
Swansea Wales **27** 51.37N 3.57W
Swansea B. Wales **27** 51.33N 3.50W
Swarbacks Minn str. Scotland **32** 60.22N 1.21W
Swartberg Range mts. R.S.A. **76** 33.20S 22.00E
Swaziland Africa **76** 26.30S 32.00E
Sweden Europe **42** 63.00N 16.00E
Sweetwater U.S.A. **96** 32.37N 100.25W
Swidnica Poland **40** 50.51N 16.29E
Swift Current town Canada **96** 50.17N 107.49W
Swilly r. Rep. of Ire. **34** 54.57N 7.42W
Swilly, Lough Rep. of Ire. **34** 55.10N 7.32W
Swindon England **24** 51.33N 1.47W
Swinford Rep. of Ire. **34** 53.56N 8.57W
Swinoujscie Poland **40** 53.55N 14.18E
Switzerland Europe **40** 47.00N 8.15E
Swords Rep. of Ire. **34** 53.27N 6.15W
Syderö i. Faroe Is. **42** 61.30N 6.50W
Sydney Australia **83** 33.55S 151.10E
Sydney Canada **95** 46.10N 60.10W
Syktyvkar U.S.S.R. **44** 61.42N 50.45E
Sylhet Bangla. **57** 24.53N 91.51E
Sylt i. W. Germany **40** 54.50N 8.20E
Syracuse U.S.A. **99** 43.03N 76.10W
Syr Darya r. U.S.S.R. **44** 46.00N 61.12E

Syria Asia **54** 35.00N 38.00E
Syriam Burma **58** 16.45N 96.17E
Syrian Desert Asia **54** 32.00N 39.00E
Syzran U.S.S.R. **43** 53.10N 48.29E
Szczecin Poland **40** 53.25N 14.32E
Szczecinek Poland **40** 53.42N 16.41E
Szeged Hungary **39** 46.16N 20.08E
Szekszárd Hungary **39** 46.22N 18.44E
Szombathely Hungary **43** 47.12N 16.38E

T

Tabarka Tunisia **38** 36.56N 8.43E
Tabas Khorā saⁿ Iran **55** 32.48N 60.14E
Tabas Khorā saⁿ Iran **55** 33.36N 56.55E
Tabasco d. Mexico **100** 18.30N 93.00W
Table B. R.S.A. **76** 33.30S 18.05E
Tabor Czech. **40** 49.25N 14.41E
Tabora Tanzania **75** 5.02S 32.50E
Tabora d. Tanzania **75** 5.30S 32.50E
Tabou Ivory Coast **72** 4.28N 7.20W
Tabriz Iran **55** 38.05N 46.18E
Tabūk Saudi Arabia **54** 28.25N 36.35E
Tacloban Phil. **59** 11.15N 124.59E
Tacoma U.S.A. **96** 47.16N 122.30W
Taconic Mts. U.S.A. **99** 42.00N 73.45W
Tacuarembó Uruguay **110** 31.42S 56.00W
Tadcaster England **29** 53.53N 1.16W
Tademait Plateau Algeria **70** 28.45N 2.10E
Tadoussac Canada **99** 48.09N 69.43W
Tadzhikistan Soviet Socialist Republic d. U.S.S.R. **60** 39.00N 70.30E
Taegu S. Korea **61** 35.52N 128.36E
Taejon S. Korea **61** 36.20N 127.26E
Tafersit Morocco **37** 35.01N 3.33W
Taganrog U.S.S.R. **43** 47.14N 38.55E
Taganrog, G. of U.S.S.R. **43** 47.00N 38.30E
Tagaytay City Phil. **59** 14.07N 120.58E
Tagbilaran Phil. **59** 9.38N 123.53E
Taghmon Rep. of Ire. **35** 52.20N 6.40W
Tagus r. Portugal **37** 39.00N 8.57W
Tahat, Mt. Algeria **73** 23.30N 5.40E
Tai'an China **62** 36.16N 117.13E
Taibai Shan mtn. China **62** 33.55N 107.45E
Taichung Taiwan **63** 24.11N 120.40E
Taihape New Zealand **85** 39.40S 175.48E
Tai Hu l. China **63** 31.15N 120.10E
Taima Saudi Arabia **54** 27.37N 38.30E
Tain Scotland **33** 57.48N 4.04W
Tainan Taiwan **63** 23.01N 120.12E
Taipei Taiwan **63** 25.05N 121.30E
Taiping Malaysia **58** 4.54N 100.42E
Taishan China **63** 22.10N 112.57E
Taitung Taiwan **63** 22.49N 121.10E
Taivalkoski Finland **42** 65.35N 28.20E
Taiwan Asia **63** 24.00N 121.00E
Taiyuan China **62** 37.48N 112.33E
Taizhou China **62** 32.22N 119.58E
Taizi He r. China **61** 41.07N 122.43E
Taizz Yemen **71** 13.35N 44.02E
Tajan Indonesia **58** 0.02S 110.05E
Tajrish Iran **55** 35.48N 51.20E
Tajuna r. Spain **37** 40.10N 3.35W
Tak Thailand **57** 16.47N 99.10E
Takada Japan **64** 37.06N 138.15E
Takalar Indonesia **58** 5.29S 119.26E
Takamatsu Japan **64** 34.28N 134.05E
Takaoka Japan **64** 36.47N 137.00E
Takasaki Japan **64** 36.20N 139.00E
Takeley England **23** 51.52N 0.15E
Takestan Iran **55** 36.02N 49.40E
Takht-i-Suleiman mtn. Iran **55** 36.23N 50.59E
Taklimakan Shamo des. China **60** 38.10N 82.00E
Talasskiy Ala Tau mts. U.S.S.R. **42** 42.20N 73.20E
Talaud Is. Indonesia **59** 4.20N 126 50E
Talavera de la Reina Spain **37** 39.58N 4.50W
Talca Chile **109** 35.28S 71.40W
Talcahuano Chile **109** 36.40S 73.10W
Taldom U.S.S.R. **43** 56.49N 37.30E
Talgarth Wales **26** 51.59N 3.15W
Taliabu i. Indonesia **59** 1.50S 124.55E
Talkeetna U.S.A. **94** 62.20N 150.09W
Tallahassee U.S.A. **97** 30.28N 84.19W
Tallinn U.S.S.R. **42** 59.22N 24.48E
Tallow Rep. of Ire. **35** 52.06N 8.01W
Talsi U.S.S.R. **43** 57.18N 22.39E
Tamale Ghana **72** 9.26N 0.49W
Tamanrasset Algeria **73** 22.50N 5.31E
Tamar r. England **27** 50.28N 4.13W
Tamatave Madagascar **69** 18.10S 49.23E
Tamaulipas d. Mexico **100** 24.00N 98.20W
Tambacounda Senegal **72** 13.45N 13.40W
Tambohorano Madagascar **75** 17.40S 43.59E
Tambov U.S.S.R. **43** 52.44N 41.28E
Tambre r. Spain **37** 42.50N 8.55W
Tamega r. Portugal **37** 41.04N 8.17W

Tamil Nadu d. India **57** 11.15N 79.00E
Tampa U.S.A. **97** 27.58N 82.38W
Tampa B. U.S.A. **100** 27.48N 82.15W
Tampere Finland **42** 61.32N 23.45E
Tampico Mexico **100** 22.18N 97.52W
Tamsag Bulag Mongolia **61** 47.10N 117.21E
Tamworth Australia **83** 31.07S 150.57E
Tamworth England **24** 52.38N 1.42W
Tana r. Kenya **75** 2.32S 40.32E
Tana r. Norway **42** 70.26N 28.14E
Tana r. Norway **42** 69.45N 28.15E
Tana, L. Ethiopia **71** 12.00N 37.20E
Tanacross U.S.A. **94** 63.12N 143.30W
Tanana U.S.A. **94** 65.11N 152.10W
Tananarive Madagascar **69** 18.52S 47.30E
Tanaro r. Italy **38** 45.01N 8.46E
Tanat r. Wales **26** 52.46N 3.07W
Tanderagee N. Ireland **34** 54.22N 6.27W
Tandil Argentina **110** 37.18S 59.10W
Tandjungpandan Indonesia **58** 2.44S 107.36E
Tanega shima i. Japan **64** 30.32N 131.00E
Tanga Tanzania **75** 5.07S 39.05E
Tanga d. Tanzania **75** 5.20S 38.30E
Tanganyika, L. Africa **75** 6.00S 29.30E
Tanger see Tangier Morocco **37**
Tanggu China **62** 39.01N 117.43E
Tanggula Shan mts. China **60** 32.40N 92.30E
Tangier Morocco **37** 35.48N 5.45W
Tangra Yumco l. China **57** 31.00N 86.30E
Tangshan China **62** 39.32N 118.08E
Tanimbar Is. Indonesia **59** 7.50S 131.30E
Tanjay Phil. **59** 9.31N 123.10E
Tanjungbalai Indonesia **58** 2.59N 99.46E
Tanjung Datu c. Malaysia **58** 2.00N 109.30E
Tanjungkarang Indonesia **58** 5.28S 105.16E
Tanjung Puting c. Indonesia **58** 3.35S 111.52E
Tanjungredeb Indonesia **58** 2.09N 117.29E
Tanjung Selatan c. Indonesia **58** 4.20S 114.45E
Tannu Ola Range mts. U.S.S.R. **45** 51.00N 93.30E
Tano r. Ghana **72** 5.07N 2.54W
Tanout Niger **73** 14.55N 8.49E
Tanta Egypt **54** 30.48N 31.00E
Tanzania Africa **75** 5.00S 35.00E
Tao'an China **62** 45.20N 122.48E
Taoudenni Mali **72** 22.45N 4.00W
Tapachula Mexico **100** 14.54N 92.15W
Tapajós r. Brazil **108** 2.40S 55.30W
Tapa Shan mts. China **63** 32.00N 109.00E
Tapti r. India **56** 21.05N 72.45E
Taquari r. Brazil **110** 19.00S 57.22W
Tara r. U.S.S.R. **44** 56.30N 74.40E
Tara r. Yugo. **39** 43.23N 18.47E
Tarakan Indonesia **58** 3.20N 117.38E
Tarancón Spain **37** 40.01N 3.01W
Taransay i. Scotland **32** 57.53N 7.03W
Taranto Italy **39** 40.28N 17.14E
Taranto, G. of Italy **39** 40.00N 17.20E
Tarbagatay Range mts. U.S.S.R. **60** 47.00N 83.00E
Tarbat Ness c. Scotland **33** 57.52N 3.46W
Tarbert Rep. of Ire. **35** 52.34N 9.24W
Tarbert Strath. Scotland **30** 55.51N 5.25W
Tarbert W. Isles Scotland **32** 57.54N 6.49W
Tarbert, Loch Scotland **30** 55.48N 5.31W
Tarbes France **36** 43.14N 0.05E
Tarboiro r. France **36** 45.57N 1.00W
Tarbolton Scotland **30** 55.31N 4.29W
Tardoire r. France **36** 45.57N 1.00W
Taree Australia **83** 31.54S 152.26E
Tarifa Spain **37** 36.01N 5.36W
Tarija Bolivia **110** 21.33S 64.45W
Tarija d. Bolivia **110** 21.30S 64.00W
Tarim Basin f. Asia **113** 40.00N 83.00E
Tarim He r. China **60** 41.00N 83.30E
Tarkwa Ghana **72** 5.16N 1.59W
Tarlac Phil. **59** 15.29N 120.35E
Tarland Scotland **33** 57.08N 2.52W
Tarleton England **28** 53.41N 2.50W
Tarn r. France **36** 44.15N 1.15E
Tarnow Poland **43** 50.01N 20.59E
Tarporley England **28** 53.10N 2.42W
Tarragona Spain **37** 41.07N 1.15E
Tarrasa Spain **37** 41.34N 2.00E
Tarsus Turkey **54** 36.52N 34.52E
Tartary, G. of U.S.S.R. **45** 47.40N 141.00E
Tartu U.S.S.R. **42** 58.20N 26.44E
Tarutung Indonesia **58** 2.01N 98.54E
Tashkent U.S.S.R. **60** 41.16N 69.13E
Tasikmalaya Indonesia **58** 7.20S 108.16E
Tasman B. New Zealand **85** 41.00S 173.15E
Tasmania d. Australia **83** 42.00S 147.00E
Tasman Mts. New Zealand **85** 41.00S 172.40E
Tasman Pen. Australia **83** 43.08S 147.51E
Tasman Sea Pacific Oc. **113** 38.00S 163.00E
Tatarsk U.S.S.R. **44** 55.14N 76.00E
Tatnam, C. Canada **95** 57.00N 91.00W
Tatsfield England **23** 51.18N 0.02E
Tatvan Turkey **54** 38.31N 42.15E
Taubaté Brazil **110** 23.00S 45.36W

Taumarunui New Zealand 85 38.53S 175.16E
Taung R.S.A. 76 27.32S 24.48E
Taung-gyi Burma 57 20.49N 97.01E
Taunton England 27 51.01N 3.07W
Taunton U.S.A. 99 41.54N 71.06W
Taunus mts. W. Germany 40 50.07N 7.48E
Taupo New Zealand 85 38.42S 176.06E
Taupo, L. New Zealand 85 38.45S 175.30E
Tauranga New Zealand 85 37.42S 176.11E
Taurus Mts. Turkey 54 37.15N 34.15E
Taveta Kenya 75 3.23S 37.42E
Tavira Portugal 37 37.07N 7.39W
Tavistock England 27 50.33N 4.09W
Tavoy Burma 57 14.07N 98.18E
Tavy r. England 27 50.27N 4.10W
Taw r. England 27 51.05N 4.05W
Tawau Malaysia 58 4.16N 117.54E
Tawe r. Wales 27 51.38N 3.56W
Tay r. Scotland 31 56.21N 3.18W
Tay, Loch Scotland 30 56.32N 4.08W
Taylor, Mt. U.S.A. 96 35.14N 107.36W
Taymyr, L. U.S.S.R. 45 74.20N 101.00E
Taymyr Pen. U.S.S.R. 45 75.30N 99.00E
Taynuilt Scotland 30 56.26N 5.14W
Tayport Scotland 31 56.27N 2.53W
Tayshet U.S.S.R. 45 55.56N 98.01E
Tayside d. Scotland 31 56.35N 3.28W
Taytay Phil. 58 10.47N 119.32E
Taz r. U.S.S.R. 44 67.30N 78.50E
Tbilisi U.S.S.R. 55 41.43N 44.48E
Tchibanga Gabon 74 2.52S 11.07E
Te Anau New Zealand 85 45.25S 167.43E
Te Anau, L. New Zealand 85 45.10S 167.15E
Te Awamutu New Zealand 85 38.00S 175.20E
Tebessa Algeria 38 35.22N 8.08E
Tebingtinggi Indonesia 58 3.20N 99.08E
Tebingtinggi Indonesia 58 3.37S 103.09E
Tecuci Romania 39 45.49N 27.27E
Teddington England 23 51.25N 0.20W
Tees r. England 29 54.35N 1.11W
Tees B. England 29 54.40N 1.07W
Teesdale f. England 28 54.38N 2.08W
Tegal Indonesia 58 6.52S 109.07E
Tegucigalpa Honduras 100 14.05N 87.14W
Tehran Iran 55 35.40N 51.26E
Tehuacán Mexico 100 18.30N 97.26W
Tehuantepec Mexico 100 16.21N 95.13W
Tehuantepec, G. of Mexico 100 16.00N 95.00W
Tehuantepec, Isthmus of Mexico 100 17.00N 94.00W
Teifi r. Wales 26 52.05N 4.41W
Teign r. England 27 50.32N 3.46W
Teignmouth England 27 50.33N 3.30W
Teisenberg mtn. W. Germany 40 47.48N 12.46E
Teith r. Scotland 31 56.09N 4.00W
Tekapo, L. New Zealand 85 43.35S 170.30E
Tekirdağ Turkey 39 40.59N 27.30E
Te Kuiti New Zealand 85 38.20S 175.10E
Tela Honduras 100 15.56N 87.25W
Telavi U.S.S.R. 55 41.56N 45.30E
Tel-Aviv-Yafo Israel 54 32.05N 34.46E
Tele r. Zaire 74 2.48N 24.00E
Telford England 24 52.42N 2.30W
Telgte W. Germany 41 51.59N 7.46E
Telimélé Guinea 72 10.54N 13.02W
Tel Kotchek Syria 54 36.48N 42.04E
Tell Atlas mts. Algeria 70 36.10N 4.00E
Telok Anson Malaysia 58 4.00N 101.00E
Teluk Berau b. Asia 59 2.20S 133.00E
Telukbetung Indonesia 58 5.28S 105.16E
Teluk Irian b. Asia 59 2.30S 135.20E
Telungagung Indonesia 58 8.03S 111.54E
Tema Ghana 72 5.41N 0.01W
Tembo Aluma Angola 74 7.42S 17.15E
Teme r. England 24 52.10N 2.13W
Temirtau U.S.S.R. 44 50.05N 72.55E
Temora Australia 83 34.27S 147.35E
Témpio Italy 38 40.54N 9.06E
Temple U.S.A. 97 31.06N 97.22W
Temple Ewell England 25 51.09N 1.16E
Templemore Rep. of Ire. 35 52.48N 7.51W
Temuco Chile 109 38.45S 72.40W
Tenasserim Burma 58 12.05N 99.00E
Tenasserim d. Burma 57 13.00N 99.00E
Tenbury Wells England 24 52.18N 2.35W
Tenby Wales 27 51.40N 4.42W
Ten Degree Channel Indian Oc. 58 10.00N 92.30E
Tenerife i. Africa 70 28.10N 16.30W
Tengchong China 57 25.02N 98.28E
Tengiz, L. U.S.S.R. 44 50.30N 69.00E
Teng Xian China 62 35.08N 117.20E
Tenke Zaïre 74 10.34S 26.07E
Tennant Creek town Australia 82 19.31S 134.15E
Tennessee d. U.S.A. 97 36.00N 86.00W
Tennessee r. U.S.A. 97 37.10N 88.25W
Tenterden England 25 51.04N 0.42E
Tenterfield Australia 83 29.01S 152.04E
Teófilo Otoni Brazil 109 17.52S 41.31W
Teplice Czech. 40 50.40N 13.50E

Ter r. England 23 51.45N 0.36E
Ter r. Spain 37 42.02N 3.10E
Tera r. Portugal 37 38.55N 8.01W
Téramo Italy 38 42.40N 13.43E
Teresina Brazil 108 4.50S 42.50W
Termez U.S.S.R. 44 37.15N 67.15E
Termini Italy 38 37.59N 13.42E
Terminos Lagoon Mexico 100 18.30N 91.30W
Termoli Italy 38 41.58N 14.59E
Ternate Indonesia 59 0.48N 127.23E
Terneuzen Neth. 41 51.20N 3.50E
Terni Italy 38 42.34N 12.44E
Ternopol U.S.S.R. 43 49.35N 25.39E
Terre Haute U.S.A. 98 39.27N 87.24W
Terschelling i. Neth. 41 53.25N 5.25E
Teruel Spain 37 40.21N 1.06W
Teslin r. Canada 94 62.00N 135.00W
Tessaoua Niger 73 13.46N 7.55E
Test r. England 24 50.55N 1.29W
Tet r. France 36 42.43N 3.00E
Tetbury England 24 51.37N 2.09W
Tete Moçambique 75 16.10S 33.30E
Tete d. Moçambique 75 15.30S 33.00E
Teterev r. U.S.S.R. 43 51.14N 30.30E
Tetney England 29 53.30N 0.01W
Tetuan Morocco 37 35.34N 5.22W
Tetyukhe Pristan U.S.S.R. 64 44.17N 135.52E
Teuco r. Argentina 110 25.37S 60.10W
Teviot r. Scotland 31 55.36N 2.27W
Teviotdale f. Scotland 31 55.26N 2.46W
Teviothead Scotland 31 55.20N 2.56W
Tewkesbury England 24 51.59N 2.09W
Texarkana U.S.A. 97 33.28N 94.02W
Texas d. U.S.A. 96 32.00N 100.00W
Texel i. Neth. 41 53.05N 4.47E
Texoma, L. U.S.A. 97 34.00N 96.40W
Tezpur India 57 26.38N 92.49E
Thabana Ntlenyana mtn. Lesotho 76 29.30S 29.10E
Thabazimbi R.S.A. 76 24.41S 27.21E
Thai Binh Vietnam 63 20.30N 106.26E
Thailand Asia 57 16.00N 102.00E
Thai Nguyen Vietnam 63 21.46N 105.52E
Thakhek Laos 57 17.25N 104.45E
Thala Tunisia 38 35.35N 8.38E
Thale Luang l. Thailand 58 7.30N 100.20E
Thallon Australia 83 28.39S 148.49E
Thame England 24 51.44N 0.58W
Thame r. England 24 51.38N 1.10W
Thames r. Canada 98 42.20N 82.25W
Thames r. England 23 51.30N 0.05E
Thames New Zealand 85 37.08S 175.35E
Thames Haven England 23 51.31N 0.31E
Thana India 56 19.14N 73.02E
Thanh Hoa Vietnam 63 19.47N 105.49E
Thanjavur India 57 10.46N 79.09E
Thar Desert India 56 28.00N 72.00E
Thargomindah Australia 83 27.59S 143.45E
Tharrawaddy Burma 60 17.37N 95.48E
Tharthar, Wadi r. Iraq 54 34.18N 43.07E
Tharthar Basin f. Iraq 54 33.56N 43.16E
Thásos i. Greece 39 40.40N 24.39E
Thaton Burma 57 17.00N 97.39E
Thaungdut Burma 57 24.26N 94.45E
Thaxted England 25 51.57N 0.21E
Thayetmyo Burma 57 19.20N 95.18E
The Aird f. Scotland 33 57.26N 4.23W
Thebes ruins Egypt 54 25.41N 32.40E
The Buck mtn. Scotland 33 57.18N 2.59W
The Cherokees, L. O' U.S.A. 97 36.45N 94.50W
The Cheviot mtn. England 31 55.29N 2.10W
The Cheviot Hills England/Scotland 31 55.22N 2.24W
The Coorong Australia 83 36.00S 139.30E
The Everglades f. U.S.A. 97 26.00N 80.30W
The Fens f. England 25 52.32N 0.13E
The Glenkens f. Scotland 30 55.10N 4.13W
The Grenadines is. St. Vincent 101 13.00N 61.20W
The Hague Neth. 41 52.05N 4.16E
The Hebrides, Sea of Scotland 32 57.05N 7.05W
The Little Minch str. Scotland 32 57.40N 6.45W
Thelon r. Canada 95 64.23N 96.15W
The Long Mynd hill England 24 52.33N 2.50W
The Machers f. Scotland 30 54.45N 4.28W
The Marsh f. England 29 52.50N 0.10E
The Minch str. Scotland 32 58.10N 5.50W
The Mumbles Wales 27 51.34N 4.00W
The Naze c. England 25 51.53N 1.17E
The Needles c. England 24 50.39N 1.35W
The North Sd. Scotland 33 59.18N 2.45W
Theodore Roosevelt L. U.S.A. 96 33.30N 111.10W
The Ox Mts. Rep. of Ire. 34 54.06N 8.50W
The Paps mts. Rep. of Ire. 35 52.01N 9.14W
The Pas Canada 95 53.50N 101.15W
The Pennines hills England 28 55.40N 2.20W
The Potteries f. England 28 53.00N 2.10W
The Rhinns f. Scotland 30 54.50N 5.02W
The Six Towns town N. Ireland 30 54.45N 6.53W
The Skerries is. Wales 26 53.27N 4.35W
The Solent str. England 24 50.45N 1.20W

Thessaloniki Greece 39 40.38N 22.56E
Thessaloniki, G. of Med. Sea 39 40.10N 23.00E
The Storr mtn. Scotland 32 57.30N 6.11W
The Swale str. England 25 51.22N 0.58E
Thetford England 25 52.25N 0.44E
Thetford Mines town Canada 99 46.06N 71.18W
The Trossachs f. Scotland 30 56.15N 4.25W
The Twelve Pins mts. Rep. of Ire. 34 53.30N 9.49W
The Wash b. England 29 52.55N 0.15E
The Weald f. England 25 51.05N 0.20E
The Woods, L. of N. America 97 49.46N 94.30W
The Wrekin hill England 24 52.40N 2.33W
Theydon Bois England 23 51.40N 0.05E
Thiers France 36 45.51N 3.33E
Thiés Senegal 72 14.50N 16.55W
Thimbu Bhutan 56 27.29N 89.40E
Thionville France 40 49.22N 6.11E
Thíra i. Greece 39 36.24N 25.27E
Thirsk England 29 54.15N 1.20W
Thisted Denmark 42 56.58N 8.42E
Thitu Is. Asia 58 10.50N 114.20E
Thjórsá r. Iceland 42 63.53N 20.38W
Tholen i. Neth. 41 51.34N 4.07E
Thomastown Rep. of Ire. 35 52.32N 7.08W
Thomasville U.S.A. 97 30.50N 83.59W
Thonburi Thailand 57 13.43N 100.27E
Thornaby-on-Tees England 29 54.34N 1.18W
Thornbury England 24 51.36N 2.31W
Thorne England 29 53.36N 0.56W
Thorney England 25 52.37N 0.08W
Thornhill Scotland 31 55.15N 3.46W
Thornton England 28 53.53N 3.00W
Thornwood Common England 23 51.43N 0.08E
Thorpe England 23 51.25N 0.31W
Thorpe-le-Soken England 25 51.50N 1.11E
Thorshavn Faroe Is. 42 62.02N 6.47W
Thouars France 36 46.59N 0.13W
Thrapston England 25 52.24N 0.32W
Thrushel r. England 27 50.38N 4.19W
Thuin Belgium 41 50.21N 4.20E
Thule Greenland 95 77.40N 69.00W
Thun Switz. 40 46.46N 7.38E
Thunder Bay town Canada 98 48.25N 89.14W
Thuringian Forest f. E. Germany 40 50.40N 10.50E
Thurles Rep. of Ire. 35 52.41N 7.50W
Thurnscoe England 29 53.31N 1.19W
Thursby England 31 54.40N 3.03W
Thursday I. Australia 59 10.45S 142.00E
Thurso Scotland 33 58.35N 3.32W
Thurso r. Scotland 33 58.35N 3.32W
Tiamen China 63 30.40N 113.25E
Tianjin China 62 39.07N 117.08E
Tian Shan mts. Asia 60 42.00N 80.30E
Tianshui China 62 34.25N 105.58E
Tianyang China 63 30.22N 104.31E
Tiaret Algeria 37 35.20N 1.20E
Tibati Cameroon 73 6.25N 12.33E
Tiber r. Italy 38 41.45N 12.16E
Tiberias, L. Israel 54 32.49N 35.36E
Tibesti Mts. Chad 73 21.00N 17.30E
Tibet d. China 57 32.20N 86.00E
Tibetan Plateau f. China 57 34.00N 84.30E
Tibooburra Australia 83 29.28S 142.04E
Tiburon I. Mexico 96 29.00N 112.25W
Ticehurst England 25 51.02N 0.23E
Ticino r. Italy 36 45.09N 9.12E
Tickhill England 29 53.25N 1.08W
Tidjikja Mauritania 72 18.29N 11.31W
Tiel Neth. 41 51.53N 5.26E
Tieling China 62 42.13N 123.48E
Tielt Belgium 41 51.00N 3.20E
Tierra Blanca Mexico 100 18.28N 96.12W
Tierra del Fuego i. S. America 109 54.00S 68.30W
Tiétar r. Spain 37 39.50N 6.00W
Tietê r. Brazil 110 20.43S 51.30W
Tighnabruaich Scotland 30 55.56N 5.14W
Tigris r. Asia 55 31.00N 47.27E
Tihama f. Saudi Arabia 71 20.30N 40.30E
Tijuana Mexico 96 32.29N 117.10W
Tikhoretsk U.S.S.R. 43 45.52N 40.07E
Tikhvin U.S.S.R. 43 59.35N 33.29E
Tiko Cameroon 74 4.09N 9.19E
Tiksi U.S.S.R. 45 71.40N 128.45E
Tilburg Neth. 41 51.34N 5.05E
Tilbury England 23 51.28N 0.23E
Till r. England 31 55.41N 2.12W
Tillabéri Niger 73 14.28N 1.27E
Tillicoultry Scotland 31 56.09N 3.45W
Tilt r. Scotland 33 56.46N 3.50W
Timagami L. Canada 98 46.55N 80.03W
Timaru New Zealand 85 44.23S 171.41E
Timbuktu Mali 72 16.49N 2.59W
Timişoara Romania 39 45.47N 21.15E
Timişul r. Yugo. 39 44.49N 20.28E
Timmins Canada 98 48.30N 81.20W
Timok r. Yugo. 39 44.13N 22.40E
Timoleague Rep. of Ire. 35 51.38N 8.46W
Timor i. Austa. 59 9.30S 125.00E

188

Volga *r.* U.S.S.R. **44** 45.45N 47.50E
Volga Uplands *hills* U.S.S.R. **43** 53.15N 45.45E
Volgograd U.S.S.R. **43** 48.45N 44.30E
Volkhov *r.* U.S.S.R. **43** 60.15N 32.15E
Vologda U.S.S.R. **43** 59.10N 39.55E
Vólos Greece **39** 39.22N 22.57E
Volsk U.S.S.R. **43** 52.04N 47.22E
Volta *d.* Ghana **72** 7.30N 0.25E
Volta *r.* Ghana **72** 5.50N 0.41E
Volta, L. Ghana **72** 7.00N 0.00
Volta Redonda Brazil **109** 22.31S 44.05W
Volterra Italy **38** 43.24N 10.51E
Volturno *r.* Italy **38** 41.02N 13.56E
Volzhskiy U.S.S.R. **43** 48.48N 44.45E
Voorburg Neth. **41** 52.05N 4.22E
Vopna Fjördhur *est.* Iceland **42** 65.50N 14.30W
Vordingborg Denmark **40** 55.01N 11.55E
Vorkuta U.S.S.R. **44** 67.27N 64.00E
Voronezh U.S.S.R. **43** 51.40N 39.13E
Voroshilovgrad U.S.S.R. **43** 48.35N 39.20E
Vosges *mts.* France **40** 48.10N 7.00E
Voss Norway **42** 60.38N 6.25E
Votuporanga Brazil **110** 20.26S 49.53W
Vouga *r.* Portugal **37** 40.41N 8.38W
Voves France **36** 48.16N 1.37E
Voznesensk U.S.S.R. **43** 47.34N 31.21E
Vranje Yugo. **39** 42.34N 21.52E
Vratsa Bulgaria **39** 43.12N 23.33E
Vrbas *r.* Yugo. **39** 45.06N 17.29E
Vrede R.S.A. **76** 27.24S 29.11E
Vršac Yugo. **39** 45.08N 21.18E
Vryburg R.S.A. **76** 26.57S 24.44E
Vung Tau Vietnam **58** 10.21N 107.04E
Vyatka *r.* U.S.S.R. **43** 55.45N 51.30E
Vyatskiye Polyany U.S.S.R. **43** 56.14N 51.08E
Vyazma U.S.S.R. **43** 55.12N 34.17E
Vyazniki U.S.S.R. **43** 56.14N 42.08E
Vyborg U.S.S.R. **42** 60.45N 28.41E
Vyrnwy *r.* Wales **26** 52.45N 3.01W
Vyrnwy, L. Wales **26** 52.46N 3.30W
Vyshka U.S.S.R. **55** 39.19N 49.12E
Vyshniy-Volochek U.S.S.R. **43** 57.34N 34.23E

W

Wa Ghana **72** 10.07N 2.28W
Waal *r.* Neth. **41** 51.45N 4.40E
Waalwijk Neth. **41** 51.42N 5.04E
Wabag P.N.G. **59** 5.28S 143.40E
Wabash *r.* U.S.A. **98** 38.25N 87.45W
Wabush City Canada **95** 53.00N 66.50W
Waco U.S.A. **97** 31.33N 97.10W
Wad Pakistan **56** 27.21N 66.30E
Wadden Sea Neth. **41** 53.15N 5.05E
Waddesdon England **24** 51.50N 0.54W
Waddington, Mt. Canada **94** 51.30N 125.00W
Wadebridge England **27** 50.31N 4.51W
Wadesmill England **23** 51.51N 0.03W
Wadhurst England **25** 51.03N 0.21E
Wadi Halfa Sudan **71** 21.55N 31.20E
Wad Medani Sudan **71** 14.24N 33.30E
Wafra Kuwait **55** 28.39N 47.56E
Wageningen Neth. **41** 51.58N 5.39E
Wager Bay *town* Canada **95** 65.55N 90.40W
Wagga Wagga Australia **83** 35.07S 147.24E
Wah Pakistan **56** 33.50N 72.44E
Wahpeton U.S.A. **97** 46.16N 96.36W
Waigeo *i.* Indonesia **59** 0.05S 130.30E
Waihi New Zealand **85** 37.24S 175.50E
Waihou *r.* New Zealand **85** 37.12S 175.33E
Waikato *r.* New Zealand **85** 37.19S 174.50E
Waikerie Australia **83** 34.11S 139.59E
Waimakariri *r.* New Zealand **85** 43.23S 172.40E
Waimate New Zealand **85** 44.45S 171.03E
Wainfleet All Saints England **29** 53.07N 0.16E
Waingapu Indonesia **59** 9.30S 120.10E
Wainwright U.S.A. **94** 70.39N 160.00W
Waiouru New Zealand **85** 39.39S 175.40E
Waipukurau New Zealand **85** 40.00S 176.33E
Wairau *r.* New Zealand **85** 41.32S 174.08E
Wairoa New Zealand **85** 39.03S 177.25E
Waitaki *r.* New Zealand **85** 44.56S 171.10E
Waitara New Zealand **85** 38.59S 174.13E
Waiuku New Zealand **85** 37.15S 174.44E
Wajir Kenya **75** 1.46N 40.05E
Wakasa wan *b.* Japan **64** 35.50N 135.40E
Wakatipu, L. New Zealand **85** 45.10S 168.30E
Wakayama Japan **64** 34.12N 135.10E
Wakefield England **29** 53.41N 1.31W
Wakkanai Japan **64** 45.26N 141.43E
Walachian Plain *f.* Romania **43** 44.30N 26.30E
Walbrzych Poland **40** 50.48N 16.19E
Walbury Hill England **24** 51.21N 1.30W
Walcha Australia **83** 31.00S 151.36E
Walcheren *f.* Neth. **41** 51.32N 3.35E
Walderslade England **23** 51.21N 0.33E

Wales U.K. **26** 52.30N 3.45W
Walgett Australia **83** 30.03S 148.10E
Wallasey England **28** 53.26N 3.02W
Wallingford England **24** 51.36N 1.07W
Wallington England **23** 51.22N 0.09W
Walls Scotland **32** 60.14N 1.34W
Wallsend England **31** 55.00N 1.31W
Walmer England **25** 51.12N 1.23E
Walney, Isle of England **28** 54.05N 3.12W
Walsall England **24** 52.36N 1.59W
Waltham Abbey England **23** 51.42N 0.01E
Waltham Forest *d.* England **23** 51.36N 0.02W
Waltham on the Wolds England **29** 52.49N 0.49W
Walthamstow England **23** 51.34N 0.01W
Walton-on-Thames England **23** 51.23N 0.23W
Walton on the Hill England **23** 51.17N 0.02W
Walton on the Naze England **25** 51.52N 1.17E
Walvis B. R.S.A. **76** 22.48S 14.29E
Walvis Bay *d.* R.S.A. **76** 22.55S 14.35E
Walvis Bay *town* R.S.A. **76** 22.50S 14.31E
Wamba Kenya **75** 0.58N 37.19E
Wamba Nigeria **73** 8.57N 8.42E
Wamba Zaïre **75** 2.10N 27.59E
Wamba *r.* Zaïre **74** 4.35S 17.15E
Wami *r.* Tanzania **75** 6.10S 38.50E
Wanaaring Australia **83** 29.42S 144.14E
Wanaka New Zealand **85** 44.42S 169.08E
Wanaka, L. New Zealand **85** 44.30S 169.10E
Wandsworth *d.* England **23** 51.27N 0.11W
Wanganella Australia **83** 35.13S 144.53E
Wanganui New Zealand **85** 39.56S 175.00E
Wangaratta Australia **83** 36.22S 146.20E
Wangeroog *i.* W. Germany **41** 53.50N 7.50E
Wangford Fen *f.* England **25** 52.25N 0.31E
Wankie Zimbabwe **76** 18.18S 26.30E
Wankie Nat. Park Zimbabwe **76** 19.00S 26.30E
Wansbeck *r.* England **31** 55.10N 1.33W
Wanstead England **23** 51.34N 0.02E
Wantage England **24** 51.35N 1.25W
Wanxian China **63** 30.52N 108.20E
Wanyang Shan *mts.* China **63** 26.01N 113.48E
Warangal India **57** 18.00N 79.35E
Waratah B. Australia **83** 38.55S 146.07E
Ward Rep. of Ire. **34** 53.26N 6.20W
Warden R.S.A. **76** 27.50S 28.58E
Wardha India **57** 20.41N 78.40E
Ward Hill Orkney Is. Scotland **33** 58.54N 3.20W
Ward's Hill Orkney Is. Scotland **33** 58.58N 3.09W
Ward's Stone *mtn.* England **28** 54.03N 2.36W
Ware England **23** 51.49N 0.02W
Wareham England **24** 50.41N 2.08W
Warendorf W. Germany **41** 51.57N 8.00E
Warialda Australia **83** 29.33S 150.36E
Wark Forest *hills* England **31** 55.06N 2.24W
Warkworth New Zealand **85** 36.24S 174.40E
Warley England **24** 52.29N 2.02W
Warlingham England **23** 51.19N 0.04W
Warmbad Namibia **76** 28.29S 18.41E
Warminster England **24** 51.12N 2.11W
Warracknabeal Australia **83** 36.15S 142.28E
Warragul Australia **83** 38.11S 145.55E
Warrego *r.* Australia **83** 30.25S 145.18E
Warren Mich. U.S.A. **98** 42.30N 83.02W
Warren Ohio U.S.A. **98** 41.15N 80.49W
Warri Nigeria **73** 5.36N 5.46E
Warrington England **28** 53.25N 2.38W
Warrnambool Australia **83** 38.23S 142.03E
Warsaw Poland **43** 52.15N 21.00E
Warsop England **29** 53.13N 1.08W
Warta *r.* Poland **43** 52.45N 15.09E
Warwick Australia **83** 28.12S 152.00E
Warwick England **24** 52.17N 1.36W
Warwick U.S.A. **99** 41.42N 71.23W
Warwickshire *d.* England **24** 52.13N 1.30W
Washington England **31** 54.55N 1.30W
Washington U.S.A. **99** 38.55N 77.00W
Washington *d.* U.S.A. **96** 47.00N 120.00W
Washington, Mt. U.S.A. **99** 44.17N 71.19W
Wasian Indonesia **59** 1.51S 133.21E
Wasior Asia **59** 2.38S 134.27E
Wassy France **36** 48.30N 4.59E
West Water *l.* England **28** 54.25N 3.18W
Waswanipi L. Canada **99** 49.30N 76.20W
Watampone Indonesia **59** 4.33S 120.20E
Watchet England **27** 51.10N 3.20W
Waterbury U.S.A. **99** 41.33N 73.03W
Waterford Rep. of Ire. **35** 52.16N 7.08W
Waterford *d.* Rep. of Ire. **35** 52.10N 7.40W
Waterford Harbour *est.* Rep. of Ire. **35** 52.12N 6.56W
Watergate B. England **27** 50.28N 5.06W
Waterloo Belgium **41** 50.44N 4.24E
Waterloo Canada **98** 43.28N 80.32W
Waterloo U.S.A. **98** 42.30N 92.20W
Waterlooville England **24** 50.53N 1.02W
Watertown N.Y. U.S.A. **99** 43.57N 75.56W
Watertown S.Dak. U.S.A. **97** 44.54N 97.08W
Watertown Wisc. U.S.A. **98** 43.12N 88.46W
Waterville Rep. of Ire. **35** 51.50N 10.11W

Waterville U.S.A. **99** 44.34N 69.41W
Watervliet U.S.A. **99** 42.43N 73.42W
Watford England **23** 51.40N 0.25W
Watlington England **24** 51.38N 1.00W
Watson Lake *town* Canada **94** 60.07N 128.49W
Watten, Loch Scotland **33** 58.29N 3.20W
Watton England **25** 52.35N 0.50E
Wau P.N.G. **59** 7.22S 146.40E
Wau Sudan **71** 7.40N 28.04E
Wauchope Australia **83** 31.27S 152.43E
Waukegan U.S.A. **98** 42.21N 87.52W
Waukesha U.S.A. **98** 43.01N 88.14W
Wausau U.S.A. **98** 44.58N 89.40W
Wauwatosa U.S.A. **98** 43.04N 88.02W
Waveney *r.* England **25** 52.29N 1.46E
Wavre Belgium **41** 50.43N 4.37E
Waxham England **25** 52.47N 1.38E
Waycross U.S.A. **97** 31.08N 82.22W
Wealdstone England **23** 51.36N 0.20W
Wear *r.* England **31** 54.55N 1.21W
Weardale *f.* England **31** 54.45N 2.05W
Weaver *r.* England **28** 53.19N 2.44W
Weda Indonesia **59** 0.30N 127.52E
Weddell Sea Antarctica **112** 73.00S 42.00W
Wedmore England **24** 51.14N 2.50W
Weert Neth. **41** 51.14N 5.40E
Wee Waa Australia **83** 30.34S 149.27E
Weiden in der Oberpfalz W. Germany **40** 49.40N 12.10E
Weifang China **62** 36.40N 119.10E
Weihai China **62** 37.28N 122.05E
Wei *r.* Shantung China **62** 36.47N 115.42E
Wei He *r.* Shensi China **62** 34.27N 109.30E
Weimar E. Germany **40** 50.59N 11.20E
Weinan China **62** 34.25N 109.30E
Weirton U.S.A. **98** 40.24N 80.37W
Weishan Hu *l.* China **62** 34.40N 117.25E
Weissenfels E. Germany **40** 51.12N 11.58E
Welhamgreen England **23** 51.44N 0.11W
Welkom R.S.A. **76** 27.59S 26.44E
Welland Canada **99** 45.59N 79.14W
Welland *r.* England **29** 52.53N 0.00
Welling England **23** 51.28N 0.08E
Wellingborough England **24** 52.18N 0.41W
Wellington Australia **83** 32.33S 148.59E
Wellington Salop England **26** 52.42N 2.31W
Wellington Somerset England **27** 50.58N 3.13W
Wellington New Zealand **85** 41.17S 174.47E
Wellingtonbridge Rep. of Ire. **35** 52.16N 6.45W
Wellington I. Chile **109** 49.30S 75.00W
Wells England **24** 51.12N 2.39W
Wells-next-the-Sea England **29** 52.57N 0.51E
Welshpool Wales **26** 52.40N 3.09W
Welwyn England **23** 51.50N 0.13W
Welwyn Garden City England **23** 51.48N 0.13W
Wem England **28** 52.52N 2.45W
Wembere *r.* Tanzania **75** 4.07S 34.15E
Wembley England **23** 51.34N 0.18W
Wemyss Bay *town* Scotland **30** 55.52N 4.52W
Wenatchee U.S.A. **96** 47.26N 120.20W
Wendover England **23** 51.46N 0.46W
Wenjiang China **63** 30.42N 103.50E
Wenlock Edge *hill* England **24** 52.33N 2.40W
Wenshan China **63** 23.20N 104.11E
Wensleydale *f.* England **28** 54.19N 2.04W
Wensum *r.* England **25** 52.37N 1.20E
Wentworth Australia **83** 34.06S 141.56E
Wenzhou China **63** 28.02N 120.40E
Wepener R.S.A. **76** 29.44S 27.03E
Werne W. Germany **41** 51.39N 7.36E
Werris Creek *town* Australia **83** 31.20S 150.41E
Wesel W. Germany **41** 51.39N 6.37E
Weser *r.* W. Germany **40** 53.15N 8.30E
Wessel, C. Australia **82** 11.00S 136.58E
West Allis U.S.A. **98** 43.01N 88.00W
West Bridgford England **29** 52.56N 1.08W
West Bromwich England **24** 52.32N 2.01W
West Burra *i.* Scotland **32** 60.05N 1.21W
Westbury England **24** 51.16N 2.11W
West Calder Scotland **31** 55.51N 3.34W
West Clandon England **23** 51.16N 0.30W
Westcott England **23** 51.13N 0.20W
Westerham England **23** 51.16N 0.05E
Western *d.* Ghana **72** 6.00N 2.40W
Western *d.* Kenya **75** 0.30N 34.30E
Western Australia *d.* Australia **82** 25.00S 123.00E
Western Cleddau *r.* Wales **27** 51.47N 4.56W
Western Cordillera *mts.* N. America **112** 46.00N 120.00W
Western Ghats *mts.* India **56** 15.30N 74.30E
Western Hajar *mts.* Oman **55** 24.00N 56.30E
Western Isles *d.* Scotland **32** 57.40N 7.10W
Western Sahara Africa **70** 25.00N 13.30W
Western Sayan *mts.* U.S.S.R. **45** 53.00N 92.00E
Wester Ross *f.* Scotland **32** 57.37N 5.20W
Westerstede W. Germany **41** 53.15N 7.56E
Westerwald *f.* W. Germany **41** 50.40N 8.00E
West Felton England **26** 52.49N 2.58W
Westfield U.S.A. **99** 42.07N 72.45W
West Frisian Is. Neth. **41** 53.20N 5.00E

West Germany Europe **40** 51.00N 8.00E
West Glamorgan *d.* Wales **27** 51.42N 3.47W
West Haddon England **24** 52.21N 1.05W
West Ham England **23** 51.32N 0.01E
West Hanningfield England **23** 51.41N 0.31E
West Hartford U.S.A. **99** 41.46N 72.45W
West Horsley England **23** 51.17N 0.27W
West Indies C. America **101** 21.00N 74.00W
West Kilbride Scotland **30** 55.42N 4.51W
West Kingsdown England **23** 51.21N 0.14E
West Kirby England **28** 53.22N 3.11W
West Lake *d.* Tanzania **75** 2.00S 31.20E
West Linton Scotland **31** 55.45N 3.21W
West Loch Roag Scotland **32** 58.14N 6.53W
West Loch Tarbert Scotland **32** 57.55N 6.53W
West Malaysia *d.* Malaysia **58** 4.00N 102.00E
Westmeath *d.* Rep. of Ire. **34** 53.30N 7.30W
West Mersea England **25** 51.46N 0.55E
West Midlands *d.* England **24** 52.28N 1.50W
West Nicholson Zimbabwe **76** 21.06S 29.25E
Weston Malaysia **58** 5.14N 115.35E
Weston-super-Mare England **24** 51.20N 2.59W
West Palm Beach *town* U.S.A. **97** 26.42N 80.05W
Westport New Zealand **85** 41.46S 171.38E
Westport Rep. of Ire. **34** 53.48N 9.32W
Westray *i.* Scotland **33** 59.18N 2.58W
Westray Firth *est.* Scotland **33** 59.13N 3.00W
West Schelde *est.* Neth. **41** 51.25N 3.40E
West Siberian Plain *f.* U.S.S.R. **44** 60.00N 75.00E
West Sussex *d.* England **25** 50.58N 0.30W
West Terschelling Neth. **41** 53.22N 5.13E
West Thurrock England **23** 51.29N 0.17E
West Virginia *d.* U.S.A. **97** 39.00N 80.30W
West Water *r.* Scotland **33** 56.47N 2.35W
West Wickham England **23** 51.22N 0.02W
West Wittering England **24** 50.42N 0.54W
West Wyalong Australia **83** 33.54S 147.12E
West Yorkshire *d.* England **28** 53.45N 1.40W
Wetar *i.* Indonesia **59** 7.45S 126.00E
Wetheral England **31** 54.53N 2.50W
Wetherby England **29** 53.56N 1.23W
Wetzlar W. Germany **40** 50.33N 8.30E
Wewak P.N.G. **59** 3.35S 143.35E
Wexford Rep. of Ire. **35** 52.20N 6.28W
Wexford *d.* Rep. of Ire. **35** 52.20N 6.25W
Wexford B. Rep. of Ire. **35** 52.27N 6.18W
Wey *r.* England **23** 51.23N 0.28W
Weybridge England **23** 51.23N 0.28W
Weyburn Canada **96** 49.39N 103.51W
Weymouth England **24** 50.36N 2.28W
Weymouth U.S.A. **99** 42.14N 70.58W
Whakatane New Zealand **85** 37.56S 177.00E
Whale *r.* Canada **95** 58.00N 57.50W
Whaley Bridge *town* England **28** 53.20N 2.00W
Whalley England **28** 53.49N 2.25W
Whalsay *i.* Scotland **32** 60.22N 0.59W
Whangarei New Zealand **85** 35.43S 174.20E
Wharfe *r.* England **28** 53.50N 1.07W
Wharfedale *f.* England **28** 54.00N 1.55W
Wheathampstead England **23** 51.49N 0.17W
Wheeler Peak *mtn.* Nev. U.S.A. **96** 38.59N 114.29W
Wheeler Peak *mtn.* N. Mex. U.S.A. **96** 36.34N 105.25W
Wheeling U.S.A. **98** 40.05N 80.43W
Whernside *mtn.* England **28** 54.14N 2.25W
Whickham England **31** 54.57N 1.40W
Whipsnade England **23** 51.52N 0.33W
Whitburn Scotland **31** 55.52N 3.41W
Whitby England **29** 54.29N 0.37W
Whitchurch Bucks. England **24** 51.53N 0.51W
Whitchurch Hants. England **24** 51.14N 1.20W
Whitchurch Salop England **28** 52.58N 2.42W
White *r.* Ark. U.S.A. **97** 35.30N 91.20W
White *r.* Ind. U.S.A. **98** 38.25N 87.45W
White *r.* S. Dak. U.S.A. **96** 43.40N 99.30W
Whiteabbey N. Ireland **30** 54.42N 5.53W
Whiteadder Water *r.* Scotland **31** 55.46N 2.00W
White Cap Mtn. U.S.A. **99** 45.35N 69.13W
White Coomb *mtn.* Scotland **31** 55.26N 3.20W
Whitefish Pt. U.S.A. **98** 46.46N 84.58W
Whitehaven England **28** 54.33N 3.35W
Whitehead N. Ireland **30** 54.45N 5.43W
Whitehorse Canada **94** 60.41N 135.08W
Whitehorse Hill England **24** 51.35N 1.35W
White Mountain Peak U.S.A. **96** 37.40N 118.15W
White Mts. U.S.A. **99** 44.15N 71.10W
Whiten Head Scotland **33** 58.34N 4.32W
White Nile *r.* Sudan **71** 15.45N 32.25E
White Parish England **24** 51.01N 1.39W
White Russia Soviet Socialist Republic *d.* U.S.S.R. **43** 53.30N 28.00E
Whitesand B. England **27** 50.20N 4.20W
White Sea U.S.S.R. **44** 65.30N 38.00E
White Volta *r.* Ghana **72** 9.13N 1.15W
Whithorn Scotland **30** 54.44N 4.25W
Whitland Wales **26** 51.49N 4.38W
Whitley Bay *town* England **31** 55.03N 1.25W
Whitney Canada **99** 45.29N 78.15W
Whitney, Mt. U.S.A. **96** 36.35N 118.17W
Whitstable England **25** 51.21N 1.02E
Whittington England **26** 52.53N 3.00W
Whittlesey England **25** 52.34N 0.08W
Whitton England **29** 53.42N 0.39W
Whitwell England **23** 51.53N 0.18W
Whyalla Australia **82** 33.04S 137.34E
Wiay *i.* Scotland **32** 57.24N 7.13W
Wichita U.S.A. **97** 37.43N 97.20W
Wichita Falls *town* U.S.A. **96** 33.55N 98.30W
Wick Scotland **33** 58.26N 3.06W
Wickford England **23** 51.38N 0.31E
Wickham England **24** 50.54N 1.11W
Wickham Market England **25** 52.09N 1.21E
Wicklow Rep. of Ire. **35** 52.59N 6.03W
Wicklow *d.* Rep. of Ire. **35** 52.59N 6.25W
Wicklow Head Rep. of Ire. **35** 52.58N 6.00W
Wicklow Mts. Rep. of Ire. **35** 53.06N 6.20W
Wick of Gruting *b.* Scotland **32** 60.37N 0.49W
Widford England **23** 51.50N 0.04E
Widnes England **28** 53.22N 2.44W
Wien *see* Vienna Austria **40**
Wiener Neustadt Austria **40** 47.49N 16.15E
Wiesbaden W. Germany **40** 50.05N 8.15E
Wigan England **28** 53.33N 2.38W
Wight, Isle of England **24** 50.40N 1.17W
Wigmore England **23** 51.21N 0.36E
Wigston Magna England **24** 52.35N 1.06W
Wigton England **31** 54.50N 3.09W
Wigtown Scotland **30** 54.47N 4.26W
Wigtown B. Scotland **30** 54.47N 4.15W
Wilberfoss England **29** 53.57N 0.53W
Wilcannia Australia **83** 31.33S 143.24E
Wildhorn *mtn.* Switz. **40** 46.22N 7.22E
Wildspitze *mtn.* Austria **40** 46.55N 10.55E
Wildwood U.S.A. **99** 38.59N 74.49W
Wilhelm, Mt. P.N.G. **59** 6.00S 144.55E
Wilhelmshaven W. Germany **41** 53.32N 8.07E
Wilkes-Barre U.S.A. **99** 41.15N 75.50W
Willemstad Neth. Antilles **101** 12.12N 68.56W
Willersley England **26** 52.07N 3.00W
Willesden England **23** 51.33N 0.14W
Williamsport U.S.A. **99** 41.16N 77.03W
Willington England **31** 54.43N 1.41W
Williston R.S.A. **76** 31.20S 20.52E
Williston U.S.A. **96** 48.09N 103.39W
Williton England **27** 51.09N 3.20W
Willmar U.S.A. **97** 45.06N 95.00W
Willow U.S.A. **94** 61.42N 150.08W
Willowmore R.S.A. **76** 33.18S 23.30E
Willunga Australia **83** 35.18S 138.33E
Wilmington Del. U.S.A. **99** 39.46N 75.31W
Wilmington N.C. U.S.A. **97** 34.14N 77.55W
Wilmslow England **28** 53.19N 2.14W
Wilrijk Belgium **41** 51.11N 4.25E
Wilson *r.* Australia **83** 27.36S 141.27E
Wilson, Mt. U.S.A. **96** 37.51N 107.51W
Wilson's Promontary *c.* Australia **83** 39.06S 146.23E
Wilstone Resr. England **23** 51.48N 0.40W
Wilton England **24** 51.05N 1.52W
Wiltshire *d.* England **24** 51.20N 2.00W
Wimbledon England **23** 51.26N 0.12W
Wimbledon Park England **23** 51.26N 0.17W
Wimborne Minster England **24** 50.48N 2.00W
Winam *b.* Kenya **75** 0.15S 34.30E
Winburg R.S.A. **76** 28.31S 27.01E
Wincanton England **24** 51.03N 2.24W
Winchester England **24** 51.04N 1.19W
Windermere England **28** 54.24N 2.56W
Windermere *l.* England **28** 54.20N 2.56W
Windhoek Namibia **76** 22.34S 17.06E
Windlesham England **23** 51.22N 0.39W
Windrush *r.* England **24** 51.42N 1.25W
Windsor Canada **98** 42.18N 83.00W
Windsor England **23** 51.29N 0.38W
Windsor Great Park *f.* England **23** 51.27N 0.37W
Windward Is. C. America **101** 13.00N 60.00W
Windward Passage *str.* Carib. Sea **101** 20.00N 74.00W
Wingate England **31** 54.44N 1.23W
Wingrave England **23** 51.52N 0.44W
Winisk *r.* Canada **95** 55.20N 85.20W
Winkleigh England **27** 50.49N 3.57W
Winneba Ghana **72** 5.22N 0.38W
Winnebago, L. U.S.A. **98** 44.00N 88.25W
Winnipeg Canada **97** 49.59N 97.10W
Winnipeg, L. Canada **95** 52.45N 98.00W
Winnipegosis, L. Canada **96** 52.00N 100.00W
Winnipesaukee, L. U.S.A. **99** 43.40N 71.20W
Winona U.S.A. **98** 44.02N 91.37W
Winschoten Neth. **41** 53.07N 7.02E
Winscombe England **24** 51.19N 2.50W
Winsford England **28** 53.12N 2.31W
Winslow England **24** 51.57N 0.54W
Winston-Salem U.S.A. **97** 36.05N 80.05W
Winsum Neth. **41** 53.20N 6.31E
Winterswijk Neth. **41** 51.58N 6.44E
Winterthur Switz. **40** 47.30N 8.45E
Winterton England **29** 53.39N 0.37W
Winterton-on-Sea England **25** 52.43N 1.43E
Winton Australia **82** 22.22S 143.00E
Winton New Zealand **85** 46.10S 168.20E
Wirksworth England **29** 53.05N 1.34W
Wirral *f.* England **28** 53.18N 3.02W
Wisbech England **25** 52.39N 0.10E
Wisconsin *d.* U.S.A. **98** 44.45N 90.00W
Wisconsin *r.* U.S.A. **98** 42.57N 91.07W
Wisconsin Rapids *town* U.S.A. **98** 44.24N 89.50W
Wishaw Scotland **31** 55.47N 3.55W
Wismar E. Germany **40** 53.54N 11.28E
Wissembourg France **40** 49.02N 7.57E
Wissey *r.* England **25** 52.33N 0.21E
Witham England **23** 51.48N 0.38E
Witham *r.* England **29** 52.56N 0.04E
Witheridge England **27** 50.55N 3.42W
Withernsea England **29** 53.43N 0.02E
Witney England **24** 51.47N 1.29W
Witten W. Germany **41** 51.26N 7.19E
Wittenberg E. Germany **40** 51.53N 12.39E
Wittenberge E. Germany **40** 52.59N 11.45E
Wittlich W. Germany **41** 49.59N 6.54E
Witu Kenya **75** 2.22S 40.20E
Wiveliscombe England **27** 51.02N 3.20W
Wivenhoe England **25** 51.51N 0.59E
Włocławek Poland **43** 52.39N 19.01E
Wodonga Australia **83** 36.08S 146.09E
Wokam *i.* Asia **59** 5.45S 134.30E
Woking England **23** 51.20N 0.34W
Wokingham England **24** 51.25N 0.50W
Woldingham England **23** 51.17N 0.02E
Wolf *r.* U.S.A. **98** 44.00N 88.30W
Wolfenbüttel W. Germany **40** 52.10N 10.33E
Wolf Rock *i.* England **27** 49.56N 5.48W
Wolfsburg W. Germany **40** 52.27N 10.49E
Wolin Poland **40** 53.51N 14.38E
Wollaston England **24** 52.16N 0.41W
Wollaston L. Canada **94** 58.15N 103.30W
Wollongong Australia **83** 34.25S 150.52E
Wolmaransstad R.S.A. **76** 27.11S 26.00E
Wolseley Australia **83** 36.21S 140.55E
Wolsingham England **31** 54.44N 1.52W
Wolvega Neth. **41** 52.53N 6.00E
Wolverhampton England **24** 52.35N 2.06W
Wolverton England **24** 52.03N 0.48W
Wombwell England **29** 53.31N 1.23W
Wonersh England **23** 51.12N 0.33W
Wonsan N. Korea **61** 39.07N 127.26E
Wonthaggi Australia **83** 33.33S 145.37E
Woodbridge England **25** 52.06N 1.19E
Woodford Rep. of Ire. **35** 53.03N 8.24W
Woodford Halse England **24** 52.10N 1.12W
Wood Green England **23** 51.38N 0.06W
Woodhall Spa England **29** 53.10N 0.12W
Woodmansterne England **23** 51.19N 0.10W
Woodside Australia **83** 38.31S 146.21E
Woodstock England **24** 51.51N 1.20W
Wooler England **31** 55.33N 2.01W
Woolwich England **23** 51.29N 0.05E
Woomera Australia **82** 31.11S 136.54E
Woonsocket U.S.A. **99** 42.00N 71.30W
Wooroorooka Australia **83** 28.59S 145.40E
Wooster U.S.A. **98** 40.46N 81.57W
Wootton Bassett England **24** 51.32N 1.55W
Worcester England **24** 52.12N 2.12W
Worcester R.S.A. **76** 33.39S 19.26E
Worcester U.S.A. **99** 42.17N 71.48W
Workington England **28** 54.39N 3.34W
Worksop England **29** 53.19N 1.09W
Worland U.S.A. **96** 44.01N 107.58W
Wormit Scotland **31** 56.25N 2.28W
Worms W. Germany **40** 49.38N 8.23E
Worms Head Wales **27** 51.34N 4.18W
Worsbrough England **29** 53.33N 1.29W
Worthing England **25** 50.49N 0.21W
Worthington U.S.A. **97** 43.37N 95.36W
Wotton-under-Edge England **24** 51.37N 2.20W
Wowoni *i.* Indonesia **59** 4.10S 123.10E
Wragby England **29** 53.17N 0.18W
Wrangel I. U.S.S.R. **45** 71.00N 180.00
Wrangell U.S.A. **94** 56.28N 132.23W
Wrangle England **29** 53.03N 0.09E
Wrath, C. Scotland **32** 58.37N 5.01W
Wrexham Wales **26** 53.05N 3.00W
Wrigley Canada **94** 63.16N 123.39W
Wrocław Poland **40** 51.05N 17.00E
Wrotham England **23** 51.19N 0.19E
Wuchuan China **63** 21.21N 110.40E
Wugang China **63** 26.42N 110.31E
Wuging China **62** 39.19N 117.05E
Wugong Shan *mts.* China **63** 27.15N 114.00E
Wuhai China **62** 38.50N 106.40E
Wuhan China **63** 30.37N 114.19E
Wuhu China **63** 31.25N 118.25E
Wu Jiang *r.* China **63** 29.41N 107.24E
Wuliang Shan *mts.* China **60** 24.27N 100.43E
Wuppertal W. Germany **41** 51.15N 7.10E
Wuqing China **62** 39.19N 117.05E
Würzburg W. Germany **40** 49.48N 9.57E